THE STRUGGLE FOR CHANGE

Carter G. Woodson Institute Series

DEBORAH E. MCDOWELL, SHAWN LEIGH ALEXANDER,
AND ROBERT T. VINSON, EDITORS

THE STRUGGLE FOR CHANGE

Race and the Politics of Reconciliation in Modern Richmond

Marvin T. Chiles

University of Virginia Press • *Charlottesville and London*

University of Virginia Press
© 2023 by the Rector and Visitors of the University of Virginia
All rights reserved
Printed in the United States of America on acid-free paper

First published 2023

9 8 7 6 5 4 3 2 1

Library of Congress Cataloging-in-Publication Data

Names: Chiles, Marvin T., author.
Title: The struggle for change : race and the politics of reconciliation in modern Richmond / Marvin T. Chiles.
Other titles: Race and the politics of reconciliation in modern Richmond | Carter G. Woodson Institute series.
Description: Charlottesville : University of Virginia Press, 2023. | Series: Carter G. Woodson Institute series | Includes bibliographical references and index.
Identifiers: LCCN 2023034109 (print) | LCCN 2023034110 (ebook) |
  ISBN 9780813950334 (hardcover) | ISBN 9780813950341 (paperback) |
  ISBN 9780813950358 (ebook)
Subjects: LCSH: African Americans—Virginia—Richmond—History. | Civil rights movements—Virginia—Richmond—History. | Richmond (Va.)—Race relations. | Richmond (Va.)—History.
Classification: LCC F234.R59 B53 2023 (print) | LCC F234.R59 (ebook) |
  DDC 908.996/0730755451—dc23/eng/20230822
LC record available at https://lccn.loc.gov/2023034109
LC ebook record available at https://lccn.loc.gov/2023034110

Cover art: Photo, Arthur Ashe statue dedication, 1996. (Bill McKelway/Richmond Times-Dispatch); background, Jullius/shutterstock.com

To Richmonders past, present, and future who wish to better understand their city's race relations

CONTENTS

Acknowledgments ... ix

Prologue: "Color Was Never Something People Were Blind To" ... 1

Part 1. A City Breaking, 1954–1970

1. The Marsh Revolution: "Build People, Not Things" ... 11
2. Annexation: "The Only Answer" ... 28
3. Dogtown: "We Never Crossed the Bridge" ... 47

Part 2. A City Broken, 1970–1984

4. Richmond Community Action Program: "Where the Grass Roots Is Forever Active" ... 71
5. Project One: "A Dividing Line Separating Whites and Blacks" ... 89
6. Richmond Renaissance and Sixth Street Marketplace: "A Bridge of Unity" ... 110

Part 3. A City Healing, 1985–Present

7. Richmond Urban Institute: "The Conscience of Richmond" ... 135
8. Moral Re-Armament and Hope in the Cities: Healing the Heart of America ... 155
9. Monument Avenue: "Richmond Is No Longer the Capital of the Confederacy" ... 177

Epilogue: "Capital of Reconciliation?" ... 199

Notes	213
Bibliography	297
Index	321

ACKNOWLEDGMENTS

Books are truly collective endeavors. Thanks to Dr. Robert A. Pratt of the University of Georgia, Dr. Julian Maxwell Hayter of the University of Richmond, Dr. Brian J. Daugherity of Virginia Commonwealth University, Dr. Steven A. Reich of James Madison University, and Reverend Benjamin Campbell for believing in this project when it was a half-baked idea with little structure and even less potential. I owe each of you more than I will ever have to repay. Thank you, too, Nadine Zimmerli of the University of Virginia Press for taking a chance on this book when it was in dissertation form. I am not an easy person to work with, as you know, Nadine. Yet God gave you the patience to do so. To the Richmonders who shared their stories with me for this project, as well as the institutions (both private and public) that opened their doors to me, thank you as well! Lastly, the biggest thanks goes to you, my loving wife Alia Quinn Chiles. This book required you to make a bigger sacrifice than anyone. You uprooted your life from Richmond, Virginia, to Athens, Georgia, and then from Athens to Norfolk, Virginia, to help me find mine. In the process, we built a life together through the completion of this book. This finished product is a testament to everything you've done for me and all that you mean to me. Although my name graces the cover as the author, the beforementioned guided my pen from the first word of the first page to the last word of the last page.

THE STRUGGLE FOR CHANGE

Prologue

"COLOR WAS NEVER SOMETHING PEOPLE WERE BLIND TO"

AT ITS HEART, this book is a hometown kid's inquiry into the city that reared him. That place is Richmond, Virginia: a southern metropole where historical burdens ensured that color was never something people were blind to, especially during my childhood, a time defined by scholars as the "Era of Colorblindness."[1]

Had my life run according to the course set by my parents, I would have never written a book about race in Richmond. I was born in 1992 to middle-class Blacks who raised me in a mostly White suburban bubble. This insular world of private schools and class-homogenous neighborhoods reinforced the notion that shared economic and educational values rendered anti-Black racism obsolete. My parents embraced colorblindness because they desired to raise me in a place and time untainted by racial discrimination, a world they wanted to see because they never knew it. Because of this, the first person to educate me on race was neither my mother nor father. Rather, it was a White female store clerk who racially profiled and falsely accused me of theft when I was but eight years old. My parents sought to pick up the pieces by explaining to me that regardless of my upbringing, my skin color would sometimes attract negative attention and undeserved accusations, a lesson they admittedly never wanted to teach me. From then on, I enjoyed the rest of my youth and adolescence in Richmond relatively free of overt bigotry, but I never lost my curiosity about race and racism. For that, I give thanks to the woman who made me aware of racism, for it was she who unknowingly bestowed upon me a kernel of knowledge about race in Richmond, a cultural inheritance that my loving parents tried to desperately withhold.

I spent my early academic career trying to reconcile that incident with my otherwise racially harmonious upbringing. That led me to learn more about the history of Richmond's Black people, which is largely the story of White city leaders confining the masses to poverty-stricken ghettoes. From there I wanted to know how and why racist attitudes and economic systems coexisted in a place where I grew up witnessing Blacks and Whites share class ideals and privileges. Putting this conundrum and book into perspective for me was the racial reckoning that facilitated the removal of Confederate statues from Monument Avenue in 2020, the result of over a century of civil rights activism—an event that symbolized Richmond's current struggle with its subtle racism.[2] The bygone relics represent the belief that Blacks are inherently inferior to Whites. That belief has long manifested in the economic and educational disparities that justify why most Black people still have separate and unequal lives from Whites. This anti-Blackness is the city's collective heart; hence, my childhood self was protected but never immune to Richmond's bigotry. Thus, efforts to remove the statues revealed the struggle that has long made up the essence of modern Richmond—the gross dissatisfaction with islands of progress sustaining the sea of White supremacy.

Richmond is more than the former capital of the Confederacy: it is a city seeking to end its complicity with American racism. One would not know that if they simply looked at recent demographic information. The numbers reflect a continuity of White wealth and Black poverty that is as old as Richmond itself. The sixty-three square-mile, medium-sized city has around 232,000 residents—47 percent Black and 45 percent White—centered amid a mostly White metropolitan area of around 1.5 million people. Richmond is Virginia's employment, government (state and federal), banking, university, medical research, and biotechnology center while also being the Commonwealth's largest producer of working poverty and public-sector incompetence. Residential distrust of local government has created an enormous nonprofit community (more than fifteen hundred known organizations) that work to mend the divide between White wealth and Black poverty. Black Richmonders bear the largest brunt of this neoliberal tragedy: they monopolize the bottom of nearly every statistical category in city life, ranging from economic prosperity to educational achievement and housing security.

Because Black Richmond's social realities are based in the historical injustices of slavery and Jim Crow, it is widely accepted by politicians, activists, organizers, and residents that current racial disparities evolved from an unyielding continuum of racism inflicted on powerless Blacks by powerful Whites and their opportunistic Black allies.[3] To many, Richmond is but an anecdote of America's urban history. That is why so many believed that a *racial reckoning* needed to take place in the summer of 2020, when city governments leaned into the era of antiracism by removing Confederate statues.[4]

This book subjects memory (both popular and personal) to the practice of history. Memory is the personal and collective lessons we take from the past. Memory is elusive, however, in that it is jaded by the myopathy of fondness, pain, and perspective, as people experience a shared past in different contexts. History is the scholarly attempt to understand the knowable past using the evidence it left behind. The two often operate in separate realms, creating contested debates about what happened and, more importantly, why it happened. Moreover, historical analysis clarifies memory, bringing its most truthful elements together in generating a common understanding of the past and present with the hopes of building a common future. This book is what I and others remember about Richmond being placed under the hard sheet of empirical facts and scholarly analysis. I found that present-day issues plaguing the city, which are issues that invariably plague the nation, have a complicated recent history that needs to be understood in order to address systemic inequities.

Through conforming memory to the practice of history, I find that modern Richmond's conflict between White wealth and Black poverty in the post–civil rights age is not the result of intentionally racist policies or the refusal to implement racial reforms. Rather, it resulted from the unintended consequences of disjointed and misguided racial reform efforts by Whites and Blacks seeking common ground. After the modern civil rights movement ended Jim Crow segregation in Richmond, residents and political leadership used urban revitalization and public history to shed their racist identity. Reform efforts after the 1960s thrust Richmond to the forefront of a regional and national reckoning on race, while producing current racial disparities in housing, public education, and economic security. Examining various progressive movements throughout Richmond that previous scholars ignored has led me to conclude that Black and White Richmonders should be judged by their agendas and desired outcomes, and not just by the systems of inequity they unintendedly reinforced. Moreover, my narrative synthesis treats Black and White Richmonders as pragmatic, rational people who prioritized coexisting as equals after segregation. They validated these expressed desires for reconciliation with actions that altered city life in ways beyond their control. Various interest groups identified the same problems but implemented disconnected and competing solutions to create a singular vision of racial reconciliation after Jim Crow.

This book builds upon a rich literature about modern Virginia. It is not the first academic monograph to analyze race and politics in Richmond during the twentieth and twenty-first centuries. It is, however, the only one that defines recent Black-White relations by the shared values, desires, and actions of each race, and not as the paradigm of White bigotry and Black resistance.[5] My book's unique take on Richmond pushes the literature on modern Virginia beyond discussions of the Byrd machine or the "Massive Resistance" of Whites against school desegregation. In centering racial discrimination at the core of Virginia's struggles with modernity in the twentieth century, historians have dispelled the long-held myth that the Commonwealth was uniquely above southern racism because of the genteel culture established by the Founding Fathers, Confederate leaders, and the mythmakers who wrote about them.[6] I seek to push the field further by focusing on Virginia's issues with urbanization well after the demise of segregation. This book offers a blueprint for future scholarship on suburban flight, urban revitalization, and the inclusive public history movement to rid the Commonwealth of "Lost Causism" in the twenty-first century. Although pushing the field forward in time, I also make the case that the activist spirit discussed in previous works lasted well beyond the 1960s.

This book is more than local history. Rather, it provides a newer interpretive model for literature surrounding the modern South.[7] The historiography of the modern South is shaped by works that see post–World War II metropolitan growth and suburban politics in North Carolina, South Carolina, Georgia, Mississippi, and Louisiana as proof that the South is no longer a *distinctly* backwards American region. However, they cast the modern South as a failed social experiment where White power-brokers and Black opportunists used neoliberalism and racial capitalism to stymy civil rights changes to maintain the political supremacy they held during Jim Crow.[8] I do not upset this grand narrative. Rather, I track how competing visions of racial progress prevented the modern South from becoming the multiracial democracy that 1960s activists so desperately fought for. My book uses Richmond to frame the metropolitan South's failure to create more equitable public services, housing, education, and economy as a struggle between historic enemies seeking common ground and not a zero-sum game for political power. I take seriously that generations of legalized segregation created the collective misunderstandings and disagreements about how the races should live without legal barriers dividing them. The failure of reformers to calculate the complex relationship between race, politics, and economy in the post–World War II era of suburbanization created policies and programs that appear on the surface to be inherently anti-Black in design. Thus, the Richmond story uniquely shows that when it comes to the issue of racial progress in the modern

South, scholars should approach the sources optimistically and weigh the intentions of liberal actors as much as the outcomes they created.

Richmond's recent issues with racial reform show that newer modern South scholars should focus on localities that, in the pursuit of modernity, openly bore the brunt of their racist history. Modern South literature is defined by an accomplished collection of metropolitan studies about Charleston, Charlotte, New Orleans, and Louisville. But Atlanta—The City Never Too Busy to Hate—undoubtedly garners the most attention. Atlanta historians conclude that city leadership successfully used boosterism and the corporate economy to hide the fact that racial policymaking made Atlanta a major city. Moreover, emphasis on Atlanta as the example of the modern South furthers the notion that the region's failures after World War II came from White and Black political and economic leaders hiding their overt racism behind corporate influx and suburban-focused city planning.[9] Richmond better represents the modern South because, like most other southern cities, it was never defined by a perception of racial moderacy or economic dominance. Richmond was like most southern cities in not having an established culture of racial moderacy that withstood seismic social changes like desegregation. Richmond's history of racial intolerance in particular handcuffed its economic and demographic growth, preventing it from becoming a regional giant after World War II. Ending racial division was essential to improving the city's political economy in a way that was not true for Atlanta. Furthermore, the Richmond story is valuable to modern South historiography because it takes an exceptional approach (study of reconciliation) to a less exceptional place in trying to better explain the South's limited racial progress after the modern civil rights movement.

Crucial to this book is my insistence on historicizing racial reconciliation as Richmonders understood it. Richmonders broadly viewed racial reconciliation as Whites and Blacks working together to resolve issues that were based in past commitments to racism. Richmond's collective understanding of racial reconciliation is in tune with some scholarship that views reconciliation as acknowledging and repenting for past sins with the commitment to correct them.[10] In the round, however, Richmonders falls woefully short of the reconciliation standard recommended by most academics who myopically see racial reconciliation through the prism of reparations and equity.[11] I do not apply the reparatory model to Richmond's reconciliation because it renders negligible the progress generated by Black and White reformers. Moreover, the reparatory model is largely disconnected from the actions of everyday people, as neither Blacks in Richmond—or, for that matter, throughout the nation—saw compensatory policy as a prerequisite for the races to coexist as equals. Time, space, custom, and reality limited even the most optimistic Richmonders' expectations of progress. Therefore, I examine those expectations to better understand and explain the realities they created.

This book's argument comprises three parts, bookended with a prologue and an epilogue. Part 1, "A City Breaking, 1954–1970," starts in 1960s Richmond, yet covers political, economic, social issues that have an even longer history. Prior to the age of modern civil rights—or before *Brown v. Board of Education* (1954), White Richmonders used the power of government and economy to oppress Black residents. Whites seized control of local government after Reconstruction through fraud and excluded Blacks from the political process. The disenfranchisement of Black men, and later Black women, allowed Whites to implement Jim Crow laws at the turn of the twentieth century. These laws allowed White leaders, at the behest of White residents, to confine Blacks to substandard housing, underfunded schools, and menial blue-collar labor. Richmond's transition from Reconstruction to Jim Crow was not uncontested. Yet it was pervasive enough in cementing Blacks beneath Whites in city life. To be Black in Jim Crow Richmond was to begrudgingly accept this fact. That was, however, until Black Richmonders engaged in a full-scale legal assault on Jim Crow segregation after World War II. When it became clear that federal court victories would not undo nearly a century of segregation, Black Richmonders used civil rights legislation to infiltrate city government and turn it into an activist agent for racial equality.

During the 1960s, Black civil rights attorney Henry Levander Marsh III successfully infiltrated city government by becoming a city councilman and vice mayor. Black political ascendance accompanied Black demographic growth, in turn compelling White leaders to use an illegal annexation to limit Black voting power and allowed middle- and working-class Whites to oppose crosstown busing by relocate deeper into the so-called crabgrass frontier. Black political ascendance, annexation, and resistance to busing ended any illusion of racial harmony that some Whites believed Jim Crow Richmond had. Moreover, annexation and White flight were the ultimate rejections of the Black freedom struggle. By the 1970s Whites had quarantined the chocolate city of Richmond between the vanilla suburbs of Chesterfield and Henrico Counties. This reality created the impetus for the next five decades of racial reconciliatory activism by Blacks and Whites, as members of both races sought to pick up the pieces and use the power of government and economy to build an interracial Richmond.

In part 2, "A City Broken, 1970–1984," White business interests and Black political leadership began the racial reconciliation movement by using urban revitalization to heal Richmond's racial divide. Newly empowered Black middle-class leaders worked with White businesspeople to construct newer glass-plated leisure and business spaces in desolate downtown areas where middle-class Whites previously fled in resistance to desegregation. Revitalization was not just a monetary investment in a dying inner city: it materialized the fundamental axiom that interracial cooperation at the highest levels of government would create racial harmony and economic prosperity in a city that had never truly seen it. Moreover, newer downtown infrastructure was the symbolic inspiration for an interracial Richmond. Middle-class White urbanites, working- and middle-class Blacks, and White suburbanites opposed revitalization, draining the city's coffers and creating more distrust between residents and local elites. Yet the failed revitalization efforts set the tone for Richmond to become a more tolerant and inclusive city, where grassroots, cultural, and academic communities would later effectuate their own vision of reconciliation beyond the halls of power.

Part 3, "A City Healing, 1985–Present," argues that city leadership's failed efforts compelled Richmond's nonelite progressives to implement their own reconciliation plans from the mid-1980s to the present. A coalition of progressives enacted crusades against redlining and gentrification while promoting affordable housing, livable-wage employment, and improved public transportation. The next decade saw a neighborhood organization, along with cultural and academic institutions, publicly celebrate the city's long-underappreciated Black history, culminating in the erection of the Arthur Ashe statue along Monument Avenue in 1996. A local civic group then traveled the nation to help other cities use their controversial history to overcome contemporary racial issues at the dawn of the new millennium. This national effort exposed that nearly four decades after the birth of the modern civil rights movement, Whites and Blacks were greatly divided about the existence and extent of racism, especially during the "colorblind era." The national reckoning convinced Richmond's elite and nonelite progressives to unite in marginalizing, reinterpreting, and disconnecting Lost Causism from the city's identity well before the tragedies in Charleston (the shootings at the Emanuel AME Church in 2015) and Charlottesville (the White supremacist–led violence in August 2017). By summer 2020 Richmond was all too ready to take the next step in shedding its racist history by tearing down its Confederate cathedral along Monument Avenue.

This book ends with an epilogue, "Capital of Reconciliation?," that articulates the social issues left unresolved by decades of reconciliation movements. Despite living in the age of antiracist rhetoric and economic abundance, many Richmond leaders and residents refuse to implement racial equity measures to remedy the highest disparities between Whites and Blacks. Richmond has the worst public school system, highest working-poverty rate, and most unstable housing situation of any city in the Commonwealth of Virginia. Yet new monuments, museums, and murals celebrating Black history and racial equality are present throughout the city. This conflict between cosmetic and systemic reform is the unintended consequence of limiting reconciliation to public history, a war that, in spite of the 2020 monument removals, Richmond won two decades prior. Richmonders' limited view on reconciliation comes not from a desire to maintain racial inequity: it is the evolution of the more recent and successful public history reform, where a shared understanding of the past became a common lens by which Blacks and Whites could see themselves as neighbors and not enemies. This new racial attitude inadvertently helped inspire corporate influx and gentrification in the 2010s, which exacerbated the racial disparities that local institutions, which focused on history and identity, were not designed to remedy.

This present study calls for twenty-first century Richmond to further the legacy of racial reconciliation by reinvesting in a more holistic outlook on city life. To prevent gentrification the white-collar middle class should send their children to Richmond public schools and live amongst the working and underclasses in dispersed patterns. City government should align with nonprofits and corporations to pipeline the perpetual Black underclass to livable-wage employment in this hostile and isolating technology-based economy. In sum, Richmond must invest its human capital in moving beyond the sins of racism wrought by centuries of slavery and Jim Crow. The deconstruction of class-centered racial segregation will help Richmond live up to the mission of past progressives who pushed for their city to win/overcome its Struggle for Change.

PART 1

A CITY BREAKING, 1954–1970

1
The Marsh Revolution
"BUILD PEOPLE, NOT THINGS"

> I was brought up under the Virginia system, Virginia values. We respected the law. And that's probably one reason why we sort of tolerated segregation, because it was the law, and we figured that everybody would go by the rules. So we thought that in a matter of time this would change.
> —Henry L. Marsh III

RICHMOND COULD NOT avoid the social and political changes happening across the South in the 1960s. During this decade southern cities became battlegrounds for civil rights protests, White suburban flight, and the rise of Black political officeholding. This fate was not a foregone conclusion for Richmond, however. The city had the distinct identity of being the former capital of the Confederacy in both body and spirit. The plethora of Confederate monuments, the racially segregated landscape, elite White control of city governance, and untapped Black political potential assured many locals that the 1960s whirlwind would bypass Richmond. Local Blacks, however, pushed the city of around two hundred thousand people toward a new racial order. They openly protested segregation in the courts and streets, all while converting their population growth into voting power. Black residents were more assertive than in years past in demanding control of city politics as middle-class Whites fled to the newly expanded suburbs. The 1960s represented the first time in city history where Blacks chartered their own destiny, one where they would be both the city's majority population and primary shareholders of political power.

This reality made the 1968 Richmond city council election a key political battle in the war over the city's soul. In one corner were wealthy White archconservatives who wished to maintain a Jim Crow–style political system where White patronage appeared to suppress Black political ambition. In the other corner was a controversial Black rookie councilman named Henry Levander Marsh III.[1] The coveted prize was a valuable seat on, and influence over, the nine-member city council—Richmond's legislative body. Marsh should have had no real chance to win in 1968. Although he won a seat on the council in 1966, Marsh's first term was filled with failed attempts to stop urban renewal, to help other Blacks get elected to office, or to mend the growing social chasm between Blacks and Whites. Marsh, a civil rights attorney, was also not wealthy, White, a descendant of a prominent Virginia family, or an elite college alumnus in a city where those elements were prerequisite for elected office. Marsh was not particularly cared for by Black leaders, either. The local Black political class refused to support his 1966 campaign or the reform efforts he pushed after being elected. Marsh also had no backing from national civil rights organizations such as the National Urban League, National Association for the Advancement of Colored People (NAACP), Student Nonviolent Coordinating Committee, Southern Christian Leadership Conference, or the Congress on Racial Equality.

What Marsh lacked in traditional credentials for public office, however, he more than made up for with the undying support of Richmond's Black population. Moreover, grassroots changes in Black Richmond gave rise to Marsh's political fortunes. He embraced the age of Black protest; challenged the Black and White power structure on public policy; and prioritized the interests of working-class Black people over the whims of the Black political class. By 1968 Richmond's Black political leadership was forced to back him, and White elites ginned up the highest voter turnout to that date (almost fifty thousand) to restrict his influence on the council. Marsh won reelection in June 1968, becoming only the second Black vice mayor and fourth Black city councilman in the twentieth century. His steady presence in the halls of municipal power reflected the rising tide of color in Richmond, exacerbating a citywide racial fracture that had previously operated beneath the surface.

Henry Marsh brought the full brunt of the modern civil rights movement to Richmond, a city where Whites were all but hiding from it. Marsh's meteoric political ascendance in the mid-to-late 1960s illustrates in detail how the modern civil rights movement ended Jim Crow segregation, yet in so doing exposed some older racial hostilities and created new ones that polarized Whites and Blacks in the Richmond region. As Julian Maxwell Hayter argues in *The Dream Is Lost* (2017), Richmond's Black political leaders had patiently and tactfully pushed to control local government since World War II. As I show, Marsh's political rise caused racial strife because it placed that hidden ambition in plain sight for all to see, even though Marsh did not make the larger dream of full Black political control a reality.

The Marsh Revolution, as I call it, was both a Richmond phenomenon and star in the constellation of American civil rights history. While sharing space with radical second-generation post–World War II Black civil rights activists—headlined by Stokely Carmichael, the Black Panthers, and Fred Hampton—Marsh believed that the traditional channels of power could be reformed to produce equality for Black people. His rise to prominence engendered more Black trust in the political system and not skepticism of it, ensuring that Richmond avoided the widespread violence that had ravaged other cities by 1968. Like other Black leaders of his generation, Marsh failed to achieve the larger goals he set out to accomplish. Yet he fundamentally changed the nature of racial politics in Richmond. Marsh pushed Black elites to expedite plans to seize control of the city council, forcing elite Whites to later go beyond the realm of legalities to ensure that they maintained political power. This turn of events, one where Black political elites no longer disguised themselves as a finger on the hand of White-supremacist policymaking, evaporated the elite White illusion of "racial harmony" that had long defined Jim Crow Richmond, an illusion that belied the notion that Blacks willingly deferred social and political power to their White "betters."[2]

"Our Democratic Way of Life"

Henry Marsh was born in Richmond on December 10, 1933, a time when racial discrimination defined every aspect of Black life in the South: it had been the law of the land since the 1660s, when Virginia's colonial government codified Black people as a slave race.[3] Fewer than 5 percent of Black people living in America had experienced even the slightest modicum of freedom between the nation's founding and the Civil War.[4] Not long after the Confederate South surrendered at Appomattox, White southerners used violence and fraud to drive newly freed and enfranchised Black men from elected office. Southern White supremacists followed this violence by codifying segregation and trapping Blacks in a perpetual state of otherness. This otherness meant "complete segregation," in the words of the *Richmond Times* in 1899.[5] This otherness, more importantly, labeled Blacks as an inferior caste that could not mix with Whites in any way that suggested racial equality.

Henry Marsh was born into a world where segregation reflected the socioeconomic subordination of Black people. The best schools, jobs, and homes were reserved for White people who saw Blacks as beasts of burden who should toil away in menial, under-skilled employment as the equivalent of slaves in the twentieth century.[6] The White South's commitment to segregation in the early 1900s forced millions of Blacks to flee the region for what they thought would be better lives in northern cities. However, on the eve of the Great Depression, roughly nine million Blacks remained in the South. Those who stayed carved out lives within slavery's former boundaries—the rural countrysides and urban centers between Wilmington, Delaware, and El Paso, Texas. Apart from a few prosperous Black communities scattered throughout this vast region, the Black South was largely a dirt-road tundra where scantly paved backroads connected shanty towns with infrastructureless neighborhoods, tarpaper-shacked schools, and pinewood church houses. Even worse, many southern Blacks lived more than half of the twentieth century without running water and electricity.[7]

The Marsh family embodied the resilience Black southerners had to exhibit if they were to thrive in a world designed to impoverish them. Marsh's parents—Henry Levander II and Lucy—were two of the thousands of rural Black working-class domestics who settled in Richmond around 1930, at the outset of the Great Depression. Lucy died in 1938, when Marsh was only five years old. Before her untimely passing, she bore four children who shared space in the dank, single-family home on 509 North 5th Street in Richmond's historically Black Jackson Ward district—the current location of the Richmond Coliseum.[8] Marsh's father sent his four children away to extended family in Newport News while he finished college at Virginia Union University (commonly called Union) and secured better-paid employment.[9] By 1944 the patriarch cemented his family's newly stable lower-middle-class position by finishing his theology degree and landing a pastorship at O'Berry Methodist Church—a parish that no longer exists. He also moved his family out of the impoverished Jackson Ward area.[10]

Marsh's father enforced a strict code of academic achievement amongst his children. "Everyone else in my . . . family was a genius except me. . . . They were all straight-A students," Marsh once said during an interview.[11] His older sister, Marian, eventually became a medical technologist; his younger brother, Fred, earned a PhD and became an analytical chemist. The youngest brother, Harold, became one of the first Black undergraduates at the University of Virginia and eventually a respected Richmond-area judge. Marsh himself earned a full academic scholarship to Howard University School of Law in 1956. Before that, he graduated from Maggie Walker High School in 1952 and enrolled in Union shortly thereafter.[12]

Richmond's racial culture undoubtedly shaped Marsh's decision to matriculate at Union. Upon returning to Richmond to rejoin his father at eleven years old, Marsh would have been more cognizant of Jim Crow.[13] The city streetcars, buses, theaters, hotels, dancehalls, restaurants, department stores, churches, schools, and YMCAs were segregated by color.[14] Marsh later admitted in his memoir and interviews that the Black community helped shield him from the indecencies of racial segregation. Black parents often refused to let Black children wander outside of their enclaves due to the reality that hostile Whites, both in uniforms and street clothes, would not be punished for attacking them.[15] They also used all-Black schools, churches, and civic clubs to instill the confidence and self-worth that Jim Crow tried to take from their children.[16] Yet the hegemonic pillar of Black Richmond resiliency was Virginia Union University. An architectural marvel and center of Black intellectual and political life, Union credentialed most of the professionals who ran Black Richmond institutions. Anyone associated with Union inherited a status in Black Richmond's highly stratified but racially prideful environment. Although he never stated it publicly, Marsh's insistence to study sunup to sundown, often taking unapproved study breaks in the bathroom of the Louis Moriconi Restaurant where he worked as a teen, was to attend not just any college, but Virginia Union University.[17]

It was at Union where Marsh decided to become a lawyer. When he stepped beyond Kings Gate and upon Union grounds, he understood full well the expectation of greatness Unionites were groomed for. As a small Baptist college located in the historically middle- and upper-class section of Northside Richmond, Union's distinction within the historically Black college world came from its commitment to a rigorous liberal arts education, Christian code of conduct, and expectation of postgraduation excellence.[18] Unionites were "to be the leaders among their race"; "to make racial goodwill" through community service; commit to a life of learning; and be at the forefront of racial activism, said famous alumnus and longtime professor Dr. Gordon Blaine Hancock.[19] Upon matriculating at Union in the fall of 1952, Marsh studied sociology, the major Hancock built at Union.[20] He became student body president by his junior term; around the same time he decided that he wanted to become a lawyer after speaking out against school segregation on behalf of Union students on November 30, 1955.

That day, Marsh saw his future flash before his eyes. He was one of 750 people who piled into the Virginia House of Delegates to witness a legislative hearing about "averting compulsory racial integration in [Virginia] schools."[21] The all-White Virginia legislature, with the support of the Commonwealth's White majority, wished to open state funds to White parents who wanted to send their children to all-White private schools to circumvent the *Brown v. Board of Education* US Supreme Court decision. Only thirty-eight of the one hundred Black spectators publicly expressed dismay over the proposal to, as one Black pastor said, "weaken our public-school system" by incentivizing Whites to use taxpayer money and segregated private schools to evade the law of the land.

Marsh was one of them. He spoke on behalf of Union's student body—Richmond's future Black middle class—accusing the legislature of "sell[ing] out our democratic way of life" with tax-funded private school vouchers.[22] Yet few speakers captivated the audience like the forty-eight-year-old Black lawyer Oliver White Hill. After taking the podium, the slender, balding man implored White legislators to "look at the facts" and refuse to "succumb to the hue and cry raised . . . by those who have no faith in democracy, public education, or anything else that makes democracy meaningful." Hill believed that undermining the Supreme Court decision with private school vouchers was "illegal, unchristian and un-American." While members of the legislature sat in disagreement, the federal courts sided with Hill six years later.[23]

Oliver Hill would help guide Marsh through the troubled waters of legal education. Marsh later admitted that Hill's courage amazed him, as he never heard "any Black person speak to White folks like that."[24] Little did Marsh know, but Hill was also impressed with him because very few Black people openly criticized the White power structure in Virginia. "What are you going to do when you grow up?" Hill asked Marsh after the hearing. "Well, I want to be a lawyer," Marsh remembered nervously telling Hill. Seeing potential in the Union upperclassman, Hill offered him a job as an assistant at his law firm. Marsh happily accepted the opportunity.[25] Hill also convinced Marsh to attend Howard's School of Law in 1956. Marsh's other option was the esteemed University of Virginia School of Law—a program that had, until then, only matriculated one Black student at the behest of a court order by Oliver Hill in 1950.[26] With that in mind, Marsh chose Howard, and their offer to pay for his education made the decision much easier.

Howard School of Law was, by the time Marsh matriculated in the fall of 1956, the premier legal training ground for aspiring Black attorneys. It groomed nearly every Black lawyer working in Virginia, and the South at large, between 1871 and 1970. Moreover, Howard's law school taught its students to become social engineers who used the US Constitution to undo Jim Crow laws.[27] Graduating second only to future US Supreme Court Justice Thurgood Marshall in 1933, Oliver Hill left Howard and became one of only fifteen full-time Black lawyers who worked for little to no profit to end discrimination in Virginia.[28] In fact, it was Hill's dogged attack against school segregation that led him to Capitol Square in downtown Richmond, the place where he met the young Henry Marsh.[29] Marsh found in Hill both a source of inspiration and an example to follow on the long road of legal and political activism. For Richmond, Hill was the Black activist past and present while Marsh was its future.[30]

"Building People, Not Things"

It did not take long for Henry Marsh to infuse Richmond's courtroom and street-level civil rights activism into the local political system. After graduating from law school in 1959 and serving nearly three years in the US Army and with the Department of Labor and Statistics, Marsh returned home to marry dentist and high school sweetheart Diane Harris and start a law firm with Oliver Hill's close friend Samuel Wilbur Tucker.[31] They did not have to search hard for work, as parent and college student activism, ignited largely by *Brown* and the Greensboro, North Carolina, sit-ins in 1960, energized Black Virginians to continue attacking Jim Crow segregation where the modern civil rights movement mostly played out: in court.[32]

Marsh took the lead in fighting school segregation. He lost his first case in 1961 involving a Black Richmond boy who failed to gain admission to a White school for "lack of academic qualification," although he tested at a genius-level IQ.[33] Marsh tried again in 1962; this time he won a class-action lawsuit against the City of Richmond for maintaining racially segregated schools.[34] By 1964 the young attorney made a decision that altered the city's racial climate for the next few decades. That decision was entering politics to better effect his civil rights agenda.[35] Marsh set his sights on the nine-member Richmond City Council, a post his mentor Oliver Hill had won in 1948 and lost in 1950. Like Hill, Marsh soon learned that his path to city hall would not be an easy one.

By the time Marsh eyed elected office, local politics was dominated by two factions: elite Whites and Black middle-class professionals. Wealthy White businessmen and oligarchs dominated city politics; the majority of voters (White) elected them to nearly every office. By 1965, however, "Richmond's Negro voters [were] rapidly moving into a position of formidable [*sic*] political power. . . . and [White] Richmonders [would] be wise not to ignore it," as the *Richmond News-Leader* had warned five years earlier.[36] The growing Black voting bloc was a product of an increasing Black population and the ability of the Crusade for Voters (Crusade) to mobilize and steer them to the polls. Influential Black doctors, lawyers, insurance executives, and professors created the Crusade in 1956 in lieu of the Commonwealth's and South's attack on NAACP activity after the *Brown* decision. Nearly a decade later, they had made the Black vote—"once the kiss of death" per the *Washington Post*—into "an asset; no candidate for city council can afford to offend it and expect to win." The *Post* went on to state, quite accurately, that "perhaps nowhere else in the country, certainly nowhere else in the South, do Negroes use their vote with more sophistication than in Richmond."[37]

Shaping this racialized political dichotomy was an unequal partnership in which White elites used patronage to keep Black electoral gains from becoming effectual political power. After World War II, Black politics in Richmond, like elsewhere in the urban South, had become what it had been for decades in Northern cities: a clientage system in which White elites controlled Black voting power by appeasing the often out-of-touch Black middle class.[38] This was not the vision of Oliver Hill and Virginia NAACP chairman Dr. Jesse Tinsley, two men who spent the mid-1930s and early 1940s growing the Black vote in Richmond. Yet they unknowingly sowed the seeds for this arrangement by aligning with powerful New Deal liberal Whites who needed Black support to change the city charter and empower the council and city manager while making the mayor a figurehead. As a result, even though Blacks throughout the South were heavily disenfranchised, White Richmond elites supported Black voter drives and helped extend registration hours. This was perhaps the only case in the South where Whites encouraged Black franchise during Jim Crow.[39] This partnership paid off in 1948 when Hill won a seat on the city council with more than three thousand White votes, making him the first Black elected to a citywide office in the entire South since 1898.[40]

Increased civil rights advocacy cost Hill his post in 1950, but his and Tinsley's efforts in previous decades mended an unholy bond between Black voting and White political power in Richmond. By the 1960s the Crusade for Voters steered Black votes toward the least conservative White councilmen during citywide elections to push "the Negro voter into the mainstream of Richmond's political current." The rewards for these often-lopsided bargains were menial "places on personnel, housing, welfare, recreation, beautification and planning boards," according to a Crusade memo.[41] This was the primary means for Blacks to access the highest levels of political power in Richmond. Moreover, this political reality buttressed Black Richmond's associationalism, where white-collar Black elites took it upon themselves to represent Black interests. A result of this came in 1964, when the Crusade secured the election of White establishment favorite Bernard A. Cephas to the nine-member city council.[42] The Unionite real estate broker was a longtime token bureaucrat and the second Black person elected to the council in the twentieth century behind Henry Marsh's mentor Oliver Hill.[43]

Marsh rose to the top of Black Richmond politics because he used the political machine against itself. The Crusade's organizational structure reflected the middle-class dominance over Black Richmond politics writ large. Professionals occupied the offices of president, executive board, research committee, and fundraising. Working-class Blacks operated the precinct clubs, where block leaders and field workers went door to door compelling Blacks to vote on election day. According to an organizational memo, block leaders and field workers were "the lifelines of communication between the organizations and the people of the neighborhood." Marsh wisely operated as a field worker and block leader upon returning home to practice law in 1961.[44] By the 1966 election cycle, he continued to work these channels, but for himself and not the Crusade, which refused to support his bid for city council. He remembered being told that "two Blacks [Cephas and Winfred Mundle] on the ticket" was "enough" by Crusade leadership.[45] The Crusade was very resistant to Henry Marsh entering city politics as an elected official even though organizational histories, as well as Marsh's own interviews and memoir, are quiet to this fact. The Crusade's rejection of Marsh's proposed candidacy was not a rejection of him per se. Rather, the Crusade refused to let a political outsider, even a well-meaning one, undermine over a generation's worth of political groundwork to seize the levers of power in Richmond. Although Marsh did not see it at the time, the Crusade was engaged in a long march through Richmond politics that was scheduled to end with Blacks being the city's voting and governmental majority.

Marsh's mentor Oliver Hill and other local Black elites had allied with White liberals for the 1948 city charter change with the secret, long-term intention of controlling the city council. This charter change turned a thirty-two-member bicameral body, elected by precinct, into a nine-member unitary group elected at large. The switch not only made city government more efficient, it allowed Blacks more access to the council. Because Blacks were confined to certain residential areas of the city by a racist real estate market, the ward system ensured that not one Black person sat on the council between 1898 and 1948. With wards no longer a factor in elections, Blacks could, in theory, and many hoped in practice, elect a majority Black council and mayoral office. Thus, what functioned as clientage politics was, in fact, a sophisticated strategy to seize power from unsuspecting White elites. This strategy required the Crusade to, as they did, operate as a nonambitious political group that served White elite interests. The candidacy of a young Black lawyer from Howard University in the mid-1960s with a strong civil rights background would have awakened White elites to, and activated them against, the Crusade's real agenda.

While it is unclear whether Marsh understood the full dynamics of his proposed candidacy, his actions showed that he was unconcerned with the Crusade's ultimate agenda. In September 1965 Marsh announced his independent candidacy, promoting himself as "a voice of the people without any obligation to consider the will of any political machine." Marsh's candidacy scared Crusade leadership because he was "an articulate young civil rights lawyer [whose] commitments and consistency were considerably different from the [Black] moneyed class," a Crusade memo documented on the eve of the election.[46] Marsh's grassroots popularity among young adults and working-class Blacks compelled local ministers to "unanimously" endorse him. Poll after poll in spring of 1966 showed that Black Richmonders were going to follow their ministerial class's endorsement.[47] To save face and keep the Crusade prestige alive and well, their leadership met with Marsh a week before the election and offered their official but empty endorsement.[48] Given his agenda to create "a coalition to take over the council . . . [and] provide [Black] leadership to the city," Marsh wisely accepted their offer and joined two other Black candidates on the Crusade slate (Cephas and fellow insurance agent Winfred Mundle). All three men won city council seats in 1966.[49]

Marsh entered city hall at a critical juncture in southern and civil rights history. By the mid-1960s the South had grown economically thanks to industrial and federal investment in its major cities. Previously backwater towns such as Atlanta, Birmingham, New Orleans, Richmond, Memphis, Charlotte, and Houston made the South the nation's fastest-growing region in terms of population growth, middle-class job creation, and housing development.[50] Leading this economic change were college-educated middle- and upper-class White urbanites, mainly lawyers and corporate executives, who also entered politics and proclaimed that they would "emphasize an attitude of cooperation and a spirit of [racial] reconciliation," according to Arkansas congressman Lawrence Brooks Hays.[51] Richmond elites took part in this regional boosterism, often touting the city as the only major southern metropole with "desegregated" schools, a Black school board member, and thousands of active Black voters. "Nondiscrimination is one of the exciting racial stories in the South, its pace astonishes many Richmonders, White and Negro," wrote the *Washington Post*, for example.[52]

The region's economic growth only exacerbated simmering racial unrest, however.[53] The White South's supposed racial moderation rarely extended beyond the color line, regardless of their "North industrial alliances."[54] Most White southerners flagrantly disobeyed desegregation orders in public schools, bus services, and public parks.[55] White officials also targeted Black voters with routine changes to voting laws.[56] This reality of economic abundance and unreformed racism compelled Black Americans to shift their support from older, traditionally white-collar, middle-class leaders to younger, more radical voices.[57] Thus, Marsh's electoral victory was both the result of his sound political maneuvering and of Black desires to infuse their leadership class with new blood.

Not long after taking office, Henry Marsh etched his legend into local lore by opposing a bipartisan, biracial urban renewal plan. Marsh's opposition, in the form of a November 1966 resolution, halted the Downtown Expressway with $95 million of public and private funding. The expressway was the centerpiece of the "Main to the James" strategy of linking the downtown business core to the growing southwest Chesterfield suburbs at the expense of eradicating some long-standing, working-class, mostly Black communities.[58] In spite of that, local Black leaders, as Marsh learned, were already on board with the plan.

By the time Marsh opposed the expressway, Richmond in particular and Virginia at large were in lockstep with the national push for urban renewal. Since the late 1940s, White Richmond leadership advocated for the growth of what historian Christopher Silver documented as a "Greater Richmond" form of planning. This plan involved decimating "slum" neighborhoods in favor of newer highways connecting the inner city to the growing suburban ring.[59] Under the Federal Highway Act of 1956 (later reenacted in 1962), Congress gave upwards to fifty thousand localities federal funds to construct new highways.[60] Where these highways would be built was no secret, as it was in the "national interest to encourage and promote the development of transportation systems" through Black inner-city neighborhoods, a congressional memo stated. These "blight fights" or "war[s] on slums" were "active on all fronts," allowing White slumlords and bureaucrats in southern cities to autocratically displace Black families.[61] More rural Virginia cities such as Lynchburg, Charlottesville, Harrisonburg, Roanoke, Bristol, Portsmouth, and Alexandria dealt with similar issues, but on a smaller scale than Richmond.[62]

Richmond's highway construction plans reveal the neglect and indifference for Black life inherent within them. The highway reports accounted for cost, expected business growth, environmental impact, and even the toll revenue needed to pay off various loan debts. The plans almost never mentioned the human cost of displacing Black families who could not afford to leave. Black Richmonders were by and large working-class people, possessing very little wealth, with even fewer opportunities to acquire it. "There was always a joke that the only 'respectable' jobs for a Black man in Richmond [were] a teacher, undertaker, lawyer, businessman, preacher, and mailman," a longtime resident said about the 1960s.[63] This was less a joke than it was fact, as Black Richmonders had limited access to the social ladder. The public sector provided very little reprieve from the economic limitations Blacks dealt with. With the exception of teachers, Black professionals were completely barred from Richmond's large governmental middle class.[64]

The private-sector middle class was small as well, given that Black businesses almost always served a segregated market of working-class customers. Those who worked for Whites were rarely promoted up the managerial and administrative ladder. This was a regional and national problem: around 42.5 percent of southern Blacks made less than $3,000 a year; in comparison, only 17.4 percent of Whites earned as little.[65] "The average Negro college graduate," said the Harvard Business School in 1966 about the nation in sum, "can expect to earn less over his lifetime than the White who does not go beyond the eighth grade."[66]

Marsh's defiance of the Downtown Expressway highlighted that urban renewal was, in the Richmond context, a White elite plan that exacerbated Black economic oppression. In spite of having a sizable Black middle class (mostly educators and businesspeople) in comparison to many southern cities, the Black working class represented over 97 percent of displaced people in Richmond prior to 1966. Much of this came from working-class Whites rallying substantial opposition to the decimation of their own neighborhoods, such as the successful fight that saved Gamble Hill in 1953. Working-class Whites, with the help of the *Richmond News Leader* and their grassroot neighborhood organization, pushed the all-White city council to reject a proposal to demolish the area. Blacks, however, did not have such success that same year, as the local papers refused to curry public favor in their direction.[67]

With overwhelming public support for demolishing Black neighborhoods, Black middle-class Richmonders navigated the city's racist real estate community by purchasing and renting their way into transitioning neighborhoods, mainly in Richmond's Northside. Many working-class Blacks—homeowners and renters—however, could not afford new homes and rising rents elsewhere. Thus, they relocated to newly constructed housing projects in the city's East End for the better part of the twentieth century (a trend that will be discussed in detail in chapter 4).[68] Black opposition to urban renewal was largely couched in Crusade advocacy for the construction of more affordable housing. Marsh, on the other hand, did not just oppose an expressway: the political outsider confronted a real systemic force of White supremacy that actively trapped many Black Richmonders in a state of helplessness. This assessment is confirmed by a populist White Richmond lawyer who said that "the downtrodden and exploited people of the poverty stricken areas of Richmond ha[d] a real champion," and his name was Henry Marsh.[69]

Marsh's resistance to the expressway exposed Black Richmonders to the reality that not all Black elected officials, even during the civil rights era, worked in favor of Black interests. All of Marsh's colleagues on the council (six Whites and two Blacks), in a combined public statement, publicly accused Marsh of being a political opportunist, declaring that "we deplore that some would undertake to make political capital out of the human problems" of urban renewal.[70] Marsh retorted to the Black and White councilmen by saying that he always "bitterly opposed it [urban renewal] as being overly and unnecessarily destructive of the homes, churches, and communities in its path."[71] Marsh's colleagues proved themselves more out of touch when they asked him to rescind his resolution by promising to place displaced Blacks in public housing with greater efficiency. Marsh would not grease the wheel of urban renewal, however, and refused to recenter the conversation on "putting roofs over heads when the real issue is not to take roofs away," a political insider observed.[72] Confronted with a united resistance by fellow councilmembers just months after being elected, Marsh learned what it really meant to be a political outsider.

Marsh's stance ultimately succumbed to the political maneuvering that trapped the dislocated into poverty in the first place. The soon-to-be-public-housing residents and Marsh held several antihighway grassroots meetings in November 1966. They channeled the spirit of the civil rights era by packing churches, community centers, and even city council meetings, all with significant media attention. Yet no victory would be won as the other eight city council members voted to remove Marsh's resolution on November 28, 1966.[73] The following year the city council outvoted Marsh again to turn other Black neighborhoods into highways, toll roads, and the Richmond Coliseum. When Richmond was selected over Hampton, Norfolk, and Roanoke by *Look* magazine and the National Civic League to be the All-American City in 1967, Marsh refused to participate in the boosterism, saying: "I do not believe Richmond deserves an award as an All-American City." A Black grassroots leader echoed that sentiment in a letter to the council, claiming that "when it comes to the attitude of this city government toward working class people—toward racial readjustment—toward housing problems . . . we do not qualify for the award."[74] The efficiency with which Richmond moved on urban renewal obscures the importance of the Black dissent that Marsh represented. Marsh's failed campaign cemented a bond between his political career and the aspirations for leadership festering in the Black working classes, putting the Black establishment on notice. From here on, opposing Marsh would have electoral consequences.

The inability to halt urban renewal convinced Marsh that he needed political allies who would help him in city hall. Although fellow Black council members Winfred Mundle and Bernard Cephas were supposed to represent Black Richmond, the urban renewal fight proved them unwilling to challenge the White power structure when it mattered. So when councilwoman and former mayor Eleanor Sheppard resigned to run for a seat in the Virginia legislature in November 1967, Marsh nominated Walter T. Kenney to replace her. Kenney did not fit Richmond's mold for a Black political leader. He was not educated at Union, nor was he a white-collar worker who lived in the Northside. Kenney was a mailman and Crusade block captain who headed many civic groups in the Black working- and underclass area of Church Hill in Richmond's East End. Most importantly, Kenney was the kind of ally Marsh needed on the city council because he "underst[ood] the poor and underprivileged," a housing project resident told the *Richmond Afro-American* upon his nomination.[75]

Marsh's nomination of Kenney helped solidify Black Richmond's political shift. He pressured Northside's Black elite to open its leadership ranks and support Kenney. Mundle and Cephas, however, "told the colored community, in essence, to go jump," the *Afro-American* opined in the aftermath of them voting against Marsh once again. While Cephas and Mundle did not know it at the time, Marsh's rookie term, while filled with failed efforts, increased Black people's expectations of political leadership. Black leaders were no longer just expected to occupy office: they had to openly represent the myriad Black interests, even at the risk of losing powerful White allies. The Crusade sensed the changing tide and refused to endorse Cephas and Mundle for the 1968 city council election. Marsh was reelected to the council. His Black colleagues, however, lost their seats and the respect of Black Richmond voters, neither of which they ever regained.[76]

"We Should Not Seek Black Power"

When Marsh took office again in 1968, the modern civil rights movement shifted hard toward the Black Power protests. This shift was largely the result of Blacks expecting more from their elected leadership than they could give. After the Voting Rights Amendment, many urban Blacks stopped demanding integration and called for livable-wage jobs, better healthcare, and more control over public education.[77] However, Black leaders could not provide these opportunities. Seeking solutions, Blacks listened closely to newer activists such as Stokely Carmichael. He rose to prominence in 1968 by articulating a message of Black Power that meant Blacks should separate from Whites within America and protect themselves from White violence.[78] White Americans, however, labeled Carmichael's Black Power a "Militant Negro nationalist movement."[79] In 1968 the Black Power movement was tainted by the eruption of riots throughout American cities following the assassination of Dr. Martin Luther King Jr.[80] The violent scenes showing over two thousand casualties in American streets made the Black Power movement more attractive to young urban Blacks, feared by most Whites, and, most importantly, visible enough for many to base their perceptions of race relations on it.[81]

Stokely Carmichael came to Richmond in April 1968 in hopes of building his Black Power nation.[82] This was his second trip to the former capital of the Confederacy in two years.[83] His presence encouraged five hundred Union students to march on the administration about implementing systemic changes on campus, ranging from the removal of mandatory class attendance to eradicating exit exams for graduation. The administration conceded to all of these demands. The comfort with which Black elites at Union accepted Carmichael and adhered to student demands for change put Richmond Whites on notice for the potential of a race riot. "Stokely Carmichael versus the Ku Klux Klan, that's the real problem in this society," a Richmond-area politician said in 1968.[84]

The Black Power sentiment did land in Richmond with the arrival of Stokely Carmichael. While it is unclear as to why, Carmichael had a negative encounter with the majority White Richmond police force upon his arrival. When the news broke of him being detained, Carmichael reportedly told Blacks to "go home and get your guns." This incident did not escalate further in the streets. It did, however, in the halls of power. White Richmond councilmembers inquired about how to prevent what they felt was an oncoming race riot. A close friend to the council, who happened to be a Washington insider, told a White councilman to "restore law and order" and militarize the police.[85] He relayed that message to the other White councilmembers, who wanted to ensure that "the police department must prepare for demonstrations and for civil disobedience." The Richmond Police Department received new weaponry, and they underwent paramilitary training during the summer of 1968.[86] The White councilmen also worked with nonprofit organizations to help create jobs for Blacks in an effort to, as one White councilman claimed, "reduce urban tensions and overcome the influence of radical extremists who seek to exploit poverty and sinister ends."[87]

The city council had much to fear. It was widely known that more than a few young Black men in the city's worst ghettos were very receptive to Carmichael's message.[88] The oldest among them began recruiting younger Black boys and teaching them "the technique of making firebombs and rioting." The Richmond Riot Commission reported that the "targets would be Broad Street, West End, and other commercial areas" that White people frequented. While no large-scale attacks happened, some adolescents "engaged in [minor] looting and burning for thrills, others for revenge" against Whites.[89] While "few Negro leaders here predict the kind of ghetto violence that is rocking other American cities," wrote the *Washington Post*, "most agree that Richmond has not guaranteed insulation from an explosion." Even Henry Marsh, a man with his ear to the ground of Black Richmond ghettoes, admitted that the "most tragic mistake" Richmonders could make was "to believe it [racial violence] can't happen here."[90]

Although violence could happen in Richmond, Marsh's political rise and prominence ensured that it did not. A Black resident wrote to the *Afro-American*, "We do not want Richmond to turn into a Watts." The resident went on to say that "we should not seek Black Power." Instead, Blacks sought empowerment through controlling city hall. As the *Washington Post* reported, "Stokely Carmichael drew a big crowd and considerable interest when he spoke in Richmond last winter but whatever aftereffect he created apparently was parlayed into an advantage for . . . the powerful Crusade for Voters."[91] For this, White political leaders should have thanked Henry Marsh. Although he was the Crusade's most ardent opponent, his advocacy for the Black working- and underclasses ensured that Richmond did not burn like peer cities such as Atlanta and the District of Colombia. "Some see Henry Marsh as the first real break from this long-standing arrangement" of White leaders telling Blacks what to do. Furthermore, as the *Washington Post* elaborated, "Many negroes see the promise of a real voice in running the city—as symbolized by Marsh—that the more violent interpretations of Black Power so far mean little here."[92] Marsh gave Black Richmonders a political avenue by which to channel their energy for racial reform. This invaluable resource came from a man who grew up as one of their own, a social engineer whose political ascendency came from the idealistic mission to "build people, not things."[93] Richmonders did not have an activist city government by 1968. Yet Marsh's political rise in Black Richmond, while the city became Blacker, made it clear that they were about to get it.

2
Annexation

"THE ONLY ANSWER"

"CHANGE IS rapidly overtaking this city of White-columned mansions, monuments studded boulevards and traditional Southern ways," wrote the *Washington Post* in 1967. The paper boldly predicted Richmond's ironic fate: "Once the capital of the Confederacy and later the birthplace of Massive Resistance to school integration. . . . [Richmond] is on the verge of becoming, like Washington [DC], a predominately Negro city."[1]

This demographic development was mainly a problem for White Richmond elites because of the economic and political ramifications of being a majority Black city in the post–World War II era. Majority Black cities, large and small, were often financially hamstrung because the middle-class (mostly White) tax base fled to the surrounding suburbs. In Richmond the citywide population of 220,000 was evenly split between Whites and Blacks by 1968. This split translated into increased public-sector poverty and growing Black electoral power. Richmond's Black population grew alongside rookie councilman Henry Marsh's winning reelection in 1968 with significantly fewer White votes than in 1966, and with the number of registered Black voters increasing by 5,300, while the White vote had only increased by 4,500 in the same period.[2] The growing Black presence in Richmond foreshadowed that the *Washington Post*'s assessment of the city's future was indeed correct. By 1970 Richmond would fall in line with cities such as Washington, DC, and be majority Black and impoverished.

I recast the often-told story of White elites trying to prevent the city from becoming majority Black and poor through a twenty-three-square-mile annexation of a portion of Chesterfield County in 1970. Historians often paint the annexation as a streamlined, racist, knee-jerk reaction to White politicians' sudden realization that Blacks were becoming Richmond's majority.[3] Although White elites certainly used annexation—the process of extending urban boundaries and incorporating occupied suburban territory to grow the tax base—to maintain political control over Richmond, annexation was the most sensible solution to prevent Richmond from becoming a municipality of the Black poor in the 1960s. The city's mounting public debt created the imperative for White leaders to aggressively seek to absorb an adjacent tax base. This strategy had been employed in many peer southern cities to satisfy public debts and maintain decaying infrastructure. The annexation strategy, however, ran against both a regional and state political culture that had been long opposed to urban expansion. Thus, the Black political ascendance and demographic shift in Richmond sped up already-existing plans to absorb the suburbs and turn Richmond into a thriving metropolitan area.

My analysis of the actions of Richmond's White elite, when put into context of local, state, and national urban expansions in this period, also shows that the politics of annexation became a racialized process because of White suburban flight and the growth of Black urban residence. In seeking to prevent urban decay, White Richmond elites, like urban elites elsewhere, preferred to form city-county mergers. These mutually agreed upon combinations of urban and suburban localities ensured that the lily-White "island suburbs," in the words of historian Matthew Lassiter, pay for the inner-city poverty they left behind.[4] White suburbanites, especially in the South, used every legal means to block urban governments from acquiring their tax dollars through municipal mergers.[5] This was the impetus for annexation efforts in the post–World War II era. Suburban resistance racialized annexations by exposing the socioeconomic fault lines among White supremacists. Urban White elites did not mind sharing a city with poor Blacks because residential segregation protected them from Black neighborhoods. The White middle and working classes, however, had less protection from Black areas. Thus, the suburbs and the political protection they afforded White tax dollars appealed to them more than urban residency. Annexation became a last resort for urban leadership to economically maintain their crumbling cities and not just a racist rallying cry for the maintenance of White political control in urban areas.

The Richmond story exemplifies the limitations of urban leaders' insistence to racialize annexation as a means of maintaining White supremacy. While both White urbanites and suburbanites agreed about the "race problem"—a dislike for Black political power and majority residency—their diverging socioeconomic interests insured that they rarely aligned on a policy solution. If the maintenance of White supremacy was the sole motivator for annexations, then Whites in Richmond, Chesterfield, and Henrico Counties would have willingly merged into one locality, drowning out the Black vote and ensuring that Whites would control the area's governmental, economic, and cultural centers for the foreseeable future. The fact that they did not, and that White Richmond leaders went through so much trouble to secure a twenty-three-square-mile annexation deal in 1970, shows that annexation was not the extension of White political and racial solidarity after World War II. Rather, it represented a contested terrain where class-centered political battles were defined by their racial outcomes, which further polarized Richmond during the modern civil rights era.

"All of the Evils of the City"

Richmond's racial demographics concerned nearly every White political figure in Virginia.[5] It was also well known that the 1968 election cycle sent shockwaves throughout the Commonwealth, as the highest number of Black candidates since Reconstruction ran for statewide offices. Most of them hailed from counties and cities with Black majorities that had never seen Black representation on the capitol grounds.[6] The word was out that Black leaders were making a political play to control Richmond, from city government to the state capitol. However, a White Virginia delegate made it clear in 1969 that "the capital of the Old Confederacy . . . will not become like our nation's capital."[7] The quote reflects the sense of ownership that White Virginians, primarily the elite, felt they had over Richmond. The "capital of the Old Confederacy" was the political and economic center of Virginia's high society. The city's very geography reflected where this power was located and how it operated.

In 1780 the Virginia General Assembly elected to move the state capital up the James River from Williamsburg to Richmond. Thomas Jefferson helped design the first iteration of Capitol Square—the Commonwealth's governmental center, consisting of Roman temples and gothic mansions that housed the Virginia legislature, Virginia Supreme Court, Richmond City Hall, Eastern Federal District Court of Virginia, the Executive Mansion, and other governmental buildings. Also lying within the borders of Bank Street to the south, Capitol Street to the north, Government Street to the east, and 9th Street to the west were monuments to George Washington, Edgar Allen Poe, Stonewall Jackson, as well as insignias honoring Founding Fathers George Mason, Patrick Henry, and Supreme Court Justice John Marshall.[8]

Outside of Capitol Square, as the capital city grew, major retailers, high-end social clubs, and swanky restaurants catered almost exclusively to local and statewide elites. Downtown's Main Street headquartered major chemical (Ethyl Corporation) and metal (Reynolds) factories, whose gross domestic output was second to none in the entire South. Richmond's economic crown jewel, the tobacco industry led by Philip Morris, then located in Shockoe Bottom, earned the city the title of Cigarette Capital of the World. Financing these firms were the First Bank of Virginia, Planters Bank, and others situated within blocks of Capitol Square. Richmond was the seat of social, political, and economic power in Virginia and was one of the most viable and growing urban centers in the South. When White attorney and Martinsville delegate William F. Stone claimed that "this capital city belongs to All Virginians," he meant that it belonged to those who were White, wealthy, and connected.[9]

Richmond's political and corporate network was founded on an exclusive social club that was so interconnected and hidden from plain sight that one of its long-term members challenged the local conspiracies about them by saying, "There is no unit of people you can call the *Establishment*."[10] The anecdotal and documentary record says otherwise. The Establishment, or "The Group" as they fancied themselves, was an archconservative, White male oligarchy that controlled the city's most powerful religious, educational, economic, and political institutions from their downtown offices and affluent Far West End neighborhoods. They frequented the same Episcopal and Presbyterian churches, attended the same private schools (St. Christopher's, St. Catherine's, St. Gertrude, and Benedictine), postsecondary institutions (University of Richmond, College of William & Mary, Virginia Military Institute, University of Virginia, Yale University, and Princeton University), and owned the key brokerage firms and banks along Main Street that controlled Richmond's, and much of Virginia's, corporate and industrial economy after World War II.[11]

Richmond's elite operated in a tight-knit circle. The Establishment made the city's most important decisions within the Chamber of Commerce, the Commonwealth Club, and the William Byrd, Thomas Jefferson, and John Marshall hotels.[12] Men such as Morrill M. Crowe (vice president of William Poythress & Co., Inc.), Robert J. Habenicht (attorney and director of trade relations at A. H. Robins Co.), Robert T. Marsh Jr. (chairman of First and Merchants National Bank), Henry R. Miller III (secretary of First Federal Savings and Loan Association), and James C. Wheat (president and CEO of the James C. Wheat and Co. brokerage firm), served several terms on the city council after World War II.[13] Other Establishment men like William M. Hill (president of the Bank of Virginia), Frank G. Louthan Jr. (president of Everett Waddey Co., Inc.), Charles P. Wilson (president of Chewning and Wilmer, Inc.), Stuart Shumate (president of the Richmond, Fredericksburg, and Potomac Railroad), J. Harvey Wilkinson Jr. (president of State-Planters Bank of Commerce and Trusts), and his vice president, Carleton P. Moffatt Jr., filled the ranks of the retail merchants committee, school board, chamber of commerce, real estate commission, and other "advisory" committees throughout Richmond.

From the comforts of their West End clubs and downtown offices, the Establishment handled Richmond and its race relations with velvet gloves. After the 1968 election the Establishment held their noses and *selected* Henry Marsh to be vice mayor "to improve race relations in the city."[14] Beneath their velvet gloves, however, lay iron fists that stamped out anyone, White or Black, who threatened their power. For one longtime Richmonder, the most important thing to remember about the Establishment was that "it was White!"[15] Yet ambitious working- and middle-class Whites learned that while White skin was a non-negotiable requirement for entry into the Richmond Establishment, it was still just one of many standards that had to be met. "There was a widespread sense that the upper classes, through their commerce and influence over government, ultimately controlled our lives," a White working-class resident once noted in his memoir. He continued, "We knew full well that there were higher rungs of the ladder of success," yet "we also knew that we had no access to that ladder."[16]

Past the nearly impenetrable walls of race was family legacy, private and university-level education, and highly skilled, white-collar employment. These walls acted as pillars that upheld the shared values that White Richmond leaders relied on to maintain power amidst the social changes of the 1960s. Every Establishment member was not obligated to think the same, but they were obligated by custom and shared interests to act the same.[17] They maintained power by using their influence in the local courts, businesses, and legislative chambers to play defense against any major social changes. By 1968 the bulk of this shared responsibility ironically fell on the shoulders of Mayor Philip J. Bagley Jr., a man whose place in the Establishment was not protected by family, church, or school affiliation but by his race and merit.

The grandson of rural Irish-born laborers, Bagley grew up among the White working poor in Richmond's East End. Bagley's father worked several odd jobs before starting his own laundry service in the 1910s. He would own this business until his death in the 1940s.[18] The outstanding Richmond City public school student later earned admission to Georgetown University in 1922 and the University of Richmond Law School in 1925.[19] Although educated at two elite private universities, Bagley quickly hit Richmond's glass ceiling. Answers to the questions "What high school did you attend?" and "What does your father do for a living?" disqualified Bagley, as well as most other White applicants, from the comfortable life that working at downtown-based law and brokerage firms provided.[20] He spent most of his post–law school years working as a laundryman with his father and as a part-time attorney in Richmond.[21] After returning from World War II, Bagley became a civic leader in the East End and galvanized White support for urban renewal.[22] This, along with the cachet of being an University of Richmond alumnus, earned him a coveted seat on the city council in 1952. Bagley took full advantage of becoming a councilman. He connected with several downtown elites and landed a lucrative career in real estate law with prominent Main Street firms. Bagley later moved his family to the Far West End, settling well into the nest of Richmond's White moneyed class.[23]

After sixteen years on the city council and with support from the White working class and Black political class, Bagley's fellow council members chose him to be the mayor of Richmond in 1968. This selection resulted largely from Richmond's city manager form of government. The popularly elected council hired a city manager to handle administrative duties. They also chose two of their own to fill the largely ceremonial, and effectively powerless, offices of mayor and vice mayor. Councilmen treated the mayorship specifically as a rotating trophy between friends who shared the reins of power for decades. However, by the late 1960s the office was changing.

Although the mayor's primary function was to propose and vote on legislation with the city council, the office required more active involvement by the time of Bagley's tenure. Bagley walked into the mayor's office during, as he stated with regret, "a time of urban crisis in America."[24] He went on to declare upon his inauguration: "We are a community of almost 220,000 people—about half Black, about half White. We are a community into which have moved thousands of impoverished families from the rural sections of our and other nearby states."[25] The phrase "urban crisis"—known mostly because of historian Thomas Sugrue's seminal book about postwar Detroit—was widely used by legislators, academics, and journalists in the mid-1960s to describe the rapid economic decay of America's inner cities after World War II.[26] America's fifty largest urban areas initially swallowed the majority of returning veterans and job seekers following the war.[27] However, rural counties just beyond the city limits worked with housing developers and financiers to create affordable homes for the emerging White middle class. As the newly suburban counties attracted affluent taxpayers from cities across the country, urban cores became filled with, as an Establishment member stated about Richmond specifically, "racial unrest, poverty, and the ghettos that Blacken our city environment."[28]

By 1968 the urban crisis had already reached epic proportions in Virginia's largest cities. "Conditions are bleak and threatening to become worse.

Downtown indeed appears to be dying," the Virginia Chamber of Commerce reported after examining the economic projections for Norfolk, Lynchburg, and Roanoke in 1967.[29] These areas, combined with Alexandria, Portsmouth, and Petersburg, carried over $1 billion in annual debt.[30] Suburban flight caused Richmond to lose around 13 percent of its tax revenue annually from the $1.1 billion in taxable real estate.[31] Most of the land that remained in the hands of taxpayers showed little to no equity growth since 1950.[32]

The City of Richmond's welfare spending revealed how dire things had gotten since World War II. The median family income was $5,200, as opposed to $6,900 and $6,100 in neighboring Henrico and Chesterfield Counties, respectively. One in four Richmond families lived in poverty and earned less than half the median income. Richmond's welfare budget was ten times that of its suburban neighbors combined. There were twice as many Blacks as Whites on every local welfare program: Aid to Dependent Children, Foster Care, General Relief, Old Age Assistance, Aid to the Blind, and Aid to the Permanently Disabled. The overall welfare budget grew from $2 million to over $20 million (a 249 percent increase) between 1959 and 1968, with no signs of slowing down. Poverty had always been disproportionately Black in Virginia. By 1968, however, Black poverty was defining the urbanizing Commonwealth, which sat in a largely urban region, in an urban nation.[33] The Commonwealth's capital did not fare much better: "A city of southern agrarian roots," per the *Washington Post*, "is now a city with northern-style urban problems."[34]

Bagley attempted several times to make Richmond financially solvent. As a councilman the laundryman-turned-real-estate-lawyer helped the Establishment divert millions in tax revenue to purchase vacant lands near the suburbs and construct competitive shopping malls, most notably Willow Lawn, Southside Plaza, and Azalea Mall.[35] Suburban areas combated this strategy with their own malls, further bleeding dry the city's coffers. The Establishment then decided to raise taxes across the board to cover the deficits, but that did not help either.[36] Days after Henry Marsh accepted his nomination as the city's second Black vice mayor, Bagley secretly crossed Robert E. Lee Bridge over the James River into Chesterfield County in search of an annexation. In most states, annexations were the means by which urban areas purchased additional territory for expansion. Annexing municipalities completed this land deal by petitioning their state legislature or conducting a referendum vote among residents in the target area.[37] Annexations in Virginia were land purchases during which cities acquired property and residents from surrounding counties who, for all intents and purposes, desired the public services that urban life offered. Bagley was aware that this had been the case with Chesterfield County since the 1950s and 1960s.[38]

Until the post–World War II era, Chesterfield was emblematic of most Virginia counties: largely agricultural, administratively limited, and more populated by farm animals and equipment than people. A prominent Chesterfield lawyer claimed that at this time, "Richmond should have annexed the suburbs." Prior to World War II, Chesterfield residents favored annexation because they "wanted services which the city could give and the counties could not." After World War II, however, Chesterfield had ample public services and a strong local government that were "all made necessary by the demands of thousands of new [White] suburbanites," the same lawyer gloated. Chesterfield leaders slightly mirrored the Richmond Establishment. They were businessmen and attorneys who were born and raised in the county, who attended private schools, elite universities, and Episcopal or Presbyterian churches. While mostly working in Main Street firms, Chesterfield's establishment maintained power by supporting and facilitating suburban growth in the county. Thus, when Mayor Bagley marketed annexation as a public benefit to the entire metropolitan area, Chesterfield leaders and residents were not receptive because they heard what Bagley was really saying: "Let us merge so you can help us pay for all the evils of the city."[39]

"Time Is Running Out Fast"

Bagley's attempt to expand Richmond fit into a hostile national political climate where cities sought annexations but found it extremely difficult to execute them. Prior to 1968, a national debate had surfaced between cities, suburbs, and state governments over the responsibility of curing the economic ills of suburbanization. Suburban leadership, growing powerful from the increased tax base and industrial and political representation, were content to let their sister cities struggle economically. White urban leaders, on the other hand, believed that they and suburban leadership shared a responsibility to further the "movement of America toward a metropolitan society," as a delegate to the Urban America Conference in 1967 said.[40] This society would in theory and practice be built largely on cooperative planning by White elites to connect cities and suburbs at the hip to prevent urban decay.[41] That connection hinged largely upon the inner city's ability to absorb suburbanites back into the cities they had left. For all sides involved, there was no middle ground.

Municipal annexations began in the late 1890s when urban politicians in the Northeast started corralling wealthy urbanites who had sprawled to densely wooded outskirts.[42] By the mid-twentieth century, the only American cities maintaining the population growth stimulated by World War II were the ones using annexation. Cities that annexed adjacent land grew more than eight times the rate of cities that did not. This reality created consensus among urban leaders that rapidly growing cities needed to continuously annex more adjacent land and people.[43] In 1959, at the height of this development, 533 American cities annexed surrounding counties, adding on average more than 5,000 people and ten square miles within their respective city limits.[44] A year later American cities used annexation to nearly double in geographic and population size, adding almost 1,500 square miles at a time.[45] Between 1950 and 1970, cities with at least 50,000 residents added around 9,300 square miles in aggregate and thousands of residents per annexation.[46] While suburbanites in northern, midwestern, and West Coast cities often, but not always, welcomed annexations because of better public utilities, southerners expressed grave concerns about annexations disturbing the already unsettling racial order brought on by the modern civil rights movement.[47]

The South was an antiurban region in spite of having some of the nation's most iconic cities.[48] Atlanta knows this struggle all too well. The Georgia legislature's strict laws against annexation went unchallenged until Atlanta desperately needed to double in size, which it eventually did by 1952.[49] White Atlanta leaders had called on the state to help them expand into the five surrounding areas of Clayton, Dekalb, Fulton, College Park, and Gwinnett Counties eight years later. They claimed that the region's continued growth relied on Atlanta's ability to expand and keep its ever-fleeing tax base.[50] This argument did not convince the legislature to help. In the meantime, the city of 500,000 residents with an economy that serviced 1.2 million people faced significant resistance from Whites in Hapeville and East Point when they tried to purchase land for what later became the Hartsfield-Jackson Airport.[51] Thus, White Atlanta leaders desperately relied on calls for White supremacy to end annexation opposition in the suburbs.

Atlanta's White urban leadership racialized their annexation efforts, seeking to generate a White consensus to keep the center of the metropolitan area out of the hands of local Blacks.[52] "If you ever allowed the Negro to become a majority in the city, the worst of their race would take over," an *Atlanta Constitution* contributor commented on the issue of annexation. He and many like him believed that "the pragmatic segregationist should be heartily in favor of annexation. His chief concern seems to be that if current population trends continue, Atlanta will be predominantly Negro and will elect a Negro city government. That probably will happen if Atlanta is restricted to its present artificial boundaries."[53] Atlanta native and mayor William B. Hartsfield took it a step further: "Atlanta must annex leadership as it migrates to the suburbs or leave husks of the city to the worst elements of the Negro race."[54] Time was of the essence to these men, as Atlanta's borders did not expand faster than the civil rights gains and White flight happening around the city. "We are on the threshold of a major catastrophe unless we develop the political capacity to prevent it.... Time is running out fast," wrote the *Atlanta Constitution* in 1963.[55]

White Georgia elites eventually agreed to help Atlanta conduct annexations when it became clear that the growing suburban bubble would not be disturbed. Since White Atlanta elites insisted on couching their annexation agenda in terms of preserving White supremacy, suburbanites responded in kind, but in the opposite direction. White suburban opposition came from them being former city residents who "remember[ed] what they were fleeing from" in terms of rising taxes and increased poor Black residency, said the *Atlanta Constitution*. Thus, they "want[ed] no part of being roped back in, never mind the civic advantages."[56] Moreover, they felt that "Atlanta has done too much for Negroes, but so little for us," in the words of one White female critic of city government. Mayor Hartsfield and the White Atlanta establishment smoothed over annexation dissent by agreeing to keep the burdens of city life (school desegregation and public transportation) outside of the White annexed suburbs of Sandy Springs, Druid Hills, and Buckhead.[57] With the baseline that suburban life would remain undisturbed, annexations in Georgia moved quite smoothly by the late 1960s. The Georgia legislature removed annexation restrictions, allowing Atlanta to more than triple its size in the following decades.[58] Atlanta was a gleaming example that annexations were not born from simple appeals to White supremacy. Rather, they relied on the political maneuvering needed to maintain White middle-class suburban autonomy.

Atlanta's issues reflected that annexations in the South were hard-fought battles where urban leaders overcame substantial anticity biases within their respective states. Urban leaders in the South would have preferred mutually agreed upon city-county consolidations, as were achieved by Jacksonville–Duval County and Miami–Dade County in Florida, East Baton Rouge Parish in Louisiana, and Nashville–Davidson County in Tennessee.[59] Others would have likely preferred the Texas model, where cities such as Dallas, Houston, and San Antonio only needed to pass a city ordinance to annex an adjacent suburb or rural area.[60] Counties in Texas were so powerless to stop urban expansion that a former Houston mayor confidently told the *New York Times* that "when White people have left the downtown, we just go get them again."[61]

However, most southern cities that needed to expand accepted whatever their legislature and surrounding suburbs gave them—namely, portions of land occupied by suburbanites who were the least resistant to being urban residents. This was the case in South Carolina cities such as Rock Hill, Greenville, Columbia, Anderson, Laurens, and Charleston, each of which fought vigorously in the state courts and legislature to streamline the annexation processes with referendum voting laws.[62] Cities in the Upper South with populations between one hundred and eight hundred thousand (such as the District of Columbia, Raleigh, Baltimore, and Rockville, Maryland) used similar tactics to double their size.[63] In Tennessee city leaders in Knoxville, Memphis, Chattanooga, and Nashville petitioned their legislature to allow annexation through simple passage of city ordinances and referendum votes.[64] The annexation issue was so pivotal to the South's regional progress that southern mayors and industrialists met in 1968 to discuss the need for more cooperation to "avoid the crumbling crisis-ridden cities of other regions."[65] Race was never divorced from the discussion, however. While some mayors defined their urban crises simply as an overabundance of poor people that "did not want to work," the more resistant suburban leaders dismissed the cry as a coded measure to recruit Whites back to the city.[66]

By the time Mayor Phil Bagley attempted to extend Richmond's borders into the growing suburbs of Chesterfield County, annexation, while generally difficult to execute in the South, was an easier process everywhere but in the Commonwealth. Virginia was the only state where cities and counties were jurisdictionally independent of each other under law.[67] Jurisdictional independence long aided the legendary Byrd machine (1924–65)—a political regime orchestrated by longtime US senator and governor Harry Flood Byrd. The Byrd machine used independent jurisdictions by coordinating with the inordinate number of tax-funded political operatives—such as judges, clerks, treasures, boards of electors, school officials, and sheriffs—to control Virginia through suppressing the vote. Proponents of jurisdictional independence also used the Virginia legislature to suppress proannexation policies for most of the twentieth century.[68] This resulted in annexation becoming a one-way street in Virginia: cities could absorb sections of adjacent counties by proving to a three-judge panel (chosen by the antiurban state legislature) that the adjacent county provided inadequate public services to its residents.[69] Even then, the court did not always grant urban areas the territory they desired. If the city did not like the award, they could refuse their rights to it, as did Richmond in 1965 after a decade-long annexation battle against Henrico County.[70] A city could also merge with a county with a majority referendum vote from both the annexing and the potentially annexed localities.[71] This was the most preferred method, as city-county mergers went unopposed by the state legislature.

Issues in Northern Virginia proved that annexations were difficult to execute because of the growing opposition to city life in the suburbs. In the wealthy White suburbs of Northern Virginia near Washington, DC, the rapidly growing cities of Alexandria and Falls Church struggled to annex the suburbanizing Fairfax County in the early 1960s.[72] Led by the Fairfax County Federation of Citizen Associations (FCFCA), Fairfax suburbanites used political and economic pressure to maintain their independence. The FCFCA recruited industrial immigrants; improved public services; voted out public officials who supported annexation; pressured the Virginia legislature into considering a five-year moratorium on annexations; called for referendum laws that allowed suburban residents to vote against annexation proposals by neighboring cities; and sought a city charter from the Virginia legislature.[73] While Colonial Heights (Richmond area) and Salem (Roanoke area) both received city charters to stave off annexation, Fairfax failed to do so.[74] But Fairfax's resistance to annexation compelled Alexandria and Falls Church officials to end attempts by the mid 1960s.[75]

Urban-suburban movements in the Tidewater proved that mergers were the more preferred method of municipal consolidation in Virginia. By 1968 Virginia's Tidewater region held just over 800,000 people, around 20 percent of Virginia residents.[76] The Tidewater was divided into two major sections: Newport News–Hampton to the north and the Norfolk-Portsmouth area to the south. Increasing political activism by Tidewater Blacks compelled local White oligarchs to block future attempts at urban expansion through annexation into the mostly White counties between 1952 and 1968.[77] The most important mergers were the White-majority South Norfolk City combining with White-majority South Norfolk County to create the City of Chesapeake, and the White-majority, ultrarural Virginia Beach City merging with Princess Anne County in February 1962.[78] Not only were these mergers done within the same year, but they happened just as White officials from the majority Black Norfolk (at the time Virginia's largest city) and largely Black Portsmouth sought annexations into those same places to offset their growing urban poverty.[79] The

Virginia legislature voted overwhelmingly to codify each merger with an 85 to 9 vote in the state senate. Efforts by Portsmouth and Norfolk leaders to block these mergers fell on deaf ears. These moves made the Virginia Beach–Chesapeake area the seventh largest urbanized area in the nation, just behind Chicago–Cook County in Illinois.[80] Tidewater Whites, asserted Virginia Beach oligarch Sidney Kellam, had the "right to live under the government of their choosing."[81] This comment amplified the fact that the Virginia legislature did not favor cities in disputes about urban expansion. Rather, they favored interjurisdictional cooperation.

The politics of annexation in Virginia was shaped by the jurisdictional autonomy and interjurisdictional cooperation and not the interests of White urban leadership. Immediately after the formation of Chesapeake and Virginia Beach, the annexation courts did not help White leaders expand the boundaries of their majority Black cities via changes to annexation law.[82] Had White supremacy been the ultimate goal and uniting force in Virginia politics, the overwhelmingly White state legislature would have helped White urban leaders expand their borders into suburban areas to dilute the Black population and political influence. But they did not, and the debate about urban expansion sparked a movement within the legislature itself. Some White urban legislators wanted Virginia to adopt a proannexation state constitution that would prevent suburban areas from shirking responsibility to help pay for the urban decay they left behind. The proposed legal change would allow Virginia cities to expand based on economic need and without the permission of a three-judge panel.[83] This fervor did not produce a new proannexation state constitution. Rather, it cemented the custom that urban expansion would come from compromise between urban and suburban leaders and not just at the whims of urban leaders wishing to maintain White supremacy in local politics.[84]

Once labeled "the dark continent of American politics," suburban areas were, according to the *Washington Post*, "beginning to assert themselves as leaders in those metropolitan areas where they long played little-brother roles."[85] American cities lost more people to the suburbs every year than they gained in the 1960s. Not one of the 168 major suburban areas recorded a net population loss during the same period.[86] This population and wealth concentration away from inner cities compelled the growing suburbs—often called the "bedrooms for the large cities"—to fight 62 percent of annexations in 1960, just one year after the most annexations in American history had taken place.[87] Their main defenses against forced mergers were to petition their legislatures for city charters, cite the tax burdens that cities would thrust upon them, or even racialize annexation by portraying it as an obvious attempt to quell a growing Black urban voting majority.[88] These methods began to work as cities found it nearly impossible to simply annex previously struggling counties by the late 1960s.[89]

"Niggers Won't Take Over This Town"

By the time Mayor Phil Bagley reached across the Robert E. Lee Bridge to broker a deal with Chesterfield leaders, annexation had become racialized by the politics of the day. "Conservative Richmond," as the *Washington Post* called White city elites, faced "the familiar equation of annexation" that vexed the entire nation: "How it affects the delicate racial balance in the former Confederate capital."[90] This racial balance was wedded to the financial vitality of urban areas because Black people were disproportionately working-class or underclass due to generations of systemic racism. Hence, Chesterfield conservatives believed that Richmond's interest in offsetting the budgetary issues of suburbanization coincided with "the fear that Richmond may in the future be a city dominated by Negroes."[91] It was when they failed that "Richmond delegates" uttered, the *Washington Post* reported, "that unless more land and people are added to Richmond. . . . the growing Negro population—which is showing an enthusiasm for voting—may outnumber Whites at the polls or swing the balance of power in city elections."[92] Chesterfield's reluctance to merge with Richmond showed that the White suburbs did not share a sense of racial responsibility with White Richmond elites. As I discuss later, the Virginia legislature's reluctance to force a merger between the two showed that while race was a part of White elite desires for urban expansion into the suburbs, it would not completely trump the state's antiurban political culture.[93]

The Richmond Establishment tried its hand at acquiring the adjacent suburbs through orchestrating a merger well before the threat of Black political power reached a fever pitch in 1968. The first attempt came in 1960, with Richmond leaders proposing that the city and neighboring Henrico County combine into one municipality. These merger talks did not include Chesterfield due to its leaders' refusal to take part. With the help of the *Times-Dispatch*, the Establishment used expansive marketing campaigns to show residents that if all three localities were combined, Richmond would be the fifth largest metropole in the nation.[94] They also used published reports to argue that should Richmond not expand, the urban core would economically decay. Thus, the marketing campaigns centered calls for efficient government and the overall prosperity of the entire metropolitan area. The combined government would have nine council members elected at large, and with that, county real estate value would increase; public services would improve; and most county employees would retain their jobs and compensation.[95]

White Richmonders voted overwhelmingly for the merger. However, the Crusade for Voters mobilized Black Richmond voters to oppose it because they knew it would dilute the growing Black vote. White Henrico residents likewise rejected the merger, and by December 1961, the motion died.[96] Whites in Henrico, and for that matter Chesterfield, fit within the national suburban trend of blocking urban expansion to protect their suburban autonomy. Siding with them were Richmond Blacks, who saw annexation as a threat to their political influence.[97] The unpopularity of metropolitan formation among the growing demographics (urban Blacks and suburban Whites) ensured that appeals to good government, and even subliminal calls for the maintenance of White supremacy in Richmond, did not cultivate unified White support for urban-suburban consolidation. Thus, more aggressive action was needed on the part of White urban elites. As then Richmond mayor Claude Woodward stated firmly after the failed referendum: "Annexation is now the only answer."[98]

Yet the Richmond Establishment found no reprieve in the annexation courts and state legislature, either. Between 1965 and 1967 Richmond put forward weak cases to annex Henrico and Chesterfield.[99] Under Virginia law they had to prove that the potentially annexed localities benefited from the merger, and not that the annexing power needed more land and residents to pay its bills. Perhaps they felt confident that the legislature and annexation judges would help them keep the Commonwealth's capital majority White. They were wrong, and a 1967 census showed that Richmond's racial makeup was split nearly fifty-fifty, making Richmond only second to Washington, DC, in having the highest percentage of Black residents in a "major" American city.[100]

The Virginia legislature slightly changed its tune after the 1968 election. Once it became clear that Richmond would succumb to the demographic realities plaguing cities across the country, the legislature aided the Establishment by increasing Richmond's bonding capacity to purchase newly acquired territories and by amending the state constitution to empower themselves to forcibly expand Richmond's borders in any direction they deemed necessary by January 1, 1970.[101] This provision would be nullified if Richmond and Chesterfield came to an out-of-court agreement before then.[102] The skeptical *Washington Post* surmised that the legislature's maneuvers were to "dilute the drowning Negro majority in the

State's capital with a large dose of White suburbanites." While noting that the new bill was "couched largely in terms of economics," the *Washington Post* advanced the idea that White supremacy was the overall goal.[103] The Virginia legislature's maneuvering, however, showed the limits and not the pervasiveness of White supremacist politics. If maintaining a White majority Richmond explained the state's new legislative zeal, they could have forcibly combined Richmond, Chesterfield, and Henrico into one majority White locality. Instead, they adhered to Virginia's political tradition of strong local autonomous governance and limited state action, allowing localities to work out a land deal that would receive little to no contest in the courts.

The state's actions brought the Richmond and Chesterfield establishments into a closer working relationship on the issue of annexation. White elites from Richmond and Chesterfield spent much of 1969 at each other's homes, golf courses, restaurants, hotel luncheons, bars, and sporting events to broker the annexation.[104] While the "new White guys" and older White elite discussed the amount of land and number of people Richmond needed, the race question was inherently at the center of the conversation.[105] "Race was not necessarily mentioned at every meeting, but we both knew what we were talking about. . . . This was the fundamental underlying feature of all of our discussions," the Chesterfield secretary at the time later testified in federal court.[106]

Chesterfield residents and leaders did not want to deal with Richmond. Yet the Establishment's agitation and subsequent state action thrust upon them a duty to help solve Richmond's financial problems and to maintain the political status quo while doing so. "Because Chesterfield is a vital part of the Richmond metropolitan area, it is extremely interested in the vitality of the entire area," a Chesterfield official said in reference to annexation. By 1968 this "interest in vitality" meant doing the dirty work of the legislature and Richmond Establishment, which would keep the city out of the political grasp of Black leadership—and its rising star, Henry Marsh.

Moreover, annexation had been so racialized by the urban crisis that leaders, who had rarely discussed the process in terms of race before, often did so as time wore on in 1969. To the racist White Chesterfield residents and leaders, White supremacy meant separating from Black Richmonders, not helping elite Whites maintain control over them. However, Chesterfield leaders understood that the times forced them to adjust to the racial realities of the day. A Chesterfield executive later explained in a deposition that the understanding between Richmond and Chesterfield over the annexation was that "the city of Richmond was gradually

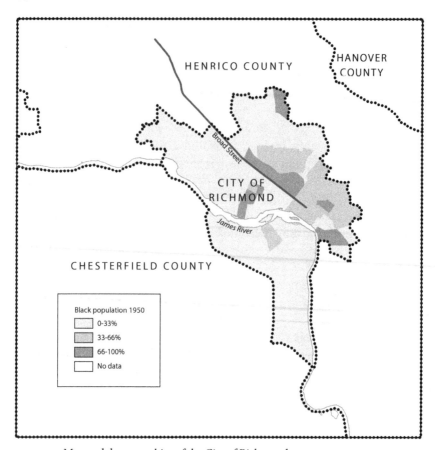

FIGURE 1. Map and demographics of the City of Richmond, 1950

growing Black[er]" and poorer.[107] Mayor Bagley allegedly described the situation more plainly. One Chesterfield official later testified under oath that Bagley told him: "We don't want the city to go to the niggers. We need 44,000 White bodies." He doubled down on that desire by allegedly stating, "As long as I am mayor of the city of Richmond, the niggers won't take over this town." While the economic vitality of Richmond was, and had always been, the impetus for annexation, the underlying racial consequences were very much understood.[108]

By late summer 1969 Bagley brokered a deal for Richmond to annex a twenty-three-square-mile territory of the north Chesterfield County suburbs. The city of 220,000 grew to around 262,000 with the addition of the more affluent areas in Chesterfield County.[109] Chesterfield residents spent much of fall 1969 fighting the annexation in court, but to no avail.[110] Made

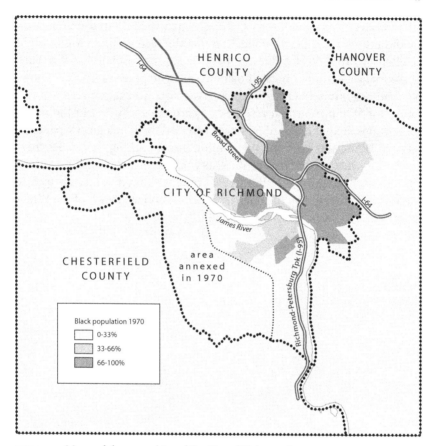

FIGURE 2. Map and demographics of the City of Richmond, 1970

official in January 1970, the deal added more middle-class taxpayers and territory to Richmond's rolls. The deal manifested in the newly annexed suburbs voting overwhelmingly for Establishment city council candidates in the election that year, stalling the Marsh Revolution by ensuring he remained the only Black councilman for the second straight election cycle.[111]

The resulting maintenance of elite White control over the city council, along with the racial rhetoric during the final stages of the annexation, led historians and the public to sum up this deal as a bargain created by the shared interest of White racial supremacy. However, local, state, and national context shows that the politics of annexation exposed fault lines in White supremacy. Annexations were last resorts for White urban leaders who understood that a majority Black city was, in the post–World War II era, a municipality of the poor. Both urban and suburban Whites saw the urban crisis in economic terms. It was when their shared understanding did not result in shared obligation that the race problem was brought in, often by urban White elites. Both sides addressed the issue of a Black urban majority from opposite positions and perspectives. Actions, however, did have consequences. The reluctant 1970 annexation set the foundation for White suburban resistance to crosstown busing in the 1970s. These issues further exposed how race revealed the ideological separation between White elites and the White middle and working classes. Furthermore, the White rejection of civil rights changes thrusted Richmond into a paradox where the end of Jim Crow brought about a new nadir in race relations, one defined by the polarized, dichotomous growth of the White suburbs and Black inner city.

3
Dogtown
"WE NEVER CROSSED THE BRIDGE"

> For we must be clear about one thing: The South is desegregating, not integrating. And in the process of desegregating, the South is making clear how few men, North or South, are willing to confront these exigencies of *real* integration.
> —Lerone Bennett Jr., *Ebony,* 1971

ON A COLD rainy night in February 1972, over one thousand Richmond-area residents flooded the cramped gymnasium on the campus of Highland Springs High School in Henrico County, Virginia. "The crowd, all White except for two young Black children," did not come to see a basketball game. Rather, they were there to listen and strategize about how to subvert the recently decided court order to consolidate Richmond, Chesterfield, and Henrico Counties public schools.

The message was quite clear about how the White suburbs should respond. Civic leader Bill Kimbrell joked about the lack of public officials at the event: "The politicians aren't here tonight!" He argued that regardless of their absence, "It is time to stop asking the politicians, and start telling them what to do." Kimbrell lived up to this message as he wrote letters to local and state school officials informing them that his children, under no circumstances, were attending consolidated schools or being bused across town. He encouraged other parents to do the same so school officials would drive empty buses, patrol empty hallways, and oversee empty classrooms. The crowd cheered and clapped as Kimbrell gave the stage to Morty Fleet, a visiting supporter from Norfolk. After giving an impassioned speech, Fleet told the crowd: "The freedom of America is in the hands of the Richmond Henrico-Chesterfield area people."[1] While it was hard for anyone in the gym to understand the gravity of that phrase upon it first being spoken, they soon learned that their defiance to crosstown busing and consolidation would end federal support for school integration across the nation. The net result was that despite desegregation, for the next few decades metropolitan areas like Richmond remained deeply disintegrated by race and space into chocolate cities and vanilla suburbs.

The issue of busing made White Richmonders' racism more overt, cementing the ill will created by Blacks overtly seeking political power and White elites trying to retain it. In this way, the modern civil rights movement, especially the implementation of civil rights law, revealed Richmond's polite, genteel racism as the mere façade it had always been during Jim Crow.

The controversy over busing reveals also that the depths of Richmond racism did not only lie with White elites but with the middle- and working-class majorities in the White suburbs. While the Richmond Establishment's opposition to Black political rule operated within the Virginia tradition of elite genteel racism, the issue of school integration showed that the White middle and working classes were less beholden to that culture when it did not satisfy their own interests. Despite their expressed desires to keep their children in schools close to home, White suburbanites undoubtedly opposed school integration because of racial prejudice.[2] Their overt methods of resistance showed that racism was an active part of suburban Whiteness, which built off of Richmond's long history of anti-Black racism. Thus, when White urban elites pushed integration on these suburban residents, they had no issue shedding Virginia's polite culture of subtle racism by taking to the streets and courts to protest at every level. The White suburbs had begrudgingly submitted to the 1970 annexation of Chesterfield. But when it came to sharing schoolhouses with Black families to satisfy court orders, they refused to be the pawns of their racial elites, igniting a social fracture that would remain at the heart of Richmond's municipal identity and social and racial relationships for decades to come.

Their protests and persistence paid off when federal court appeals blocked the consolidation of Richmond area schools into one unitary district, even though the latter would have created a foundation for the metropolitan consolidation that White Richmond elites desired most. Left behind were Black Richmonders, who lost all hope that civil rights changes would improve race relations. White rejection to racial equality was nothing new in Richmond, the South, or the nation. What was unique to Richmond, however, was the openness of that rejection by White suburbanites. Richmond was a town where Blacks and Whites regularly exercised politeness in public discourse. The busing issue undid that custom completely, as any hopes at racial goodwill through educational equality seemed unreachable. Thus, the busing issue represented that the twilight of Richmond's modern civil rights movement was also the lowest point in race relations after World War II. The very public anti-Black racism made clear that the city and its metro area were severely broken by a class-based, racial division that future leaders and residents would spend decades trying to heal.

"When Too Many Negroes Move into a School"

Richmond's 1970 annexation of twenty-three square miles of Chesterfield County, along with approximately 45,000 White suburban residents, helped the White Richmond establishment maintain control of city hall. The architects of the deal, however, failed to recognize that the annexation was not a compromise between brethren. It was a forced parting gift that Chesterfield surrendered only to maintain its independence as a county from the city. That gift involved the necessary sacrifice of suburban Whites who were now a part of Richmond's Southside, an area known at the time as Dogtown.

Dogtown contained the middle-class neighborhoods of Forest Hill and Westover Hills, but when city residents thought of Dogtown, they mostly had in mind White and overtly racist trucking, tobacco, and aluminum manufacturing workers and their families. Around the time of the annexation, Richmond's newly hired city manager Alan F. Kiepper noted that Dogtown was "a large area which is now in the state of decline."[3] Richmond residents already knew what the city manager discovered. Southside's neighborhoods, although home to Black as well as White families, were widely known as undesirable places to live.[4] Racism was so rampant and overt in the Southside that Richmonders assumed that any incidents of interracial violence and Klan activity reported in the news had happened there.[5] "We never crossed the [Robert E. Lee] Bridge," a White Southside resident later said in an interview. That bridge represented the psychological distance between the proud blue-collar Southsiders and the refined, conservative city that they deemed too liberal.[6]

Yet the three-quarter-mile bridge could not separate Dogtown from the city's lingering racial issues. In January 1970 the annexation forced them to welcome new, middle-class White neighbors into their area. A month later a group of Black Richmond parents sued the school board for maintaining racial segregation in defiance of the *Brown* decision.[7] While this suit was one of several desegregation cases Richmond faced after 1954, the overwhelmingly White school board did not deny the allegations. To the surprise of many, they asked the federal courts to make a "recommendation as to a plan that would ensure the operation of a unitary school system."[8]

Richmond schools had exited Virginia's infamous Massive Resistance-era of the late 1950s by adopting the widely used Freedom of Choice plan. This allowed parents to select their children's school regardless of race.[9] Over 60 percent of southern school districts (1,140 of 1,900) used Freedom of Choice to maintain their federal funding in lieu of the Civil Rights Act of 1964.[10] However, almost every Richmond school remained either 90 percent or more Black or White.[11] Pushed by Black parents who were fed up with Richmond's unwillingness to adhere to *Brown,* the US District Court for the Eastern District of Virginia ordered the use of busing to integrate public schools in March 1970. Newly annexed and older Dogtown residents quickly discovered that this judgment required yet another sacrifice, as they saw it, on their part. Not only were their property taxes and votes surrendered to the City of Richmond to help maintain the White majority: their 8,135 school-aged children (97 percent White and 2.5 percent Black) would be guinea pigs in the first real attempt to integrate southern schools.[12]

The busing order was a result of popular sentiments about how to achieve racial equality in the civil rights age. The federal courts' goal was to ensure that as many public schools reflected the city's racial makeup (split nearly evenly between Blacks and Whites) as possible. With that in mind, and the reality that city schools were disproportionately Black (nearly 70 percent) in comparison to the overall population—due to White families fleeing to the counties—most of the busing participants would be the poorest Black children from the East End and middle-class Blacks from the Northside. They were to be bussed to schools in the majority White West End and Southside. That part did not raise as much alarm as the logical adverse of that plan: White suburban children would be sent to majority Black schools in the East End and Northside. The only children of both races to be spared from the lottery were high school seniors.

Prior to 1968 the NAACP had little success in fighting to end school segregation. In the fourteen years after *Brown,* less than 10 percent of Black students and faculty attended and worked in "integrated" schools. Not one White student was recorded as attending a previously all-Black school anywhere in the South. This all changed after *Green v. County School Board of New Kent County* and the election of President Richard Nixon in 1968. With *Green,* NAACP attorneys—Henry Marsh being one of them—proved that "Freedom of Choice" was not freedom at all because White school boards employed token admission policies and disparate spending practices to maintain segregated and unequal schools. While the federal courts struck down Freedom of Choice, many school districts

(Richmond included) still practiced it as an integration plan. Very few school districts around the nation (and none in Virginia) were under a judicial busing order in 1968. That gave school districts temporary leeway to integrate schools as they saw fit. However, a shakeup in national politics, as well as Black parental activism, ensured that the future of integration involved more judicial oversight and direction.

The uncertainty of school integration after *Green* played into Richard Nixon's hands. The lifelong California moderate earned the growing southern White vote by running on an antibusing platform. This helped the Republican Party trade its liberal White and Black voting blocs for White suburban moderates and rural conservatives who were dissatisfied with the Democratic Party's support for civil rights. Upon taking office, Nixon put into practice his now-infamous "Southern Strategy" by taking a centrist vow to enforce only the most limited interpretation of civil rights laws already on the books.[13]

The irony of Nixon's limited civil rights agenda was *Alexander v. Holmes County Board of Education.* The 1969 unanimous Supreme Court decision concerning Holmes County, Mississippi, was handed down and articulated by Republican appointee Justice Earl Warren. The court opined that segregated school districts would be given no more slack on adhering to the *Brown* decision.[14] By the fall of 1970, every school system receiving federal funding would have to operate on a racially integrated (also called "unitary") basis.

Schools outside the South were the testing grounds for this Supreme Court edict. Long before 1954, civil rights organizations had placed tremendous pressure on northern and midwestern school districts to end their Jim Crow–style segregation. Cities such as Boston, Hartford, Providence, New York, Philadelphia, Detroit, Cleveland, Chicago, Milwaukee, Topeka, and others used the "quicksands of legal interpretations," as US Secretary of Education Harold Howe II, once described it, to evade integration mandates. Those quicksands were the fact that very few schools outside the South had statutes barring Blacks and Whites from attending the same schools. Rather, school systems in the North and West relied on their de facto racially segregated housing markets, ensuring that the best public schools remained upper and middle class and, most importantly, White. West Coast public schools did not have a much better record, either. California cities such as Sacramento, Oakland, San Francisco, and Pasadena, along with Portland (Oregon), Phoenix, and Denver, used housing patterns, school zones, and sometimes outright violence to keep Blacks and Latinos out of White schools.[15]

Yet the federal courts and civil rights attorneys predictably focused most of their attention on the South, the nation's most defiant region. The aftermath of *Holmes* compelled Black parents to sue fourteen separate school districts in Georgia, Florida, Alabama, Mississippi, and Louisiana. The courts sided with them, ordering the districts to devise and implement busing plans by February 1, 1970, just one month before the ruling in Richmond. These decisions were not requests, as they had been phrased in years past. Rather, delinquent school districts risked losing their federal funding. Those preventing the implementation of busing orders, such as Florida governor Claude R. Kirk Jr., were subject to fines and jail time.

In response, southern governors acted in the spirit of Massive Resistance as pioneered in Virginia by encouraging the growth of private schools; firing school officials who complied with busing orders; and proposing state and federal antibusing legislation. It did not help that many White parents sided with their governors and moved their children out of public schools. Some more radical dissenters started school fights, attacked buses, and burned crosses on the lawns of parents who obeyed the order.[16]

In Virginia the federal courts encountered a very different environment, where Whites rarely resorted to violence in defying school integration. Instead, they relied on school bureaucracies (state and local education boards) to maintain segregation through testing requirements and pupil placement plans. And when those plans failed, they fled to suburban and rural counties or created private schools, also called segregationist academies. Black parents, regardless of income, did not have this option. The Richmond school board attempted to offset this disparity by helping talented Black students—one of them future state delegate and councilwoman Viola Baskerville—gain admission to New England preparatory schools at no cost to the parents.[17] Southsiders in the 1970s, both new and old, did not benefit from either scenario. Most of their children were chosen to fulfill the federal busing order. With this reality ever-present, Dogtown channeled their racism and stalled busing by barking and howling their way through the federal courts, the General Assembly, and Congress over the next half-decade.

Whether Southside parents knew it or not, the Richmond City Council and school board were well aware of the issues surrounding their recently invalidated Freedom of Choice plan. Implemented in spring of 1964, Freedom of Choice facilitated Richmond's first concerted effort to integrate city schools. Praise for this plan was short-lived after the publication of research findings by well-respected sociologist and University of Richmond professor Dr. James A. Sartain. He and a group of academics from the University of Richmond, the University of Tennessee, and the University of North Carolina at Chapel Hill formed the Urban Team after being awarded a $61,000 federal grant to study the effects of school choice. The Urban Team focused their attention on Richmond's Northside schools, as they were the most integrated in the city and perhaps in the South. After collecting a plethora of faculty and parent interviews, as well as observing daily school activities, the Urban Team found out what residents already knew to be true: Freedom of Choice was nothing but a tool to circumvent school integration. Most importantly, Sartain concluded that school integration would eventually require a more metropolitan busing plan to force Whites and Blacks to attend the same schools.[18]

Before Southsiders were forced to integrate their schools, Richmond's Northside neighborhoods had long operated as both a Black refuge and White purgatory. The once-exclusive White, middle-class community received a large influx of Black middle-class doctors, teachers, lawyers, ministers, and businessmen between 1930 and 1970 because, as one local put it, "many Negro neighborhoods have been destroyed by urban renewal projects."[19] Whites often lived in the upscale Ginter Park or Highland Park neighborhoods, while the Black bourgeoisie resided in Barton Heights, Battery Park, and Laburnum Park. "If people did not walk outside their doors, you would not be able to tell the Black neighborhoods from the White neighborhoods," a White observer told a Black Northsider.[20] The Black and White middle classes were so alike that the school board, with persistent pressure from Black Northside parents and civil rights activists, chose its Chandler Middle School and John Marshall High School to be among the first integrated schools in Richmond prior to Freedom of Choice.[21] This class homogenization was never mistaken for racial harmony, however.

Whites were keenly aware that their majority control in the area was coming to an end. As Richmond's economy grew in the decades after World War II and Whites began flooding the nearby suburbs of Henrico and Chesterfield Counties, upwardly mobile Blacks sought the nicer homes, neighborhoods, and schools that Northside had to offer. Local White real estate firms jumped at this opportunity and engaged in blockbusting to fill the area with middle- and working-class Blacks against the wishes of middle-class Whites. Local Black realtor and political organizer Milton Randolph admitted to the Urban Team how this process worked. Local banks pressured White realty firms to turn new suburban plots in

Chesterfield and Henrico into mortgages; to gin up demand, they often contacted Black realtors to spread rumors that Blacks were looking to buy homes in certain areas of Northside. For a slight fee, Black realtors sent young Black married couples, and in some cases just two Black adults, along with some children to walk through the areas in question. Then White realtors helped White Northsiders relocate before the housing prices declined. They often lied about sales to scare some stubborn White couples into selling their homes.[22]

White realtors also listed certain homes in Black newspapers to steer members of the two races toward the homes they wanted to sell. A local resident summed up blockbusting in the Northside: "If a home is sold to Negroes, For Sale signs still spring up all around."[23] White realtor James S. Watkinson Jr., a member of the Board of Realtors, and the board's president, Morton G. Thalhimer Jr., both adamantly claimed Randolph's account to be false. Later real estate studies (which will be discussed in chapter 7), however, proved Randolph's account to be just the tip of the iceberg. Randolph claimed with certainty that "the Establishment has created controlled areas into which the Negroes are allowed to move." That control led to Blacks funneling into the Northside area, and by proxy, into its public schools.[24]

Integration in Northside schools began in the fall of 1960 after a controversial school board decision. While the local media largely ignored the often-painful realities of integration for Black children and their families, the Black students and their parents who entered formerly all-White schools were routinely harassed with disturbing phone calls to their homes from terrorists, as well as constant unchecked bullying inside of school. From simple class sessions to after-school activities, Black students were treated by most White schoolmates as contaminants not to be touched or dealt with.[25] Notwithstanding this tense and toxic atmosphere, the fear of court orders compelled the school board to allow more Black student enrollment in Northside schools after 1960. Racial tensions only heightened, as some White children and residents routinely harassed Black students on their way to school with taunts and threats of violence. Some students were even assaulted within the schools.[26] Thus, when the Urban Team entered Northside schools, they encountered an environment rife with White hostility to integrated schooling.

Sartain and the Urban Team found that "opening new [city] blocks to Negroes," as a Black realtor optimistically saw it, actually hurt the city's chances of achieving school integration.[27] As more Blacks moved into Northside schools after Freedom of Choice, racial turmoil ensued. White teachers and administrators, many of whom parented children within the school system, were completely invested in maintaining the White Northside majority. They understood that if Northside gained the reputation as a Black school area, Whites would flee. Hence, White school officials marginalized Black students as much as possible. The front line of White teachers at these schools were well-regarded "old timers" known for their discipline and instruction. The "moderates" were typically thirty-to-forty-year-old White women who were more concerned with maintaining their salaries and tenure than anything else. The old timers and moderates implemented a dual system within the schools by methods as small as frequently calling Blacks "nigra" (pronounced "niggra") in front of White children.[28] They also aided White Northside parents in preventing interracial mixing in every meaningful way. Parents and teachers believed that most Black children came from broken homes and were too undisciplined to share classrooms with Whites. Thus, they argued that interracial encounters would lead to the lowering of White children's' academic and moral standards. Almost all of them voiced some concern over miscegenation, as they felt that Black "male students were slightly aggressive" due to their "fascination with a White woman." Given these prejudices, White teachers routinely overpunished Black student wrongdoers, especially if they were known to associate with White children.[29]

Liberal White teachers were not immune to the bigotry that permeated Northside schools. This minority of teachers were fresh out of college and labeled liberal "too much by the rest of the faculty" because they were not parents, and they tended to be more supportive of racial integration. Fellow faculty "considered [them] to be more lax in their discipline and agreeable to lower standards" for Black students.[30] This agreeableness was in reality the bigotry of low expectations. Even these so-called liberal White teachers did not nominate Black students for advanced classes; they assumed that they could not keep up. Although some Black students slipped academically due to the constant isolation and fear they experienced, pessimistic liberal Whites feared that White students and parents would abandon advanced classes should Black students infiltrate them.[31] Some Black students who achieved academic accolades did so against their liberal White teachers' wishes.[32] This created the widespread belief among Black children that they had to be twice as obedient and intelligent as Whites to be treated half as well.[33] Regardless of the slight differences between White teachers, the Black students used their experiences to form a consensus, as one Black girl said about 1960 in particular: "They did not want us there."[34]

White administration also treated Northside Black students as interlopers. "What we have seen at J[ohn] M[arshal] [High School] has been continued resistance by the administration in a subtle form to integration," the Urban Team documented.[35] They went on to note that "guidance persons do not seem to have a grasp, or a knowledge of the needs, abilities, aspirations, etc. of the Negro pupils."[36] Some Black students experienced a double isolation; by attending racist White schools, they also lost their Black friends. Because they went to a White school—a sign that they were better than other Black children—former Black schoolmates wanted nothing to do with them.[37] Many Black students admitted that they wished to return to all-Black schools.[38] When the final school bells rang, Black students sought familiarity and comfort and traveled across town to commune with fellow Black students and faculty at their former schools. Consequently, after-school activities in the Northside were nearly all White.[39]

While attending Black sporting and community events offered some reprieve, turning back to the days of segregated, unequal schools was not an option for upwardly mobile Black Northsiders. The Urban Team watched as Black students led protests, marches, and lunchroom boycotts after Dr. Martin Luther King's assassination in 1968. Richmond city manager Alan Kiepper treated Black students as insurgents, ordering the installment of command posts and armed police officers in every integrated school shortly after Dr. King's murder. The racial tensions rose to the point that some of the White teachers who boldly targeted Black students before the assassination stopped completely, citing that they feared "physical harm."[40]

The Black students' resistance to racism made many uncomfortable, particularly the few Black teachers they encountered. In between a rock and a hard place, Black teachers had to walk the tightrope of supporting Black children and maintaining their careers. Black teachers resisted favoring Black students, but that earned them little respect among their White colleagues. Many White parents refused to engage with Black teachers and help them correct even the simplest of issues, such as White students calling them by their first names as if they were janitorial staff. White teachers often ignored Black faculty in teachers' lounges and hallways. Blacks would never be invited to dinners, movies, or any other events that White faculty organized.[41] Black male teachers were probably the most vulnerable, as they kept a safe distance from White female teachers and students to ward off "some speculation" that they were sexual predators.[42] As racial issues were evident even between faculty and administration, an Urban Team member wrote about the area's flagship high school that "there really are two separate John Marshalls—a Black and White one."[43] As integrated Northside schools fractured along racial lines, White parents had to decide on staying in their beloved Northside or fleeing to the county or private school system.[44]

Many Whites and the Urban Team were "very pessimistic about the future" of integration in Northside schools at the conclusion of the spring 1968 semester. As the Urban Team saw it, "This is because of two things—racial prejudice and belief that quality programs suffer when too many negroes move into a school."[45] Some White parents pulled their children from after-school programs as Black children began joining them. Others simply removed their children to prepare them for the move to the suburbs or private school. The reasons for removals varied, as some parents claimed that education standards had dramatically decreased since integration. "The quality of education will go down here; if you don't want to teach all basic classes you'll have to leave," one teacher told the Urban Team. Others complained that White teachers spent too much time trying to learn "the Negro speech pattern" and help Black students keep pace with Whites.[46] Race was "far and away the most important factor" in White families leaving Northside schools.[47]

Sartain concluded that Freedom of Choice, in the southern context, was shaped by racism, and therefore created what later scholars deemed "re-segregation."[48] From 1967 to 1968, the Richmond Black school population increased from 65 to 70 percent.[49] This was no coincidence: Sartain found a direct correlation between developers announcing medium-income housing developments in Northside as being "for Negroes," and Whites, out of "great concern" for Northside schools, "moving to the suburbs."[50] "As the percentage of Negroes living in this area increases," he concluded, "more White students will exercise their option under freedom of choice and attend other schools."[51] The White Northsiders who remained often enrolled their children in private schools or sent their children to stay with relatives and attend suburban schools.[52] By 1969 Northside schools were filled with Black working-class students who believed that risking mistreatment by White teachers was a better option than attending the understaffed, underfunded all-Black schools across town.[53] Thus, as the 1970 busing order came down, White Southsiders had a clear picture of what would happen to their schools when, not if, integration happened. Their schools would fracture at nearly every social level because the incoming Black presence would bring White bigotry to the surface, compelling parents, students, faculty, and administrators to enact the indecencies of segregation within a space that was long reserved for Whites only.

"Can't You See We Whites Want the Blacks to Stay Away?"

The complete "resegregation of the public schools under a freedom of choice policy" left the Richmond school board with little defense against the desegregation lawsuit filed in 1970.[54] By the time annexed suburbanites became a part of Dogtown, White liberals such as longtime schoolteacher and civic leader Virginia Alden Crockford had secured positions on the school board and saw to it that city schools obeyed the busing order.[55]

Crockford hailed from a working-class family in Virginia's poor White southwest. She earned degrees from Virginia Polytechnic Institute and State University—now known as Virginia Tech—and Madison College—now James Madison University—before moving to Richmond to become a teacher. After settling into her new hometown, she married *Times-Dispatch* executive William Hamilton Crockford. While not born into the White Richmond establishment, Crockford ascended the ranks by using her limitations as steppingstones. Her background made her an authority on progressive issues among the city's elite. She headed many progressive causes that promoted racial tolerance, charity, youth employment, and sex education. Along the way she joined and eventually headed the Richmond Committee for Youth, the Richmond Federation of PTAs, and the Richmond Council of Women's Organizations, to name just a few.[56] This teacher and civic leader quickly became an Establishment fixture as Richmond's elites supported her nomination in 1962 to be only the second female Richmond PTA president. The city council later appointed Crockford to serve as the president of the Richmond school board.[57] No one was more qualified to lead the charge for school integration than Crockford.

With the March 1970 busing order in effect, Crockford tried to ease the fears of Southside parents.[58] Black and poor White parents in the East End generally supported the busing order, as it provided their children with access to schools with better facilities and teachers. It was the White middle-class Southside parents who refused to accept busing as the new normal. They were not confrontational at first, as they simply avoided every public meeting and discussion about the busing order.[59] A White Southside father justified his refusal to attend PTA meetings by saying that "it is extremely hard to keep whatever latent prejudice that I might have from rising to the surface."[60] He was not alone. Other Southside Whites wrote angry letters opposing what they felt to be an unfair busing system. One parent rhetorically asked Crockford, "Is this the kind of equal justice now being dispensed by the federal court system? The rich can buy out and the average citizen will be forced to accept FORCED government integration plans [sic]."⁶¹ Southside parents, many of whom were recent migrants from other parts of Richmond, wanted to keep their children in the public school system. They were crystal clear, however, that "if busing takes place," they would "have no alternative than to seek out private school at great expense."⁶²

Organized busing opposition reflected that geographic affiliation and racial interests bred political association. Whites in the recently annexed Southside formed the West End Concerned Parents and Friends (WECPF). Composed of about five hundred families from the newly built Bon Air suburb in the northwest corner of Southside, WECPF outwardly supported school integration, feeling that it was "the crucial factor" in "preserving the public-school system." Yet they objected to forced busing as a method of achieving it.⁶³ The Citizens Against Busing (CAB) had a different message entirely. These 1,700 lower-middle-class families were from the more established area (central Manchester district) of Dogtown, where race relations were among the worst in the city.⁶⁴ While being more adamantly against busing, they did not use overtly racist rhetoric to promote the mass "opening [of] churches as private schools" and the complete defunding of public education.⁶⁵ Between June and August 1970, these groups, while having different missions and outlooks on public education, found common ground. They worked together and petitioned the governor, state delegates, and the US Congress to pass antibusing legislation. They also used rallies and motorcades to recruit other White families in opposing the March 1970 busing order.⁶⁶

Local and state leaders did not succumb to the pressure. The Richmond city council, Virginia General Assembly, and Governor Linwood Holton refused to pass and support antibusing legislation. Suburban residents would later learn the depths of Holton's resistance to their cause, in that he exercised a form of elite reconciliation by sending his White children to majority-Black East End schools. The legislature was more practical. They understood that supporting antibusing advocates with anything more than lip service (such as passing laws) would lose them federal funds and out-of-state industry. Therefore, Southside's persistence was "a futile gesture."⁶⁷ The lack of state support compelled White Southside parents to pester Crockford personally and to implore her to stop supporting the busing order.⁶⁸ A White single mother of three once wrote in anguish that "it just won't work for either race. The Negroes will not feel at home in our neighborhoods and the Whites in the inner-city neighborhoods." The longtime White liberal refused to budge, however, responding to every dissenting letter with: "The Richmond School Board is working and will continue to work for the best education possible for ALL of Richmond's children."⁶⁹

Although it took the entire summer, the federal courts, in conjunction with the Richmond school board, US Department of Health, Education and Welfare, and education specialist Dr. Gordon Foster of the University of Miami, approved a busing plan. Around six thousand White Southside and West End students, along with seven thousand Black East End and Northside students, would be sent to opposing neighborhood schools.⁷⁰ Those involved felt that the busing plan would work given that "racial balance" was not required; annexation made city schools 60 to 40 percent Black and White, and high school seniors were not required to participate.⁷¹

They also felt secure in their plan because it combined myriad cases and remedies used around the country to bring school districts into compliance with *Brown*. The first began at home with *Wanner v. Arlington County* (1966), *Green v. County School Board of New Kent County* (1968), *Brewer v. School Board of Norfolk* (1968), *United States v. Franklin* (1970), and *Green v. School Board of Roanoke* (1970) which allowed school systems to end Freedom of Choice plans and purchase and use buses to ensure that "racial discrimination would be eliminated root and branch."⁷² Decisions outside of Virginia also allowed the federal courts to form "unitary" school districts "within which no person is to be effectively excluded from any school because of race or color."⁷³

On behalf of the Richmond city council, Mayor Morrill Crowe "urge[d] all Richmonders to comply" with the recently decided busing order. WECPF followed by issuing support for the public school system during these trying times. Yet when the first buses arrived in the WECPF stronghold of Bon Air, 650 of the 900 assigned students were already enrolled in private schools.⁷⁴ Other families, a Southside realtor told the *Times-Dispatch*, were "trying to buy homes farther out so they'll be beyond busing."⁷⁵ The less fortunate Dogtown parents bypassed legalities and withheld many of the remaining five thousand children from city schools. Whites expressed few qualms about their decisions. One student responded to critics outside of the area by saying: "You'd be upset and scared. You wouldn't want your kid to go to a Black school."⁷⁶ Others were less inclined to solicit empathy: "We do not want to be cruel, but no thanks. We want our children in our schools."⁷⁷

The few White parents who obeyed the busing order were looked down upon and treated as traitors by fellow Whites. A local professor recalled his "liberal" colleague asking him one day, "Where do your children go to school now?" When he said Richmond Public Schools, the colleague responded with vitriol: "How could you do this to your children?!" The conversation about schools escalated into a heated argument about race and Richmond's future. The two longtime friends never spoke again.[78] Another White parent had similar experiences when, as he said, "In some social settings, conversations would dry up the minute we mentioned our children went to the city's public schools." Those who obeyed the order "did not realize how alone we would be."[79]

The flood of White complaints, suburban flight, and flagrant truancy were compounded with the inefficient busing system itself. The Virginia Transit Company—the only local bus provider—took some of the burden off the city by donating older buses and offering reduced rates for students traveling across town to school. Still, with upwards of ten thousand (mostly Black) students riding buses every day, neither the Virginia Transit Company nor the school board could make the bus rides more efficient. White Dogtown parents who did comply constantly complained about how slow and overcrowded the busses were.[80] The mix of White defiance and the city's logistical issues made many admit that less than two weeks into the 1970 fall semester, "Richmond's new desegregation plan appears to be a flop," per the *Times-Dispatch*.[81] White liberals encouraged Crockford to continue reworking the busing plan until it achieved integration.[82] Others, including city leaders and fellow PTA members, called for her resignation.[83] Crockford refused to quit, and she had enough Establishment allies to ensure that she did not have to.[84]

Crockford's issues mounted as the city's troubles with race infiltrated the schools. A White parent remembered telling his daughter, "You have to do it, we have to save the public schools," as she cried after receiving her busing order through the mail.[85] The White female student had much to fear. White students who obeyed the busing order were alienated and unfriended by fellow Whites, as if they had betrayed their race.[86] As that same parent recalled integration, this isolation made "throwing White kids to the wolves" even harder. "During that first year, there was a fight everyday [between] Blacks and Whites" a Black woman who attended Dogtown's George Wythe High School later recalled. Another Black George Wythe alumnus said that as he remembered it, "I don't think much learning went on."[87] The issue of interracial violence in schools hit a fever pitch in the middle of the 1970 fall semester when Crockford called several PTA meetings to address the "negative newspaper coverage and publicity about the Richmond Public School System and how to combat it."[88]

The local newspapers were active agents against the busing order. The coverage Crockford referred to specifically involved one major incident that made the months of rumors and anxiety visible to the world. On September 3, 1970, twelve hundred students, parents, faculty, media, and police converged on the front lawn of Southside's Elkhardt Middle School. The scene was chaotic as parents parked along Route 360 and began walking to the middle school campus to retrieve their children. At the same time, the principal and other faculty tried to corral students back inside the schoolhouse. Local police stormed the lawn in search of the suspected wrongdoers. Rumor held that a group of Black students planned to shoot the principal as well as fight and stab some White students because of a fight that they had lost a few days before. The rumors alone drew the 845 White and 280 Black students (up from 25 Blacks the year before) out of school around one p.m. As students used school phones to call their parents in fear, the parents called local radio stations and police in hopes to stop the anticipated bloodbath. When the officers arrived, Chief Frank B. Wright Jr. was already telling the press that "unfortunately, rumors of stabbings, shootings, and other incidents of physical violence have been circulating throughout the city"—but were untrue. Crockford also made it clear to the press that there was "no reason for parents to withhold their children from Elkhardt School. No one has yet produced a shred of evidence that anything of a serious nature took place." While this false alarm was part-and-parcel of the stream of negative busing coverage, Wright later admitted that violence was an issue that plagued almost every integrated school.[89]

Indeed, every middle and high school where busing took place suffered from conduct issues. White students fought Blacks; Black students fought Whites; and no one who attended integrated schools has denied that this was a daily occurrence.[90] However, the prevailing narrative among White Richmonders was that the violence was one-sided. Stories of Black students using bus stops, cafeterias, and bathrooms to unleash waves of physical assaults on innocent White children ran rampant in White parent circles. Rumors even traveled about Black males raping White girls, stabbing White boys, and threatening to harm White teachers who dared to discipline them. The rumors spread like wildfire, leading people as far away as Charlotte, North Carolina, to call local radio stations asking about the shootings and stabbings in Richmond schools. And of course, the local newspapers never missed an opportunity to spread such rumors.

While it is unclear who started these rumors, some suspected the CAB parents. Many of them had vested interests in growing the newly opened private schools in the Southside and Chesterfield. In fact, CAB leader Reverend John Butler Book was present at several public events to "investigate" the status of public schools.[91] One of his investigations led to a group of angry Dogtown parents meeting with the Richmond school board to accuse them of ignoring the violence in city schools. This conflict between White parents and the school board was covered extensively by the Richmond *Times-Dispatch*. "We have certainly not tried to cover up incidents," assistant superintendent James W. Tyler told several parents. They were not buying it, however, and the flood of parent reports about bus stop and bathroom beatdowns went allegedly unaddressed both publicly and privately. "Child protection, not busing, is the problem now," a Southside parent told the *Times-Dispatch*.[92] As the fall turned to spring, CAB parents and supporters continued using rumors of Black predators to transition Whites out of public schools.[93] On the other hand, Crockford, while "doubt[ing] the attitude of the newspapers would change in the foreseeable future," told White and Black parents to tell everyone that "a large majority of students in the City of Richmond have tried to make school mixing work."[94]

In this period, Richmond was not completely marred by racism. A group of Near West End parents, mostly White but also a few Black, spent years begging the city to establish a "model" elementary school in their neighborhood. The council and school board granted their wish shortly after the Urban Team's study revealed the depths of racial division in city schools. At John B. Cary Elementary School, admissions were not done by neighborhood zoning or competency tests. The school board and faculty conducted a citywide lottery system where they selected students based on the city's racial, gender, and class demographics. This resulted in a student body of 350 students who were, as the *Times-Dispatch* noted, "rich and poor, blue and White collar" Black and White students "from all over the city."[95] This admission policy exempted them from the federal busing order. At Cary there were no rumors of threats of violence; no police stationed outside, or parents sending their children to school with grave fear. Black and White parents, teachers, and students sought to create a harmonious culture where academic excellence, not racial supremacy or uplift, was the shared value. Regardless of race and economic class, Cary's students tested among the city's elite in every subject, making admission there the most sought-after among Black and White parents.[96]

Unfortunately for Cary parents and faculty, Richmond's race issues made their way into the school. Racial and economic balance became harder to maintain as the 1970s turned into the 1980s. When demographic realities of White suburban flight resulted in Black and working-class children becoming Cary's majority, the White middle-class parents removed their children from the school because, as a White liberal parent once said aloud at a PTA meeting, "We are proud of our diversity in this school, but we don't want to have too much diversity."[97] She meant that too many working- and lower-class Black children were harmful to the school's reputation and everyday function. Many parents shared her subtle bigotry; Cary later lost its "model" classification and became just another public school in the 1980s.[98]

Even at the height of Cary's success, Richmond Public Schools could not shake the reality that integration through a targeted busing strategy was a colossal failure. While it would have been easier to quit and allow resegregation to be the norm, Crockford saw the consolidation of Richmond, Henrico, and Chesterfield schools as the key to school integration. The proximity and jurisdictional independence of Henrico and Chesterfield made them safe havens for White families who could not access private or model schools. The White exodus from city schools was so common that newcomers to the area were quickly recruited to follow suit. For example, a White Air Force major told Crockford in a letter that after speaking with many locals, "I refused to even talk to six Richmond realtors regarding Richmond area homes. By choice, I purchased a home in Henrico County because I felt that the educational system in this county would offer my children a better education."[99] After losing thousands of White parents to the suburbs in 1970, Crockford bypassed the city council and motioned the federal courts to enjoin Chesterfield and Henrico into the desegregation case. The federal courts, after much dismay and resistance from suburban parents over busing, granted her request on December 14, 1970.[100]

After another failed busing order in 1971, Judge Robert Merhige consolidated Richmond, Chesterfield, and Henrico into a unitary school district. As a result, around 80 percent of school-aged children in all three jurisdictions were to be bused to schools outside of their neighborhoods. Some believed that the consolidation order was long overdue, as it "will mean that Richmond, the Capital of the Confederacy, will also represent a milestone towards true equality," per a television news editorial.[101] Yet that milestone would continue to be miles away as Chesterfield and Henrico attorneys filed separate appeals and halted the implementation of the order. White suburbanites from both counties joined the annexed Southsiders in resisting the court order as well. The PTAs and other parent organizations wrote several letters of protest to Crockford.[102] A Henrico parent who had recently relocated to evade the busing order wrote to Crockford that her efforts were futile because other White parents were "equally determined that their children shall not be hauled ridiculous distances across the metropolitan area."[103] Some merely picketed the federal court building while others organized rallies that drew up to four thousand people at a time.[104] School consolidation created a new classless White consensus that had not existed in Richmond since the end of Reconstruction. As one parent told Crockford, "I don't believe you understand the depth of this sentiment, and I don't believe you understand how widespread it is."[105]

The consolidation order not only unified Whites along the color line, it exposed the depth of racial hatred and vitriol rarely seen publicly in Richmond. Public officials were under constant police protection because angry parents and residents made numerous threats to their lives. The threats were not centered on the busing and consolidation order itself, but more on the hypocrisy displayed by city leaders. "What is all this bull shit—your decision to integrate was for the 'other people'—not your family," an angry parent wrote to public officials.[106] The reality was that many White city leaders, as well as the federal judge himself, sent their children to private school after the orders came down. Even some within Black leadership enrolled their children in private schools to escape the busing crisis.[107] Earlier letters of dissent usually featured the names, identities, and addresses of the senders, along with well-articulated formal complaints about the social impact of busing. After the consolidation order, the letters were so vulgar and filled with anger that "kiss my ass" is the title of the most respectful one now housed at the University of Richmond Law Library. Researchers will never grasp the full picture of what White leaders dealt with because the federal marshals kept most of the letters to build cases against those who threatened to harm public officials. However, the most representative letter that is available to historians reads:

> You must have Black relatives to do what you have attempted to do. Can't you see we Whites want the Blacks to stay away? Can't you see we do not want to live and socialize with them? None are so blind as those who will not see! We truly hope you have children that will be bused to nigger areas—we hope these children, or perhaps grandchildren, will be raped [and] molested. Girls . . . in general can turn and thank you for there [sic] nigger babies. We lived among them Blacks until we could afford to buy away from them—now jackasses like you are forcing them on us. We do not want to be with them or near them—what does it take to make this clear?

These letters were often sent with newspaper clippings about integrated schools failing in northern and midwestern cities, and reports about White Richmond students being assaulted in city schools.[108]

Luckily for suburbanites, their leaders made it to the biggest political stage. Washington, DC, became the site of one of the largest publicized rallies against school consolidation in the country. On a snowy day in February 1972, around 3,261 White suburban Richmond parents traveled to meet with US Congressmen about proposing and enacting federal antibusing legislation. A White parent told the *Times-Dispatch*, who sent reporters to cover the motorcade, that "this is middle-class America speaking out." White congressmen did not openly agree to the requests of their suburban visitors from south of the Potomac. They did greet them with a warm reception, though, describing the peaceful demonstration and movement as "democracy in action."[109] The DC trip provided much needed exposure for the anticonsolidation movement. Throughout the spring and summer of 1972, White parents and supporters from Southside and the counties conducted motorcades and rallies to display their growing dissatisfaction with the federal court's orders.[110]

In June 1972 the US Court of Appeals for the Fourth Circuit overruled the consolidation by a five-to-one vote. Richmond's consolidation order suffered its final death in the US Supreme Court less than a year later.[111] Justice Lewis F. Powell, a Richmond resident and former school board chairman, cast the deciding vote by recusing himself from the case, resulting in the four-to-four tie that upheld the lower court's decision. He would be the deciding vote against school consolidation in a similar case involving Detroit, Michigan, just a few years later.[112] Therefore, it is not difficult to ascertain his real sentiments or how he might have voted in the Richmond case. This development was one part of a larger political and judicial retreat from school integration. While some federal judges—many appointed under Presidents John F. Kennedy and Lyndon B. Johnson's administrations—continued ruling in favor of Black plaintiffs, the appellate courts, and eventually the Supreme Court, fell in line with the national consensus that *Brown* was unenforceable. While overt racial segregation in schools remained undone, covert tactics such as White flight and segregationist academies proved too powerful and elusive to overcome.

The Supreme Court's indecision left a festering, open wound in Richmond's collective body. Longtime civil rights attorney and resident Oliver Hill lamented that the city's issues with busing and school consolidation "have taught us that the majority of. . . . Virginia. . . . is so steeped in racial bigotry that it is unable to accept the Black man as a human being."[113] This inability to see Black people as equal manifested into instances of affinity for disintegration. Clara Silverstein, a child during the busing and consolidation crisis, later published a record of her experiences and noted the psychological toll the festering racial divide had on her. Upon visiting a local preparatory school, she lost her desire to attend integrated city schools: "I wanted to look like everyone else. I wanted to go out for the track team. I wanted the guidance counselor to tell me that if I kept up the good work, I could get into Harvard." Silverstein went on to admit that "I hated myself for feeling this way."[114] She was not alone.

The failures of busing and school consolidation corroded the few interracial friendships that had formed during the initial turmoil. A former Black student recalled, "I remember being confused a little bit by my friends from Tee Jay [Thomas Jefferson High School in Northside] who happened to be White, over the years disappearing." He went on to say that upon asking them why they were leaving Richmond schools, "They were sad they had to go. But their parents were pulling them out."[115] While the reasons for their parents removing them remained unsaid, everyone, from school administrators to faculty to the students themselves, knew why. Hence, this episode in city history remains, for many, a past that will never be revisited. White students who graduated from integrated schools during this time often refuse to attend their high school reunions. While it is possible that many of them may be deceased or live outside of Richmond, a Black alumnus of John Marshall High recently said during an interview that he "really do[es] believe that it's a racial thing."[116]

The busing episode both revealed existing racial tensions and created new ones that plagued the Richmond region as it exited the civil rights era. Before the 1960s and 1970s, White Richmonders relied on the rule of law and a culture of politeness to disguise the depths of the anti-Black racism inherent in Jim Crow segregation. However, as the Black push for educational equality meshed with White elite desires for a metropolitan Richmond, White suburbanites were forced to say the quiet truth out loud: Whites rejected the modern civil rights movement because they were unwilling to sacrifice their centuries-long privilege in the name of racial harmony. The area's physical and political landscape reflected this development from here on. City schools became nearly 90 percent Black and impoverished, while suburban schools were majority White and affluent. The schools belied the racial divide that defined the Richmond region. Richmond became the progressive chocolate city surrounded by vanilla conservative suburbs filled with middle-class Whites who wanted little to do with city life. Nearly every political issue from here on reflected this fundamental reality.

With the White middle class gone, racial politeness done with, and race relations broken seemingly beyond repair, city leaders and residents chose to rebuild in the coming decades. Elite Whites and politically powerful Blacks attempted to set the example for the majority of their respective races by engaging in interracial cooperation at the highest levels of government and economy. Behind them were the consequences of the modern civil rights movement. In front of them was their vision for an interracial city unburdened by racial hatred. This was the foundation for the politics of racial reconciliation.

PART 2

A CITY BROKEN, 1970–1984

4

Richmond Community Action Program

"WHERE THE GRASS ROOTS IS FOREVER ACTIVE"

> No issue is more urgent; no problem is more serious than the problem of poverty here in Richmond.
> —City Councilman Winfred Mundle, 1968

ISSUES WITH Black activism, annexation, and busing reflected that Richmond was changed by the civil rights age and attendant Black political empowerment. Scholars of the modern South chronicle the story of Black empowerment in urban centers as an inevitable process in which demographic destinies became political realities. As these chroniclers tell it, middle-class Whites turned their backs on the inner cities to face suburbia, and Blacks became the populational majorities who rode the Civil Rights Act of 1964 and Voting Rights Act of 1965 to city halls, state legislatures, and the chambers of the US Congress. Yet they often ignore the inner workings of Black urban politics during the twilight of the modern civil rights movement.[1] Black political empowerment did not take place at the polls, city hall, the state house, or in Congress: it took place in the ghettos and projects, places that conjure up "pictures of bleak urban-renewal blocks, ridden with crime and fear," as the *Richmond Times-Dispatch* put it in 1970.[2]

After World War II, Black ghettoes became the epicenters of urban politics. Whites feared that these areas and their people would grow beyond their predetermined boundaries and engulf their cities.[3] The emerging Black political class (i.e., middle- and working-class professionals) needed the ghetto and housing project residents to legitimize their claims to electoral power. Their vision of a fulfilled civil rights movement involved professionals occupying elected office and poor Blacks supporting them in the process. The Black poor, however, saw their condition of poverty as an unfixed status that could be remedied with their participation in administering sound government action. Thus, poor Blacks used federal civil rights law, the courts, and electoral politics to take an active part in improving their lives. In Richmond poor Blacks quickly learned that their empowerment compromised the long-range plans set forth by the Black middle class to assume a controlling interest in city government.

In Richmond Black political empowerment in the form of control over city governance emerged from the failed "war on poverty." The Black poor regarded the war on poverty as their civil rights movement. They used the antipoverty programs of the Economic Opportunity Act of 1964 to wrestle control of their lives from paternalist White and Black leadership. Yet their bids for self-determination and political autonomy succumbed to the fleeting implementation of federal antipoverty programs by White elites, and, crucially, by Black leaders who saw themselves as "the" representatives of the race who should remain unobstructed in their pursuit of political control.[4] Moreover, the active incorporation of the poor in political decision making was not only a missed opportunity by Black and White Richmond elites in their pursuit of racial reconciliation, but it also exposed the rifts between the Black poor and their middle-class political leadership who, until the late 1960s, had complete control of race politics.

Curtis Holt, a Black activist from the Richmond ghetto of Creighton Court, sued the city council over the 1970 annexation of Chesterfield. Holt hoped that the federal courts would undo the annexation and restore the Black voting and population majority to better his chances at gaining access to the city council. He believed that an underclass Black representative on the highest governmental body in Richmond would provide the Black ghetto, or, as he often said, the "grass roots," with the resources and representation that had long been denied to the Black poor. The result, however, was that the Black middle class undermined his lawsuit to further their long-term agenda to control city hall.

Black middle-class control of Black Richmond politics was not a foregone conclusion. Rather, the Richmond story proves that the aphorism documented by Henry G. Bohn in 1855—that "the road to hell is paved with good intentions"—is indeed true. The often-celebrated age of Black empowerment in Richmond came with the disenchantment and disempowerment of the Black poor. The failed war on poverty and the successful Holt lawsuits meant that the Black poor ironically lost their bid for political leadership as their city became majority-Black and working-class. While Black middle-class politicking played a major role in this development, it was the federal government and its efforts to remedy past discrimination with war on poverty programs and federal court rulings that transferred political power past the Black poor and to Black middle-class professionals. Both the failure of antipoverty programs and Holt's lawsuits crystalized the norm that the Black middle class should be the gatekeepers of Black progress after the modern civil rights movement.

"Richmond's Version of the War on Poverty"

Beneath Richmond's racial strife between the Black political class, the White Establishment, and the White middle class lay the political impotence of the Black underclass. Each group cultivated its political power from the shared understanding that in Richmond, the Black poor were a vulnerable group to be "represented" by Black professionals, pitied by White elites, and avoided by the White middle and working classes. More than anything, they were a group who were to remain beneath all others. The Establishment sought to "modernize" Richmond by removing the Black poor with urban renewal in the 1950s. In the next decade, Black leaders like Henry Marsh and the Crusade for Voters rose to power by representing the Black working- and underclass and consolidating their vote. When the White middle and working classes fled the city to avoid sending their children to school with Black Richmonders, the Establishment tried to annex the poor Black majority out of political existence. The pursuit of Black political empowerment, and White resistance to it, were connected by the suppression of the Black underclass.

A Texas Democrat shook the foundation upon which the battle between Black progress and White resistance usually rested. In January 1964 President Lyndon B. Johnson delivered one of many speeches he would roll out that year about "The American Promise." Originally devised by assassinated President John F. Kennedy, that promise was an "unconditional war on poverty." Half of the unconditional war involved increasing federal funds and eligibility for existing welfare programs. The other half involved breaking the glass ceiling that local elites, both White and Black, had over their poor. The Economic Opportunity Act of 1964, which created the Office of Economic Opportunity (OEO), funded and oversaw local nongovernment entities that administered federally funded education, healthcare, and jobs programs to the poor.[5] The OEO's main requirement was that antipoverty groups must include poor people in the design and implementation of every program for which they sought federal money.

Nearly every nonprofit antipoverty group across the country accepted federal money and kept the poor at arm's length after receiving it.[6] The OEO, under the direction of R. Sargent Shriver Jr., threatened to defund local antipoverty groups that did not incorporate the poor in their decision-making processes. These threats were unsuccessful; as many historians have noted, the OEO often caved and sent grant money anyway. In a way, the OEO was in a bind and had to rely upon local antipoverty programs because those who ran them were local "experts" who had experience administering resources to Black communities.[7]

Scholars argue that the war on poverty's perceived failure came from these local experts—or welfare paternalists—who formed community action programs.[8] All told, between 1961 and 1965 the OEO oversaw the creation of over a thousand locally run community action programs. While their purpose was to bypass the political pitfalls of local government and responsibly funnel federal funds—in the form of aid programs—to the poor, they did the exact opposite.[9] Local government agents (both White and Black) infiltrated community action programs to become the gatekeepers of federal money and ensure that the poor and powerless remained just that.[10]

Richmond fit within this national mold when thirty-six of its White liberals and Black middle-class professionals quietly formed the Richmond Community Action Program (RCAP) in June 1965.[11] RCAP's organizational structure consisted of a president and high-level directors who created antipoverty programs and drafted the federal grant applications to fund them. Supervisors then implemented the various programs on the ground. Upon incorporation, RCAP selected local White oligarch (attorney and former mayor) Thomas P. Bryan as their first president. Under his direction RCAP enshrined a college degree requirement for employees within its initial charter, effectively prohibiting the poor from becoming presidents, directors, and midlevel supervisors. The OEO took issue with RCAP's initial charter, and when RCAP refused to amend it, the OEO treated them like other community action programs and refused to fully fund their first grant application for $137,000.[12] The heads of Black working-class civic groups offered to serve on RCAP to help satisfy the OEO requirement, but RCAP refused because they believed the poor should remain reliant on their betters.[13]

There was a general assumption in the local media that White and Black RCAP founders were birds of a feather, in that they placed a tight lid around their leadership positions to ensure that RCAP remained, in the words of a cynical White city councilman, "a cross-section of wealthy, [and] not poor."[14] Much of this belief came from the words White RCAP members used to describe welfare and the poor. RCAP director Nell Pusey told the *Richmond News Leader* that "welfare handouts rob recipients of self-respect," so antipoverty programs should be run by professionals who "promote self-help efforts."[15] Bryan better articulated the White RCAP sentiment by saying that "Richmonders who desire to be aided by the [RCAP] program can't expect to sit back and have their aid dropped in their laps"; this was RCAP's "most essential ingredient," he once bragged.[16] Perceptions of interracial elitism only worsened when White director Weston A. Hare, upon stepping down to help grow Black leadership in RCAP, said that "most important, the White community has to listen to Black folk who haven't been paid off."[17] These public statements hid the internal tensions and divisions between Black and White RCAP leadership.

Whites and Blacks in the RCAP struggled for power and control of the organization among themselves. It was indeed true that Blacks in RCAP—such as directors psychologist John R. Chiles, Councilman Henry Marsh, banker J. Jay Nikens, sociologists Randolph Kendall, Theodore E. Thornton, and Spencer Roberts, social workers Grace Harris, Mrs. Betty Duhamel, Clifford B. Chambliss, and other well-connected Virginia Union University and Virginia Commonwealth University alumni—were, because of their education and income status, "far removed from the grass roots."[18] Their reluctance to suggest the inclusion of Black working-class people to positions of leadership lends credence to beliefs that they were just as paternalistic as vocal White RCAP directors. In criticizing Black RCAP members in 1966, Thomas Bryan publicly alluded to them being careerists who used RCAP as "a political springboard"—a salaried resume-builder in an age of increasing Black political empowerment.[19] Black RCAP members did break rank with fellow Whites in a few ways. For one, they supported the popular election of presidents and directors when Whites did not.[20] Black RCAP members got their wish, and J. Jay Nickens was elected to serve as president at the conclusion of Bryan's term in 1967.[21] They further defied their fellow White members and the local media narrative about their unrelatability with the Black poor by supporting the directorship bid of psychologist John Chiles—the son of a well-respected dentist.[22] Chiles was like most Black RCAP officials in having respect among the Black Richmond poor because they either grew up without means, or they descended from local Black elites. To many, Chiles was, as a White RCAP director claimed while nominating him for a directorship, "the only man who would be accepted by the black people." A Black Gilpin Court resident validated this assessment when he told the local press that "if John Chiles is not elected [to be a director], we don't want any part of the RCAP in our court."[23] Like Nickens and the RCAP presidency in 1967, Chiles eventually gained his directorship two years later.

RCAP's original structure, where White and Black elites controlled and administered every program, proved wildly unstable. The OEO either denied or underdelivered on every RCAP grant application between 1965 and 1966 because the requirement that "proper minority group representation and representation from the areas being served" remained unmet.[24] RCAP's defiance was matched by poor Richmond Whites who followed the national trend of refusing to partake in antipoverty programs alongside poor Blacks.

It was poor Black women, in the end, who compelled RCAP to reform its policies. They cost RCAP millions in federal grants by not participating in many surveys and funded programs. There was no mistaking this lack of participation for ignorance. Poor Black mothers often vocalized their "chief complaint" to nearly every well-dressed man and woman who went door-to-door in Richmond's six housing projects.[25] "Negroes in poverty areas don't believe the Community Action program is doing anything for them and that [poor] Negroes are not involved enough in workings of the social agencies," Black RCAP advertiser Ronald K. Charity bluntly told the press. He continued that "persons in the poverty areas wonder why don't we see more young Negro men and women working in these programs? Why do we have a White person coming to see us? I wonder this, too."[26] A local White director agreed that change needed to happen, as "we have not been able to reach the grass roots level."[27] Faced with extinction like other community action programs across the country, White RCAP directors—against the wishes of those like Thomas Bryan who saw it as "really impractical"—allocated portions of their thin administrative budget to renting and staffing thirteen offices near the Richmond housing projects.[28]

Over a year after its founding, RCAP finally (albeit roughly) resembled the image President Johnson had when he issued his "unconditional war on poverty." Poor Black mothers became bookkeepers, aides, and assistants within the newly staffed project offices.[29] Although the college requirement made the salaried director and supervisor positions unavailable to them, poor Black women turned the RCAP offices (called Central Neighborhood Centers) into hubs that brought "together the haves and the have-nots," according to a data assessment. When poor Black people entered these offices in search of nutritional, mental health, educational, transportation, housing, and job services, they felt more comfortable seeing their own, who often "voice[d] the needs of the people to those agencies." Poor Black women's presence as low-level facilitators made them authority figures on whom directors and supervisors had to rely to organize and "attend various community meetings to keep in touch with the pulse of the community."[30] These Central Neighborhood Centers embodied the potential of empowerment that elites of both races had long denied the Black Richmond poor.[31]

Poor Black Richmonders quickly realized that economic stability incentivized political activism. Some Black single mothers became more vocal about the issues concerning their communities shortly after receiving RCAP offices and the jobs that came with them. Local civic groups organized and protested the lack of bus stops, traffic lights, and functional parks in housing project areas. They also raised concerns about broken appliances that the Richmond Redevelopment and Housing Authority (RRHA) routinely refused to fix.[32]

RRHA employees, some of whom were RCAP directors and supervisors, fought back quickly by weaponizing the number one issue that hurt the Black Richmond poor—housing.[33] Understanding that Richmond had a shortage of affordable housing and that racist realtors mostly refused to rent homes to Blacks outside of largely Black underclass areas, the RRHA began a series of rent hikes and evictions to quiet the vocal Black poor by spring of 1966.[34] The Department of Housing and Urban Development (HUD) and OEO allowed local housing authorities to exempt income earned from antipoverty programs in welfare assessments, yet concerns about poor people's activism prompted local officials to ignore the federal income exemption. The RRHA reasoned, as was articulated by director Frederic Fay, "that a person working for the antipoverty program ought to have to bear the same kind of obligation to pay rent based on income as the person living next door to him." This new rent policy created the intended effect, as many young women quit their RCAP jobs. As an RCAP worker told the *Times-Dispatch,* many poor Black women asked: "What good does it do to raise the aspirations of these people if they are going to be penalized for doing it?"[35] The RRHA also evicted Black single mothers for allowing suspected boyfriends to spend the night, which was a violation of their lease agreements.[36] "We feel that no program to relieve poverty will be successful as long as the number of needy children multiply twice as rapidly as they are well cared for," a RCAP director said in defense of the RRHA's de facto chastity clause.[37] They also banned civic organizations from meeting on RRHA property. These rules and policies were intended to effectively clamp down on poor people's activism, and that is exactly what they did.[38]

The RRHA's attacks on poor Black women happened as many in Virginia and the nation felt that community action programs had run their course. Richmond was one of fifty-five Virginia localities that received $14 million in federal antipoverty grants to create and run community

78 THE STRUGGLE FOR CHANGE

action programs. Only the Tidewater and Southside regions cooperated well with the OEO's requirements by fully incorporating the input of the poor. Most Virginia cities and counties either did not form functioning community action programs, or they merely had dysfunctional coalitions that excluded the Black poor from decision making.[39]

Virginia's insolence in the war on poverty was a star in a constellation of national resistance to President Johnson's plan. A congressional poll showed that most Americans wanted to nix antipoverty programs altogether by 1966.[40] Republican congresspeople used political attacks, similar in nature to those in Richmond targeting Black women from the projects, along with a national budget crisis over the Vietnam War, to argue that the war on poverty had become a partisan bureaucratic scheme to funnel federal money into the hands of "overpaid administrators and poorly organized field workers."[41] Only $1.5 billion of federal funds—less than 1 percent of federal spending—went to community action programs by 1966. The war on poverty in its entirety only made up 2 percent of the federal budget.[42] The dollar amount did not matter as the nation grew tired of funding a project that had largely devolved into petty infighting between the poor and welfare officials.

"The Grass Roots Is Forever Active"

Within a few short years, RCAP had become a shell of itself, a zombie organization feasting on small federal and private funds to hold off death. The spirit of the war on poverty had effectively vacated the RCAP, if it ever existed in the first place. Yet that spirit was alive and well in the Richmond ghettoes like Creighton Court, where men such as Curtis Holt Sr. pushed for poor peoples' inclusion in the decisions made about their lives. Curtis Holt is given slight mention in the overall narrative of Black political power in Richmond. This treatment is understandable given that extracting Holt's story from the archives and public sources is difficult. While the result of Holt's activism—the successful lawsuit that ushered in a majority Black council—is well known, his efforts in the local and national battle to grow the political power of the poor has received hardly any attention.[43] Curtis Holt was more than the man who lost a city council bid and sued a corrupt city government shortly thereafter. He symbolized the pushing and prodding of poor Black people, which the Black middle class then subverted in their own push for power.

Holt was born to sharecroppers from Rocky Mount, North Carolina, in 1920. After the untimely death of his father, he moved with his mother and seven siblings to the poor section of Richmond's Church Hill neighborhood. Holt was the oldest male in his household by the time they reached Richmond, so the intellectually curious boy became a hardworking man at the tender age of sixteen. He worked several odd jobs in trucking and manufacturing to make ends meet. In an industrial city like Richmond, the most frequent work that Holt found was in construction, where very few employers asked questions as long as one could swing a hammer and dig a ditch. Holt nearly died after falling from an elevated surface on one construction site. With his physical prime taken from him at the age of twenty-one, he was unable to work and lucky to be alive. The undereducated Holt would no longer work manual jobs after this fall. Bad fortunes forced him and his new wife Alto Mae—a maid in Richmond Public Schools—to relocate to the Creighton Court housing projects in Church Hill.[44] The Holts reportedly lived on a meager $3,000 a year—$1,800 a year came from disability and the remainder from Alto's salary as a maid.

By the mid-1960s, Holt, now the father of four children with Alto Mae, had become politically active. In 1964 he worked with various single mothers to help start the Creighton Court Civic Association (CCCA). They envisioned the CCCA to be a representative organization that crystallized, facilitated, and converted the collective energy of Church Hill's Black poor into meaningful forms of activism. The CCCA started some of the first autonomous childcare programs in the Church Hill area. They also held voting drives and "poor people's meetings" to draft petitions and letters to city government. It is in these public records, and the archived collections of some elite men and newspapers, where the CCCA's activities and their impact come to life.

Curtis Holt's CCCA was the group that complained to RCAP and city government about the lack of bus stops, traffic lights, and functional parks in housing-project areas. They also raised concerns about broken appliances that the RRHA routinely refused to fix and replace. When the RRHA began evicting Black single mothers, Holt protested.[45] Holt also garnered negative attention for exposing the RRHA and local housing barons for using federal funds to maintain segregated housing in defiance of the Civil Rights Act of 1964. Richmonders generally understood that city officials used HUD funding to construct and expand housing projects almost exclusively in the majority poor and Black East End to "preserve a pattern of segregation in the city," as city council members honestly answered on a questionnaire. Holt and the CCCA wrote to HUD director Philip G. Sadler about the city using federal funds to construct and maintain segregated housing, and his letter halted the release of federal funds to construct additional public housing in the Gilpin Court housing projects, located just outside of downtown.[46] This letter, along with his other forms of activism, put him on the Establishment's radar. In April 1966 the RRHA accused Holt of fraud, claiming that he earned more money (from cutting hair as an unlicensed barber) than he had listed on his housing project application. Thus, they wanted him and his family evicted from Creighton Court.

After receiving his eviction notice, Holt sued the RRHA in federal court, claiming that the eviction was a political attack against him. Judge John D. Butzner—the same judge who had protected school segregation in Virginia by allowing Freedom of Choice plans—ironically ruled against the RRHA. He opined that Holt "was being threatened with eviction because he was instrumental in organizing a civic group that sought improvement in living conditions at the court." Judge Butzner continued that his court found Holt's "lease was terminated because he was organizing the tenants and was exercising his first amendment right of freedom of speech and assemblage."[47] Furthermore, Judge Butzner's ruling validated Holt's belief that, in the age of the war on poverty, poor people could improve their circumstances and defeat tyrannical forces if they remained politically active.

The RRHA's issues with Holt were part and parcel of the retreat from the war on poverty and RCAP just as the Black poor became more politically active. By 1966 the OEO funded RCAP's $400,000-a-year operation at 90 percent. Per their agreement with the OEO in 1965, RCAP had promised to find additional funding to help reduce OEO's contribution to 50 percent.[48] The general idea was that city government would pick up the tab, but Black working-class activism led by Holt was a major reason why RCAP failed to convince the city to do so. Between 1966 and 1968, city councils in Hampton, Fairfax, Charlottesville, and Newport News funded their community action programs at nearly full capacity.[49] This compelled OEO to ask the mostly White Richmond city council (six Whites and three Blacks—Marsh, Cephas, and Mundle) to help cover RCAP's tab by 1968. The White Establishment utterly refused, and it was nearly impossible to "change community attitudes" on the subject, a White councilwoman told the press.[50]

The questions surrounding the permanent public funding of RCAP came to the forefront when Richmond was desperately holding on to the economic prosperity it had acquired after World War II. The city of 220,000 (evenly split between Black and White residents) had an annual $16 million welfare budget. This number was steadily climbing as one quarter of Richmonders lived below the poverty line, as opposed to less than a tenth of residents in Henrico and Chesterfield.[51] The Virginia legislature helped subsidize some of Richmond's welfare costs, but they refused to ensure the city's economic well-being as the short-lived war on poverty was effectively over.[52] RCAP looked "something like a bride who was left behind at the altar," said the *Times-Dispatch*, and local welfare issues ensured that is where it would remain.[53] A local contractor made this reality abundantly clear when he frankly told the council that "the Richmond Community Action Program is a complete waste of the Richmond Taxpayer' money and I trust that you will vote against it."[54] Not only did the White councilmen vote against it, one of them went a step further in voting against a token "gesture of cheap politics": namely, approving a resolution to defund a RCAP fundraiser in which they would solicit newer sources of private funding.[55]

Informing the local consensus to defund RCAP was the belief that the war on poverty failed because the poor were simply too lazy to work. War on poverty policy centered on job training because of the commonly held axiom that poverty resulted from a lack of education and not opportunity. Believing this sentiment, conservative Black city councilman Winfred Mundle did not propose funding RCAP. Rather, he wanted the council to allow local capitalists to reshape the public-school curriculum and create a direct pipeline to industrial and manufacturing employment. He touted that his plan would come "without extra cost to the people of Richmond and without additional federal aid or interference," and, most importantly, that "everything gained will be earned."[56] While capitalists such as Henry Ford II and David Rockefeller lauded plans like this around the nation, Mundle's plan received no support from local businessmen or his colleagues on the council because of the unverified belief that, as one business owner wrote to the council, "there are jobs available in the City of Richmond that are going unfulfilled not only because of the lack of educational requirements" but because Blacks did not want to work.[57] Former mayor Morrill Crowe once agreed by rhetorically asking "why the City of Richmond has so many job vacancies if poor people want to work?"[58] He, like many businessmen, believed that the poor were lazy and that programs like RCAP perpetuated that pathological behavior. "The local war [on poverty] hasn't done much"; thus, "We cannot apply the hard-financial sheet to any effort to aid the disadvantaged," Crowe said in his final objection.[59]

While the Richmond Urban League and councilman Henry Marsh boldly demanded that the city council permanently fund RCAP, other advocates focused on the reality that rejecting RCAP could result in violence.[60] "This is a serious matter" because "the thought of having one of these neighborhood agencies dissolved because of lack of financial aid certainly would not be to the best interests of an All-American City," a White RCAP director bluntly stated.[61] The director said the quiet part out loud: many local Whites and Blacks feared that the growing Black Power movement might seep into Richmond's ghettos.[62] Poor Black Richmonders were watching civil rights legislation bypass them and benefit the Black middle class exclusively in terms of job access, housing, and political appointments. The war on poverty was their civil rights movement, but the city and nation gave up on it. A local White stockbroker and war on poverty supporter argued that RCAP "provides an opportunity for these people to speak and be heard; I question whether these people had an opportunity to speak and be heard prior to the formation of RCAP."[63] RCAP was, for the Black Richmond poor, the only tie they had to policymaking that effected their lives. To take that away was, in essence, to aid in their reduction to a powerless class of people.

The gridlock on RCAP funding magnified the sense of hopelessness that permeated the Black Richmond ghettoes. "Poor People have so little to build faith on, promises are not forgotten," said one civic leader after acknowledging that over 2,074 people wrote letters of dissent to the city council.[64] The promises that the civic leader referred to pledged that the war on poverty would put them in conversation with elites to improve their lives. Areas like Fulton, Hillside, Creighton, Mosby, and Gilpin needed these promises to be fulfilled because, as former state delegate Viola Baskerville remembered about her childhood in Church Hill, "people relied on each other" so much because life was, generally, a carousel of hardship defined by the shortage of resources.[65]

The denial of the promises for economic justice and political representation resulted in Blacks growing "tired of promise[s] those White folks downtown make" when "nothing ever happens (referring to better jobs, better housing)," a group of poor Black Richmond parents told a social worker. Had Black Power advocates set up shop in Richmond, they would have found a breeding ground because the poor felt en masse the "lack of interest by [Black middle-class] leaders in the [poor] community," the parents continued. As RCAP's childcare services diminished from a lack of funding, Black boys were, by 1968, found in abundance "wandering aimlessly through the community; first one corner then the other." Many allegedly landed in back alleys, pool halls, and drug dens engaging in many forms of debauchery.[66] Others resorted to random acts of violence that caused a thirty-eight-year veteran of Richmond Public Schools to tell the city council, "We feel that an appropriation for the maintenance of R-Cap is a fight against anger, frustration, and despair for a large percentage of our population." She continued, "I can assure you that we have witnessed too many evidences of frustration and despair among the under-privileged in our community."[67] Hopelessness and despair were commonplace in the Black Richmond ghetto; however, Curtis Holt did all he could to ensure it would not remain so.

Curtis Holt wrote a dissenting letter to local business leaders and councilmembers that reflected poor Black Richmond's anger over the refusal to permanently fund RCAP. "We have been asking and begging for your assistance, and now the time has come for us to not do any begging for your assistance, and now the time has come for us to not do anymore begging, asking or pleading with you peoples in City Government [sic]. We are not going to beg, plead or ask any longer, since we have not many steps forward. . . . From now on we are going to demand," Holt wrote to White councilman and prominent businessman James C. Wheat.[68] Holt was no radical; he never promoted the use of violence for political gain. Yet his words created worry that Richmond's poor Blacks were going to pay attention to the protests in over one hundred cities where antipoverty programs had been abandoned. The Dallas *Times Herald* noted that these protests were a clear sign that "negroes are fed up with overcrowded, overpriced, rat-infested ghetto housing . . . which no White neighborhood would tolerate."[69] When Holt claimed that "we are going to demand," White Richmond leaders paid close attention. Monitoring riots elsewhere, according to a local businessman, "should give us greater insight into the problem as we relate it to our city."[70] Furthermore, Holt's words were twofold, in that they made visible the growing dissatisfaction in the Black Richmond ghettoes and signaled his plan to do something about it.

Seeing that "there is no end in sight" to the anger over the city's decision to not fund RCAP permanently, the Establishment and Black leadership effectively killed the local war on poverty and RCAP discussion with the politics of representation.[71] In the summer of 1968 they formed the first ever human relations board. The board operated outside of the OEO's purview, in that it was not legislative or regulatory. The board maintained "daily contact with public establishments, churches and social groups," connecting the underserved to public services and fielding complaints about discrimination and presented them to the city council.[72] The board was highly political as local civil rights legends such as attorney Oliver White Hill and W. Lester Banks worked with welfare paternalist and councilmember Nell Pusey to select Curtis Holt and others to represent poor Black Richmonders.[73] The city council chose the board members, who then served either a two- or three-year term.⁷⁴ Although poor Blacks served as members, the council made sure that "the human relations commission directorship [was only given] to a qualified Black person," someone with the "ability to speak and write effectively."⁷⁵ Unfortunately for Holt, whom the *Times-Dispatch* by that time had labeled a "self-styled grassroots coordinator for the city," he would never qualify for the role of director.⁷⁶

"Henry L. Marsh Won His Election; I Was the Man Who Was Denied"

Although the human relations board provided poor Blacks some level of representation and interaction with those in power, that was not enough to satisfy their desires for more say in city government. Curtis Holt knew that; he served on the board and regularly watched his proposals and requests get dismissed by Whites and Blacks alike. Thus, he ran for city council in 1970 to better represent the Black poor's interest in city hall.⁷⁷ He made it clear that he intended to bring power to "the slums, ghettos, and Housing Projects within the city, where the Grass Roots is forever active," given that, as he once stated, "Richmond does not care for the needs of the poor."⁷⁸ Holt's populist platform was not policy-heavy; rather, it emphasized his role in city government as a human relations board member and as "the poor people's coordinator, a poor man who has been working with the poor."⁷⁹ While Holt wanted his activism to translate into a position of leadership, Black middle-class politicians felt otherwise. It is well documented that they publicly supported his campaign while privately asking him to concede.⁸⁰ They felt that Holt's lack of formal education and unrefined dialect and mannerisms reinforced White stereotypes of Black inferiority. While Blacks may have seen a charismatic leader, Whites would have undoubtedly labeled him a "Sambo." The uncomfortable truth about Black politics in Richmond was that it was largely about racial representation. Therefore, Curtis Holt should not, the Black middle class largely felt, represent the race.⁸¹

Curtis Holt finished seventeenth in the field of twenty-seven candidates for city council, receiving around 13,000 of the 51,509 votes.⁸² The aftermath of his failed campaign taught Holt how tight the bonds were between economic class and political power. He believed that his electoral loss came from the recently annexed parts of Chesterfield County (see chapter 2) that had turned the Black voting majority into a slight minority. His response reflected the belief that poor people should, as he once said about the issue of public housing, "test our strength" in the federal courts. Holt, like many poor people throughout America who participated in the modern civil rights movement and war on poverty programs, saw the federal government as a bulwark against local tyranny. "If you do not get justice here in Richmond, you can try Washington, DC," Holt once said publicly.[83]

His initial attempts to sue the city council over annexing twenty-three square miles of Chesterfield County fell on deaf ears within the local Black political class.[84] Not one Black lawyer took his case to court. Likely, they did not want to work pro bono, as Holt made it abundantly clear to all of them that he could not afford litigation.[85] Yet the most telling rejection came from Henry Marsh, the same attorney who had successfully represented Holt's pro bono case against the RRHA years before. Marsh rose to political prominence as a man who represented the interests of the Black working- and underclass. Yet his position in city hall made him a part of the Black middle class's long-range plans to control city politics at a time when Richmond needed a newer tax base and the inclusion of the suburbs to help desegregate public schools. If Holt won his lawsuit as he envisioned it, it would have guaranteed Blacks control of a financially strapped city with hypersegregated schools. In sum, the Black middle-class political establishment needed the annexation to financially bolster the city they were on the verge of controlling. Holt's inability to retain Marsh as a lawyer likely hinged upon this fact. Holt's personality also played a factor; a longtime Richmond resident who knew Holt personally believed that while Holt fancied himself a race leader, the Black political class saw him as a symbol of Black inferiority who would, once Blacks seized power in city hall, be politically sidelined.[86]

With this new, disappointing sense of his actual place among Richmond's Black political class, Holt found a White attorney to represent his cases against the city council. Holt claimed in three separate suits, which were litigated by six separate courts beginning in February 1971 and ending November 1976, that the 1970 annexation violated Section IV of the Voting Rights Act of 1965, which required the Department of Justice (DOJ) to investigate any municipal land deal that turned a voting majority into a minority. Holt won his first suit (Holt I) in which he requested a new election. The US Court of Appeals for the Fourth Circuit overturned the US District Court's decision. By 1972 Holt's remaining case against the city council was in the federal courts in Richmond while the DOJ, under Section IV of the Voting Rights Act, opened a parallel case against Richmond in the Federal District Court of Columbia. Although the city council faced two separate federal cases—one in Washington, DC, and the other in Richmond—the judges joined their cases at the hip by unofficially agreeing to render rulings that did not conflict with one another. The federal court in Richmond waited on the district court in Washington to make a recommendation. By 1972 the DC court decided that Richmond should be able to keep the annexed suburbs because of the economic benefits to the entire area. The main stipulation was that the city council had to create a new voting system to reempower Black voters.[87] The US Supreme Court, for its part, eventually suspended city council elections until the creation of this newer, fairer voting format.

At this point the Black political class, namely the Crusade for Voters under the leadership of Henry Marsh, hijacked Holt's case by successfully petitioning the courts in DC for entry into the DOJ's case against Richmond. This ensured that they worked closely with federal judges and the Department of Justice on shaping the outcome of the case, as they argued that their advisory presence was "protecting the interest of the total Black community." When asked about the hypocrisy of refusing to represent Holt while requesting to enter the case as advisors to shape the outcome, Marsh claimed that he and the Black political class were "not anti-Curtis Holt, but we've learned we can't put all our eggs in one basket."[88] The pro-Crusade *Richmond Afro-American* newspaper revealed the underlying logic by writing that "the Crusade could help bring a decision in which Black voters would obtain fair district representative on council while allowing the city to retain the rich tax base of the annexed areas."[89] The Black middle class wanted to recapture the city's majority while keeping the newly added, affluent White tax base of North Chesterfield. In sum, they wanted to have their cake and eat it, too.

Holt's insistence on pointing out the Crusade's opportunistic involvement marked the end of his push for the political empowerment of poor Blacks. Black Richmond politics had long operated on a few fundamental axioms. For one, Blacks acted as if Whites, whether rich or poor, could not be fully trusted. The second was that Blacks could bitterly disagree in private, but they were to never, ever disagree or personally attack each other in the public view of Whites.[90] Holt violated the latter when he consistently pointed out that in 1970 "Henry L. Marsh won his election, I was the man who was denied."[91] He also wrote opinioned editorials about how "Henry Marsh has had six years to show that he does not intend to do anything for people." When Holt said "people," he meant poor Black people. Holt further accused the Crusade of being "hungry Black people who only care about what they get for themselves." Later, he criticized the

Crusade organ, the *Afro-American,* after a gubernatorial election by saying, "This is unbelievable that you would give credit to the Crusade. You know deep down in your heart the Grass Roots, first of all, put thousands of newly registered voters' names on the books before Election Day." Furthermore, "It is time that credit is given to those who deserve it."[92] Holt's vocal criticism likely cost him his seat on the human relations board. Crusade leaders were not too shy about booting Holt, telling the press that they "viewed the formation of a new commission as getting rid of 'some' people" that they no longer cared for.[93]

The irony of Holt's demise was that *his* court cases, rather than the previous attacks on urban renewal, school segregation, voting discrimination, housing, and job discrimination, provided the Black middle class with access to the political power that they had clamored for since the Crusade's founding in 1956. With Holt's cases plowing through the courts, it became clear to the White Establishment that Black Richmonders would benefit from the courts' impending decisions.[94] Thus, they divested from city affairs and appointed Crusade members to prominent positions in city government. Between 1975 and 1976, White leaders named Black appointees to be their race's first in several citywide posts, ranging from circuit court judgeships to school board chairman.[95] By the spring of 1976, the Washington, DC, and Richmond courts lifted their injunctions on local elections and the city council (composed of five White men, a Black man—Henry Marsh—and a Black woman named Willie J. Dell) replaced the at-large voting system with a ward system. The formation of one mixed, four White, and four Black wards excited the Black political class as they confidently felt that they "could elect five Blacks to the city council," Marsh told the *Afro-American.*[96]

Black Richmonders produced over fifty new candidates for the 1977 special election, the first citywide election in seven years. By organizing symposiums and promising to support Black candidates who were backed by local civic groups, the Crusade shrewdly tamped down on any populist political sentiments that Holt may have created.[97] Yet it was clear to all, especially in the Fifth District (downtown), that the Crusade would only pick Blacks who toed the party line. One political organizer disappointedly said that "the Crusade has persistently engaged in undesirable, unrepresentative, and undemocratic activities" by recanting on their promise to back the favorites who emerged from within the Black community.[98] Another disenchanted Black organizer similarly claimed that "Blacks in this town had the chance for political freedom" after the annexation cases. Yet the refusal to accept Black grassroots candidates who operated outside of the Crusade pipeline assured many that "the Crusade [had] sold them out" come election day.[99]

All five Crusade candidates secured electoral victories on March 2, 1977. While they were well-respected among Black Richmonders en masse, not one of them hailed from the "grassroots" in the Curtis Holt sense. This reality was the ultimate insult for Holt, a man who helped turn the fractured war on poverty into a poor people's movement for political empowerment and representation. His efforts led him, like many civil rights activists before, to the federal courts seeking justice. Yet those efforts only empowered those above him, revealing that the Black political gains during the civil rights age, in general, came at the expense of the Black urban poor: a group who had their own aspirations that differed greatly from those of the middle class. Poor Black Richmonders' activism was, however, like the mythical phoenix: it temporarily died only to give birth to a new age of city politics. From 1977 on, leaders of both races would shoulder the burden to rebuild a racially divided Richmond, metaphorically and literally. While the grassroot communities tried to function in a city where civic pride had suffered from decades of political turmoil and residential flight, those in city government and the business community, not the ghettoes, would set the foundation for determining what a post–Jim Crow Richmond would look like.

5
Project One

"A DIVIDING LINE SEPARATING WHITES AND BLACKS"

IN THE FALL of 1982 approximately three hundred Richmond women organized a roundtable discussion with Henry L. Marsh III and representatives from the chamber of commerce that quickly devolved into an indictment of the Marsh administration. The Junior League of Richmond wanted to know why Marsh and the White establishment could not articulate their consensus view on the city's flagship revitalization project. The answer was simple: they could not provide what they did not have.

By 1977 Richmond had become a fully engaged participant in the national urban revitalization movement, where White businesspeople and Black politicians allied on infrastructure improvement in downtown areas.[1] Yet despite the biracial consensus on urban revitalization in Richmond, there was more stalemate than movement, costing Marsh the mayorship in 1982—although he remained on the city council. When asked during the fall roundtable in 1982 whether the agenda for infrastructural modernity would eventually "enhance racial cooperation and racial harmony" in Richmond, both Marsh and chamber representatives sat in silence. It took moderator Virginia Ritchie to break "the embarrassing silence by saying she would come back to that question after allowing some time to think," the *Times-Dispatch* reported.[2] The silence, as this chapter will show, said more than any words could have.

Richmond's political and business leaders both Black and White created an "urban regime" to promote downtown revitalization as racial reconciliation. City leaders used bipartisan and biracial public projects to cultivate Richmonders' desire for reconciliation through so-called Project One: the first ever attempt by city leaders of both races to implement a shared vision for Richmond's future.

That vision was a city where Black and White leadership worked together to rebuild the desolate economy created by White suburban flight. Urban regimes, a term coined by political scientist Clarence Stone, are formal arrangements between public officials and private interests that result in government action.[3] Between 1977 and 1982 the creators of Richmond's urban regime agreed to invest tax money into the private development of Project One—new downtown hotels, businesses, and mixed-use buildings. Yet Richmond's urban regime faced a formidable taxpayer revolt that threatened to undo Project One. When faced with difficulty, Richmond leaders revealed that in spite of the inclusive rhetoric, they had no interest in sharing credit for the city's economic rebuild. Rather, they envisioned their own respective races leading the economic comeback with the help of the leadership of the opposite race. When it was all said and done, Project One did not become "one project."

Still, this first attempt laid the cornerstone of racial reconciliation after the modern civil rights movement. The image of Black and White leaders coming together to fulfill a singular project served as inspiration for themselves and later other nonelite organizations to fix the city economically and politically. Imbedded in this interracial cooperation was the collective desire to heal race relations by rebuilding a post–Jim Crow city with Black leadership at the helm. While Project One succeeded in coalescing the reconciliation energies of Black and White leadership, it failed to fix the economy and highlighted that during the initial phases of racial reconciliation in Richmond, both sides worked together without wanting to lead together. Acknowledgement of this failure in later decades then shaped subsequent revitalization projects, forcing leaders of both races to work in tandem to socially engineer and run an interracial Richmond.

"Bridging Barriers between Peoples"

Following the 1977 election, Richmond reluctantly embraced the changes happening throughout the region. That same year, the *Atlanta Constitution* claimed, "We are entering the era of a new relationship between the South and the rest of the nation." The widely read newspaper continued by claiming, "As far as the race issue is concerned, the nation once looked upon the South as a peculiar problem area." Yet now the civil rights revolution, and the influx of more liberal middle-class professionals and corporations to southern urban centers, showed the region's leaders and residents that "the system of segregation by law [that] long held the South back" was no longer.[4] By 1977 the South exported more poor people than it took in for the first time in American history. The majority of southerners (over 70 percent), both new and old, lived in metropolitan areas, assuring that the *city* and the *suburb* were the region's cultural and economic present and future.[5] As this "Newer" South grew wealthy and powerful on the foundation of interracial cooperation at the highest levels of government and economic growth, Dallas and Houston took the population lead. Atlanta and Charlotte became the region's face and flagship cities.[6] Richmond, however, struggled to keep pace in this new mainstream, corporation-controlled deracialized Southland.[7]

The former Confederate citadel tried its hand at transitioning away from being just "a convenient tourist stop between Washington, DC, and Williamsburg." Richmond's White business community began with a massive advertising campaign, recruiting northern and western industries to headquarter their firms in the largely vacant downtown area. Charlotte, North Carolina, had succeeded with a similar plan by attracting West Coast banks (mainly Bank of America), while Atlanta focused on technology firms such as the New York–based IBM. Richmond—the nation's leading tobacco and synthetic fiber producer—attracted the likes of Figgie International, CSX Corporation, and ten other Fortune 500 companies to share space with local giants Philip Morris (tobacco), James River Corporation (paper), Reynolds Metal (aluminum), and DuPont (chemicals). Out-of-town companies relocated to Richmond because of its geographic position between Atlanta and New York City, as well as its suppressed union activity and probusiness political culture.[8]

Although geography mattered, the most attractive draw for Richmond was the perceived improvement in race relations. The unusual sight of Black men and women walking into the newly built, glass-plated city hall along East Broad Street as high-level bureaucrats was, according to *Ebony* magazine, "a sign of the changing times" in Richmond and the region. "Out in Hollywood Cemetery," *Ebony* continued, "Confederate President Jefferson Davis must be turning over in his grave."[9] Richmond was a place where people could "leave your car door unlocked," enjoy suburban malls, and "seek sameness through private clubs and private schools," the *Wall Street Journal* touted on the city's behalf. With lowered taxes, suburbanization, and new racial moderation, out-of-town leaders of industry came to realize that the traditionally hidebound Richmond was, like Charlotte and Atlanta, open for business.[10]

The sins of the past still haunted Richmond, however. Some corporations' relocation to Richmond did not cure the economic ills created by White middle-class flight. Richmond's leaders needed the property taxes from middle- and upper-class residents to perform the essential functions of a city. Southern cities such as Atlanta, Charlotte, Memphis, and Nashville relied heavily on formal and informal partnerships between local and state leaders in the private and public sectors. These partnerships resulted in annexations and metropolitan governments that ensured the inner cities and suburbs shared expenses, and, in some cases, state funding.[11] Cities that could not rely on such cooperation, such as Dallas and Houston, had urban-friendly annexation laws that allowed them to take the land—and by proxy the property taxes—they needed to pay the bills. Richmond had recourse to neither. This makes Project One all the more important, because here was a southern city that did not have suburban cooperation on fixing urban decay. Supporting the suburban neglect was a state legislature that shut the door on Richmond's annexation pursuits.

The Virginia General Assembly, once willing to pay lip service to Richmond's economic vitality, all but turned its back on the city. The suburban-leaning legislature passed state laws in 1971 and 1980 that prevented future annexation requests by cities. For Richmond, that meant closing the door on annexing surrounding Henrico County and what remained of Chesterfield County.[12] Suburban leadership followed the state's lead by refusing to voluntarily form metropolitan governments with urban areas that would have shared the expense of public resources (infrastructure, police, and schools) between the Richmond, Henrico, and Chesterfield area. As remembered by Richmonders, this suburban political conservatism reflected the disdain White leaders had for the majority Black and cash-strapped Richmond.[13]

Without state and suburban help, Henry Marsh and his four Black allies on the city council looked for temporary solutions to their seemingly permanent issues with both race and poverty. The equation was simple: as Richmond became demographically Blacker, its coffers became dryer.[14] With the exception of a few exclusive neighborhoods, both the White and Black middle class largely refused to live within the city once the federal courts and state legislature had protected the suburbs from urban rule. This trend created the paradox of metropolitan wealth and urban poverty that scholars studied at length and continue to study.[15] How do Blackening, or already Black, cities obtain a share of metropolitan wealth when they are economically and politically cut off from the suburbs? The search for an answer was aided by a meeting of the National Conference of Black Mayors held about two hours north of Richmond in Washington, DC. The October 1977 gathering included Henry Marsh and 160 other Black mayors who passed two dozen resolutions about leading their cities toward the path of economic prosperity. Each resolution included aspects of extremely popular downtown revitalization programs.[16] This agenda came largely from the Congressional Black Caucus pressuring newly elected President Jimmy Carter to issue "a comprehensive economic package linking full employment, urban revitalization and equal opportunity through affirmative action."[17]

Urban revitalization was a national movement whereby city leaders sought to reverse White suburban flight by repairing downtown commercial areas through federal, state, local, and private real estate investments. Like urban renewal in the 1950s and 1960s, revitalization plans catered to the White suburbanites who made their money in the inner city while spending it in the suburbs. Unlike urban renewal, however, these new infrastructure projects were designed to repopulate cities and not aid in their depopulation. According to Jon C. Teaford's seminal monograph *The Road to Renaissance* (1990), this phase in urban history was unique in that it gave leaders a bipartisan, singular focus. Plans to construct new downtown high rises, mixed-use corporate headquarters, and upscale bars and restaurants took center stage and pushed more divisive topics to the periphery. This consensus plan, never easy, was the second phase (urban renewal being the first) in a series of expensive attempts by urban leaders after World War II to keep their middle-class tax bases from fleeing to suburban areas.[18]

At the federal level, Georgia native and moderate Democrat Jimmy Carter allocated funds to failing cities that had viable public-private partnerships (or urban regimes) and revitalization plans.[19] These billion-dollar block grants combined with the millions raised by local governments and industries to literally build their cities out of poverty.[20] Before Carter's support, northern cities had been "pumping new life into downtown and its fringes" since the mid-1960s. These projects included new office buildings, premier hotels, and riverfront mixed-use facilities underwritten by banking and manufacturing firms.[21] The largest southern cities matched the northern zeal for revitalization.[22] Although the White House and southern urban leaders were fully committed to revitalization by the time Henry Marsh came to occupy the executive office in 1977, Richmond's first Black mayor may have been hesitant to take up the task. Marsh was a longtime opponent of urban renewal, and he assumed power after years of political and social disintegration in the Richmond area. Urban revitalization projects often required strong cooperation between the public and private sector that then empowered a mayor to act as a strong executive. Before Marsh took power, the Establishment's dominance in city government, although pervasive, had rarely resulted in streamlined government initiatives. This newer Richmond, however, would be different because Blacks had a majority share of the city's legislative offices, and White leaders were desperate to restore their hometown to prominence.

Interracial cooperation was probably the last thing Marsh assumed he had as Richmond's mayor. However, he took office when his agenda of "bridging barriers between [White and Black] peoples" was in the

Richmond establishment's interest as well.[23] Some of them wrote to him privately in a group letter that "we needed to help more individuals in the White business community, the so-called Establishment, to get to know and trust responsible individuals in the Black community."[24] The Establishment generally respected Henry Marsh for his intellect and his standing within Black Richmond. They did not, however, care for him as a person. Many Whites felt Marsh to be arrogantly radical in his political advocacy. Unlike the Black leaders he had usurped in 1966, Marsh demanded that city government work to the benefit of its Black people. The Establishment cared even less for his fellow Black council members Walter T. Kenney, Claudette Black-McDaniel, Willie Dell, and Henry Richardson. These four were low-level bureaucrats, academics, and civic leaders who, largely because of their race and working-class backgrounds, the Establishment deemed unqualified for public office.[25]

What Black and White Richmond leaders lacked in comradery, they made up for in pursuing a common goal, which became the foundation for their new urban regime. Both groups had, as a White minister later said in an oral history interview, "a genuine care for Richmond as a place." The Establishment were mostly born, raised, and would later die within the city limits. They took pride in Richmond's reputation. Although the Establishment did not particularly care for racial integration, they grew leery of watching White middle-class flight and defiance to busing tear the city apart at the seams. Even worse, they hated seeing White flight deplete Richmond's coffers and ruin its economic, social, and political life.

Richmond—home to nearly a quarter of a million Virginians—was, after the turbulent decades of the 1960s and 1970s, a municipal area that trapped the area's poor and Black residents in inferior housing, jobs, and education within its boundaries; an area in which many Whites worked but never took up residence; where Blacks saved enough money to exit if the opportunity arose. This was Richmond's present, but both Black and White leaders did not believe it should be; more importantly, this should not be its future. "We too hold the conviction that Richmond can demonstrate to the nation and the world answers to racial division," a group of wealthy White women told Henry Marsh just days after his historic inauguration. Marsh agreed with this sentiment, telling a fellow public servant, "We'd like Richmond to be an example to the rest of the world of how [different races of] people can live like brothers."[26] While generally distrustful of White leadership, Black Richmonders understood that Black governance required the financial and political support of White business leaders, as generations of slavery and Jim Crow had endowed them with an inordinate control of city resources. Thus, cooperative city planning was not as much a desire of Black Richmonders as it was a fundamental reality for successful Black governance. This realization, along with the vocal support of White leaders and some residents, set the foundation for downtown redevelopment being interracial and bipartisan in a city where few policies had ever been that before.

"It Is People, Not Concrete and Steel, That Makes a City Viable"

Henry Marsh believed that urban revitalization could help reform Richmond and rehab its race relations by bringing its economy in line with the rest of the region and even the nation.[27] He was not alone in believing that revitalization was the corrective agent Richmond needed to heal after the civil rights years. Local White lawyer Andrew J. Brent Jr. volunteered to help Marsh make Richmond into that model.

Brent was the most prominent member of the Establishment, descending from an upper-class family from the Far West End. He had attended both the St. Christopher's Preparatory School and the University of Virginia Law School, where he graduated with a law degree in 1941. Following his brief stint as a naval officer, Brent practiced law with his father, Andrew Senior, at Christian, Barton, Epps, & Brent. Brent chaired several civic organizations between 1946 and 1977, serving on the chamber of commerce, the Board of Visitors at Virginia Commonwealth University, and the Greater Metropolitan Authority. Brent became an enemy of Henry Marsh in the 1960s as he helped lead the urban renewal charge. In the 1970s Brent also brokered annexation talks between Mayor Phil Bagley and Chesterfield officials. Yet by 1975 Brent understood that the Establishment's days were numbered in city hall, so he started Downtown Development Unlimited (DDU). He designed this nonprofit organization to fight the tide of suburbanization by recruiting private investments and businesses back to downtown Richmond. Brent's lineage and accomplishments made him arguably the most influential man in Richmond. This distinction was only matched by Brent's desire to see his home flourish as a modern southern city.[28]

Only a few months after the 1977 election, Brent worked with Marsh to develop Project One: a series of new construction ventures that would result in a convention center, core hotels, and business buildings in the retail center of downtown Richmond's East Broad Street.[29] This proposed development was one of around 250 multiuse developments being built along the East Coast in the late 1970s. Combined, they all cost around $10 billion.[30] The DDU board—composed of some of the wealthiest White men in Richmond—had concocted Project One in 1975. Yet the plan was at a virtual standstill until Brent reached across the aisle to work with Henry Marsh. Before proceeding, however, DDU wanted to know if Marsh and his Black allies in the council would fully support downtown revitalization. These men had deep pockets and an even longer memory. Marsh had garnered much of his political clout by opposing urban renewal. But he surprised many DDU members by attending their meetings as an honored guest to assure them that he would act in support. Marsh's willingness to work with Brent signaled a true break from the past.[31]

With Black leaders supporting Project One, Brent raised hundreds of thousands of dollars from local tobacco, railroad, and investment firms. Hilton Hotel Corporation, Thalhimers, and Miller & Rhoads department stores each gave $25,000 to underwrite the entire project.[32] Richmond was unique in this regard as most cities relied heavily on federal grants to begin revitalization projects. By the time Project One was gaining steam, other US cities had already received significant portions of the billions doled out by the Carter administration.[33] This cash flow came from a concerned White House and liberal Democrat US Congress that understood that without federal funds, private investment into urban areas was nearly impossible to secure. Richmond's insular mentality, while hindering its progress in other ways, provided a leg-up in this regard; White elites did not wait for the federal government to fund its downtown rebuild. This perspective was unique for this age, as major southern cities had begun relying on federal funds like northern and midwestern cities had for decades. In rallying local funding for Project One, Richmond leaders were attempting to retain the city's conservative political culture and in the process resist Richmond's transition to becoming the typical all-Black city of the day.

While raising money, Brent helped the housing authority buy the downtown properties needed to begin Project One. Marsh's job was much harder, as he had to figure out how the cash-poor city would buy the selected properties. After careful consideration by the city council, Marsh decided to make Richmond taxpayers the primary shareholders in the prospective revitalization project. The council agreed in a unanimous secret vote to bond and sell the city's debt to out-of-town shareholders for cash. Brent used this cash to buy the vacant properties and retain the services of Houston-based designed firm Gerald D. Hines Interests. Cities much larger, wealthier, and more politically stable than Richmond also placed bids for Hines's services. Richmond had an advantage, however, because its leaders appealed to Gerald Hines himself, emphasizing that they were a self-funded southern city looking to rebuild as a functional means to healing racial wounds.[34]

In November 1977 Marsh and the eight other council members voted to bond the city's $32.2 million debt and sell it to shareholders for the cash needed to begin Project One.[35] The racially divided council—four White and five Black—cast unanimous votes, which was an extremely rare occurrence and has to be regarded as an accomplishment for its time. The November vote took place in front of over one hundred Richmond residents, many of whom vehemently opposed the use of public funds to rebuild downtown. This resistance crystallized into a makeshift group of Black and White middle-class property and business owners named the Richmond Independent Taxpayer Association (RITA).[36] Days before Christmas 1977, RITA petitioned the local and state courts to block the bond sale. A minor technicality sank the initial petition. They then asked Governor Charles S. Robb—a vehement supporter of urban revitalization—to propose antibonding legislation at the state level. He, unsurprisingly, rejected the request. RITA members then filed individual lawsuits against the city council. By the spring of 1978, however, various courts had dismissed all of their cases.[37]

City leaders publicly denounced RITA as a group of dissenters attempting to disrupt budding racial harmony.[38] The truth was that RITA members did not see biracial support for revitalization as the key to economic prosperity or racial reconciliation. Rather, they wanted to use public resources to develop quality neighborhoods and not downtown business buildings for corporations. In other words, they embodied Marsh's initial political agenda to "build people, and not things."

RITA members were mostly White (and some Black) housewives, small downtown business owners, and college professors who, an investigative report concluded, "have felt cut out of power for decades by the White Establishment."[39] This isolation from power should not be confused with an ignorance of how power operated. They had witnessed the Chesterfield and Henrico suburbs successfully resisting the Richmond city council's efforts to take them over in the 1960s and 1970s. The political and economic strength of suburban populism—or in this case taxpayer populism—led RITA founders to assume that the Virginia legislature and courts would not support the city completely in political and economic matters. Should taxpayers like themselves cause enough upset, so they thought, Richmond would surely lose its valuable time, partners, and resources in court.[40] These assumptions fueled taxpayer resistance. RITA used its opposition to Project One as a catalyzing issue to propose that city council should pass several radical tax cuts and referendum voting laws. Only then would they reconsider their resistance to urban revitalization. Although these attempts were voted down by the city council, RITA represented a serious obstacle as it challenged the contemporary axiom that urban revitalization was an inherent step toward good government and racial harmony.[41]

Richmonders who did not know much about RITA might have assumed them to be antiprogressive rabble rousers. But Henry Marsh and Andrew Brent knew better. On more than one occasion, RITA representatives met with them about ending Project One. The cordial discussions often ended with both sides refusing to concede to the other because of ideological differences. When formal negotiations failed, RITA sent both the mayor and DDU chairman packets of information that "attempt[ed] to point out that Richmond's conventional wisdom is 30 years out of date," as one letter began. Attached to that same letter was a news article about Lancaster, Pennsylvania. Similar to Richmond, Lancaster had suffered tremendous tax debt from White suburban flight. Unlike Richmond, however, Lancaster leaders worked with grassroots organizations to redevelop residential areas and attracted Black and White middle-class residents back to the city. If Marsh and Brent needed a more local example, RITA reminded that the Richmond Coliseum (finished in 1968) had yet to stimulate commercial and residential real estate investment and divert convention and concert traffic away from rival cities such as Roanoke, Norfolk, Hampton, Charlotte, Birmingham, Nashville, and Memphis.[42] RITA made it clear that "it is people not concrete and steel that makes a city viable." They concluded the letter by asking city leaders to "immediately act to bring a stop to the waste of millions of taxpayer dollars for a project that will ultimately cost more millions and put us years behind other cities." This request, like others, was flatly rejected by Marsh and Brent.[43]

RITA arose among a plethora of grassroots movements that sprang up against urban revitalization. Political and business leaders in northern and midwestern cities built massive downtown buildings in the face of tremendous grassroots resistance.[44] Southern city leaders also battled with taxpayers on using public funds to turn dilapidated, often all-Black neighborhoods into newer mixed-use areas with facilities that would go unused decades later.[45] City leaders, both Black and White, saw the development of malls, business buildings, hotels, and restaurants as the key to bringing stable, middle-class jobs back from the suburbs.[46] These jobs would, in turn, generate massive private investment into inner city housing as seen in places like Charlotte.[47] There, local banks moved to Independence Square in the decaying downtown area and invested millions of dollars to revitalize older neighborhoods in the famous Victorian Fourth Ward section.

However, RITA and other taxpayer groups like it understood that most cities that invested tax dollars into building glass-plated skyscrapers rarely generated a profit. Studies concluded that "despite encouraging signs of rejuvenation, the nation's oldest cities are continuing to decline in population and per capita wealth." Revitalization projects in America's sixty wealthiest cities (twenty-two of them in the South) created "isolated improvement" where downtown retail and business parks succeeded in attracting both highly specialized jobs and premium housing, while at the same time solidifying low-wage, unskilled employment. In other words, the rich got richer and the poor got poorer.[48] Even worse, these projects did not inspire suburbanites to become "urban pioneers" and resettle within city limits.[49] In response, taxpayer organizations wanted to redirect the revitalization zeal toward rebuilding decayed inner city neighborhoods.[50] They believed this investment would attract young, upwardly mobile couples back toward the city center.[51] The refusal by city leaders to invest in urban housing led grassroots dissenters to agree with *Businessweek* magazine's assessment in 1979 that "there is very little data current enough to say that an urban revival is taking place" in downtown areas.[52]

Although RITA could not persuade Richmond's Black and White leadership to end Project One, they received a bit of good news. Gerald D. Hines and the Hilton Hotel Corporation called Andrew Brent on Friday, November 10, 1978, nearly a year after the bond vote. The short conversation began and ended with Hines telling Brent that Hilton and his firm "would have to withdraw from participation in the project." The developer generously allowed Brent to control the public narrative by refusing to tell the media until after Brent spoke with them. DDU and Henry Marsh informed the public that they agreed to part ways with Hines and Hilton over a slight disagreement about which party would underwrite vacant office spaces. Secretly he and Marsh knew that, as Brent stated, "the withdrawal was prompted because of the delay of more than a year resulting from the litigation instituted by the Richmond Independent Taxpayer Association." With Project One missing a developer and hotel chain, and the city being stuck with unsold bonds, "it seems to me that the Project is now in real jeopardy," Brent disappointedly told Marsh.[53] There is no record of Marsh's response to Brent. However, the mayor later told reporters that Project One was "strong enough to stand on its own" and that it would not require a developer or hotel partnership to survive. Brent feared that these kinds of comments would scare off other investors, so he told the mayor that "if this is to be the method of operating, then we [DDU] do not want to be a partner or held responsible for the decisions in which we do not participate."[54]

The RITA issue revealed how divided the leaders of both races could become on this reconciliation project. Brent represented White leaders in feeling that although Blacks controlled city governance, the Establishment was to be made aware of every important decision in city affairs. Marsh disagreed, as he and many Black leaders saw revitalization as led by the Black mayor (supported by White leadership) and his coalition in city government. While Marsh and Brent's disagreement did not end the revitalization plan, it exposed existing divisions that later issues would exacerbate.

Project One's struggles coincided with a retrenchment in national support for urban revitalization projects. Days before Brent scolded Marsh, President Carter had announced the end of two urban programs. Combined, they had allocated upward of $3 billion to ailing cities every year. This reduction in aid was a part of a $60 billion cut in spending toward urban revitalization grants from HUD. The Carter administration made these cuts because of the failing national economy, which inflated the cost of living while keeping wages stagnant for the first time in over a generation. Suburbanites, many of whom did not vote for Carter, agreed with the spending cuts because they saw inner cities as, in the words of an urban studies professor, "the cancer of urban existence."[55]

Suburban America dominated the political landscape in the early 1980s. Bolstered by Richard Nixon's rise in 1968, overwhelmingly White homeowners saw the federal government as a protective agency over their racially defined class interests. Thus, their parent generation's support for New Deal federal spending, which allowed for the expansion of colleges and universities, homeownership, and industrial economy, was not out of sync with their disdain for federal spending to aid the often Black and brown urban working class. Suburban Whites believed that federal money should go to those whom they considered deserving groups of people. Their biggest gripe with Carter's urban aid programs was that these funds apparently did just the opposite. In other words, urban aid or revitalization, as suburbanites saw it, was a coded phrase that meant transferring the nation's wealth to Black and brown cities, helping to satisfy their bloated welfare budgets and not capital improvements.[56]

President Carter was not his predecessor Lyndon B. Johnson. When Johnson spoke of urban aid, he meant war on poverty programs. Carter, on the other hand, wanted federal money to be invested in real estate projects. Economic realities, however, forced him to disperse general block grants because recipient cities such as Newark, St. Louis, and Detroit spent almost double the amount of money they generated on payroll and public services such as water, sewage, and electricity.[57] Many of the recipient cities ran almost exclusively on the federal aid that Carter's administration gave them.[58] The *Washington Post* reported that "the flow of federal dollars that has fueled this measure of revitalization is slowing to a trickle, and officials here are wondering how they are going to pay for such capital improvements in the future."[59] While Richmond's revitalization program did not have federal investment, many of its city services did. Thus, declining federal support made Project One's success all the more important for the city's financial future. After Black mayors failed to reverse the White House decision, and state governments refused to fill the void, they used more local tax revenue to solicit private investments and complete revitalization projects.[60] The retrenchment in federal support, both political and social, was only the beginning of a larger governmental de-emphasis on urban life; a trend that would not be reversed until the early 2000s.[61] For cities like Richmond, this federal retrenchment coupled with grassroots resistance, putting urban revitalization on life support.

"A Dividing Line Separating Whites and Blacks"

In the summer of 1981 the Hilton Corporation announced that their new $70 million, 825-room grand hotel in New York was open for business. Located between office buildings and retail stores, this glass-plated structure was equipped with restaurants, spas, luxury penthouses, conference rooms, and pleasant staff who would accommodate everyone's needs. Some months before, the rival Marriott Company had announced the grand opening of a few two-thousand-room luxury hotels in New York located near bars and several upscale restaurants.[62] The ribbon-cutting ceremonies for these premium hotels reeked of optimism for downtown revitalization, and with good reason.[63] As cities across the nation constructed midsized arenas to benefit from the growing conference, tourism, and convention market, they relied on corporate hotel chains to provide affordable and luxury accommodations near high-end retail stores and restaurants.[64] In contrast, many older, more established inner-city hotels had suffered financially from suburban flight.[65] The southern chains of Hilton (Texas) and Marriott (DC), however, worked with city governments across the nation to become anchors in various revitalization projects. It did not hurt that partnering with various cities came with tax breaks and federal funds.[66] Hanging in the balance of this corporate hotel land grab was Richmond, a city that was, by 1981, too politically hamstrung to build anything.

January 1980 marked five years since Project One's inception. Years of court cases and grassroots resistance had cast serious doubts over Richmond ever seeing Project One, or any other form of urban revitalization, materialize. RITA suffered a final defeat that winter, however, when the Virginia Supreme Court allowed the city council to sell its bonds to prospective bondholders. The court went a step further by spelling out the quiet part and acknowledging that RITA had used the courts as a political weapon. Thus, they refused to accept any new cases brought by RITA or its members.[67] Marsh aided the city council in selling the long-held bonds less than a year later. This gave the city and DDU the needed funds to begin building Project One; and build they did. Richmonders must have been annoyed by the barrage of traffic cones, jackhammers, pile drivers, cranes, and moving trucks that cluttered East Broad Street in the spring and summer of 1981.[68] Those sounds, however, masked a tension that boiled over in city hall between Marsh, DDU, and the four White members of the city council.[69]

Like revitalization projects across the country, Project One relied heavily on the construction of an anchor hotel. RITA's years-long court battles had compelled the Hilton Corporation to withdraw from the project. The bond sale and subsequent construction allowed Marsh and Brent to begin courting new vendors. Although the documentary record is not definitive on the matter, there is little doubt that the Hilton Corporation had maintained its interest in Richmond. Its executives did not, however, reply to Marsh's and DDU's requests to renew negotiations. Marsh and Brent then spoke with competitor Marriott Incorporated.[70] Unlike the Texas-born Conrad Hilton, John Willard Marriott had Virginia roots. He had begun his entrepreneurial ventures in the 1920s with a string of root beer stands in Richmond, Washington, DC, and Baltimore. Forty years later his company—Marriott Incorporated—became publicly traded on the stock market. The first Marriott Hotel opened in 1967 in Arlington, Virginia. By the 1980s Marriott was the fastest-growing hotel chain in the world.[71]

After the initial round of negotiations, Marriott representatives made it clear that they were extremely interested in adding Richmond to its hotel empire. They were not, however, "interested in Project One." Instead, they wanted to build a hotel about four blocks south, just above the largely underdeveloped James River basin. However, it was clear that Marriott could be persuaded to build on the Project One site if DDU and Marsh offered them a favorable deal. Brent wanted to entertain other suitors and offers to gain leverage on Marriott, while Marsh, on the other hand, did not.[72] The mayor correctly assessed that his legacy, and the reputation of Richmond's flagship generation of Black officeholders in general, depended on the completion and success of Project One.[73] Five years of stalemate and the city's existing economic issues must have pushed Marsh and his supporting Black council members to forge ahead and secure Marriott against the wishes of Brent.

Marsh bypassed Brent's advice and brokered a forty-nine-year lease agreement with Marriott to build and operate a hotel as a part of Project One, although not along the James River as they previously desired. What sweetened the pot was that the four-hundred-room hotel would, at the expense of a $24 million loan from the city, come with an additional 89,000-person capacity convention center and an 80,000-square-foot exhibition hall. Marriott was to pay the city the minimum of $500,000 per year to lease the facilities; the city would receive 40 percent of the interest accrued on the convention center and exhibition hall, assuming that Marriott turned a profit and paid off its $44 million loan—$24 million from the city and the rest from Richmond-area banks.[74] Marsh also promised that taxpayers would allocate up to $9 million to cover Marriott's debt should they struggle to turn a profit. Marriott took the deal because, as Executive Vice President Gary Wilson later noted, "Mayor Marsh very creatively put together a financing package we just couldn't pass up." Yet that lucrative deal in favor of Marriott disappointed Brent and other White executives, given that Marsh had once again excluded them from a key Project One decision. Brent had little to say when the deal became public, only that "I think Henry Marsh is an ambitious rascal."[75] The official record of Brent's and Marsh's correspondence runs cold after Project One's intricate details manifested into actions. "It appears that the business community, on whose active financing and advocacy the Project was predicated, has left it to the council majority to make a go of it," a political insider documented.[76] Brent's silence guaranteed that Project One would be the legacy of Marsh and Black leadership, for better or for worse.

The reality of Black Richmond leading the city's structural rebuilding sparked tremendous resistance from the four White city council members, who had mostly stayed in the background when Brent and DDU were seemingly at the helm. Their dissent arose not because of the hotel chain involved but because of the hotel's proposed location. Marsh and the Black councilmembers wanted the Marriott hotel north of Broad Street—"a euphemism for that side of the central city that is predominantly Black," as the *New York Times* accurately assessed.[77] White councilmembers wanted the hotel located south of Broad Street, where Marriott originally wanted to build. This seemingly minute disagreement became a major one since the White councilmen knew that "no respectable White person would dare sleep north of Broad Street," a political scientist once heard a local say aloud.[78] The divide along Broad Street was so stark that a local executive once said that, upon relocating to Richmond, he learned "when North was north and South was south, Broad Street divided the Black and White sections of Richmond. And there are still some blue-haired ladies in tennis shoes who won't walk on the northside of Broad."[79] North of Broad Street lay well-known Black enclaves such as Jackson Ward, Navy Hill, Battery Park, Barton Heights, and others. South of Broad were the pillars of White Richmond power—St. Paul's Episcopal Church, Capitol Square, the Jefferson Hotel, Thalhimers, Miller & Rhoads, the First Bank of Virginia, as well as Establishment-owned brokerage and law firms.[80] The majority of Whites and Blacks rarely frequented the opposing sides of town, especially in the early 1980s.

Although Project One's design was meant to bridge the racial gap in Richmond, things had not significantly improved since Marsh's inauguration on May 8, 1977. After being sworn in, Marsh defied local tradition by hiring full-time assistants and fully occupying an office in city hall. His fellow Black council members followed suit soon after.[81] These moves were controversial because Richmond city council members followed the recently established precedent (as of 1948) of elected officials remaining part-time public servants. Occupying offices insinuated that city affairs needed the full attention of government, which was antithetical to Richmond's political conservatism. Office spaces and full-time staff were also not "done" because in previous years, all of the real decisions had been made at the Commonwealth Club—the once all-White West End haven of the Establishment.[82] However, the newly sworn-in Black council members broke with tradition by trying to remake city government into a responsive, progressive agency that placed Black Richmond's needs at the center of city planning.

The racial divide on the council widened when Marsh and his four Black colleagues flexed their political muscle for the first time and fired White city manager William Leidinger. The Establishment fixture and holdover from the previous administration irritated Black leadership by overseeing every aspect of city government that they now controlled.[83] This led to constant clashes between Leidinger and Marsh, and eventually to Leidinger's dismissal on August 14, 1978. "For fifteen months he

[Leidinger] tried to sabotage us," Marsh said in a later interview. When the four White councilmembers learned of the impending dismissal, they set up a meeting with the Black councilmembers in which White business leaders threatened to remove their economic interests from the city if Marsh did not recant the decision.[84] The mayor could not be moved. Three weeks later Marsh addressed the five-to-four city council vote to fire Leidinger. To protect himself and the city from a lawsuit, Marsh drafted an eighteen-page document outlining the various reasons for Leidinger's dismissal. He even added insult to injury by requiring Leidinger to vacate his offices sooner than normal because of the need to make room for Emmanuel Deese, Richmond's first full-time Black city manager and Leidinger's former second in command.[85]

A year after Leidinger's dismissal, the White and Black council members were divided once again, but this time over redrawing voting districts. Richmond had nine voting districts: four White, four Black, and one swing district that was roughly half Black and half White. After Curtis Holt's lawsuits in the mid-to-late 1970s, the DOJ advised city leaders to redraw the voting districts after every major population shift. This would keep the city in line with the Voting Rights Act of 1965 and avoid another lawsuit. Marsh privately instructed the city attorney to compile a census record to help his offices redraw the voting districts. The ad hoc census revealed that the city should, based on continuing White flight, have five Black voting districts. White councilmembers heard of Marsh's maneuvers and used city council meetings as a forum to accuse him of corruption. They went so far as to conduct secret investigations of Marsh with the hopes of ousting him from office. Their efforts failed as the federal courts cleared Marsh of any wrongdoing. His newly drawn districts were voted into existence by a predictable five-to-four vote in June 1981.[86]

The once bipartisan Project One largely sat in the background of this council turmoil. Unfortunately, the hotel controversy pushed it to the forefront as the location became what it was not designed to be: the latest move in a zero-sum chess game over which race would dictate Richmond's future. Marsh made it clear that as long as he was mayor, the Marriott would be constructed north of East Broad Street. His stance confirmed for members of the White establishment that "the Black majority on the city council is incompetent, and that the mayor is arrogant," an internal survey found.[87] White council members froze the passage of a new city budget, halted Project One construction, and threatened to remove their businesses from downtown.[88] This aggressive stance confirmed for some Black council members that "the White majority wanted Project One to fail as long as Henry L. Marsh 3d was Mayor. . . . They [Whites] wanted to be the ones to say they made Project One work."⁸⁹ Others were even more pessimistic, believing, as another Black council member put it, that "there are some people who'd rather see this city run into the ground than [run correctly] under Black leadership."⁹⁰ In the midst of this disagreement, the Richmond Hilton Associates—a franchise licensed under the Hilton Corporation, who had previously backed out of Project One, purchased from the Capital Square Associates a plot of land just blocks away from the Marriott site. Because both groups were filled with Establishment fixtures, there was widespread speculation that the White council members facilitated this purchase to ruin Project One. Decades of hearsay stand in contrast to scanty documentary evidence to support this reading. Hilton's reasons for buying near Marriott might also have been simply the result of healthy competition between two southern-based hotel chains.

Marsh found out about the land deal just days before its official announcement in August 1981. The Virginia National Bank—a key financial institution of the Establishment—financed the 350-room downtown hotel complex.⁹¹ Marsh reached out to the Hilton developer and reminded him that the city council had not approved the placement of new sewer lines to that area. Without sewage pipes, there would be no hotel. Hilton representatives saw Marsh's letter as a tyrannical threat, so they had it reprinted in the local papers.⁹² The Hilton representative later invited the mayor to the hotel's public announcement. Marsh did not formally respond to the invitation "for reasons which I am sure you will understand," he told the press. The mayor later contracted a consulting firm to investigate whether Project One's hotel could survive with a competitor nearby. They told Marsh that there was no feasible way to assure that the city would recoup its investment if White visitors had the option to stay in an equally priced hotel in a perceived nicer section of the city.⁹³

With Project One falling apart, Marsh and his four Black colleagues on the council proposed Resolution 81-R132-125.⁹⁴ This would prohibit any hotels from operating near Project One. This stalled Hilton's plans to build a hotel along Sixth and Canal Streets, a few blocks south of the Project One site.⁹⁵ On November 9, 1981, Hilton representatives visited city hall and pleaded with the council to reconsider bringing it to a vote. The local law would force Hilton, and any other hotel chain, to pay the city for operating near the Project One site. With a five-to-four vote, the resolution passed. The Black council members continually bypassed the Establishment and crafted more legislation to prevent Hilton from operating near Project One. When criticized by residents for using legislation to dominate Richmond's revitalization efforts, Marsh responded by saying, "If you're giving a $35 million loan to a company and you're putting that much money on the line, wouldn't you take all the steps necessary to protect it?"[96]

These laws were not enough to stop Hilton, so the Black city council members filed a suit on behalf of the city council to block Hilton from operating near the Project One site.[97] Hilton filed a countersuit in December 1981, seeking over $250 million in damages over claims that Marsh and his Black council members had conspired against their business interests in an unconstitutional manner.[98] Capital Square Associates—the group that purchased the Sixth and Canal Street location for resale to Hilton—sued the city as well, claiming that its prohibition on hotels near Project One was an unconstitutional blow to their economic interests.[99] In January 1982 the US District Court for the Eastern District of Virginia initially sided with Marsh in ruling that his laws were not unconstitutional.[100] This was the only victory Marsh and his Black councilmembers would get during this ordeal.

As the cases dragged through the appellate courts, Marsh experienced legal backlash from White councilmembers. They rallied together and petitioned the federal courts to block Marsh from selecting the law firm to represent the city. They further compromised the city's case by openly stating that they believed that Marsh, alone, "ultimately be held liable for intentional acts of misconduct."[101] The White councilmembers also sought court injunctions to prevent Marsh from voting on Hilton-related matters before the city council due to his political interests in the case.[102] As the legal battle turned into a political quagmire, and the city paid out around $900,000 in legal fees to fight Hilton, the White councilmembers forged a settlement with Hilton. Taxpayers ended up footing around $5 million in restitution ($2.5 million in investment loans and legal fees to Hilton and $1.25 million to purchase the Sixth and Canal lot back from Capital Square Associates) to end the litigation between the city council and Hilton hotel chain.[103] When legal fees are included, the city paid out over $11 million to keep Hilton away from Project One.[104]

The Marriott was completed along Sixth and Broad in 1984. A year later, Ramada Renaissance Hotel purchased the former Hilton lot from Capital Square Associates and built a three-hundred-room hotel in 1986. Fearing litigation, the city not only allowed the purchase, it sat back and watched Omni announce their intentions to build a downtown hotel as well.[105] With three hotels within blocks of each other in downtown Richmond, Hilton opted for greener pastures in the crabgrass frontier, locating their three-hundred-room hotel "across the street from the city limits" in

Chesterfield. This represented a real death of what racial reconciliation was supposed to be with the original deal between DDU and Richmond. Hilton solicited mostly out-of-town financing to create "a country club atmosphere" in the White suburbs instead of a downtown hotel located in the mostly Black city.[106] The Hilton currently resting along East Broad Street in downtown Richmond—ironically in the former Project One site—resulted from another firm buying the old Miller & Rhoads department store (closed in 1990) in 2005. The hotel opened "with little fanfare" on February 9, 2009.[107]

The breakdown of racial harmony during Project One had political consequences that its prime mover could not avoid. The main consequence was that it gave Marsh's political enemies more ammunition to use against him come election season. The local press did not miss opportunities to print polls showing Marsh's unpopularity among White Richmonders at large. These subtle press attacks only made the stream of death threats he regularly received more real. His White colleagues did not help his cause, as their constant opposition to him appeared to have emboldened the White opposition he faced. Luckily for Marsh, the newer ward-style voting system protected him from those Whites at the ballot box, ensuring that he remained in city hall until 1991, when he won a seat in the Virginia General Assembly. However, Marsh would not remain mayor. His White colleagues supported Dr. Roy Alexander West—a Black school principal whom Marsh had demoted for criticizing him in the past—for a seat on the council in 1982. With that seat, the Establishment recaptured the majority and, adding insult to injury, replaced Marsh with the man he had demoted.[108]

Project One represented one of the largest political and economic blunders in Richmond's history. In the end, the centerpiece hotel, and the legal issues caused by maintaining it, cost the taxpayer nearly $50 million.[109] With three hotels later built in the area, the Marriott struggled to generate the property-tax boom that city leaders expected of Project One upon its inception.[110]

Richmond's urban regime project was what the *New York Times* claimed it was in 1982: "A new attempt at cooperation between Blacks and Whites in a city with a history of racial acrimony and nearly consistent interracial bickering on its city council."[111] Project One was a historic endeavor for Richmond because it reflected how leaders of a traditionally hidebound city embraced a contemporary political movement (urban revitalization) to heal deep racial wounds. Its failure was the logical result of naivete, as leaders believed that interracial cooperation would create interracial harmony. Furthermore, it symbolized the difficulty of achieving racial progress with interracial planning. Richmond could not avoid the natural evolution of history: age-old divisions between Black and White leaders birthing competing interests among them, even when they supported the same plan. From Project One, city leaders learned that although they shared similar goals, they would have to assure that both sides had an equal stake in the desired results. If not, city leaders would taint future planning with the racial division that was prevalent throughout the city, further etching racial division deeper into the landscape. Project One proved that racial reconciliation in Richmond was difficult but not hopeless, and that the city's soul was worth fighting for. With this in mind, city leaders continued that fight in the late 1980s.[112]

6

Richmond Renaissance and Sixth Street Marketplace

"A BRIDGE OF UNITY"

> The worst thing that can happen is to add disintegration of the center of the city.
> —James Rouse, 1984

"TEN YEARS ago today," said the *Richmond Times-Dispatch* in September 1995, "hundreds of balloons were released and fireworks exploded as more than 50,000 people gathered for the opening of the 6th Street Marketplace." When it had opened a decade prior, it was the centerpiece in Richmond's downtown revitalization plans for the new millennium. Its visionaries expected retail giants and corporate leaders to bring new life to the desolate downtown area. More importantly, they expected the new 65,000-square-foot glass-plated super structure to generate racial harmony in a region that had little of it since the *Brown* decision in 1954. This hope for an economically thriving, racially harmonious Richmond is why fifty thousand people came to the intersection of Sixth and Broad Streets to celebrate the opening. A local said that "everyone thought it was going to be like opening day every day"; however, ten years later the *Times-Dispatch* reported that "the party [had] been long over." By fall 1995 the city was still politically and economically reeling from a $25 million mall they spent $60 million in bonds and subsidies to keep solvent. Due to a severe lack of revenue, the city council tried to sell the mall that had infrastructurally and symbolically sunken beyond repair.[1]

A few months later, fireworks did go off again at the Sixth Street Marketplace, but not in the way anyone wanted to see. Police officers radioed "mayday" to backup units as they converged on a series of massive brawls erupting between dozens of amateur basketball teams in the Marketplace food court.

The fights stemmed from a local streetball tournament in which over 850 teams played three-on-three basketball on handmade courts barricaded along Sixth and Broad Streets. While it was unclear who or what started the melees, police confirmed that most were schoolyard in nature, resulting from trash talk and joning (verbal sparring through the use of jokes). As crossovers and dunks turned to insults and insults turned to jabs, Richmond police feared that gun violence was not too far behind. A young Black male brandishing a loaded semiautomatic handgun confirmed their suspicions. At that point, police shut down the Marketplace food court and eventually the downtown tournament in its entirety.[2]

Highly publicized catastrophes like this reflected Richmond's failure with the Sixth Street Marketplace. The downtown mall went unpatroned by White suburbanites because of the perception that Richmond was unredeemable and filled with Black inner-city violence. The fall 1995 shooting at the Marketplace during an overwhelmingly Black basketball tournament reaffirmed that widely held belief. However, events like this played cover for the reality that White suburbanites rejected the Marketplace and the motivations behind it long before amateur basketball tournaments occupied space where shoppers should have been. Moreover, the Marketplace's economic failure was part and parcel of 1980s America, where the divide between the White suburbs and Black inner cities reached its apex. White suburbanites condemned their majority Black cities to poverty and completely remade their lives in the crabgrass frontier. Richmond's urban regime quickly learned that no downtown infrastructure project was going to change that.

While it no longer exists in Richmond's downtown, the Sixth Street Marketplace remains a sore subject for those who remember it. Locals have called it a "pie-in-the-sky" plan and a "spectacular failure" because it never yielded the economic and social results its visionaries promised. Because of this, the Sixth Street Marketplace is a cautionary tale to city officials and residents as a history that Richmond should never relive.[3] Residents are as shortsighted as the politicians they criticized for bringing the Marketplace into fruition.

Although the Marketplace was a colossal economic failure, the effort needed to create it helped further racial reconciliation in Richmond after the modern civil rights movement. In the aftermath of Project One, Black and White elites used racial capitalism to build the Sixth Street Marketplace and continue their revitalization agenda in the 1980s.[4] Racial capitalism—the commodification of race for profit—was a political strategy that grew out of Richmond's Black and White leaders effectuating an ideology I deem "elite reconciliation."[5] This involved White elites paying recompense for past Black exclusion in city planning by incorporating Black leaders at every stage of revitalization. Elite reconciliation provided city leaders with a united image of interracial harmony that they felt residents should follow. Thus, they worked together to rebuild Richmond's economy with a downtown mall equipped with a literal bridge connecting the Black and White sides of town. In constructing the Marketplace, Richmond leaders created a sense of racial goodwill that had never existed at the highest levels of government and economy. This project was more than a play at economic gain: it was an act of social engineering where elites sought to use industry to heal race relations by recruiting middle-class Whites back to the Black inner city.

The Marketplace failed because of a major flaw in Richmond's elite reconciliation effort. White and Black leaders came together with a paternalistic understanding that they—the elites of both races and not the people—should take the lead in rebuilding a city broken along the color line. This shared belief blinded them to the fact that by the mid-to-late 1980s, metro area residents did not "rejoice in being a multiracial, multiethnic city," in the sobering and truthful words of the *Washington Post*.[6] While city leaders faced the Black inner city and saw it as the solution to fixing Richmond, middle-class metro area residents faced the White suburbs and saw them as their only salvation from a dying city. Leadership's failures did, however, turn "the road from the past to the future," in the words of the *Times-Dispatch*.[7] Elite reconciliation generated the interracial goodwill that inspired more successful grassroots efforts between the late 1980s and early 2000s. Therefore, the chapters included in part 2 show that even failed, misguided elitist projects have redeemable value, as even they can lay important cornerstones for social progress.

"Securing Richmond's Future"

In January 1981 it was clear to some that charity, kindness, and sense of community had not completely passed with the recently ended Christmas season. In fact, both White and Black Richmond leaders converged on St. Paul's Episcopal Church to organize and publicize the work being done to shelter, feed, and clothe the city's homeless. While every race, gender, and age were represented among Richmond's poorest of the poor, the overwhelming majority of the city's forgotten were Black men.[8] Richmond's White churches were charitable enough to occasionally cross the line between bigotry and reconciliation, but very few, if any, would take in groups of homeless Black men. Thus, the decision to feature the community service project at St. Paul's was no coincidence. City leaders understood that the church had a transformative influence within the city. Thus, they felt that should racial harmony exist among themselves, as well as throughout the city, St. Paul's was a perfect place to, once again, start that process.

St. Paul's is located in the heart of downtown Richmond, just south of the Project One site on East Broad Street and west of the Virginia State Capitol. The beautiful Greek Revival building is equipped with grand stone pillars, a marble-covered foundation, and stained-glass windows. Housed within this iconic building is a history of people who helped transform the city at large. Prior to the Civil War, St. Paul's—located along East Broad Street at the time—attracted the city's elite, their slaves, and some free Black members. The enslaved members helped build the current chapel along East Grace Street in 1843. After the Civil War St. Paul's bucked the local church trend of relocating toward the suburbs. The decision to remain at the center of Richmond was both symbolic and a foreshadowing of the church's functional importance to the city's rebuild. St. Paul's elite members were among the industrialists, bankers, and white-collar professionals who fixed Richmond's post–Civil War economy. As the nineteenth century came to a close, these same members supported the Lost Cause mythology that justified the statues that once adorned Monument Avenue and the Jim Crow laws they represented. Other White members worked within charitable organizations to promote Black uplift, and when confronted with the inherent hypocrisy between racial segregation and human decency in the mid-twentieth century, they decried discriminatory laws and practices in housing, education, and healthcare.[9]

The issue of homelessness allowed Black political and White business elites to present a public face to the private meetings they were having about their role in generating racial goodwill within the city. On the surface they were feeding and sheltering the city's destitute. Below that, however, they examined why the politics of Project One perpetuated the disdain and distrust among themselves. These secret meetings broke the unspoken racial norm that Whites and Blacks did not associate with each other outside of workplaces, schools, and, now, city hall. Segregation in homes, neighborhoods, churches, and social clubs was more interwoven into the fabric of Richmond than any Jim Crow law ever was. Yet a few wealthy White Richmonders (mainly women) defied that norm and befriended Blacks of a similar cultural ilk through the use of various charity and civic organizations.[10] A common meeting place for White and Black elite women was St. Paul's Church.

There, in the twilight of Project One negotiations, a White socialite told her Black friends that they needed to stop "the movers and shakers, the people with power," from "isolat[ing] themselves with their own kind."[11] These women wished that their husbands and relatives conducted business like they did. As in any other city, Richmond saw the majority of policy and business deals done around tee time, over dinner, at lunch, at backyard barbeques, and at sporting events. The socialites felt that class interests should usurp Richmond's color line among the elite, given that obedience to it left "few opportunities for forming friendships between Blacks and Whites."[12]

In the winter of 1982 the wives of wealthy White men and well-to-do Black men used St. Paul's Church as a neutral meeting ground to plan future "gatherings of members of the Black and White power structure for a series of dinners and lectures." They expected these events to stimulate more interpersonal relationships between their husbands, who were among the leadership of both races. Because of the general Black dislike for the local media and laws allowing press access to congregations of more than five public officials, a Black doctor's wife suggested that the social engineering project "be launched quietly, [and] without publicity." They crafted lists of Richmond's most powerful people. Only the most notable lawyers, academics, doctors, businessmen, ministers, politicians, and high-level city employees from both races received official invitations to join. Those seeking admission would later send formal applications with their name, address, education, occupation, marital status, and salary to prove that they were important enough to attend the secret gatherings.[13]

The first crop of Black and White attendees did not have the easiest time sharing their opinions with each other. When asked about who or what kept the races apart in Richmond, an unnamed White CEO (more than likely T. Justin Moore Jr. of the Virginia Electric and Power Company—VEPCO) said that "[Mayor Henry] Marsh has not kept avenues open between the races." This sentiment was very common among White Richmonders more broadly. Marsh's refusal to do the bidding of the Establishment made him appear "arrogant," as he was often called. A Black doctor rejected the notion that Marsh was the cause of racial discord in the city. To him and many others, "Blacks [as a whole just] don't trust Whites" because of the way they (mainly the middle class) abandoned Richmond as civil rights legislation came down in the 1960s. Those who forgave Whites for their intolerable rejection of busing probably could not forget the more recent efforts by White leadership to foil Project One over the hotel location.[14] The earliest discussions between Black and White elites devolved into fruitless buck-passing. These early tensions showed the socialites that Richmond's longstanding color barrier had, indeed, sprouted into an ideological separation between groups who shared similar class values.

Early discord did not keep White members of the Establishment from attending future meetings. In fact, they were happy to sit in a room and dialogue with Black leaders outside the presence of the troublesome and divisive Richmond press. Black attendance varied, however. "Some [Black] people don't want it to succeed," a Black socialite said sadly about the initial meetings. The deep-seated Black distrust for Whites succumbed to the few Blacks—mostly highly skilled professionals who had recently moved to Richmond—who optimistically believed that "if it is handled right," more Blacks would attend the secret meetings. This meant that Whites had to make Black attendees feel welcomed beyond the initial invite.

It was well known that wealthy White Richmonders knowingly and unknowingly mistreated Black guests in spaces that they were not expected to be in. What awaited Black visitors to elite all-White spaces such as downtown executive suites, boardrooms, preparatory schools, country clubs, martini lunches, steak dinners, and bourbon nightcaps were cold stares, small talk, and all-too-frequent discussions about Confederate victories in the Civil War.[15] Within the walls of St. Paul's Episcopal Church, White elites promised to form a new club—ultimately named the Richmond Urban Forum—where a common love and care for Richmond's vitality, and not a dedication to racial segregation, would bond the city's elite. Realizing how special and unique an opportunity this organization offered—and later would become—the attendees made sure all invited and applied guests knew the core tenant: "Don't come if you don't believe in it or want to tear it down."[16] Some Blacks and Whites heeded this message and refused to attend, even after receiving several invitations.

Whatever skepticism remained melted away after the group moved beyond St. Paul's into Richmond's Downtown Club. Founded in 1967 along the Main Street business district, the Downtown Club was an exclusive, male-dominated middle ground between Black and White Richmond (unlike the Commonwealth Club) where the elites of both races could listen to stimulating lectures from leading academics while enjoying high-priced liquors, seafood hors d'oeuvres, and premium steak dinners. The choice to meet downtown was, as the next revitalization project would be, symbolic. Because the Far West End was de facto White and affluent, the Forum women may have felt that Black attendees would not feel comfortable meeting out there. Also, downtown was a more female space in general, where White women often shopped at department stores along West Broad Street. With race and gender factored in, the Downtown Club made sense as the host for Forum meetings.

At the Downtown Club, Black and White leaders formed in the dark what the rest of the city would later see come to light: a collective identity. This identity did not end the core political division between White and Black leadership. Whites were still in favor of a limited city government while Blacks typically favored strengthening the council. Rather, this new identity was built on a paternalistic notion that the elite of both races should work together as equals to dictate Richmond's future. This consensus set the gap that years of racism had created among the city's elite on the path to extinction. A White Establishment man once wrote to the planning committee that "only a Richmonder could fully appreciate the unique quality of the evening in a city where people tend to revolve in their own social circles."[17] At one of these meetings, where over a hundred people attended, then-mayor Henry Marsh pitched his idea for a second revitalization project. This one, however, would be the physical manifestation of the vision set forth by the wives of elite White and Black men, a credit that no historian has given to these visionary women.[18]

The Richmond Urban Forum put Marsh in contact with enough people of both races to create two advisory committees, staffed by sixty prominent residents and split evenly between Blacks and Whites. The committee's job was to create a new revitalization strategy that would be structured to avoid the political pitfalls of Project One. Around January 1982 the committee recommended Marsh help create another nonprofit development group. The board, they further recommended, should mimic the advisory committees' interracial makeup to ensure Blacks and Whites had equal say, even if they did not have an equal share, in "securing Richmond's future." Marsh agreed with the committee and helped them form Richmond Renaissance, Inc., still in existence today. A local museum director who later worked closely with Richmond Renaissance remembered the earliest group: "While having a different public persona, [they] committed to each other that they would meet every week; even if there was nothing to talk about."[19] Richmond's most powerful White (economic) and Black (political) men equally made up the executive board. Never before had the city's most powerful willingly come together equally across racial lines in any official and public capacity. The first organization of its kind in the city, Richmond Renaissance symbolized "a new beginning for Richmond," as stated in its promotional brochure.[20]

Almost as quickly as Richmond Renaissance incorporated its name and received a 501(c)(3) tax exemption, they publicly pledged to raise over $2 million for a new downtown mall called the Sixth Street Marketplace, a major glass-plated structure that would rest next to the ongoing Project One business development.[21] While a downtown mall was new for Richmond, other cities had applied this urban planning strategy for much of the twentieth century.

Fewer than a thousand malls decorated America's urban landscape before World War II. After the last troops came home, that number grew to more than twenty thousand urban malls that became popular epicenters of city life. City leaders relied heavily on urban malls to help attract and keep affluent residents from fleeing to the suburbs. It was the growing middle-class dollar, however, that suburbanized city planning.[22] By the 1980s urban shopping malls—primarily the newly constructed ones—represented Black politicians and White businessmen coaxing suburban tourists to bring their disposable income back to the urban areas they left.[23] Most of these ventures resulted in economic failure from delayed construction and Whites refusing to shop in the inner city.[24] The promise of downtown mall construction, however, was that it brought politicians and capitalists together; the peril was that it often illuminated the racial animus that urban-suburban divides kept silent.

In this regard, Richmond was more akin to its fellow Virginia city, Norfolk. Like Richmond (population 219, 214), Norfolk (population 266, 979) lost its luster after decades of White flight to Virginia Beach and Chesapeake.[25] As an out-of-town developer once said in an interview: Norfolk was in the 1980s "a very discouraged city with a ratty waterfront and not much of a downtown."[26] During the day the adjacent waterfront and downtown operated as bedrooms and panhandling dens for the homeless. At night, however, the empty warehouses and office buildings became vice dens and red-light districts where anyone looking for drugs and prostitution would undoubtedly find both.[27]

Plans to renovate Norfolk's urban core evolved in the late 1970s with the construction of newer housing developments.[28] They picked up steam in the early 1980s when local Chevrolet dealership owner Joshua P. Darden—a man whose family name graces several college campuses throughout the Commonwealth—convinced over twenty local businesses to invest $500,000 in the Waterside Redevelopment Project.[29] Intended to be completed in 1983, White Norfolk capitalists designed Waterside to accommodate twenty eateries, bars, and small shops, attract $5–6 million in real estate investments, create 800 to 1,000 permanent jobs, and $500,000 in annual revenue for the city.[30]

Trouble haunted Waterside from the very beginning. For one, Black residents, from powerful city leaders to the powerless underclass, did not support the project. Many used church services, city council meetings, and newspaper editorials to articulate their belief that Waterside sounded like urban renewal. Like Richmond, Norfolk had drastically underfunded government agencies that struggled with high Black unemployment, fleeing industrial and healthcare systems, dying shopping centers (mainly Granby Mall), and deplorable housing decay.[31] The most talked-about issue, however, was the severely underfunded schools. "We felt that the city was more concerned about economic development than the rights of Black children," said Norfolk vice mayor Reverend Joseph Green. The largely unrepresentative Norfolk city council, however, worked with Darden and other capitalists to dump around $13 million ($9.8 million in federal funds) into Waterside. The city council even agreed to pay the developer's firm $225,000 a year to run Waterside, while also splitting the revenue (rents, sales, and property taxes) fifty-fifty. This lopsided deal in favor of the developers compelled Black city councilmember Claude Staylor to opine, "If we treated every developer this way we'd be in serious trouble."[32]

Adding insult to injury, the city council overlooked Black-owned construction firms in favor of the White-owned Lynnhaven Marine Construction Co. from Virginia Beach. Lynnhaven failed to deliver on the $1.1 million contract because their Black workers boycotted alleged workplace discrimination with the local help of Reverend L. P. Watson of the NAACP.[33] The Norfolk Housing Authority assumed full control of the project in March 1982, but thirteen months passed before Waterside came into fruition.[34] While it is now just a yacht parking lot and set of overpriced bars, Waterside was a Black Virginia city's most concerted effort to prevent flight to neighboring Virginia Beach, a hyper suburbanized city that by 1981 had become the largest in the Commonwealth—a status that they have yet to relinquish.[35]

When Waterside construction neared completion, a White Richmond CEO told the *Times-Dispatch*, "I think Richmond," and not Norfolk, "should start acting like the capital city."[36] While Richmond could not compete with the overwhelmingly White and affluent Virginia Beach, they sought to mimic the spirit of Norfolk. Business and political interests designed the Sixth Street Marketplace, like Waterfront, to attract suburban residents back to a majority Black city and, as then-mayor Marsh said, capitalize on the "economic progress of Project One."[37] Unlike Waterside, however, Black and White Richmond leadership wanted the infrastructure to represent the new spirit of racial harmony that now existed between them. The Marketplace's centerpiece would be a "glass-covered pedestrian bridge across Broad Street," called the Bridge of Unity. Upon completion the bridge would "link a Black populated area of the city to the [White] downtown business, commercial, and shopping center," said the *Richmond Afro-American* newspaper.[38] Richmond leaders hoped that the bridge would be more than a symbolic architectural handshake; it was to reflect a new mentality that, as a local Black Richmond Renaissance board member once told a potential investor, "affect[s] how Blacks and Whites live and interact with one another."[39]

"Everyone Is Ready to Embrace a New Richmond"

On a chilly day in March 1982, a Black man named Clarence L. Townes Jr. received a warm welcome from an acquaintance who should have been a stranger. Townes understood that these circumstances were not normal, as the invitation came from T. Justin Moore Jr., one of the wealthiest and well-connected White men in Richmond. Moore sent a letter and left a message with Townes to set up a martini lunch for "a brief discussion." The letter ended with even warmer and inviting language that made it clear, as Moore stated, that the group hoped "very much that you will be able to join us." While Moore felt that "it is not appropriate to try to describe our discussion topic in this notice," Townes may have known why Moore wanted to meet with him so urgently.[40]

Townes and Moore were both card-carrying members of the Richmond Urban Forum. At least twice a month both men ate, drank, communed, and talked with fellow elites from the opposite race about ways to improve Richmond. The offshoot of this club was Richmond Renaissance, the newest nonprofit that White businesspeople felt Moore should represent. A perk of the position was picking a partner, someone who would work hand-in-hand to ensure that racial harmony and reconciliation were sown deep into the fabric of the Sixth Street Marketplace. Townes, who was aware of the inner dealings of Richmond Renaissance, knew that Moore could have chosen any Black leader to work with. Some of the more notable candidates were Virginia Union University president Dr. David T. Shannon, Urban League director Randolph Kendall, Richmond's first Black school superintendent Dr. Richard C. Hunter, longtime state delegate and attorney Roland "Duke" Ealey, Fifth Street Baptist Church's Reverend Roscoe Cooper, local podiatrist and political boss William Thornton, state delegate and future first elected Black governor of Virginia L. Douglas Wilder, and *Richmond Afro-American* editor John Templeton. With this impressive list of candidates, Townes must have wondered why Moore chose him.[41]

It is not definitively known why Moore chose to work with Townes, but he was obviously head and shoulders above the other candidates. Born to one of Richmond's few well-to-do Black families in 1928, Townes attended the all-Black Armstrong High School and Virginia Union University when they were both premier academic institutions. After serving in the US Army, he returned home to become the assistant manager of the Virginia Mutual Benefit Life Insurance Co., a plush job at one of the most profitable Black-owned life insurance companies in America and a firm his father helped found. In the 1950s and 1960s, Townes was one of the few Blacks selected by the Establishment to sit on the Richmond City Republican Committee and Richmond Forward, both of which were influential civic-minded committees filled with high-level executives. Townes later became the first Black Virginia delegate to the Republican National Convention in the twentieth century, and with tremendous local White support, he also ran for US Congress in 1966. While serving on several Republican committees in Washington, Townes owned and operated the Metropolitan Coach Corporation, one of the largest charter bus companies in the region.[42] Although he was born across the color line, Townes was cut from the mold of the Establishment. He was well-educated, socially refined, and conservatively business-minded. These were the characteristics that Moore appeared to look for while selecting a Black partner to work with. Fellow White elites more than supported Moore's top candidate. If Richmond had a "Black Establishment," Townes would have undoubtedly been a long-term staple within it.

Richmond did have a White Establishment, however, and Moore was born into it. The son of an upper-class lawyer and housewife from the Northside, Moore was a baseball and basketball standout at John Marshall High School and Princeton University before earning a law degree from the University of Virginia in 1950. He joined the family business and practiced law with his father, a Harvard alumnus and University of Richmond law professor who had a dormitory named in his honor upon his death. Both Moores worked at Hunton, Williams, Gay, Moore and Powell, arguably the most powerful law firm in Richmond.[43] While specializing in commerce and real estate law, Moore and his father were most known for representing Prince Edward County in its pursuit to maintain segregated public schools after 1954.[44] After his father's untimely passing in 1958, Moore worked to mend any divides his father's controversial decision to defend school segregation may have created. He assumed his father's place as a partner in the law firm, and he represented it by serving on public and private philanthropic boards that provided financial resources to Blacks and Whites alike.[45] By the late 1970s Moore transitioned out of law and into a lofty position as CEO of VEPCO, a role he assumed after the retirement of John M. McGurn, another Establishment fixture.[46]

Townes met with Moore and agreed to help bring the Marketplace into fruition. In the spring and summer of 1982 Moore and Townes held several luncheons, dinners, and meet-and-greets to solicit service and money from over one thousand of the city's most prominent businesspeople.[47] The image of Townes and Moore side-by-side was more than a truly "biracial and bipartisan" effort (in the words of Moore) to rebuild downtown Richmond: it was the physical manifestation of what racial reconciliation should look like in the minds of elite Richmonders. Reconciliation was a sense of goodwill and common economic goals exercised by the smartest and most connected Black and White men. This belief connected the long-separated leadership of both races at the hip in reshaping the landscape to attract the middle-class back from the suburbs.[48] With Moore and Townes both preaching and embodying that message, the city's elite were largely on board with doing everything possible to see that the Marketplace became a reality.[49]

"Everyone is ready to embrace a new Richmond," Moore told a group of White donors in April 1982.[50] The city council echoed this message; however, it took more than comforting words to sell residents of the cash-strapped City of Richmond that retail would be their economic and social savior. Investing current and future tax and grant funding into building a downtown mall was extremely risky considering the city's other six shopping centers struggled to compete with suburban malls in Chesterfield and Henrico. Fortunately for Richmond, cities with similar population sizes such as Toledo, St. Louis, San Antonio, Flint, and Portland had success attracting suburban retail dollars with newly built urban malls. The secret to their success lay only two hours southeast down Interstate 64, in Virginia Beach's Pungo township, at the vacation residence of a man name James Rouse.

The "low-key-unpretentious" Rouse descended from a White, upwardly mobile Baltimore family.[51] In 1937 Rouse secured a $20,000 loan to start the Rouse Company, a firm that became one of the most lucrative mortgage lenders in America.[52] Rouse believed in developing urban environments into communally oriented spaces that could alleviate poverty, crime, and racial segregation. However, he never let his ideology take precedent over economic reason. The Rouse Company became famous for developing suburban shopping malls for Whites around the majority-Black Baltimore and District of Columbia during the White flight of the 1950s.[53] It was not until the 1970s that Rouse shifted toward social engineering by producing mixed-use urban spaces that included shopping malls, small storefronts, kiosks, corporate offices, entertainment venues, and restaurants. His firm would run these properties and use a sizable portion of the revenue to help construct affordable housing for the urban poor.[54] He pitched this idea (called Urban Renaissance) to over one hundred American cities, and more than half agreed.

Rouse worked with over fifty-three city governments to construct downtown shopping malls. His firm broke proverbial ground in 1977 with the completion of the Gallery at Market East in Philadelphia and the Renaissance Center in Detroit, where suburban shoppers and tourists came and regularly spent retail money in downtown for the first time in over a decade.[55] Rouse's success in Philadelphia and Detroit convinced local banks in Boston and Atlanta to finally open their coffers and finance urban malls such as Boston's Faneuil Hall Marketplace and Underground Atlanta in 1978.[56] Boston's project in particular earned Rouse tremendous praise as locals, both White and Black, lost faith in the inner city after the busing fiasco. "Boston created a lot of believers," lighting "a lot of fires of hope around the country," according to Rouse. His projects helped generate civic pride in places where racial turmoil had all but ruined it. As he once pointed out in a later interview: "The fact that these kinds of places exist and succeed is because of the spirit rather than just the retailing function."[57] His work did more than help ailing cities balance their budgets: it gave urban American cities hope in economic resurgence and White middle-class immigration when by all available metrics they should not have had any.

Rouse's next career shift ultimately led him toward Richmond, a city that normally would not garner the attention of a major developer. As Rouse earned a place in the Business Hall of Fame in 1981—alongside the likes of Edwin Herbert Land of Polaroid, Pierre S. Du Pont, Andrew W. Mellon, and Owen D. Young of General Electric—President Ronald Reagan entered the White House and cut federal spending on inner cities in half.[58] This meant that major cities had to use any federal dollars they received on public services and not capital investment. Rouse shifted his focus to help smaller regional cities that were looking to revitalize and had less public-sector debt. His first experiment was in his hometown of Baltimore, where he built the downtown Harborplace in spite of industrial firms such as Bethlehem Steel and General Motors fleeing the city in droves after World War II.[59] Rouse's success in Baltimore compelled city leaders (mainly blue-blooded Virginians from the Tidewater) in Norfolk to contact him about designing and running the Waterside project, a task he accepted with open arms because his wife was born in the area.[60] After successfully setting the Norfolk Waterfront project on course for completion, Rouse, at the behest of his Tidewater friends, accepted a meeting with T. Justin Moore and Clarence Townes about developing the Sixth Street Marketplace.[61]

Rouse's decision to work with Townes and Moore generated excitement throughout the region. White-owned businesses and corporations who originally donated money (VEPCO, Bank of Virginia, and Philip Morris) gave hundreds of thousands more to underwrite the project. Even smaller Black civic organizations, such as the Church Hill Association and Parents of Richmond City Public Schools, contributed to the project by July 1982.[62] The excitement did not hide the fact that the city and the region remained racially segregated. There was no real indication that the Marketplace, if completed, would generate social integration; Blacks and Whites, while mixing well in workplaces, generally lived, worshiped, and communed in segregated spaces. Rouse, Townes, and Moore conducted surveys to identify the issues that perpetuated racial segregation in Richmond. They found that Whites disliked the physical decay and high crime rates in Black dominated areas, one of which surrounded the Marketplace site.[63] From this moment forward, Richmond Renaissance grounded the Marketplace's reconciliation agenda in rehabbing Black Richmond for suburban Whites. This vision of reconciliation appealed to neither side, as Whites still refused to patronize the downtown mall and Blacks distrusted the process as a new form of urban renewal.

"Spillover"

In August 1982 a Black Richmond man was shot in the head during an attempted robbery in broad daylight.[64] In December of that same year, another Black man was shot to death in a home invasion just two hours after midnight on Christmas Day.[65] A few months later another Black man was shot in the afternoon by men to whom the police believed he owed money.[66] Only one of the three above-mentioned homicides made it to trial, and the suspects were exonerated due to lack of eyewitness testimony and physical evidence.[67] These events had a common cord: they all appeared to be assassinations in the Jackson Ward neighborhood.

This was an area where cancerous vice gangs brazenly set up open-air drug and prostitution markets. City police often looked no further than this eight-block radius to catch Richmond's most wanted Black fugitives. By the 1980s cops and those looking to buy drugs and or sex were the only White people visiting Jackson Ward. They, along with the Black residents, probably could not imagine that this area was the first Richmond neighborhood to earn a spot on the National Register of Historic Places.[68] A White investment firm once noted that "the official statistics understate the extent of the crime problem" in Jackson Ward. They went on to suggest that "in any event, the widely held view that there is a significant crime problem in the area must be recognized as a major deterrent to [downtown] investment."[69]

Just one block north of the Sixth Street Marketplace site, Jackson Ward was Richmond's oldest Black enclave. In the eighteenth century mixed-race and Black barbers, artisans, and craftsmen established the neighborhood as a safe haven for free Black people. That legacy of Black freedom in the heart of the city gave birth to the Jackson Ward business and political community that gained national prominence a century later. Some of America's oldest Black-owned banks, insurance companies, fraternal organizations, and self-help enterprises were started by Jackson Ward Blacks in the twilight years of Reconstruction. The ward also housed the largest concentration of Black voters in Virginia. Thus, in the early twentieth century White city and state leaders used gerrymandering and voter disenfranchisement to put the ward out of political existence. While Black Richmond still treated the ward as a cultural and business center after its political demise, Whites used segregation ordinances, redlining, and poor public services to stymy its economic power.[70] The systemic attacks on the ward finally took their toll after World War II. When the Black middle class fled the area for better homes in the Northside and Near West End, the Black working- and underclass became Jackson Ward's majority.

By 1980 most Jackson Ward households operated on less than half of the city's median income for a working adult ($5,000 per year). Half of Jackson Ward's residents never attended high school; less than a quarter of those who did earned a diploma; and under 6 percent graduated from college. Ninety-seven percent of Jackson Ward residents, ranging from single mothers to the elderly, relied on public assistance while working menial service jobs.[71] The other 3 percent thrived on the vice trade as "pool halls, beer taverns, massage parlors, adult book stores, night clubs, and prostitution" were the only factories hiring within the neighborhood.[72] The city invested some money in renovating and reselling thirty-five housing units in Jackson Ward to buyers who were "younger and more affluent than average for the community." This plan did not solve the area's long-term divestment problems. Jackson Ward was a source of pride for Black Richmonders, so it hurt them to know that it was a community afflicted with the worst levels of poverty and crime. For Richmond Renaissance and their investors, however, they resented that the neighborhood, which rested between Broad Street to the south and Interstate 95 to the north, would be the natural gateway to the emerging Sixth Street Marketplace.[73]

James Rouse, Clarence Townes, and T. Justin Moore banded together to infrastructurally improve Richmond's inconvenient eyesore of Jackson Ward.[74] What they did not expect was that their attempt to mend fences between Jackson Ward and White Richmond (whom they unfortunately represented) created further racial division and distrust between Whites and Blacks. Rouse, Townes, and Moore convinced Richmond Renaissance to approve a token revitalization plan for Jackson Ward named "Spillover." Instead of making long-term economic investments in the desperate area, the board wanted to give facelifts to only its most historic buildings and streets between I-95 and the proposed Marketplace. This plan, they hoped, would spark private investment after the Marketplace came to fruition. Townes, Rouse, and Moore reluctantly pushed this plan as they reported to the board that the "expected 'spillover' benefits associated with Project [One] and the Sixth Street Festival Marketplace development" would not fix the image or function of the community.

Fuller real estate and business investment was needed by Richmond Renaissance and the city to revive this dying downtown area; only then would it be an asset to the Marketplace and city. This message fell on deaf ears, but some Black Jackson Ward residents got wind of the proposed plan. They assumed that White moneymen were working with a few Black leaders to remove poor and working-class Blacks from the ward.[75] A Black businessman told his neighbors (who represented eighteen industries and thirty-five businesses in the area) that "it is clear that even as middle-class Blacks, we do not have the necessary financial clout to build a three million dollar development individually." Thus, they banded together and promised to keep their property for as long as they could.[76]

Between January 1983 and May 1984, Richmond Renaissance met with Jackson Ward business owners about combining their visions for the area. In these meetings it became clear that Richmond Renaissance wanted to displace Black people.[77] But that displacement also included inculcating Black businesses into the Marketplace. Rouse once told *Baltimore* that for true revitalization to happen, "Black businesses need[ed] to be formed, supported, nourished, into healthy development."[78] In the context of the Marketplace, that meant selling their properties and entering the mall as tenants.

They systematized this sentiment by creating a minority business package that included 51 percent of the parking lot contracts and revenue, low-interest capital improvement loans, and pro bono legal services be given to participating Jackson Ward businesses.[79] Townes, Rouse, and Moore marketed this plan as a beginning to "attract a growing secondary office market among small service and professional firms who wish to locate outside of the expensive downtown financial district."[80] The only issue was that some of the Black businesspeople would have to sell their premium property to Richmond Renaissance. Most were willing to sell; however, the offers were well below what the business owners expected. They asked for more money, and Richmond Renaissance saw the counteroffers as "assign[ing] values to their property greatly in excess of the appraised value." Negotiations fell apart and Richmond Renaissance, to the dismay of Townes, Moore, and Rouse, looked for "alternative sites to do business."[81] The alternative site solution, and any hopes of making Jackson Ward an actual part of downtown revitalization ended less than a month after Marketplace construction began. As punishment, Richmond Renaissance rerouted its traffic and trash deliveries through Jackson Ward, a petty decision that they later reversed after resident complaints.[82]

While Richmond Renaissance lost out on a critical opportunity to reconcile the city's relationship with the long-neglected Jackson Ward, they made significant progress with those who participated in the Marketplace. Townes's Affirmative Action and Minority Tenant Opportunity Program tasked Rouse's management firm with recruiting Black business owners to become Marketplace vendors. Upon accepting a lease agreement, Black vendors would be assigned financial advisors who would conduct analysis, projections, and recommendations for improvements, inventory, and advertisements.

Townes and Moore worked with local White banks to set aside a $1.25 million loan fund for the Black vendors.[83] Richmond Renaissance reserved at least 15 percent of rental space, 30 percent of construction contracts, 30 percent of administrative positions, and 50 percent of clerical jobs for qualified Black applicants. Every business was required to reserve at least 35 percent of its employment opportunities for Black applicants as well. Any business caught violating the minority agreement would have their lease terminated. After reading the agreement, city manager Manny Deese told Rouse, Townes, and Moore: "I am extremely pleased with the support that I have been able to obtain from local bankers, universities and law firms assisting in the development of minority business opportunities in the City of Richmond." He went on to claim that "to my knowledge, this is the first time that a city government and the private sector have developed a program which will afford an opportunity for minorities to enter the mainstream of economic development."[84] While this was not the first public-private economic step towards racial harmony in America, or even the South, it was the most impactful for Richmond to date. Once a hegemonic pillar of White supremacy and racial division, downtown reflected the idealistic vision of Black and White elites and the possibilities of racial reconciliation. Richmond did not become racially harmonious or healed with the completion of the Sixth Street Marketplace; however, with its opening in September 1985, elites felt that it would be.[85]

"It Has Become a Symbol of Failure and It Must Come Down"

There was tremendous fanfare surrounding the ribbon-cutting ceremony on September 18, 1985. Over fifty thousand people (around twenty thousand residents) witnessed T. Justin Moore, Clarence Townes, James Rouse, and other city leaders give impassioned speeches about how the Marketplace and Unity Bridge would mend the city's racial divide and fix the economy. The Marketplace's opening weekend saw thousands of shoppers and visitors of both races. The Project One hotel, which was built on "the historic wrong side" of Broad Street, operated at an 85 percent capacity. The Marketplace also spurred over $1 billion in real estate and corporate investments that resulted in renovations to the Richmond Diamond (baseball park), Main Street Train Station, and other venues in the late 1980s.[86] While prospects were high for Richmond, those closest to the project remained grounded. Clarence Townes told *Minorities and Women in Business* magazine that he was not too sure that the Marketplace would survive financially. "The jury is still out, and ultimately only time will tell if the Sixth Street Marketplace will be more than just a symbol."[87]

Urban Reporter magazine conducted a follow-up report on the Marketplace less than a year later. They were expecting to see a thriving downtown mall that city leaders advertised before, during, and after its construction. What the reporters found, however, mimicked many other urban revitalization projects around the country. The storefronts were empty; the food courts were also empty; even the parking decks, which were used to park at the Marketplace and downtown in general, were empty. In search of answers, the journalists interviewed several Black and White marketplace vendors and found that White women between the ages of eighteen and forty—the marketplace's intended client base—mostly refused to shop there. "They think they'll get mugged or raped," the Black business owner sadly told one of the reporters.[88] The fear expressed by potential White female shoppers was largely unjustified. "Walking beat patrols, the canine corps, horse troops, plainclothesmen, and cruise cars in large numbers" were around the Marketplace "before any other section of the city," Townes once said in anger after local news reporters flooded the airwaves with negative press about the downtown area.[89] Like with the 1982 survey conducted by Townes, James Rouse, and T. Justin Moore, crime continued to play cover for the reality that White suburbanites spurned downtown because of their disdain for Blacks.

The Marketplace was erected in a city where "[White] people were still leaving," a longtime resident remembered.[90] Potential suburban shoppers, both Black and White, were repulsed by the idea of the Marketplace itself. Many of them had grown accustomed to shopping in lily-White suburban malls. The Marketplace, being filled with Black vendors and Black shoppers, however, perpetuated the idea that, as was previously said by White Richmond elite Thomas Boushall: "[Poor] Black people have literally taken over Broad Street shopping."[91] Richmond, and more so its Marketplace, suffered greatly from a middle-class disdain and fear of the Black working- and underclass. Tom Soto, owner of local restaurant Zippy's on East Grace Street, near the Marketplace, confirmed this modern-day assessment in 1991 by saying, "I see many moving vans, but I see people moving out, not in." Therefore, it is "what you see [in] downtown [that] counts more than what people say about Richmond."[92] Wherever the majority of Blacks were, either places of leisure or education, those with means mostly stayed away from them. When discussing this undeniable truth of Richmond life, a former city councilwoman and state delegate said that with the Marketplace, "we put the cart before the horse" by ignoring the obvious divide between the idea of elites and sentiments below them.[93] Moreover, city leaders refused to acknowledge that it was in the suburbs where city life was now happening.[94]

Middle-class Richmond area residents, mostly White and some Black, largely believed that their futures lay in the suburbs filled with manicured lawns, cookie-cutter subdivisions, highly rated public and private schools, and class-exclusive shopping malls. Richmond's Black and White elites largely ignored this reality when constructing the Marketplace. Their wishes to interracialize the Richmond of old—a place where elites controlled every facet of city life—blinded them from accepting the race and class realities of the 1980s.[95] Although they were facing forward in terms of race relations between themselves, they looked backward as they sought to reinstall a sense of economic and social normalcy in their hometown. As one city planner suggests, they were "[too] captured by the idea of building a bridge between the Black and White communities" and not enough by fixing the communities people were fleeing. Because of this failure, the city planner went on to conclude: "Despite the efforts to bridge the Black and White communities, the effects of racial segregation were still evident . . . [and] the magnitude of change generated by the marketplace was simply not enough to make a difference."[96]

While crime was the excuse Whites used for refusing to shop at the Marketplace, it was also a serious problem that Richmond failed to solve in the 1980s, a time when the city was the epicenter for Virginia's violent and drug-crime spike. Issues with drug gangs such as the Brown and Johnson families from Southside and with killers such as the Briley brothers and Russell "Block" Gray compelled even the most distrusting residents to beg city and state leadership for harsher crime laws and more law enforcement in their neighborhoods.[97] As local government uncomfortably implemented a tough-on-crime agenda, resulting in antidrug task forces and stricter gun laws, Richmond Public Schools suffered a crisis in leadership and direction. Dwindling student achievement, rising delinquency, a federal lawsuit, and high-level corruption coincided with the resignation of three superintendents, retirement and transfer of several veteran staff, and deprioritizing by city government in the 1980s.[98]

The systemic issues plaguing Richmond race relations manifested in the Marketplace's economic demise. While the Marketplace was a social engineering project between the city's elite, economics still ruled the day. Issues began after the Marketplace opened, as the retail space along East Broad and Grace Streets remained mostly vacant for months. The smaller, but profitable, retailers who once promised to relocate from suburban malls such as Regency Square (Henrico) and Cloverleaf (Chesterfield) and to share space with giants like Thalhimers, Miller & Rhoads, Woolworths, and G. C. Murphy reneged on those handshake agreements. A prominent downtown merchant said, "It [Marketplace] really hasn't brought people out of the suburban malls."[99] After a year, "most merchants in the Marketplace remain upbeat"; however, fewer businesses than expected opened in the area, especially after neighboring retailers limited their operation hours to the daytime.[100] By 1987 the Marketplace management firm had to sue tenants (some minority-owned) for delinquent rents.[101] A year later

City Manager Robert C. Bobb was tasked by the city council with working with the Marketplace management firm and struggling tenants to solve the legal issues and help make the project solvent.[102]

Bobb's plans for the Marketplace were as infected with the spirit of elite reconciliation as the original plans to construct it. The popular city manager wanted to expand the Marketplace in the 1990s to help attract newer retailers with larger facilities. "The heavily subsidized marketplace is far from being able to hold onto sufficient retailers or attract enough new ones to fill up its existing space and Mr. Bobb is talking about expanding it," the *Times-Dispatch* sarcastically opined.[103] Just as the plans were released, and increased rents were expected to be the net cost of expansion, neighboring retailers fled the area faster than they did before. The first was Berry-Burk Co. (clothing); Cokesbury (books) followed them shortly after in July 1989. Both left for bigger space and more affordable rents in Henrico County.[104] Others such as Greentree's, Montaldo's, and Biggs left soon after.[105]

The demise of the Marketplace cemented its fate as arguably one of the city's largest economic failures. In late 1989 Miller & Rhoads and Best Products underwent Chapter 11 bankruptcy, closing in January 1990. For Miller & Rhoads in particular, this ended a 104-year run, sparking more anxiety among the remaining retailers about staying downtown. Miller & Rhoads ownership eventually sold their assets to national department store Hecht's, who subsequently expanded into the Chesterfield suburbs after 1991.[106] Even fellow Richmond-based retailer and Marketplace partner Thalhimers sold its assets to Los Angeles firms to stay afloat.[107] As the major local partners and investors in the Marketplace folded in the new decade and national retailers flooded the Richmond-area market with suburban storefronts, it became clear to all that "the joyride of the 1980s shuddered to a crawl in 1990."[108]

Richmond transitioned toward a "knowledge-based technology economy" anchored by Motorola, Siemens, and Capital One in the following decade. This economic shift closed the door on the Marketplace and its architectural handshake of racial unity.[109] Other Sunbelt cities that embraced revitalization faced similar fates, as major projects absorbed millions in tax subsidies, took out tremendous loan debts, and rarely, if ever, turned a profit.[110] As the Sixth Street Marketplace's struggles became front-page news, along with the not-so-private revitalization issues throughout the region, city leaders began to openly change their tune and side with the rising "tax revolts" against subsidizing the dream that was, by now, undoubtedly a nightmare.[111] As one longtime homeowner told the

Times-Dispatch, he and many other residents predicted that "by the end of the decade the city will have dumped [the] 6th Street Marketplace," a structure that helped to nearly double city taxes while operating a nearly $4 million deficit every year.[112]

Eventually, city leaders faced the music that had been playing for a while. They were hesitant to admit their failures and adhere to popular cries to demolish the Marketplace that rang out as early as 1991.[113] Yet as the 1990s carried on, the Marketplace became a public eyesore: a haven for the homeless and delinquent teens and a magnet for other vices that use to remain in the city's East End and Jackson Ward areas. It did not help that the *Times-Dispatch* hammered that point home almost campaign style with the help of former Richmond mayor Phil Bagley's regular contributions to the editorial pages.[114] The civic dislike for the Marketplace became clearer when a planned ten-year anniversary was canceled by city leaders, as celebrating the Marketplace in any way would have been the ultimate irony. Many "question whether the mall will be around for a 20th anniversary," the *Times Dispatch* stated in 1995. The civic neglect was extended to even the most ambitious within the business community. When the city put the Marketplace up for sale in May, not one group or firm issued an offer.[115]

Just days after the Marketplace's seventeenth anniversary, the Richmond city council announced its demolition, citing that it "has become a symbol of failure and it must come down."[116] While the council promoted the obvious slum-clearance project as the beginning of a series of downtown renovations, one business owner bluntly told the local press that the Marketplace and Unity Bridge were being demolished because in his opinion, "Who shops here? It's not White people. It's Black people."[117] With respect to the minority tenant owner(s) who lost everything with Marketplace demolition, the decision was not a simple act of racism by city government. It was an acknowledgement that interracial cooperation among leadership was not nearly enough to overcome the burden of racial division in the Richmond area.

The paternalism by Richmond Black and White elites authored the demise of the project before it even started. Moreover, the Sixth Street Marketplace's economic failure resulted from the use of elite reconciliation and racial capitalism at a time when metro area residents were quite comfortable remaining separated by race. Yet Richmond leaders did in fact lead the city, but not in the ways they planned. They publicly broke down generational racial barriers to construct the failed Marketplace. By showing Richmonders that Blacks and Whites at the highest levels could work together as equals, elites inspired nonelite groups to join the reconciliation movement. Nonelites had a different vision of racial reconciliation. Instead of focusing on attracting White suburbanites back, later groups prioritized systemic improvements for the Black working class, such as improving access to affordable housing, transportation, and childcare. In working across the color line to create a racially harmonious city, later groups, whether knowingly or unknowingly, enacted at a granular level the mission started by the movers and shakers of the infamous Sixth Street Marketplace.

PART 3

A CITY HEALING, 1985–PRESENT

7
Richmond Urban Institute
"THE CONSCIENCE OF RICHMOND"

I FOUND myself quite irritated on an extremely chilly morning in March 2019, as I sat in the downstairs breezeway beneath the sanctuary of St. Paul's Episcopal Church. At least ten people stopped by to ask me if I needed assistance. They all received the same "no" answer, followed by the assurance that I had a meeting with someone who was at least an hour late. That someone was Reverend Benjamin Campbell, a longtime minister at the church. My assurances and admittedly unpleasant demeanor prompted St. Paul's staff to call Campbell and remind him that he had a visitor waiting to speak with him. Shortly after the final call, Campbell rushed out of the elevator with a Styrofoam cup of coffee in hand and a smile on his face. He welcomed me back to the sanctuary that I had visited years before while conducting research for my master's thesis. I returned the kindness with a slight smile, handshake, and subtle request to immediately conduct the interview that we were already an hour late for.

As Campbell and I entered the ministers' study room, he asked about the status of my dissertation that was, at that time, nearly completed. I told him that the dissertation was coming along well; however, I needed to talk with him again about some local groups whose details remained unclear to me. After we both sat in the large, comfortable leather chairs facing a grand fireplace, I asked Campbell about the Richmond Urban Institute (RUI). This was a nonprofit organization that Campbell helped found in the basement of St. Paul's church in the 1980s. His face lit up like a Christmas tree before telling me that RUI was one of the most impactful groups he had ever worked with. After hearing that, I expected to get an earful of meaningful information about the mostly forgotten biracial nonprofit that reclaimed racial reconciliation for the city's grassroots communities. What I received, however, was a short conversation that revealed the difficulty nonelite groups faced while trying to racially reconcile a city that was all-to-comfortable functioning against the interests of those without money or power.

The most interesting aspect of this short conversation was that for Campbell, his past and present were diametrically opposed. At the time of the interview, Campbell was still celebrated for his well-received book titled *Richmond's Unhealed History*. In it, Campbell argued for a more metropolitan and wholistic outlook on city life; more plainly, that Richmond needed, somehow, to align with its wealthy suburbs to improve public services, and, by proxy, undo the centuries of systemic racism that has ruined race relations.[1] Campbell still feels this way today; however, there is reason to believe that he may not have felt this way in the past. In fact, I am certain that he did not.

Upon moving to Richmond as a young minister and activist, Campbell (and those like him) shunned the traditional thinking that prosperity and progress inherently relied on Richmond reaching out to its suburban neighbors. Rather, RUI worked within Richmond's working- and underclass communities to improve city life for those who, whether by choice or force, remained city residents after the modern civil rights movement. My suspicion that Campbell may have changed his mind on this issue is because his 2012 monograph, which relied heavily on the notion of metropolitan consolidation, rarely, if ever, mentioned the urban-focused RUI he helped found.

RUI started the groundswell of grassroots reconciliatory activism in Richmond after the modern civil rights movement. While contributing to the racial reconciliation movement started by city elites, RUI filtered their own notions of it below the realm of Richmond leadership. While city elites prioritized the recruitment of suburban Whites, RUI and the groups who worked with them focus on ending racism in city housing and transportation, while also trying to provide adequate childcare and economic independence within Richmond's working- and underclass communities. Their efforts were most important because they placed Richmond in step with grassroot efforts across the nation to end housing discrimination and improve public transportation for the poor. While RUI's "un-Richmond" ideas of bottom-up reform resulted from the desires of everyday people, the fruits of their labor did not become ripe until after the organization's demise in 1990.[2] Yet this largely forgotten group implemented fundamental progress in the Richmond area racial climate.

"A New Jerusalem—A Place More Acceptable to Change"

Benjamin Campbell was quite silent about RUI. For a man who often has a lot to say about everything, his quietude raised serious red flags about the organization and his role in it. I do not suggest that he withheld valuable information; rather, as our conversation developed, it became clear that he wanted to know what I knew before he would speak.

Archival research revealed that almost thirty years to the day I met with Campbell, around fifteen Whites and Blacks met in the very same room we sat in to create RUI. "The most critical question before the institute is membership," the group determined almost immediately.[3] The small collection consisted of a school board member, assistant school superintendent, city councilwoman (Willie Dell), as well as Virginia Commonwealth University (VCU) professors and area ministers. This admittedly apolitical group vowed, no matter what confronted them, to remain "a body of individuals who functioned without institutional control in pursuit of a common goal."[4] Binding them together in this new organization was a commitment to removing racism from urban life by using social science "research and education" to fix the "issues affecting the people." They grounded this commitment to make decisions based on racial equity and not interracial representation. To RUI, elite organizations like Richmond Renaissance based their mission of racial harmony on White suburban appeal. Richmond Renaissance and their flagship project—the Sixth Street Marketplace—was run biracially, but they were focused on improving race relations by attracting Whites back to the city. RUI ignored the White suburbs in "advocating the needs of those who are unheard." This was an utter defiance to what was deemed progressive by Richmond standards.[5]

RUI's mission to turn Richmond into a "New Jerusalem—A Place More Acceptable to Change," in the words of a prominent member, belonged primarily to two full-time employees called urban missioners.[6] The first so-called co-missioner was Benjamin P. Campbell, a descendant from a First Family of Virginia, a Rhodes Scholar, and White minister who led and served on many local civic and religious groups since arriving in the city in 1970.[7] The other co-missioner was Edythe M. Rodgers, "a high school dropout who went on to earn a law degree," the *Times-Dispatch* bragged in her honor.[8] The selection of Campbell and Rodgers was a change of pace in terms of reconciliation work in Richmond. Both Downtown Development Unlimited and Richmond Renaissance relied exclusively on locally born and groomed leadership—wealthy and well-to-do people—who placed custom before reason in working on projects dealing with race. It was the custom of racial segregation that compelled White and Black leaders to debate the location of the Project One hotel. Even racial integration planning succumbed to the custom of elite gentility, compelling city leaders to ignore race relations among the masses in building the Sixth Street Marketplace. Old-stock, oligarchical Richmond leaders limited themselves to the past in ways that neither Campbell nor Rodgers was willing to do. The co-missioners felt their job was to guarantee that RUI would "question old truths and traditions held dear by many" and create systemic change on the ground, as the *Times-Dispatch* said about Rodgers's selection specifically.[9]

RUI's strength lay in its ability to amorphously adjust to community needs. Upon inception in 1977, the co-missioners internally "struggled to find out what the organization was," as they "had general principals as a guideline—but no clear agenda."[10] This internal uncertainty went away when Campbell and Rodgers met with several civic groups throughout Richmond on RUI's behalf.[11] The co-missioners saw themselves as conduits who brought local aspirations under the practical application of professionals. The civic groups saw the co-missioners and RUI as an intelligent bunch who were both relatable to the working people and powerful enough to help them make changes within the city.[12] This disconnect between what RUI was and who people believed they were compelled Rodgers and Campbell to turn RUI into a multifocused organization that echoed popular sentiment. In a series of brown-bag lunches and seminars where RUI and civic groups spent "time on the subject of racism on a regular basis," the city's housing segregation emerged as a consistent problem.[13]

The academics in RUI and co-missioners "concluded that there needs to be a comprehensive approach to the subject [racism] that can be presented to the public."[14] They hoped that a comprehensive report, one grounded in both academic inquiry and social justice, would compel local groups to work more toward a united effort to dismantle the vestiges of racism in Richmond. While taking over two years to complete, RUI's first report concluded that housing segregation in Richmond resulted from a top-down, anti-Black agenda being deeply interwoven into the fabric of the local housing market, a fact that shocked very few lifelong residents.

Housing in Richmond was, like in every major American city and suburb, heavily segregated by race in the early 1980s. Urban scholar Christopher Silver and historian Robert A. Pratt noted in their groundbreaking monographs about twentieth-century Richmond that housing segregation created irreparable damage to both urban planning and the implementation of civil rights law.[15] Neither scholar included RUI's detailed 1981 report, in which RUI found that housing segregation came from the real estate community—a tight-knit coalition of real estate agencies, lending institutions (banks and credit unions), and brokerage firms.

Coming to this conclusion was not easy because housing segregation appeared to be, at least on the surface, a result of White consumer choice. During Jim Crow, White Richmonders openly intimidated Blacks from moving into their communities. If that did not work, as was the case with local Black newspaper editor John Mitchell Jr. in 1907, they compelled the all-White city government to pass codes and withhold permits from Blacks seeking to own and occupy property in White areas.[16] RUI found that after World War II, however, White Richmonders did not need intimidation or city government to maintain housing segregation. Black realtor Milton Randolph made Richmonders privy to the real estate community's role in blockbusting the Northside during the late 1960s.[17] The real estate community (mainly the Board of Realtors) publicly denied Randolph's account, knowing that he and others had little beyond anecdotal and circumstantial evidence to support it.

RUI's conclusion fit well with what urban historians have long concluded as the cause of housing segregation. They found that segregated housing was not just an organic outgrowth of Whites and Blacks buying homes in separate areas. Rather, it came from real estate communities operating segregated housing markets.[18] They also found that local and state governments, run by White "progressives" who believed that racial segregation was in the best interest of societal order, set the legal foundation for segregated housing at the local and state levels in the early twentieth century.[19] The federal government cemented the practice of state-sponsored housing segregation with the Federal Housing Authority (FHA) and its mortgage insurance, created by Title I and II of the Federal Housing Act of 1934. The FHA federalized segregated housing markets by refusing to insure mortgages to Blacks in general, and to Whites who wanted to live in and near Black-dominated and interracial areas. At the same time, they insured mortgages and subsidized suburban housing with White-only occupancy requirements. These policies placed monetary power in the belief that Black residency ruined property values; thus, White home buyers and lending institutions operated as both swords and shields that kept Blacks trapped in dilapidated inner-city neighborhoods. While the FHA created the modern mortgage industry, as Americans relied more heavily on mortgages to buy homes after 1934, they also wedded racism to it.

Urban America's Black middle class used the federal courts to prevent the public and private sectors from maintaining dual housing markets. With victories in *Deans v. Richmond* (1930), *Hurd v. Hodge,* and *Shelley v. Kraemer* (1948), Black homeowners effectively ended housing segregation ordinances by city governments and restrictive covenants by private citizens. Real estate communities picked up where governments left off by blockbusting and contract-selling.[20] While most Whites were perfectly fine with these practices, some of the more liberal ones (usually left-leaning academics) opposed blatant and subtle attempts to maintain racially segregated neighborhoods.[21] The combination of White and Black resistance brought the modern civil rights movement to the housing industry, as it did with education, private business, and political life. Civil rights organizations compelled US Congress to pass the Fair Housing Act of 1968 (FHA), Home Mortgage Disclosure Act of 1975 (HMDA), and Community Reinvestment Act of 1977 (CRA), some of the last original civil rights legislation to come about in the twentieth century.[22]

Although passed during three separate presidencies, the FHA, HMDA, and CRA worked in unison to end America's dual housing markets. The FHA prohibited the use of race to determine the financing, insuring, renting, purchase, and sale of any dwelling by both private and public agencies. The HMDA ensured that redlining was no longer an open secret, requiring federally insured mortgage lenders—those covered under Federal Deposit Insurance Corporation and Federal Savings and Loan Insurance Corporation—to keep and make public record of every mortgage they approved. The CRA required banking regulators to encourage real estate communities to invest mortgage and business loans in moderate- and low-income urban areas.[23] A top this triangle was the Federal Reserve System, which provided the necessary forms for record and, should it be necessary, levied fines to ensure compliance. These pieces of legislation originally did not apply to nondepository institutions and lenders who held less than $10 million in assets. Congress ended this loophole by the mid-1990s, as all lending institutions, large and small, depository or not, had to remove race from their lending criteria.[24]

Armed with newly passed federal laws, Ben Campbell, Edythe Rodgers, and RUI academics went to local banks, mortgage lenders, and realtors between 1978 and 1981 to collect as much information as the law allowed. Their efforts were monumental because the Federal Reserve Board—the primary regulatory agency in charge of enforcing the recently passed acts—publicly refused to archive any data that could help citizens combat redlining. Rather, they followed the letter of the law and provided the forms for lending institutions to fill out and keep. They also heard cases made by citizens who collected the information themselves, but they would not police the process by which citizens collected the information.[25]

The Federal Reserve's decision compelled interracial groups like the National People Action on Housing in northern, midwestern, and West

Coast cities to testify in front of Congress that their respective real estate communities remained largely unpunished for ignoring lawful information requests, omitting valuable information from documents, and charging as much as $0.75 per page for reports that could span over a hundred pages.[26] To prevent costly litigation, bad press, and increased federal oversight into their monetary practices, lending institutions everywhere followed southern cities like the District of Columbia, Memphis, and Atlanta by providing the necessary information that proved they maintain dual housing markets. At the same time, they made commitments to dispense with millions in mortgages to areas that were depressed by White suburban flight.[27] Like urbanites elsewhere, Richmonders would have to follow the same course of action to get the same result because, as RUI co-missioner Edythe Rodgers stated, "The problem of overall divestment and economic decline of the city of Richmond continues to be addressed in concerted fashion by no one."[28]

RUI's years of research and analysis about segregated housing led them to a Saturday night meeting at a community center in the heavily working-class Black section of Church Hill's Chimborazo area. There, local bank presidents and Richmond's Federal Reserve Board uncomfortably sat in the Black ghetto and listened to RUI accuse the local real estate community of unscrupulous and unlawful behavior. RUI charged that while Richmond was "about evenly divided between White and Black," almost all of the mortgages (over 80 percent) were in the majority-White areas of Far and Near West End and surrounding Chesterfield and Henrico suburbs. Majority-Black areas in the East End, Southside, and Northside had virtually no mortgage activity at all. Most Richmond neighborhoods were either dying or dead from a deliberate lack of financial investment by White lenders.[29]

When asked to answer for these accusations, representatives from the Board of Realtors claimed that lenders merely met the market demands of the White middle and upper classes. They claimed that these groups wanted to live among those with similar socioeconomic values. Thus, the conditions that RUI referred to were not the results of illegal tampering but of lenders legally acquiescing to realtors who responded to consumer demands.[30] The Rhodes Scholar and longtime Virginian must have grinned, as he often does, before retorting that he had more proof that "metropolitan Richmond contains two separate, distinct, and unequal sales housing markets—one for Whites and another for Blacks."[31] He argued that while the real estate community could no longer hide behind White intimidation and local and state laws, they used a subtle form of "racial steering" where White realtors appealed to the "whiteness" or racial loyalty of White homebuyers or renters while simply refusing to show homes to Blacks.[32]

Little did the Board of Realtors know, but Campbell himself had been racially steered upon arriving in Richmond. In Winter 1970 he and his then-wife Anne met with a local realtor about renting an apartment until they could afford to buy a home. Campbell remembered the realtor being very plain in his "request" that should the married couple rent the apartment, no animals or Blacks would be allowed in. When Campbell confronted the realtor for his blatant bigotry, the realtor responded with an apologetic appeal for the Campbells to consider the racial integrity of the area they were moving into. If the Campbells hosted Blacks, he argued, others would be encouraged to do so, putting the entire area at risk of transitioning into a Black neighborhood. Campbell and his wife refused to live in the apartment or deal with that realtor again, but further inquiries produced the same outcome. Campbell then sought to obtain a $12,000 mortgage to live in the heavily Black Church Hill area. Although he had dozens of high-level bank officials within his church, three of whom sat on the board, he could not get even the smallest of mortgages to live in a Black neighborhood. Eventually, the Episcopal Bishop of Virginia—Campbell's boss, convinced a prominent bank president and church member to give him a $10,000 mortgage loan to live in Church Hill.[33]

This experience sat at the front of Campbell's mind when he revealed that beneath the Board of Realtors' noses, RUI had convinced over seventy-five "prospective buyers," Black and White, to visit Richmond's fifty-nine real estate firms (thirty-four of which had been represented on the Board of Realtors for at least a decade) between May 1978 and February 1979 and request assistance buying and renting homes and apartments. RUI paired the results based on race, income, body type, gender, and occupation, so that Blacks and Whites with similar body types, gender, and incomes requested the same type of housing under the same conditions.

RUI found that realtors showed Blacks fewer than half of the dwellings in White-dominated areas as opposed to Whites of equal and lesser income, who saw all of them. Blacks mainly saw homes in majority Black areas, while Whites saw homes in both White and racially mixed areas where the percentage of Black population appeared to be both low (less than 20 percent) and stagnant. Realtors never showed Whites and Blacks available dwellings in neighborhoods that were exclusively occupied by the opposite race. Further inquiry into the city's housing history concluded that home turnover rates, or the amount of emigration and mortgage default, were nearly identical in racially homogenous and interracial neighborhoods. Thus, as Campbell told the Federal Reserve Board, "Real estate agents themselves stimulate racial resegregation" by controlling the dwellings people saw and determining if neighborhoods were considered too "unstable" to invest in. "Illegal racial steering is rampant throughout the local real estate industry," Campbell concluded, as the available evidence left little doubt that realtors were the foot soldiers who set the racist housing market that lenders financed.[34]

RUI did not solely blame realtors. Mortgage lenders approved and dispensed more than three times as many loans to the West End, Chesterfield, and Henrico suburbs than to the other parts of Richmond combined. Seventy-five percent of Richmonders lived in areas with little to no mortgage activity at all. While housing 49 percent of the metropolitan area's population, Richmond had less than 25 percent of the mortgage investment. Chesterfield County, the smallest locality by population (over 95 percent White), had over 50 percent of the mortgage activity in the metro area, totaling $100 million. Henrico had $89 million in mortgage loans, while Richmond ranked dead last with just around $43 million. Virtually fifty thousand Richmonders, nearly all of them Black, had no access to mortgages because lenders deemed their areas as too risky for investment.[35] Lenders were the financial wing of Richmond's racist real estate community, ensuring that Blacks remained renters in low-income neighborhoods while Whites and the few middle-class Blacks could evade such a fate.

RUI's report created systemic change in Richmond's housing market. After showing various civic groups copies of the final report, RUI gained enough signatures to petition for congressional intervention into Richmond's housing market. It was that petition that landed Campbell and RUI in the Saturday night meeting where the Federal Reserve Board and real estate community agreed to broker a deal in the Black Richmond ghetto. Both parties understood that no one was leaving the meeting without a deal being brokered. The CRA gave urban communities the right to block potential bank mergers if they had evidence of shoddy or illegal lending practices.[36] RUI produced this report around the time that banks in Richmond and around the country were consolidating into the megalenders and depositors we see today. The bank merger RUI targeted was between the Norfolk-based Virginia National Bank and First and Merchants Bank from Richmond.[37]

Before both institutions could combine to later become a part of the growing Bank of America, RUI and the real estate community brokered a deal that included nearly every realty firm and banks such as First Merchants Bank, Virginia National, United Virginia, Bank of Virginia,

Dominion National, and First Virginia Bank Colonial. They all agreed to work with RUI on ending racial steering and stimulating mortgage activity in previously neglected areas.[38] While the documentary evidence is not definitive on whether racial steering remained in the Richmond area, the explosion in Black suburban flight and White gentrification after 1981 suggests that realtors and lenders ensured that qualified Black and White applicants who wanted mortgages to live in areas around the opposite race received no pushback. Lenders took it a step further by agreeing to provide mortgages for lower-income (Black) applicants who would have never qualified for mortgages under normal circumstances. At the time, the average home price in Richmond was around $40,000. One had to earn at least $18,000 a year to get the highest fixed-interest rate of around 11 percent. Lenders like Central Fidelity Bank eased their interest policies to provide current working-class people home loans, and for working-class homeowners who lived in depressed areas, lenders provided capital improvement loans.[39]

RUI's tactical approach to ending redlining was a part of movements by neighborhood associations throughout the nation. National housing organizations found that lenders in around 180 cities agreed to reform their lending practices to buy their way out of fines and regulation. The most important aspect of these agreements was that neighborhood organizations agreed to forgo litigation that prevented lenders (mainly banks) from merging into bigger entities.[40] While these efforts helped both working-class Blacks and Whites to buy homes, they undoubtedly facilitated the largest migration of Black people to the suburbs in American history, a migration that Richmond was undoubtedly a part of.[41] That massive migration would not have happened without urban communities putting regulatory and judicial pressure on realtors and lenders.

RUI's equal housing efforts, mainly chiding the real estate community for its long-held racist lending practices, were not enough to strip racial inequity from inner city housing. Above RUI's efforts at racially integrated housing was urban revitalization and its natural outgrowth: gentrification. Although coined by British sociologist Ruth Glass in 1964 to describe the changes within inner-city London, gentrification is the process by which middle- and upper-class people—gentry—move into traditionally working- and underclass urban neighborhoods and reshape the collective identity.[42] Scholars largely ignored this activity until the late 1970s and early 1980s, when urban revitalization movements in America spurred the privileged children of suburbia to live, if at least temporarily, in the cities they worked in.[43] The first group of American gentrifiers, or urban pioneers, as contemporaries called them, embraced the revitalization spirit by purchasing and renovating older homes in decayed neighborhoods in cities across the country, from San Francisco to Atlanta.[44] While city governments embraced this slow-moving trend that would not fully mature until the early 2010s, poor and working-class Black urbanites feared that the influx of moneyed Whites would mix with downtown revitalization efforts to raise housing prices beyond their reach.[45]

It was not until the early 1980s that young, affluent, and upwardly mobile couples—many of whom were associated with the expanding VCU—began immigrating to the once-fashionable homes and apartments in Richmond's Fan District, Church Hill, Oregon Hill, and Jackson Ward.[46] While local economists and low-income Black residents foresaw that this slow inward migration of White yuppies was a low-risk pitstop for future suburbanites who could not yet afford to move to the $100,000-plus homes in the suburbs, the biracial city council passed gentrification-friendly legislation allowing homes to be turned into duplexes and allocating more city resources (streetlights, police presence, and newer roads) to the areas.[47] City government, and even VCU, invested in gentrification zones with the belief that they would grow and provide a much-needed return to the already depleted Richmond tax base.[48] RUI, acting in the interest of those already in the city, used calculated measures to ensure that city government's middle- and upper-class-focused investment did not come at the peril of the working and underclasses.

RUI believed that a healthy urban community relied on financial investment into the democratization of homeownership and neighborhood integrity. Property ownership for the working class was important because it meant that members of city government, both White and Black, could not ignore their concerns. It also protected them from the potential political and economic disempowerment that gentrification presented. RUI worked tirelessly to promote both economic growth and neighborhood integrity. Their second housing strategy involved bringing the spirit of downtown revitalization into Richmond neighborhoods so that the city's mostly Black renter class could become homeowners.[49] In March 1982 RUI used funding from local churches, corporations, and banks, and the elbow grease from homeowners in depressed areas of Church Hill, Highland Park, Oregon Hill, Oak Grove, and Jackson Ward to generate "community-based-efforts for neighborhood housing development through rehabilitation and purchase."[50]

RUI's housing effort was, unlike their first housing project, truly a citywide endeavor. Over sixty-two local businesses and banks funded the populist housing platform to help reconcile the city's long history of racist lending.[51] The co-missioners used local civic groups to identify working-class urbanites who could not ever get a mortgage but desired to become homeowners in Richmond.[52] RUI then purchased dilapidated and abandoned homes from slumlords and city government. With the help of Richmond Public Schools and J. Sargent Reynolds Community College, RUI started a youth employment program in which Black teenagers spent their summers helping rehab the purchased homes. Not only did the jobs provide working-class Black parents with childcare, but the youth also earned high school and, in some cases, college credits. Upon completion, RUI then sold the homes at cost to the prospective homebuyers who had nontraditional financing through local participating banks.[53]

While RUI's housing rehabilitation plan was one meaningful victory in the war for open housing and racial reconciliation, two parallel streams of American urban destiny ended RUI's efforts. Covert racial steering and lending remained pillars of urban housing despite an onslaught of federal law and grassroots activism. Studies done on cities across America proved that poor federal oversight allowed most lenders and realtors to continue housing discrimination. Most real estate communities never received requests for mortgage information, and even fewer were compelled by regulatory boards to field the requests they received.[54] Black urban neighborhoods still received significantly less lending investment than the overwhelmingly White suburbs, ensuring that the equity gained from owning homes in Black communities would not be worth the investment for any potential homebuyer.[55] The maintenance of devaluing Black working-class neighborhoods mixed with the easing of racist housing practices elsewhere to kill neighborhood integrity. While some notable Black inner-city neighborhoods withstood racist lending and capital flight, most Black neighborhoods in Richmond, like those in many southern cities, experienced a large exodus of upwardly mobile Black professionals to the suburbs, a process otherwise known as "Black Flight."[56] This flight was economically driven for Blacks, as they desired premium housing and quality schools—the trappings of American life and the fulfillment of the promises of the modern civil rights movement. The intersection of racist lending and Black flight perpetuated the "two societies" that Illinois governor Otto Kerner Jr. warned about in 1968.[57] While the chocolate city–vanilla suburb dynamic remained largely undisturbed in the early to mid-1980s, RUI's housing fight, by all measurable indication, effectively ended redlining in Richmond, allowing Blacks and Whites to, should they wish, live among each other as equals for the first time in city history.

"Everyone Should at Least Consider Getting a Piece of the Pie"

Around 8:30 every Wednesday morning in the summer, groups of volunteers met with Black inner-city youth—ages twelve through sixteen—and their parents at the Capitol Square grounds.[58] The volunteers, children, and parents then boarded charter buses to spend the day at Camp Fernlake in New Kent County or the Oceanfront area of Virginia Beach. This program, known at the time as Wednesday's Child, put RUI in closer connection with local YMCAs, churches, civic leagues, and the local, Black-owned Metropolitan Bus Co. to create a safe summer program for inner-city youth.[59]

For those who liked the forest, "the heat of the summer streets was turned into the cool of the wooded slope," as they spent six hours hiking thirty minutes southeast of Richmond. Those who did not like the woods had the option to go further east toward the ocean, where they could enjoy the summer days along the beach.[60] In both locations RUI required the three hundred or so youths to spend some allotted time reading books provided for them by the Richmond Public Library. The children also participated in arts-and-crafts projects, and some even learned interpretive dance.[61] This type of summer program was normally reserved for middle- and upper-class children, often White children. "It would be arrogant for us in the Richmond Urban Institute to claim to be the conscience of Richmond," the group openly touted in newsletters, "but we can certainly claim to be part of its conscience. And part of its consciousness."[62] RUI, under the direction of Edythe Rodgers specifically, believed that it had a moral responsibility to remain amorphous enough to provide inner-city families with childcare options that their wallets denied them, even if it required RUI to spend much of its entire summer budget (around $15,000) to maintain it.[63]

RUI's community engagement work went well beyond charity: it challenged the very nature and unresponsiveness of Richmond city government. "It is clear that city revenues can no longer keep pace with a basic minimum of services for the preservation of a healthy city," Rodgers once told RUI members in disappointment. She continued: "Richmonders must address this crisis first on a local level, with whatever weapons we can muster. If the citizens of greater Richmond cannot respond to it on the local level, then (as we have seen), it is highly unlikely that they will support state or federal policies which address it."[64] She understood the racial undertones of blaming the inadequacies of local government on incompetence. Thus, she helped RUI fill in the void as best it could.

While the organization could not provide any of the social services that city government did, or even make up for all of city government's pitfalls, Wednesday's Child was but one iteration of RUI further entrenching itself deeper into the Richmond community by working to correct real life issues. While the group was heavily involved with the youth, RUI also focused much of its energy on helping parents. One of the major issues they dealt with was transportation inequality.

Richmond had a long history of racial inequality in mass transportation. During the days of slavery, free Blacks and slaves received segregated and unequal service on commercial carriers. Blacks received some reprieve after April 1865; however, the first streetcar provider (1888), taxi cab services (1920), and bus systems (1943) implemented and enforced segregated services, even when local and state law did not require them to do so.[65] It was not until the arrest of two Black women named Sarah Pettaway and Lavinia Wilder in 1943 and, eventually, Black attorney and NAACP member Samuel Wilbur Tucker in 1946, that Richmond dealt with Black defiance to transportation inequality.[66] Local carriers, notably the Virginia Transit Co., ended any and all segregated services in 1956 when dozens of young Black adults made a habit of forcing bus drivers to enforce segregated seating. The Richmond Hustings Courts gave Black protestors petty fines for almost a decade until the US Supreme Court nullified all state segregation laws dealing with transportation in 1964.[67]

Like with housing and education, the passing of Jim Crow did not create racially equitable transportation services in Richmond. White flight to the suburbs and increased ownership of automobiles forced bus companies to consolidate their services into a city-owned, nonprofit firm named Greater Richmond Transit Company (GRTC).[68] Upon its inception in September 1973, Henrico and Chesterfield Counties refused to accept GRTC services. This prohibition remained until the early 2010s because of the racist fears, expressed by both Black and White suburbanites, that public transportation operated as a one-way system that allowed inner-city Blacks access to areas of town that money and status clearly denied them. The wealthy White West End also refused public bus services, yet working-class and poor Black Richmonders still had little to no access to quality public transportation. GRTC's directors drew ineffective bus routes that made it impossible for poor people to navigate the city in a timely manner. Some areas of town became "transit deserts": places where public buses refused to go.[69] RUI members worked within various civic groups to form a bus-rider committee composed of an equal number of Blacks and Whites.[70] This committee drafted a list of complaints and requested to meet with GRTC officials about creating more effective transportation services.[71]

RUI's public transportation mission faced more obstacles than the previous fight for more equitable housing. Whereas urban grassroots communities pushed legislators at the regional and national levels to create America's first wave of open housing, they all but closed the door on providing meaningful public transportation for the working and underclasses that were left behind by the economy.[72] By the 1970s and 1980s, mass transit providers across the nation suffered financially from poor management, reduced ridership, and increased urban crime. In sum, fares went up while rider safety and quality went down. Legislators in every region pushed for the creation of publicly owned transit authorities that would buy and effectively run their failing, privately owned bus companies. Taxpayers in densely packed, transit-friendly northeastern and midwestern cities supported the public takeover of mass transportation.[73] Sunbelt cities, however, wanted nothing to do with public transportation. Not only were they more automobile-friendly in terms of infrastructure and population density, the politically active White suburbanites resisted public transportation because of the fear that it would bridge the suburban-urban divide and allow poor Blacks access to their neighborhoods.[74] The few places that did implement metropolitan transit systems (Atlanta, Houston, and Washington, DC) compromised greatly by creating inefficient routes that did not penetrate the affluent suburbs that rested within Atlanta's Buckhead and Marietta, Houston's River Oaks, and DC's Georgetown area.[75]

Richmond's efforts to reform the GRTC did not fit in the national or regional mold because White suburbanites had no political say in the process. The failures of annexation cemented the independence of Virginia localities, ensuring that meaningful White suburbs had no say in urban governance. This privilege was also a burden. City leaders cared little about improving public transportation because it, unlike malls, could not attract suburban Whites back to Richmond. RUI then embedded their transportation reform efforts within the classist revitalization agenda. They argued that public transportation was imperative to revitalization because the shoppers, employers, and the few yuppies needed affordable access to every part of the city.[76] It was not until RUI spoke the language of revitalization that they gained an audience with members of city council and Richmond Renaissance.

RUI spent much of 1982 and 1983 "urging the city and areas businesses [to] make a long-term commitment to full service transit."[77] While RUI and city political and business leaders agreed that transportation was vital to Richmond's present and future, they did not agree on which form of transportation—buses or cars—should take precedent in urban planning. Richmond Renaissance wanted to construct more parking decks and meters to cater to the suburban tourists who saw downtown as a place to work and shop. In believing that downtown should be a space occupied more by people than buildings, RUI wanted the GRTC and Richmond Renaissance to prioritize mass transit with the creation of more bus routes and fewer parking spots. "Development is not simply a matter of dollars and buildings. One must look for the creation of urban spaces which are busy, buoyant, habitable, and peopled, rather than desolate parking lots, concrete parks, and potted plants," RUI told Richmond Renaissance and GRTC leadership. RUI used contemporary literature that showed how America's fastest-growing cities, many of them in the South, had adopted some form of efficient public transportation. Furthermore, they warned that the continued strategy of "development without people" would result in empty downtown spaces and corporate buildings filled with suburban residents who used expressways to take the money they earned away from the city.[78]

Richmond Renaissance and GRTC, like city government as a whole, were well aware that, as said in a RUI statement to them, "the interests of low and moderate income persons, healthy city neighborhoods, strategies for housing and control of displacement, public transportation, job creation, etc.—are not peripheral to the life of a healthy city."[79] However, realism ruled the day. Richmond Renaissance and GRTC refused to centralize public transportation within revitalization plans. Most Americans and Richmond-area residents with means used private forms of transportation. They reasoned that this fact alone made centralizing bus services counterproductive. Looking back on the failed negotiations, Campbell remembered that local elites felt that public transportation should operate like public housing; since it mainly served the poor, there was no need to improve it. City elites did compromise some by working with RUI to mitigate political and economic barriers that prohibited quality transportation services.[80]

GRTC made it clear to RUI and Richmond Renaissance that federal cuts to the city budget "will reduce GRTC revenue by 20% and require either a 40% curtailment in GRTC services or an increase in fares."[81] Richmond Renaissance secured some funding for the GRTC from local banks, which, because of their constant mergers and troubles with redlining in the past, needed every reason to "reinvest" in the community. Black state delegates Benjamin J. Lambert III and L. Douglas Wilder—both members of Richmond Renaissance—advocated, although unsuccessfully, for the Virginia legislature to help subsidize the GRTC at RUI's request.[82] GRTC

FIGURE 3. Richmond Urban Institute brochure. (Courtesy of the Richmond Urban Institute Collection, Virginia Commonwealth University Special Collections)

and Richmond Renaissance also agreed to improve some transportation routes, make newer ones available, and maintain fares as low as they could.[83] Still, public transportation would not become a priority for Richmond until the maturity of gentrification in the 2010s, when Richmond was under the leadership of Mayor Levar Stoney.

While Richmond Renaissance largely worked at an arm's length from RUI, the latter focused much of its work around efforts "to complement . . . citywide economic development efforts, such as Richmond Renaissance."[84] The line-item failures with transportation made RUI accept that both income and race combined to disempower the city's largely Black working class. "Economic development," RUI once stated in disgust, such as "banking and business were fields that poor and minority people were not privy to."[85] They collected census data for unemployment, poverty, home ownership, family dynamics, and race throughout Richmond before setting in motion a plan to create small-business consolidation and growth within the most depressed communities.[86]

RUI's food co-ops temporarily "employ[ed] the unskilled and hard to employ" while also "teaching entrepreneurial and financial skills to those who would not customarily be exposed to them" and "involving minorities,

152   THE STRUGGLE FOR CHANGE

FIGURE 4. Richmond Urban Institute–run Community Co-op. (Courtesy of the Richmond Urban Institute Collection, Virginia Commonwealth University Special Collections)

women, and other excluded groups in economic decisions." Urban Black neighborhoods filled with underskilled adults and youth, such as Hillside, Oak Grove, and Bellemeade, engaged in gardening, farming, and selling their own goods at places called the Potato Patch and Food Buying Club.[87] These programs only lasted a few years, as they were largely unsuccessful due to spotty community participation and low return on investment. RUI had to abandon their vision for Black working-class economic autonomy. As a substitute, RUI worked with Richmond Public Schools, local manufacturers (allied as the Private Industry Council of Richmond), and VCU to create A Joint Venture in Youth Education: "A unique year round work-learn program designed to provide employment for Richmond area high school youth while training them to find and hold jobs with 'major' employers."[88] Local businesses (around thirty-four in total) donated almost $400,000 to run the program over a decade, creating five hundred new jobs for those who would have normally been locked out of the local economy.[89] While RUI did not create a new economic independence for the Black working class, they "introduced hundreds of Richmonders to the idea that everyone should at least consider getting a piece of the pie."[90]

"The Demise of the Institute"

As I sat and chatted with Benjamin Campbell on that chilly day in March 2019, he remained surprisingly silent. It was as if he had forgotten that RUI helped transform Richmond by filtering the racial reconciliation sentiment down to the grassroots. In the process, RUI redefined its meaning by prioritizing improvements to city life for the majority of city residents. The archives were painstakingly clear about RUI's birth and peak. What was not clear, however, was RUI's demise. The organization of about thirty swelled to around a hundred in 1983.[91] By the late 1980s, RUI's membership was back down to a meager fifteen.[92] This loss in membership coincided with the clear distress calls in their later memos about declining funds. RUI had somehow lost its place in Richmond's body politick, relying on selling pre-packaged dinners and hosting antiracism talks to raise money.[93] An internal memo from 1986 stated that while "we do not at all envision the demise of the institute, next year RUI will conduct its operations with part-time or no staff." For the future, they proposed making RUI "an organization which will be significantly different in structure, one that gives less effort to fundraising but more effort to provide research, mediation, and vision within the Richmond Community."[94] A year later, they became less than that.

Although the "what" was crystal clear, the "why" was beyond baffling. Was money the real reason RUI closed its doors? Campbell quickly dismissed that assumption and summed up RUI's collapse as a typical Richmond race issue. While the complete narrative is not clear, Campbell claimed that the deeper RUI dug into the city's issues, voices of dissent rang louder about racism within the organization. RUI's work ran afoul of the Black political power structure because it pointed to the obvious systemic issues that they could not fix from city hall. In a city where politics was divided along the racial line, RUI's work appeared to be targeting the competence of Black leadership. The worst part was that the voices of dissent rang louder within the organization, as some Black members—namely the Black female co-missioners—accused the White members of racism. Campbell would not give details that day, but the issues paralyzed RUI from the inside out, draining its membership and crippling its impact on city affairs. Campbell spoke with regret in revealing that he was one of the members accused of racism. The accusation itself did very little to his reputation, but the handling of it made him and others, both Black and White, disengage from RUI, especially after the organization agreed to fire Campbell in 1987. With the intellectual founder of the organization gone, RUI dissolved soon after in summer 1990.

RUI is not just an item in a catalog of failures by Richmonders to rid their city of racism. Its demise is proof that Richmonders worked beyond their elites to redefine what racial reconciliation meant after the modern civil rights movement. While RUI's efforts were, like urban revitalization, too compromised by the issues brought on by suburbanization, these residents refused to give up on their city. They envisioned a Richmond that was inner-city focused, where Blacks and the few remaining Whites prioritized the improvement of urban life for themselves and not the anticipated suburban tourists and newcomers. RUI envisioned a Richmond that did not exist, yet they sought to use every mechanism at their disposal to create it. While it took decades for city government to deprioritize the suburbs in its economic planning, RUI emboldened later residents to reimagine Richmond as a place where both races acknowledged their division as rooted in an uncomfortable history. RUI died a very Richmond death; its spirit, however, did not.

8

Moral Re-Armament and Hope in the Cities

HEALING THE HEART OF AMERICA

THERE ARE very few American neighborhoods that have maintained their cultural integrity longer than Richmond's Oregon Hill. Today, the residents are largely young urban professionals and students at Virginia Commonwealth University. However, the area's origins lie not with yuppies—the current manifestation of gentrification and urban revitalization, but quite the opposite. The neighborhood that sits above the James River area was long home to the White working class who labored along the docks of the Kanawha Canal. The neighborhood expanded along with the city in the twentieth century, housing many blue-collar manufacturing and service workers and their families. For most of Richmond's history, Oregon Hill was a poor White community that did not, until recently, receive meaningful bank investment. In 1990 around 90 percent of the homes were more than fifty years old and had been mildly updated. Most occupants were renters who earned less than $14,000 annually. Fewer than half of the residents attended high school; even fewer finished high school and earned college degrees. Most importantly, this dying inner-city community was known for being the most racist neighborhood in Richmond.[1]

Black Richmonders knew for most of the twentieth century, as was said by a current Black bureaucrat about his childhood in the city, "to stay away from Oregon Hill. There is a part of town that is not safe for Black kids; because you know, they're racist."[2] He remembered being told that in the 1970s; however, little had changed by 1990. Even as the city helped elect one of its Black sons (L. Douglas Wilder) to be governor of Virginia in 1989, Oregon Hill residents, living just one mile west of the Executive Mansion, still hoisted Confederate flags on their front lawns and picket fences. Black policemen were often dissuaded from patrolling the area. Black bus drivers and mailmen were often rerouted away from the neighborhood by their supervisors as well.[3] While all of Richmond knew that Oregon Hill was "mostly White and middle-to-low-income," as the *Times-Dispatch* said in 1990, a Black grandmother named Celestine Edmonds jumped at the chance to own her first home, which happened to sit uncomfortably in the area. The tight-knit neighborhood refused to accept Edmonds as one of their own. Instead of being welcomed with freshly baked goods, sweet tea, and moving help, Edmonds woke up one morning to smashed windows and notes on the front door telling her to "go home."[4]

This act of terrorism resulted from Edmonds ignoring the previous attempts to scare her out of the neighborhood. She remembered that her house guests (all Black) were often stared at by her White neighbors. Those who spoke were often greeted with cold shoulders, and in some cases, racial epithets. The consistent maltreatment and hostile environment were not strong enough to keep Edmonds from living in the area. Thus, Edmonds's White neighbors violated the sanctity of her home with "smashed windows, verbal threats, racial epithets, [and] spray-painted KKK letters" on her doors and gate, as reported by the *Afro-American* in August 1990. In that same report, Edmonds admitted that "she had heard about Oregon Hill's reputation," yet Edmonds insisted that she "didn't realize things would get this bad."[5]

Another racist incident happened two months later, across town in the majority Black East End neighborhood of Church Hill. While this area also suffered from decades of divestment and racial isolation, Church Hill was distinctly different from Oregon Hill. Working-class Blacks were moving into Oregon Hill. Middle-class Whites sought to reclaim the East End. They purchased dilapidated properties and placed them on the local historical register. This gentrification strategy forced Blacks to either renovate their homes and pay higher property taxes or leave the neighborhood. Some Black homeowners appealed to the mostly Black city council in protest. "Leave us alone. . . . If you want restrictions for yourself, fine, but don't impose them on me," a disgruntled Black resident stated after receiving word that the council originally sided with gentrifying Whites. The incoming Whites insisted that they wanted to raise the property and aesthetic value of the area. Blacks saw it as a clear effort to remove them from their ancestral homeland, a sentiment and battle that is still being fought in Richmond's East End.[6]

Both stories placed pressure on city government to, once again, address its racial history. The council and police conducted community discussions and door-to-door visits with White Oregon Hill residents to hopefully end the recent acts of terrorism. The discussions were fruitful in that both the council and police assured the public that, as was said by a Black councilman to the *Times-Dispatch,* "Black and White citizens can co-exist in

Oregon Hill."[7] White Oregon Hill residents enacted this sentiment by helping restore Edmonds's home without cost to her or the city.[8] The council also reluctantly sided with Black Church Hill residents by voting to overturn the establishment of Church Hill as a historic area where residents had to renovate their homes and pay higher property taxes. By getting out in front of both issues, and essentially coaxing them out of the public limelight, city leaders proved that they were not isolated incidents. In fact, they were reminders that after decades of interracialism among local elites, Richmond was nowhere near racially reconciled, and that division was best seen not downtown—where Richmonders worked and voted—but at the neighborhood level, where, three decades after the modern civil rights movement, residents still lived their lives along the color line.[9]

To solve this, progressive Richmond residents helped bridge the city's Black-White racial divide through acknowledging and investigating their shared history of racism. The growth of newer interracial neighborhood groups and civic-minded academic organizations inspired the museum community to interpret Black public history. This emphasis on celebrating Black life within traditionally White institutions, in a city known for venerating its Confederate past, allowed residents to understand that their contemporary divides were historical in nature. This realization helped Black and White Richmonders identify as one citizenry for the first time ever. Richmonders displayed their new racial understanding through a national conference where they proclaimed to the world that their city was ready to set racial division on the path to extinction. While this awakening did not lead directly to policy changes that remedied past discrimination, it was this crucial period, primarily between 1990 and 1993, when residents acknowledge that they had a race problem that could no longer be ignored.

"A Different Vision for Richmond"

Not too long after the Oregon Hill and Church Hill episodes, the city council took a major step toward the twenty-first century by removing Confederate symbols from the city flag. This decision was not monumental given that the flag had been out of use since the 1940s. Even worse, the long-overdue change did next to nothing to address why Richmond's racial issues festered to the realm of being newsworthy.[10] The reality was that Oregon Hill and Church Hill, not an out-of-use flag, were very representative of Richmond's lingering racial divide. Neighborhoods bore the largest brunt, as racial segregation reflected socioeconomic disparities between Blacks and Whites. While the elite of both races shared neighborhoods, schools, and occupations, the middle and working classes stayed within their enclaves, and they had little to no interest in interacting with the opposite race.

Richmond's racial division was not all-encompassing, as seen by the Carillon neighborhood. This mixed-race, middle-class community was a Richmond anomaly. By the 1990s Carillon did not have to worry about racial terrorism or the threat of city-sponsored gentrification. They also did not experience severe divestment, decay, and rebirth; nor was it integrated against the will of longtime residents. Carillon was an all-White neighborhood on its inception, located just steps away from the famous Carillon Bell Tower and William Byrd Park in the Near West End. Its White residents loved their neighborhood enough to resist suburban flight between the 1960s and 1980s. When upwardly mobile Blacks moved in, Whites stayed and made their neighborhood a beacon of light in the sea of darkness that was modern Richmond.[11]

Carillon's unique makeup came from the formation of a mission-driven civic organization designed to maintain residential integrity. "The neighborhood was in an utter panic," said White Carillon resident Frank Gilbert about the late 1960s. His home sat in an area that was rife with realtors looking to blockbust and racially steer prospective buyers. Realtors were not shy about signaling prospective Whites to not live there by letting them know that the neighborhood was "in transition." Between 1964 and 1968, Carillon went from all White to 40 percent Black residency. The reason was simply that a glut of affordable homes were being newly constructed in the area; another bumper crop emerged from Whites flowing to bigger homes in the suburbs. Unlike then-mayor and real estate attorney Phil Bagley, who moved out of the neighborhood when Black residency increased, Gilbert and a number of Whites loved living in the Carillon. More importantly, they valued living in what was then called a "mixed community." Thus, some Whites formed the Carillon Civic Association (CCA) in 1968 (later incorporated in 1970) and invited new Black residents—such as local professors Timothy Langston and Rutledge Dennis and attorneys JeRoyd Greene and Harold Marsh Sr., for example—to join. The CCA met weekly in each other's homes to create familiarity and community, where Blacks and Whites combated racial segregation by simply becoming neighbors who were neighborly. Some of their efforts manifested in the races sharing a neighborhood school and placing "Good Neighbors Come in All Colors" ads for the neighborhood in the local papers.[12]

Interracial communion was difficult to come by for most of Richmond; the reason may be that it all appeared to be in Carillon. Just a few miles from both Oregon Hill and Church Hill, in the heart of the former Confederate capital, Black and White Carillon residents communed with each other daily. They had dinners, barbeques, game and movie nights; their children had sleepovers and playdates. Whites and Black picked each other's children up from school and supervised them until their parents could retrieve them. Whites and Blacks in Carillon even housed each other's guests from out of town. "Nobody had ever asked if their White friends could stay in my house before," a Black Carillon resident once said when describing her neighborhood.[13]

While its interracialism was widespread, touching every home within the tight-knit community, Carillon's centerpiece eventually became 1103 Sunset Avenue. This two-story colonial home was built in 1955. It was not until the late 1970s that it was occupied by Rob and Susan Corcoran. Rob and Susan were British immigrants who worked for a nonprofit, multifaith international organization called Moral Re-Armament (MRA)—now known as Initiatives of Change. Started as a peacebuilding group in Oxford, England, in the 1930s and funded by wealthy philanthropists and nonprofit organizations, Moral Re-Armament specialized in connecting diverse and rival communities along the commonalities of faith and goodwill. It was this mission, to connect disparate communities in America, that helped the Corcorans land in Richmond in 1977. They were two of the several MRA members who would travel and settle in the states around this time.[14]

Most MRA members had exact plans for how they would reshape the areas they moved to. The Corcorans had no such plans. They intended to help make Richmond a more harmonious place, but most importantly, they wanted to make Richmond the city to raise their prospective children. Part of that plan was finding a place to live. Upon accepting a request from fellow white and elderly MRA members to settle in Richmond and touring homes, it appeared as if every city neighborhood was largely segregated by race and class. They later found that most neighborhoods in their price point were, indeed, segregated or "in transition"—except for Carillon. After moving into 1103 Sunset Avenue, what would be their home for more than thirty years, Black neighbors Collie and Audrey Burton approached them and welcomed them over for dinner, as was the custom for prospective new neighbors. While not being Americans, Virginians, or Richmonders, the Corcorans knew that the invitation was abnormal: the races in Richmond were very much self-segregated. With the help of MRA, the Burtons, and others, the Corcorans turned 1103 Sunset Avenue into a community gathering place that would eventually export the Carillon attitude throughout the rest of the city.[15]

Settling into Carillon was not difficult for the English couple. Almost immediately after the move, they integrated into the neighborhood by first attending, and later hosting, potlucks, barbeques, and block parties. The most controversial discussions at these events were not about race: rather it was that everyone read the "please bring a vegetable, salad, or dessert" request and brought another meat instead.[16] Moving to Carillon was as seamless as putting the right slipper on the right foot; however, dealing with a city that was nothing like Carillon was uncomfortable and required constant readjustment. When the Corcorans grocery shopped or paid bills, they noticed that Blacks and Whites largely avoided each other. The issue became more obvious when they sought out interracial civic groups and found that they were few and far between. The couple wanted to make sense of Richmond's racial division, but residents outside of Carillon were more comfortable allowing the ghosts of slavery, Jim Crow, Massive Resistance, urban renewal, busing, redlining, and the recently failed urban revitalization remain at rest. The quietude about the city's racial history did not prevent all from describing how deep the racial divide was. Richmonders cared so little for the racial harmony of the Carillon that a friendly White resident once told the unfamiliar couple that because they lived there, "[other] White folks will not come into your house."[17]

The Corcorans found that Richmond's race issues were deeply rooted, but not impossible to overcome. After several in-depth conversations with their Carillon neighbors, the Corcorans learned that in general, White Richmonders did not see the racial divide as a problem that infected every facet of city life. Blacks, on the other hand, distrusted even the most well-meaning Richmond Whites. They saw the continuation of de facto segregation as proof that Whites hated them; and in many ways, that feeling was mutual. This revelation helped the Corcorans recruit members for Moral Re-Armament. When approaching White civic groups, they spoke to the political and social issues that racial division caused by not proclaiming to be the authority on racial matters. Rather they sat, listened, and asked how their organization could facilitate better race relations. These efforts produced a harvest where, as Rob later said in an interview, "enough people, within the [Black and White] communit[ies], who had a different vision for Richmond" decided to work with them.[18] The original members of Richmond's branch of MRA were housewives, college students, social workers, and teachers. The most notable members were local Black civil rights activists Collie and Audrey Burton and assistant city manager A. Howe Todd.[19]

The Corcorans made a point to bring their new members into the Carillon, where Whites and Blacks formed a functioning interracial community. The base of that community was 1103 Sunset Avenue, the site of many potluck dinners where discussions about race were shared over fried chicken and deviled eggs. It was at those dinners where the Corcorans came to understand that the racial divide was a product of Richmond being insularly trapped in its racial history. The majority of residents were born and raised within the city limits. Even those who traveled did so with family and friends of the same race. Division was all they knew; it was a shock that even this many were willing to imagine a city where it did not exist. These discussions were furthered by the urban revitalization headed by city elites and the improvements to housing and transportation by the RUI. Although both movements failed to deliver an interracial Richmond, they generated, as one Black Richmonder stated, "the most positive seasons" for race relations the city had ever experienced. She went on to describe the mid-1980s by saying that upon returning from college, "I found White and Black people very hopeful, and I had not seen that before I left."[20] The 1103 Sunset Avenue potlucks became a major expression of this hope. As Robert stated: "Those potluck dinners were an important foundational piece of building the network." To move the group beyond communion, the Corcorans decided to bridge the interpersonal gaps created by racial division. They helped Richmond MRA members travel abroad together between 1983 and 1990.[21]

The overseas travel brought to the surface how Richmond's deeply embedded racial issues infected even the most well-meaning Black and White locals. The Corcorans had an inkling that their group was "not the best pick from a recruiting point of view," as Rob once said reflectively. They were an insular bunch who, in the round, had not traveled much beyond Richmond and the American South. The Black members were mostly working- and middle-class college students and professionals who had little experience around non-Black people. The White members were mostly middle-class professionals. A few were affluent, "predominantly elderly and predominantly conservative." In sum, the Whites, according to Rob, were "happy to talk about reconciliation[;] they weren't so happy to talk about racism."[22] Their few life experiences with the opposite race made the initial trips through Africa, Europe, and Asia difficult.[23] The group often disagreed about the reality and effects of racism, as well as how to achieve even the slightest bit of reconciliation. Opinions about these key issues were, like most things in Richmond, divided heavily along the racial line.

There was not a single, catalyzing moment when the group came together and agreed to work through their differences. Rob remembers that it took a series of events to bring the group together. A White member recalled that through the heated debates and hurt feelings, "we learned that when we talk about problems, what we must have is a spirit of sharing and a willingness to hear the other person." The majority of the problems—most of which were not recorded in the documentary record—came from a collective sense of doubt that Moral Re-Armament's emphasis on putting Blacks and Whites in close contact could bring racial healing to their own lives, let alone the rest of the city. After all, as one Black traveler remembered thinking while overseas, "Some of us had been antagonists for years." This delegation, most of them housewives and college students, may not have thought of themselves as part of a chartering group for racial reconciliation in Richmond and the nation, but they were. They learned how to teach Black and White people without power and influence to acknowledge and resolve issues created by historical discrimination. Perfected during the overseas trips between 1983 and 1990, these lessons would be key as they laid the foundation for residents to follow, given that Richmond was a city quite comfortable with being divided.[24]

Their summers traveling and the news headlines that appeared in along the way made, as a Black member recalled, "so many White organizations, churches, as well as individual leaders in the Richmond area want to be a part of what we were doing."[25] Before departing on one of the first overseas trips, Rob Corcoran told the original MRA members that "there needs to be a greater awareness of MRA as a force in the city."[26] When they came back, public officials and civic leaders began attending the Corcorans' monthly potlucks and workshops on interracial dialog at 1103 Sunset Avenue. This massive movement reflected the emergence of the once hidden, now public racial progressives (both White and Black) who shared Moral Re-Armament's vision for a truly interracial Richmond.[27] Joining these local ministers, councilmembers, museum curators, professors, and journalists were foreign MRA visitors from Africa and Europe, as well as members from other cities across America. These potlucks emerged into invitations for Richmond members to speak at civic meetings about interracial dialog from New York to California. Of those interviewed for this project, most agreed that there was a distinct difference between the outpouring of progressivism in Richmond in the 1980s and 1990s, yet they mostly struggled to identify why that was. The documentary evidence shows that it was MRA's efforts that galvanized a newer sense of hope among residents who were looking to improve race relations at the most granular level. Rob Corcoran said it best: "I don't think we could have done it if we did not have the international experience" with Moral Re-Armament.[28]

Those who attended MRA events left the Carillon neighborhood more emboldened to systematize their new interracial feeling throughout the city. A major site for this was Virginia Commonwealth University (VCU). Located downtown, VCU was an "urban university" that resulted from the 1968 merger of the Medical College of Virginia (founded in 1838) and the Richmond Professional Institute (founded in 1917). VCU's place in Richmond is unique for many reasons, the most relevant being that it emerged, as recently chronicled by historian John T. Kneebone and former VCU president Eugene P. Trani, in the nexus of the urban crisis and twilight of the national consensus to fund the expansion of higher education. VCU grew into a comprehensive research institution while being seated within a politically unstable and economically dying Richmond in the 1980s. A vital part of this growth was its forward-thinking agenda to maintain an above-average Black student population, progressive curriculum, and civic-minded faculty.[29]

This faculty, mostly Whites and some Blacks, used research and civic engagement to revive Richmond from its broken political and social state, some of which resulted in the rise and fall of the Richmond Urban Institute. The most notable were political scientists John V. Moeser, Rutledge M. Dennis, Robert D. Holsworth, and W. Avon Drake, along with social work and education professors Willie J. Dell (the first Black city councilwoman), Grace Harris, Joyce Beckett, psychologist Maxine Clark, and historian Phillip Schwartz. This core, along with others, helped transition VCU from being just a commuter school located within an urban setting to a socially conscious university focused on growing within an increasingly integrated city.[30] By 1990 this core worked with newly inaugurated President Trani to improve the university's rotting relationship with its Black neighbors, who for decades saw the university, in sum, as a gentrification vehicle to push them out of the inner city.[31] With the communally engaging Afro-American Studies umbrella program, VCU faculty and administrators created projects such as VCU Mentoring, Varieties of Undergraduate Experience, Going-for-the-Goal, and Adopt-a-School. These programs helped ensure that Black residents saw VCU as a neighbor who, in the midst of its expansion, helped tear down the wall between progrowth urban policy and Black progress.[32]

Whereas VCU used community engagement and uplift to mend Black residents' relationship with city planning, the museum community reinterpreted Richmond's lily-White public history narrative. "Particularly in the [19]90s, there was a greater push for diversity of audience," a local museum director remembered.[33] This national and local push came from both academics and museum curators who wanted public history to serve the cultural interests of more than just wealthy White people. They understood that diversity of audience required museums to become more than repositories of local artifacts: they had to be the interpreters of the past who helped explain a relevant present. In a city such as Richmond, that meant abandoning hero-worshipping exhibits about southern White men to take a critical approach to race. The Valentine Museum took the first major step in 1990 when its newer curators acknowledged to their board that since "race will remain the most important issue in the area," the museum should become "a partner in creating public policy." Being this partner required the museum to become "a catalyst to create an image for Richmond, organized around the city's history" with race and racial discrimination. Creating this image, they believed, required race history to be "both implicit and explicit in the museum's plans."[34]

Incorporating Richmond's uncomfortable history into its exhibits was not new for the Valentine. Founded in 1898 by patriarch Mann S. Valentine II, Richmond's oldest museum was an urban-focused institution that had always taken a "bottom-up," social approach to constructing and interpreting its exhibits. Even if they were unoffensive and lacking nuance, histories of women, immigrants, Blacks, and the White working class always had a home at 1050 East Clay Street. It was not until 1985, however, that the Valentine (undoubtedly informed by the urban revitalization movement) addressed the history of race relations more directly. This shift cost them in terms of the "number and composition of the museum's [traditional] audience, which was then a primarily, elite [White] audience."[35] Yet newer staff, such as Frank Jewell, Marie Tyler-McGraw, and Gregg D. Kimball, ensured that their exhibits interpreted Richmond's racial history through the lens of racism. At the dawn of the 1990s, the Valentine earned national acclaim, as well as millions in grants, for reinterpreting southern history and becoming "a leader among American museums [by] setting new standards and developing an agenda for history museums throughout the nation."[36]

While incorporating Black people into the broader story about Richmond, the Valentine discussed every phase of America's racial history. The African Presence in the Americas exhibit, for example, used colorful artifacts, griots, dancers, and cuisines from the various ethnic groups represented in the Middle Passage to tell the story of African resistance to the dehumanization of slavery.[37] Shared Spaces, Separate Lives continued that discussion, as curators informed their visitors that antebellum Richmond was more than gaudy mansions and factories along Tobacco Row.

Rather, the Valentine used reenactors and materials to tell the story that Richmond, and the antebellum South as a whole, was built on the "interdependence of unequals," namely slaves and working-class Whites.[38]

The museum was well ahead of its time by partnering with premier historians Eric Foner, Barbara Fields, Ira Berlin, Edward L. Ayers, David Goldfield, and others to lead a "powerful reexamination of Reconstruction" in "the capital of the Confederacy." Making Richmond the chief vector for the public reexamination of Reconstruction, the Valentine helped wash the public consciousness of the Dunning School interpretation that Reconstruction was the folly of opportunist northern Whites and ignorant southern Blacks.[39] They continued this narrative with the Second Street exhibition. With over fifty oral history interviews, resident and guest curators used the history of Black Richmond's notorious Jackson Ward, more so its place in the Black entertainment and entrepreneurial network, to discuss how racism informed America's transition from the Jazz Age to World War II.[40]

The Valentine did not shy away from the recent past of the modern civil rights movement. Instead of featuring sanitized exhibits on beloved figures such as Dr. Martin Luther King Jr. and Rosa Parks, the Valentine connected the historically Black Virginia Union University with the historically White University of Richmond and VCU to discuss the impact of Black Power and the controversial Malcolm X. With exhibits like these, the Valentine wished to simply become an interpreter of relevant histories in the Richmond area. The long-term impact of these exhibits, however, was that public history became the language to discuss race as the prime agent of social change, a development that, while continuing into the present day, the Valentine can claim itself to be a prime mover of.[41] The proof of their success can be found in their growth and diversity in audience. In 1985 fewer than 25,000 people (less than 1 percent of them Black) visited the Valentine annually. By the mid-1990s Black attendance was around 12 percent, and over a hundred thousand people visited the museum on a yearly basis.[42]

The Valentine's push toward a more inclusive public narrative was a product of a desire for more diversity within public history, and that came from a desire for racial reconciliation among Richmonders themselves.[43] Their efforts trickled across town, to the Museum District, where the once-ultraconservative Virginia Historical Society (now Virginia Museum of History and Culture) opened its doors by hiring a Black curator (Dr. Lauranett Lee) and integrating the story of slavery and racism into its normally Civil War–heavy, Lost Cause programing.[44] Its neighboring institution, the Virginia Museum of Fine Arts, also known for being a former

Confederate Veterans Home, joined the city's movement by answering charges of racism by diversifying its collections and interpretations.⁴⁵

None of them outdid the Museum of the Confederacy, however. In August 1991 the institute tried its hand at reconciliatory public history with its first annual Down Home Family Reunion festival in Jackson Ward's Abner Park. The events included an exhibition entitled Before Freedom Came: African American Life in the Antebellum South, as well as traditional West African dances and food—fried chicken, corn-fried fish, snaps, and hoe cakes. The all-White Museum of the Confederacy did not conduct this event on its own; rather, it sponsored the Elegba Folklore Society (EFS), a group that had the cultural competency to run such activities.⁴⁶ In sponsoring this organization, the museum effectively linked the long-disconnected Black and White museum and arts communities, solidifying the foundation of racial reconciliation created by the grassroots movements before them.

Founded in 1990 by Janine Bell, a Black native of Greensboro, North Carolina, EFS taught interpretive dance in the Richmond area to spread awareness, knowledge, and appreciation for African culture in a city where it was rarely ever acknowledged.⁴⁷ EFS also provided "cultural history tours" that "interprets unmarked sites in Richmond's history." Helping the folklorists were the Richmond and Henrico parks departments, who helped them produce musical dramas and popup art galleries about Richmond's antebellum slave market. Influencing Bell's and EFS's activities was the Ezibu Muntu African Dance Company, a group founded at VCU in 1973. Seeing this cultural shift toward interpreting Black history, leadership at the Museum of the Confederacy, a group who, at the time, were seen as anti-Black, reached out to Bell and the EFS to conduct the Down Home Family Reunions as well as other programs about Black history and culture. The partnership between EFS and the Museum of the Confederacy not only netted around 25,000 visitors per event, but it also helped crystalize and disseminate the idea that Richmond could begin shedding its racist identity through reconciling its once–White supremacist public history scene.⁴⁸

"Such a Richmond Occasion"

On a spring day in 1993, Reverend Benjamin L. Campbell was in the middle of a conversation he had little interest in. While people talked around him, Campbell sat facing a window that overlooked downtown while thinking about the history of the very place he sat, a retreat center named Richmond Hill. Located along East Grace Street in the historic Church Hill neighborhood, Richmond Hill was originally a mansion built and occupied in the 1790s by some of the city's wealthiest White families who profited from the slave trade. A year after the Civil War ended, the Order of the Sisters of the Visitation purchased the property, converted it to an all-girls school, and improved the infrastructure with new chapels, dormitories, and enclosed gardens along the perimeter of the property. Their century in Richmond ended with the school closing, the property falling into disrepair, and their Catholic Diocese helping them relocate to suburban Maryland. Soon after, in 1987, an inter-Christian coalition purchased the old property. They eventually turned the dilapidated campus into a prayer retreat for various churches and a common ground for local civic groups to meet. A leading figure in the purchase and purpose of Richmond Hill was Reverend Campbell.

Even in his advanced age, the reverend could recall Richmond Hill's history with painstakingly granular detail. Yet he could not, for the life of him, remember the details of the conversation he was ignoring. What he does remember about this spring day is more important, however. As Campbell gazed out of the window, thinking about Richmond Hill's place in a city that was actively investigating its racial history, he saw a group of Black teenagers walking in an organized fashion near Richmond Hill. The extroverted reverend desperately desired to exit the meeting he sat in, so he used the odd sight of what appeared to be school children outside the center as an excuse to leave.

Upon exiting the front doors, Campbell noticed that the students were led by a Black female teacher. "This was a really important moment in my life," he emotionally said in a later interview. Campbell approached the teacher and inquired about what they were doing near Richmond Hill. The teacher smiled, introduced herself as Nancy Jo Taylor—a history teacher in Richmond Public Schools. She then explained that they were visiting "the unmarked historic sites in the East End of Richmond." Campbell felt a bit baffled because he, a long-time Church Hill resident, "didn't know there were any unmarked sites." Taylor invited Campbell to join the walking tour of his own neighborhood. He accepted the invitation and took a place among the two dozen students. As the tour commenced, Campbell understood that Taylor was no ordinary teacher and that the unmarked sites were a key to better understanding how to advance local conversations about race.[49]

The first stop was just an open field located a few blocks east of Richmond Hill, where English settlers and the Powhatan Confederacy fought for control the densely wooded forest that would later become Richmond. Taylor then took the group south toward the James River. There, she gave a brief history of the many Black Africans who would pass through the Manchester Slave Docks en route to a lifelong sentence of servitude. Slaves who resisted their life sentence often ended up at the next site of the tour: the Lumpkin Slave Jail, otherwise known as the Devil's Half Acre. The tour concluded with a trip to St. John's Church, where American Founding Father Patrick Henry uttered the ironically iconic phrase of "Give Me Liberty or Give Me Death." As Campbell left the eye-opening tour to return to Richmond Hill, he was happy to know that good people were combatting both the city's Lost Cause public history and the poor reputation of city schools. More importantly, he felt compelled to make Taylor's tour the foundational narrative by which Richmonders discussed racial issues. Campbell may have forgotten the original conversation he ignored in Richmond Hill, but he did not forget that tour, and he has "never forgotten her."[50]

Campbell's plan involved the coming together of the growing Moral Re-Armament movement with local Black, museum, and academic communities. This was easier said than done, as Black Richmonders generally distrusted even the most well-meaning Whites. To overcome this barrier within Richmond's grassroots communities, Black civic leaders—those with few meaningful political ties—had to involve themselves in shaping the (up to this point) mostly White and middle-class reconciliation movement. A man named Sylvester Turner remembered this crucial moment in city history all too well.

Today, he is great friends with Campbell, and he works within notable White liberal organizations. When the two first met in spring 1990, however, Turner was as "Black Richmond" as it gets, in that he did not trust most White people beyond where he could see them. At the time he was a Church Hill reverend who was born three years before the conclusion of *Brown* in 1954. When asked about his childhood in Gilpin Court, he briefly and succinctly responded that "you sort of knew your place in Richmond. Certain places were off-limits, primarily because of color," a quote and sentiment that many Black southerners born around that time would empathize with. After a fulfilling career in the US Air Force, Turner returned to 1980s Richmond, where racial harmony among elites was the only visible form of reconciliation. While Black political and White business leaders schmoozed over expensive dinners and collaborated to build new downtown business buildings and malls, Turner remembered that from his experience, most "[White] attitudes and mindsets were not in step with the law."[51]

Turner returned to Richmond as an ordained minister who wanted to serve the community he came from. After just a few years, he became the director of the Peter Paul Development Center—an organization designed to provide family services to Black Church Hill residents. After heading this operation for a few years, Turner realized the limitation of working within Black communities exclusively. Much of the funding and resources for Peter Paul came from White donors and organizations that he had no real access to. Turner's desire to connect with those in power, for the benefit of the families he served, led him to Moral Re-Armament in spring 1990. Peter Paul's staff accepted an invitation to participate in an interracial dialog with MRA at Richmond Hill; a request that emerged from conversations between a Peter Paul employee and MRA members. When Turner arrived, he noticed that "around that table were individuals who were making decisions about the community that I cared the most about."[52] Thus, he knew that he was in the right place.

Turner joined MRA at a time when it confronted the obvious chasm between activity and involvement. Turner felt that, as he later said in an interview, "I knew some things that they didn't know." What he knew was that the spark that MRA created would eventually fizzle out if it was not converted into more formal efforts throughout the city. MRA merely hosted events (informal potlucks and dialog sessions) where Richmonders—ranging from everyday people to the elite—met, ate, and discussed city affairs as equals. They did not, as an organization, directly involve themselves in the events and projects that emerged from their meetings. Turner felt that MRA's power and relevance lay in its ability to unite people; thus, they should be directly involved in shaping, connecting, and growing all reconciliatory programs around the city. Rob and Susan Corcoran and other MRA members were not prepared to go in that direction, given that Richmond already had strong, sustaining grassroots organizations. Turner's dissent cemented him on the outside of the favored group of members; hence, the Corcorans and others did not select him for the delegation to represent them at the annual Moral Re-Armament retreat in Caux, Switzerland, for summer 1990.

As the group boarded their flight in July, Turner waited back in Richmond. The group he encountered a week later was not the same group he wished safe travels to a week prior. As a whole, the travelers came back more receptive to his vision for the organization. The reasons why cannot be extracted from the full-bodied Moral Re-Armament sources currently located in the Richmond offices of Initiatives of Change (the group's name as of 2001). They can, however, be understood when considering changes around the nation that were brought to light by a group of young Black men out of Atlanta, aptly named Black Teens for Advancement (BTA).[53]

BTA was, like the Richmond Moral Re-Armament group, one of the seventy-three delegations representing MRA in Caux. The group was not, however, filled with well-off White liberals and Black middle-class urbanites. These Black boys, and the Black male teachers that mentored them, traveled from a small, one-story home office along Ponce De Leon Avenue in Atlanta. According to the *Atlanta Journal-Constitution,* this corridor was once "the grandest of boulevards" with "oak-lined thoroughfare dotted with drug stores with soda fountains and kiddie matinees." By 1990 the once-desirable suburban outskirt failed to weather the storms of White flight. Longtime residents "bemoaned its passing from the safe, shady thoroughfare it once was." Except for a few well-maintained neighborhoods, Ponce De Leon Avenue was nothing short of "a horror story," a corridor "overrun by bums and drunks" who shared sidewalk space with prostitutes and violent drug pushers.[54] Besides being an undesirable place to live, this unsavory area impacted local public schools by grooming Black boys for the criminal underworld. As crime along Ponce De Leon increased, the Black male school delinquency rate did as well.

In April 1989 Dr. Ed Johnson and his wife Harmon organized around twelve Black male Atlanta-area history teachers to begin combatting the issues plaguing Black boys.[55] BTA charter members spent the summer identifying and recruiting some of the area's most troubled Black youth for a series of seminars on ending street violence and drug use with a shared responsibility of manhood. Most of the young men did not accept the message. The ones who did pledged to abandon the street life and helped recruit more young Black men to do the same. From the seemingly endless series of seminars, workshops, after-school events, and recreational activities, BTA's ranks eventually grew to around five thousand students across metro Atlanta high schools. Wherever its members went, in-school delinquency decreased at least 40 percent.[56] This success was rapid, but it was anything but easy. In an interview with the *Journal-Constitution,* Ed Johnson admitted that readjusting the life trajectories for so many young men was "rough, tiring, trying, taxing, and demanding," but he ultimately felt "it's easier than going to funerals, trials, and hospitals."[57]

BTA's path to Caux, and its inevitable run-in with Richmond Moral Re-Armament members, began with a phone call that later turned into an official invitation. After learning about BTA's impact on metro Atlanta, Rob and Susan Corcoran convinced the international board that governed MRA to invite and fund BTA's passage to Caux in summer 1990.[58] For most BTA teens, Caux was the furthest and Whitest place they visited outside of the Atlanta area. They handled this cultural shock well, however. A Black Richmond delegate to Caux recalled that only "in positive ways, they turned the place out." Outside of the ease with which BTA teens cozied up to the young White European girls, MRA comfortably welcomed them and their call to "move towards action, and not just talk."[59] At the international level, MRA remained a dialog-centered organization. Its various branches, such as those in Richmond, took heed and began heading in a slightly different direction.[60]

Sylvester Turner awaited the return of his fellow MRA members. When they landed, he remembered a few people discussing BTA and its call for action by MRA groups. According to Turner, "When they came back [to Richmond], they took on that challenge. And the good thing for me was that I was in the room, on the ground floor of that new challenge."[61] The Richmond members took part in the MRA's urban outreach program called Hope in the Cities. The group would not replicate BTA in focusing on inner-city youth; rather, it stayed in its wheelhouse and became more involved in structuring and systematizing the various racial reconciliation efforts happening throughout the city. It began this transformation by hosting weekend retreats between Black and White civic groups at Richmond Hill between fall 1991 and summer 1992.[62] Within these meetings, the regular 114 attendees acknowledged and discussed the collective mental shift among them. They felt that the public expression of reconciliation required, as Benjamin Campbell said, "the Black leadership of White people" on racial matters.[63] It was only with that consensus that Richmond was ready to make its first real grassroot attempt to show the outside world that they the city was actively investigating its issues with race.

BTA's efforts in Caux also compelled Richmond progressives to confront their own racial issues. No one understood this struggle better than Reverend Dr. Paige Chargois, a Black female minister and longtime member of both Moral Re-Armament and Hope in the Cities. It was with much difficulty that she earned the title of national assistant director of Hope in the Cities in 1991. In a recent interview, she attributed the struggle for a title befitting her contribution to the organization as a racial one. The Southampton County native, an admirer of Nat Turner and a Richmond resident, recalled her fellow White members often taking the lead and tossing her requests and suggestions to the side. The reputation of patriarchy among White Richmond liberals was so pervasive that fellow Blacks intentionally referred to Hope in the Cities as "Hope for the Cities." This misnomer reflected that, as Chargois stated, "[Black] citizens cannot say hope in.... They changed it to hope for the cities because they don't have a real sense that there is hope in the city." This feeling was also shared by the White liberals she worked with.[64]

While the patronizing tone and sense of authority on race issues did not die among White liberals, interracial gatherings did help suppress them. Chargois remembered that at a community workshop for professional Black and White women in 1992 at the Museum of the Confederacy, an unnamed White attendee shocked the entire room. She said that the races cannot reconcile without first acknowledging that White efforts to improve racial issues centered on the same level of Black suppression that many claimed to have wanted to see ended. She embodied the spirit of accepting Black leadership by admitting that she and her husband, to the dismay of their parents, moved from neighboring Henrico County to Richmond, a city run politically by Blacks. The memories of busing and White flight collided with this moment, compelling Chargois to tear up. "The attitudes of most White people had changed," in that "there were [many] White people who did not just want to call it [Richmond] a chocolate city anymore."[65] That day, she saw firsthand what other Hope in the Cities members discussed in the Richmond Hill retreats. She saw that there was a desire among some Whites to follow Black people on their path to racial reconciliation.

Black Hope in the Cities members, led by Chargois, Sylvester Turner, and Mayor Walter T. Kenney, spearheaded an international convention called Healing the Heart of America Conference: An Honest Conversation on Race and Responsibility. Set for June 1993, the conference was the result of Mayor Kenney inviting several reconciliation groups to Richmond while at the 1992 MRA conference in Caux. The stated goal of the conference was to "begin the process of healing for the nation, through acts of repentance and forgiveness in the setting of the former capital of the Confederacy."[66] The underlying mission was to connect the disparate reconciliation efforts under an interracially supported Black leadership. By doing this, they would help disconnect Richmond from its long-held, and recently unfitting, reputation as one of the most racist cities in America. Kenney secured funding from local White corporate sponsors by using the political connections cultivated during the urban revitalization efforts in the 1980s. The academic (VCU) and museum communities (Valentine) were not too far behind, as they levied their support for the conference almost immediately after being asked.[67] The mayor and Turner worked very closely to get Black organizations involved as well. They had to show Black ministers and bureaucrats the same deference they showed White elites. Specifically, Turner remembered that "we went to a number of places engaging individuals that had some notoriety . . . [and] made sure that they could sit at the fifty-dollar meal table without having fifty dollars."[68] Various Black organizations agreed to participate in the conference if they could shape various workshops and events in their image, as they eventually did.[69]

It was at this moment, after MRA spawned Hope in the Cities and White liberals accepted leadership from Blacks on race issues, that Reverend Campbell encountered Nancy Jo Taylor outside of Richmond Hill. Hope in the Cities scheduled a meeting to discuss the various events that would take place at the conference when Campbell scurried off and returned with what seemed like a crazy idea.[70] Campbell wanted to make Taylor's makeshift tour into the featured event at the conference. Not one person in the meeting felt that organizing a walking tour of Richmond's unmarked sites was feasible, given that they expected thousands of people to attend. Campbell insisted that the walking tour would bring the message of the conference to life. If attendees could walk together "through" Richmond's history with slavery, they would have a better appreciation for the city's efforts to heal itself. After much convincing, Hope in the Cities members agreed to give the idea a chance. Campbell and Taylor spent much of spring 1993 identifying and unearthing over twenty sites that would be included in the "walk through Richmond's history," or as it was later called, the Unity Walk.[71]

The Unity Walk and conference gained tremendous steam after a meeting between Campbell, the Corcorans, and journalists and editors from the *Richmond Times-Dispatch*. This daily newspaper outlet was the longtime bane of Black Richmond existence. Its owners, editors, and, for a long time, journalists, opposed school integration and the Black political leadership who sprang forth afterward in the 1980s. By the early 1990s, the more liberal journalists—headlined by future Pulitzer Prize winner Michael Paul Williams—infiltrated the *Times-Dispatch* and fought against the newspaper's reputation, a task that required winning over some of the conservative ownership. Hope in the Cities agreed to facilitate a discussion with the two groups if they agreed to visit some of the unmarked sites around Richmond. The historic sites and walk itself generated discussions about the *Times-Dispatch*'s reluctance to embrace its destined role in pushing Richmond past its racist image. *Times-Dispatch* leadership did not agree with everything Hope in the Cities and their journalists said. They did agree that, as Campbell once stated, since "racism had started in its worst form here, on this ground . . . this was where the beginning of the end should take place."[72] Thus, the newspaper needed to be a more active

FIGURE 5. Promotional material for the Healing the Heart of America Conference, 1993. (Courtesy of the Initiatives of Change Collection, Richmond, Virginia)

partner in helping Richmond get over its longstanding racial issues. From this agreement came a pledge by the newspaper's leadership to cover any event held in the name of racial reconciliation.[73]

Between June 16–20, 1993, visitors from fifty cities and twenty-four countries attended the workshops and seminars at the Healing the Heart of America Conference.[74] The second half of the conference ended up being the centerpiece and, as Campbell remembered, "such a Richmond occasion."[75] Of the 1,500 people who attended the conference, around 500 Black and White people walked together in ninety-five-degree-plus heat to visit various historic sites where they witnessed historical reenactments of slavery. While out-of-town visitors did their best to ignore the humidity to enjoy the festivities, some Richmonders were thinking, as Campbell remembered telling Chargois that day, "We shouldn't be able to do this [in Richmond]."[76] Richmond was, for a long time, a city where creating a common understanding about race and history was nearly impossible. Many Whites ignored the plight of Black people and saw their city, in historical terms, as a staple in the founding of America, and the aspiring capital of the failed Confederate States of America. Blacks generally passed down a historically sound counternarrative that describe Richmond as ground-zero for America's original sin of slavery and racial discrimination. During the Unity Walk, however, Blacks and Whites were just Richmonders seeking to understand how to turn the wall of race into a bridge of reconciliation.[77]

By publicly examining the city's racial history, Richmonders legitimized the notion that, in the words of Chargois, "we had the capacity and the capability of moving beyond just being the former capital of the Confederacy."[78] Shortly after the conference, the city council worked with Hope in the Cities, along with "a city-wide commission, foundation money, and the involvement of major institutions such as VCU, and the museums," to permanently mark the previously unmarked sites.[79] This long-overdue gesture reflected the tethering of racial reconciliation to Richmond. Rob Corcoran and Benjamin Campbell admitted that before the conference, "generally speaking [everyday] people were not talking about race, and certainly there was no discussion about Richmond's racial history; none!"[80] After the conference, Campbell remembered that upon traveling between civic groups and churches, "nearly everybody in town was asking themselves whether they were racially prejudiced or not."[81] Civic groups used the lessons about slavery that they learned at the conference to structure talks about contemporary race relations. "Talking about the history of the 1600s and 1700s enabled me to say things that I could not say if I were talking about the 1900s or the twentieth century," according to Campbell. Many discovered that using history to discuss contemporary issues worked well because the evils of slavery and the city's complicity in it were undeniable truths that had contemporary consequences for Black people.[82] After the conference, Richmonders no longer ran from that truth; rather, they discovered that, as was said by a VCU professor: "Painful history can become a source for healing."[83]

The Healing the Heart of America Conference in summer 1993 crystalized the emerging racial reconciliation movement happening throughout Richmond. This movement was not spearheaded by Black and White political and economic elites as in years past. Rather, neighborhood organizations, universities, and museums worked independently and together to use Richmond's shameful history of anti-Black racism to create a common

176 THE STRUGGLE FOR CHANGE

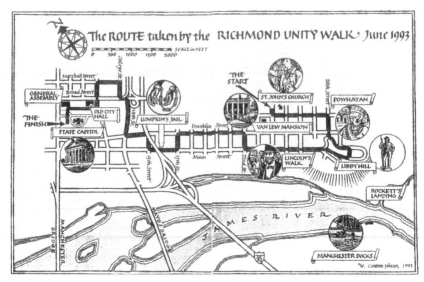

FIGURE 6. Map of the route of Unity Walk drawn for the 1993 Healing the Heart of America Conference. (Courtesy of the Initiatives of Change Collection, Richmond, Virginia)

civic culture of reconciliation. This development was so unprecedented that locals used a national conference with international attendance to display that they were ready to combat current and future racial issues not as Blacks and Whites but as one interracial city. The belief that Richmond's racial situation was indicative of a national racial crisis became the precedent by which residents would later travel the nation to help other cities start healing in the late 1990s.

This collective identity based on racial goodwill was later tested and strengthened by local and national controversies over race and representation in public history. Richmonders later learned in the late 1990s and 2000s what their elites figured out the hard way in the 1970s and 1980s. Future debates about erecting the Arthur Ashe statue, the Canal Walk, and Confederate veneration exposed that common understanding and goals do not produce commonly agreed-upon outcomes and that newer understandings on race required newer actions that were completely divorced from past discrimination. Richmonders learned that for their home to become the interracial city it aspired to be, they had to sacrifice their Lost Cause history and identity.

9

Monument Avenue

"RICHMOND IS NO LONGER THE CAPITAL OF THE CONFEDERACY"

RICHMOND ENTERED the new millennium with vandals burning a public mural of the once-revered Confederate general Robert E. Lee.[1] The burning and mural removal reflected how quickly the former Confederate capital moved beyond Lost Cause veneration. In 1977 the *Richmond Times-Dispatch* praised Lee's image and legacy for spurring national interest, investment, and development in Richmond.[2] As late as the 1980s and 1990s, the same paper referred to Lee as a one of Richmond's "most important heroes," a "statesman," and "too heroic."[3] Yet Richmond entered the new millennium with a collective sense that Lee's image, and more so the Lost Cause and Jim Crow legacy it embodied, painted Richmonders as backward-facing, hero-worshipping racists. Richmonders cemented this collective mental shift by juxtaposing Lee's image with other murals to civil rights heroes like John Mitchell and Maggie Lena Walker. This move made it clear to the world that Richmond was, by the year 2000, a city shedding its racist past for a more inclusive future. This paradox, alone, showed how far Richmond had come in just a few short decades.

"They already took away the Lee mural. This is really an all-out war not just on Confederate history but on Richmond's history," lamented Brag Bowling of the Sons of Confederate Veterans (SCV). This group was founded in Richmond in 1896 by veterans and their descendants to preserve Confederate history.[4] The SCV understood the vandalism, removal, and apathy over punishing the culprits as Richmonders quietly distancing themselves from Confederate history. Thus, in March 2000, the SCV officially requested that every major Virginia locality deem April as Confederate History Month.[5] "All we are doing is recognizing our history," said SCV's Robert Pettus.[6] In reality, they were cultivating White resistance to majority Black Richmond's marginalization of Confederate history.

Most Virginia counties vehemently rejected the SCV request, while Chesterfield County quietly accepted it.[7] Chesterfield's decision led to Black church protests and retail boycotts, as well as a visit from highly controversial Ku Klux Klan leader David Duke. While Duke's arrival resulted in a rally punctuated by civil unrest, it undoubtedly inspired around fifty White students at Henrico's Varina High School to arrive on campus in Confederate regalia, an act that led to mass suspensions that were overturned and expunged due to lawsuits filed by their parents. The White support for the SCV came as no surprise: just a few months prior groups of White Richmond workers openly protested the prohibition of Confederate symbols in the workplace.[8]

The issue over Confederate imagery and memory worsened when state officials got involved. Virginia governors George F. Allen (1994–98) and Jim Gilmore (1998–2002) both proclaimed April to be Confederate History Month during their consecutive administrations. Gilmore claimed that Confederates should be celebrated because they were "noble" and filled with "inspiring leadership." Thus, as he once stated, "We need to acknowledge each other's history and learn to be tolerant of each other."[9] That tolerance ended when Gilmore later rescinded his Confederate support. Succeeding governor Mark Warner refused to entertain the SCV's request because, as he stated, it "would not advance the healing process" already in existence. Even congressional candidate and former *Dukes of Hazzard* star Ben Lewis Jones echoed Warner's message by saying: "We need to bring Virginians together" by seizing the "opportunity to show the South and the nation how to lead on this."[10] Separating Allen and Gilmore from Warner and Jones was the understanding and acknowledgment that for Richmond to become racially reconciled, and a model for reconciliation around the nation, the city had to end its Confederate veneration. No longer could the city celebrate its Black history and Confederate history in the same space. This was a fight that played out in the late 1990s. "The reluctance to defend Confederate history and culture above all else," said a Virginia historian in 2002, showed the underrecognized "new thought pattern in the Capital of the Confederacy" that would later be revealed with the decision to remove Lost Cause relics from the landscape in summer 2020.[11]

As the twentieth century succumbed to the twenty-first, cities across the South began the decades-long exorcism of Confederate memory from the public sphere.[12] Yet for a time, it appeared as if Richmond somehow evaded this trend. "If ever a city was ripe for calls to remove Confederate monuments, it is Richmond," said *Smithsonian* magazine in 2017. I was a second-year doctoral student at the University of Georgia when *Smithsonian* printed an editorial in which a historian openly questioned how Richmond evaded the same monumental controversies that befell cities such as

New Orleans; Austin, Texas; and Durham, North Carolina, in the wake of Charlottesville. Instead of tearing down Confederate statues, Richmonders (mostly leadership with the support of residents) wanted to reinterpret them for a twenty-first-century audience. The *Smithsonian* explained this countercultural move, asking why "beyond scattered acts of vandalism, locals [had] remained largely quiet" about monument removal. It appeared that whereas other cities got it wrong, "Richmond has gotten [it] right," *Smithsonian* claimed. The magazine argued that Richmond's contextualization of Confederate history, as well as its balancing act with Black history, somehow shielded the city from reaping the whirlwind of monument removal.[13]

Richmond experienced a massive mental shift over the issue of Confederate monuments well before city government voted to remove them in 2020. Because the statues along Monument Avenue withstood national tragedies in Charleston (2015) and Charlottesville (2017), many simply ignored the seismic shift in public opinion over their existence. Public relics are not easily removed because they are riveted to the collective body and mind. White southerners erected Confederate statues out of an ingrained love for the inaccurate interpretation of history they represented. The relics symbolize the bond (more so a marriage) between the people and their history. Thus, removing these relics is a form of divorce. While many people see the results of this divorce—the physical removal of the monument—the years of separation between the people and their history, like separation within a marriage between two people, often go undetected. Other southern cities completed their divorce from Confederate monuments in 2017. At that time Richmond was still in a successful state of separation from its Confederate history, a fact that eluded *Smithsonian*. What long masqueraded as a balancing act between Confederate and civil rights history was, indeed, a longer separation process in which Richmond first decentered and then detached Lost Causism from its collective identity as a means of racial reconciliation.

Richmond spent the late 1990s and early 2000s marginalizing its Confederate history in hopes of becoming a more inclusive city. The decision to detach the Lost Cause from the city's identity resulted from a previous decade where Richmonders first erected a statue in honor of Arthur Ashe along Monument Avenue after much controversy. Locals then took their experiences with the Ashe controversy to various US cities en route to generating a national racial reconciliation movement in Richmond's image. The decision to make Richmond's identity shift into America's racial reckoning in the early twenty-first century unearthed the reality that America was not a colorblind society. Rather, it became more apparent that divided historical experiences and understandings wedged the races further apart.[14] As the nation drifted apart during its reckoning, Richmonders came closer together on the consensus that the city's images should reflect their desire to detach themselves from any symbols of racism. This meant that Richmond could no longer celebrate its Confederate past while becoming a multiracial, harmonious city. Between the mid-1990s and early 2020s, Confederate history transitioned from *the* city's identity, to *a part* of the city's identity, to representing everything that was wrong with Richmond. When Mayor Levar Stoney ordered the removal of Confederate statues from Monument Avenue in July 2020, it was obvious to the world what had been long known to locals: "Richmond is no longer the Capital of the Confederacy," touted the *Times-Dispatch*.[15]

"We Have Changed"

Arthur Ashe (1943–93) was an all-time great tennis player and civil rights advocate from Richmond. When many people think of Ashe, rarely do they think of the relationship between him and his hometown. On the off chance that people do associate Ashe and Richmond, they often revert back to the controversy surrounding his statue being placed at the intersection of Roseneath and Monument Avenue in 1996.[16] While being the most symbolic and impactful way Richmond honored Ashe's life, the statue's placement was a contested and calculated decision in which leaders aided previous efforts to reform the city's racist identity. Moreover, the statue's placement unearthed a more complicated relationship between the city and its native son; a relationship defined by Richmond's collective identity.

On February 2, 1966, White city councilmembers hosted an amateur tennis match and ceremony to showcase the twenty-two-year-old Ashe, then a homegrown talent that, ironically, they had driven away with racially segregated athletic events. This event was an obvious ploy to show that Richmond, then in the throes of the modern civil rights movement, was tackling its race problems through embracing one of its most famous Black people. Ashe was not naive; he understood that White leaders paraded him around for their political benefit. Still, he wore his Sunday's best and attended the ceremony and match with a bright smile, as if the honor was all his.[17] Returning home must have been partially bittersweet because, as he once stated in his memoir, "the most powerful local tennis officials had tried to kill my game by shutting me out of any competition."[18] Now that he had become a "globally renowned Richmonder," the White establishment wanted him to come back and play tennis where they previously refused him.[19] Nevertheless, Ashe accepted the praise bestowed upon him by city leaders with the double-consciousness that many successful Blacks learned to master. While the city fathers may have believed they "honored" Ashe, he nobly accepted their adulation knowing that the honor was all theirs.

While racism drove Ashe and Richmond apart, efforts to combat it ultimately brought the two back together.[20] The pursuit of tennis greatness kept Ashe away from Richmond, but his civil rights activism almost ensured he would never return.[21] "When I decided to leave Richmond . . . I left all that Richmond stood for at the time—its segregation, its conservatism, its parochial thinking, its slow progress toward equality, its lack of opportunity for talented Black people. I had no intention then of coming back," Ashe once reflected bluntly.[22] Little did he know that Richmond, with the help of residents and leadership, would make tremendous strides toward racial healing in the decades following his departure. Ashe's personal growth and Richmond's racial climate intersected with the creation of Virginia Heroes Incorporated in 1992. Ashe allied with a group of White West End liberals to form a mentoring program for Black youth that helped close the psychological and cultural gap between wealthy Whites and working-class Blacks.[23] This organization had tremendous public and private support before Ashe died of pneumonia in February 1993, almost twenty-seven years to the day he had first returned home as the city's beloved son.[24]

Ashe's death riveted his legacy of civil rights to Richmond's evolving collective identity. Governor L. Douglas Wilder ensured the deceased Ashe received a hero's memorial at the Executive Mansion before being laid to rest.[25] The city council, looking to capitalize on the potential tourism opportunity, planned to construct either a Black sports hall of fame or festival park named after him.[26] Virginia Heroes, however, suggested that the city council help fund and place the statue already being sculpted in his honor. Private meetings between Virginia Heroes and influential residents compelled the council to appropriate some of the $400,000 needed to erect and place the sculpture at "an appropriate memorial [site]."[27] They also formed a site committee that, after months of informal canvassing in Richmond and private meetings among its members, decided to place the statue along Monument Avenue.[28] This decision was based on the idea that local leaders would show the world that "Richmond is changing. We have changed. . . . We're a city for all people. . . . It's more than symbolic. It's real," City Manager Robert C. Bobb once said.[29] Most importantly, the site selection reflected that Ashe's death was an important platform for city leadership to help reshape Richmond's image.

Placing the twenty-four-foot bronze statue along Monument Avenue added to the long-held custom of elites using public art as a political statement. Since the early 1900s White Virginia elites had used history to cement their control over the public sphere by determining what history was worth remembering, emulating, and existing in the present through physical form. No place better exemplifies this tradition than Richmond's Monument Avenue, where the city's New South elite used Lost Cause relics to ingrain White supremacy deeper into the landscape and public consciousness in the twentieth century.[30] Located just west of downtown, slicing through the adjacent Fan and Museum districts, Monument Avenue served as the tree-lined cathedral where White southerners worshipped the Lost Cause by frequenting the statues of Confederate heroes Robert E. Lee (erected in 1890), J. E. B. Stuart and Jefferson Davis (both erected in 1907), Stonewall Jackson (1919), and Matthew Fontaine Maury (1929). Monument Avenue, and the inaccurate historical narrative it solidified, cemented the relationship between race, space, public history, and collective identity in Richmond. While Richmond became a majority-Black city run by a majority-Black city government and entrenched in a reconciliation movement, Monument Avenue remained the sacred ground where the institutionalization of White supremacy and Black inferiority was on full display. If one forgot which race controlled Richmond affairs, the statues along Monument Avenue were there to remind them.

Placing the Ashe statue along Monument Avenue not only contested Confederate history's monopoly on Richmond's identity, it also reflected how far the city's racial pathology had come. The Arthur Ashe monument should have been erected downtown. Business leaders had already used newer public art in the 1980s to reflect their revitalization-heavy, racial reconciliatory agenda. Corporate-sponsored relics such as *First Cross* (1983), *Corporate Presence* and *Quadrature* (1985), *Winds Up* and *Boatsman Tower* (1986), *James River Divide* (1987), and *Wind Chimes* and *Headman* (1988) were seemingly deracialized, ahistorical figures symbolizing Richmond's business and political class overcoming racial turmoil. Initial desires to place the Ashe statue downtown not only reflected a transition away from the recent trend of ahistorical public art, but it also represented city leadership reshaping Richmond's public image in Ashe's likeness.[31]

Placing Ashe along Monument Avenue was city leadership's acknowledgement that the landscape needed to better reflect the active racial reconciliation efforts going on throughout the city.[32] Outsiders knew very little about the racial changes happening within Richmond. While neighborhood organizations and museum and academic communities regularly engaged in reconciliatory work, newspapers outside the city portrayed Richmond as a place "where the name of your forbears is more important than the size of your paycheck"; and where failing city schools "reminded many people of the dark days of segregation and of the history of massive resistance in this capital of the Confederacy," the *Washington Post* once opined.[33]

While the *Washington Post* was long critical of Richmond's political and cultural conservatism, its portrayal of Richmond as a backward-facing city compelled leadership to become more serious in proving the opposite. They needed to show the world how far Richmond had come, and that began with "bringing racial justice to Monument Avenue," Black longtime city councilman Henry "Chuck" Richardson said emphatically.[34] Because Richmond's reputation as a racist city hinged heavily on the whiteness of Monument Avenue, site committee members believed that the Ashe statue had to be placed there. "People all over the world are watching what we do," said Marty Drumette of Virginia Heroes.[35] While we do not know how true that was, the *Washington Post* was most certainly paying attention. It once suggested that the addition of a "Black achiever" to Monument Avenue "would be a potent symbol of racial progress and healing" in a city in need of it.[36] The addition could not be of any Black man; it was clear that it had to be Ashe, as "Richmond could not craft a stronger symbol of racial reconciliation than placing a Black man of Ashe's heroic stature among the Confederate monuments."[37]

Public fallout over the official announcement showed that residents were not on board with altering the city's White identity through reforming Monument Avenue. The site committee closed its meetings to the public well before the official announcement, but "the decision continues to trouble me," said councilman and future mayor Timothy Kaine. Other committee members assured him that "public airing will [not] reduce controversy and emotionalism," and "the public will question the recommendation" regardless.[38] Beneath the refusal to consult the public was a belief that the *Times-Dispatch* would help them advertise the decision in a favorable manner. To the site committee's surprise, the editors refused to help them. Had one solely read the *Times-Dispatch* between June and July 1995, he or she would have believed that Richmond's "African American Community is divided. The White community is [also] divided" on the issue, according to one site committee member.[39] The reality was that most Blacks wanted to see Ashe's image along the avenue, while many Whites, even some of the most liberal, did not. The most vocal White dissent revealed that many residents were riveted to the notion that Richmond's reputation as a monument city relied on the sanctity of Monument

Avenue.[40] Excuses, however, ranged from Ashe being "the wrong man" to be placed on the Confederate avenue to the completed sculpture being too "second class" to be in Richmond's first-class, tree-lined neighborhood.[41]

Beneath the surface of cordial dissent lay tremendous political pressure to keep the Ashe statue off Monument Avenue. Many Richmonders believed that Monument Avenue was a Confederate boulevard, thus keeping Ashe off it was "not about American history, [or] it's not Civil War history, it is [about preserving] Confederate history."[42] This sentiment was not lost on committee members, according to Thomas Chewning (Ashe's lifelong friend, CEO of VEPCO, and staple within the local establishment).[43] Because many of them were elected officials (mostly city council), they faced the constant threat of losing reelection. Some corporate executives suggested that they would pull funding from future downtown public-private projects and Black political campaigns if the statue ended up along Monument Avenue. Black councilmembers, most notably the later-disgraced mayor Leonidas Young II, were allegedly offered bribes to oppose the decision.[44] While it appears today that the council held firm with their moral decision, the reality was that challenging Confederate memory elicited the kind of overt and covert backlash that often ruins political careers. Richmond was one of the first American cities to openly use painful history to heal race relations. Public opposition to Ashe, however, proved that, as was said by the *Afro-American:* "Phrases such as racial harmony and healing of the past floated around the city like pollen. . . . [But] now the reality [is] that the city is far from healed or harmonic."[45]

City leadership and the public eventually ended up on the same page. The council called a hearing for July 17, 1995, to field public opinion and issue a final decision regarding the statue's placement. Guiding the council was the consensus they formed during a "coming-to-Jesus moment" just hours before the hearing. The nine councilmembers (six Blacks and three Whites) initially voted seven to two in favor of not placing the statue along Monument Avenue. Chewning challenged the council to confirm that Richmond was no longer unwilling to relinquish the vestiges of White supremacy, a perception that many Richmonders rejected but a stigma that outsiders regularly placed upon them.[46] After intense debate, the council crafted a mostly united answer to the "essential questions of our collective identity," as Mayor Young later said to open the public hearing. The council's eight to zero vote—with one abstaining—in favor of making the Ashe statue a monument to reconciliation was easier because most attendees agreed with them. Dissenters, possibly fearing major reprisal from the national media and supporting residents in attendance, were but a sliver of those who made their voices heard that day.[47]

Residents legitimized their leadership's decision by embracing the Ashe statue as a platform of reconciliation. Chewning once looked back on the fiasco with nostalgia, claiming that "it was amazing to me how quickly after that monument was up, that people forgot all of the fuss. Many [White] people who were a part of the fuss went to see it, and they took their children and grandchildren to see it, and still do." Some Black people saw the statue as yet another milestone where Ashe, even upon his death, had broken barriers in the hometown he long loathed.[48] Public relics and the politics of their placement reflect how people use their past to shape the present and future. Ashe's statue showed that Richmonders were willing to use their civil rights history to slowly detach themselves from Confederate memory. If Monument Avenue cemented Richmond's embrace of Jim Crow, the Ashe monument marked Richmond's clumsy steps toward reconciliation.[49]

"Richmond . . . Set the National Standard"

Unbeknownst to many, local group Hope in the Cities helped Richmond shed its racist identity by working outside of city limits. Not too long after the Arthur Ashe controversy, a few Richmonders seized the opportunity to implement their vision of racial reconciliation throughout the nation. This vision was of Blacks and Whites cooperatively dialoging about contemporary issues with a shared understanding of the past. This culture of historically based interracial dialog hinged on a commitment to fix past issues that caused racial conflict. Richmonders by and large never fully lived up to this utopian aspiration themselves, but a select few most certainly tried to. Despite its many shortcomings on race, Richmond had a strong civic culture where the local media, leadership, and grassroots organizations rallied behind the trope, performance, and, in some cases, reality of racial harmony. The city was heavily interrelated in ways that did not exist elsewhere. Local group HIC sought to transplant Richmond's civic culture elsewhere. Yet they learned that in many cities across America, people wished to remain divided.

The Arthur Ashe incident happened within a national climate in which rates of interracial marriages, births, friendships, neighborhoods, schools, social clubs, and workplaces reached heights never before seen.[50] The racial achievement and opportunity gap that had long divided Black and White Americans was rapidly closing as well. Yet social improvements did not create more racial harmony. Rather, social scientists found that improvements led to the most disharmony since the 1960s.[51] Contributing most to this decline was the growing White belief in colorblindness: the idea that Black economic ascendance to American middle-class life (suburban neighborhoods, elite schools, and decision-making positions in major firms) proved that racism was a thing of the past.[52] Conversely, Black academics, politicians, and activists took offense to the notion that racism was over. They argued that disparate outcomes in education, healthcare, employment, housing (lending and renting), consumption, incarceration, and media coverage of crime proved the exact opposite. White resistance to welfare and affirmative action also contributed to the argument that Americans were exiting the twentieth century more racist, and not less.[53] This divide between White and Black perceptions of race relations was revealed in polling data. The majority of Blacks saw race as an issue, while most Whites did not; nearly two-thirds of Whites felt that Blacks used racism as a convenient excuse to demand political and social gain.[54]

National incidents exacerbated the differing perceptions about the existence of racism. The police brutality against Rodney King followed by the officers' acquittal and subsequent riots in Los Angeles in 1992; White flight from urban centers; resegregation of public schools; and the O. J. Simpson murder case (1994) furthered national discussions about racism. Many Whites condemned police misconduct as public-sector corruption. They also defended public school resegregation and White flight as racially neutral decisions to separate from undesirable Black areas where the "culture of poverty" had run amok.[55] The belief in colorblindness was so powerful that even when White supremacists torched over 225 Black churches between 1995 and 1998 (one of which was in Richmond's neighboring Chesterfield County in 1996), many Whites insisted that these were random acts of violence and not reflections of American racism.[56] "In my lifetime, race relations are as bad as I have ever seen them," one New York City pastor said as Whites and Blacks reportedly engaged in less frequent contact with one another by the mid-1990s.[57]

Some Richmonders felt compelled to help heal America's racial fracture shortly after the Arthur Ashe incident. HIC silently pushed the city council and site committee to place the Ashe statue along Monument Avenue in 1996. They felt that remaining quiet, however, "revealed deep divisions and hurts in our community," as HIC national director Rob Corcoran told a friend privately.[58] The Corcorans, Dr. Paige Chargois (Black), Sylvester Turner (Black), Dr. Benjamin Campbell (White), and others decided to remake HIC by setting "ground rules to which elected officials, business, and community leaders will commit themselves and agree" to rebuild communities torn by race. Drafted by HIC in 1995, the "Call to Community" was a national agenda to distill Richmond's culture of interracial dialogue into a transplantable method to heal broken communities. It was first successfully tried in Cincinnati and later Chicago before being announced as the plan for a national racial reconciliation movement. The dialogues centered on historical truths (such as recognizing that the Civil War was about slavery) that compelled Whites and Blacks to acknowledge, discuss, and "heal" racial divides together.[59] HIC dealt heavily with politicians; however, the group did not directly push for public policy initiatives. Policy involved politics, and politics inevitably divided people. Dialog sessions were to be the biracial and bipartisan "philosophical base from which. . . . local affiliates operate," Corcoran insisted. Even when supporters tried to push HIC toward political activism, Corcoran adamantly refused by issuing several statements to make it "clear where we stand."[60]

HIC's movement helped "Richmond . . . set the national standard on public conversations," in the words of Rob Corcoran.[61] In 1996 HIC alerted over a hundred grassroots and political leaders around the country (many of whom had attended the Healing the Heart of America Conference in 1993) of their national project. Realizing that race was "America's Achilles heel," most of them vied for HIC's assistance with the hopes that "the Richmond experience could be replicated in some way."[62] HIC selectively chose to work within twelve cities that represented each region of the country. Funding this national project was the W. K. Kellogg Foundation, a Michigan-based philanthropic organization long dedicated to racial improvements.[63] Optimism among HIC leaders and donors was extremely high, yet archival evidence and later interviews reveal that they had not the slightest clue how difficult healing the nation's racial wounds might be. Their work mostly validated pollsters and social scientists who surmised that race was and would remain America's biggest issue entering the twenty-first century.[64]

The extent of racial division in America's cities and counties during the colorblind era was truly dejecting to HIC.[65] Designed to connect White suburbs to Black inner cities, the northeastern and midwestern projects ended before all others with the least amount of grassroots cooperation. The extreme diversity between minorities out West (Latinos, East Asians, and Blacks) ultimately stymied HIC's efforts with the religious organizations that solicited them. Southerners, mostly wealthy White businesspeople and Black politicians, allowed folkway persuasion to prevent discussions about systemic racism from "go[ing] deep enough to result in institutional as well as attitude change." In every region, liberal Whites (typically ministers and academics) and Blacks (working- and middle-class grassroots organizers) aligned on using the history of racial oppression as a language to discuss potential policy changes. The most commonly discussed solution to every problem was municipal resource sharing across city (Black) and suburban (White) lines. Because of this, many Whites, and even some suburban Blacks, refused to take any serious part in HIC efforts.[66]

HIC discovered that the national discussion about race and racism resulted from divided Black and White opinions at the ground level. Nationally speaking, many Whites believed in colorblindness. This sentiment was also true in the cities HIC worked with as, "[White] people define racism so narrowly. If they are not calling people niggers, they think they are not racist," a disappointed Black Cincinnati executive told Corcoran.[67] HIC also found that in the Northeast and on the West Coast, "many Whites seem to think that there is no real racism problem," and because of that, "Blacks are doubtful that dialoging will accomplish much."[68] Even worse, "the media practically ignores these activities and White folks do not normally join in."[69] "The main impression right now is that HIC is stalled out" a southern representative once sadly stated in the early 2000s.[70] Their tangible success lay in guiding Portland, Oregon, to implement racial education in their public school system. They also encouraged the passage of antiracist labor legislation in Dayton, Ohio. Both efforts not only emerged from the interracial dialogs fostered by HIC, but they directly targeted the history of racism in Portland and Dayton. HIC's failure to create sustainable dialog cultures loomed larger, as in the words of Paige Chargois: "No matter where we went, it was almost exactly the same."[71]

HIC's national movement received more national notoriety when President William J. Clinton's administration colonized the movement to cement his ill-defined legacy. By the late 1990s Clinton had spent much of his political career remaking the Democratic Party into a moderate right-wing coalition to recapture the White House from Reagan-era Republicans.[72] This push compelled Clinton to offend his Black Democratic base by condemning Sistah Soulja and the Los Angeles riots after the Rodney King incident in 1992. In 1993 he pulled support from strong civil rights advocate and University of Pennsylvania law professor Lani Guiner for US Assistant Attorney General. Clinton is most remembered, however, for endorsing and signing the infamous Violent Crime Control and Law Enforcement Act of 1994, also known as the Three Strikes Law or '94 Crime Bill. This bill led to the largest incarceration of black men in American history since the end of slavery.[73]

He tried to balance this conservative push by publicly reaffirming his commitment to affirmative action, appointing the most minorities in US history to cabinet-level positions to that point, increasing earned-income tax credits for low-income families, funding urban opportunity zones, expanding eligibility for food stamps, and creating the first ever White House Commission on Civil Rights.[74] Still, Clinton's approval ratings on race tanked significantly along with race relations by the late 1990s. This reality compelled Clinton to shore up the weakest part of his presidential legacy by taking the lead on an already existing racial reconciliation movement headed by HIC.[75]

Clinton introduced the "One America in the 21st Century: The President's Initiative on Race" during a scheduled speech at the University of California at San Diego on June 14, 1997, less than a month after issuing an official apology to Black Americans for the abhorrent Tuskegee Experiment.[76] The initiative spawned from Executive Order No. 13050, which established a committee of seven led by Black historian John Hope Franklin. At the behest of Chris Edley, director of the White House Review of Affirmative Action, and Mike Wegner, deputy director of the Race Initiative, HIC and five other reconciliation groups were pulled into Clinton's initiative. The committee tapped into HIC's network of over 181 known local organizations to create national "town hall" discussions between academics, grassroots leaders (religious and secular), and political figures.[77] The most radical plans involved the need for monetary reparations to poor Black communities.[78] Public disfavor of programs focusing on race, however, made the final recommendation far from compensatory.[79] The HIC's dialogue guide for the various town halls was the blueprint for what became the One America guide on race, which articulated racial conflict as an outgrowth of America's increasing multicultural society and not as a continuation of systemic, historic racism. Thus, the White House guide was as colorblind as most Americans, advocating for local dialogues that centered on forgiveness for past sins and commitments to future improvements. The solution to America's race problems, according to the president's commission, was a national embrace of Richmond's dialogue culture.

Clinton's push to nationalize Richmond's racial reconciliation model was not well received. For one, critics—mainly liberal academics and politicians—chided the lack of policy proscription. Clinton knew better, however. He was not too far removed from the Republican Revolution of 1994, in which Americans (mostly White suburbanites) expressed their disdain for any race-based policy.[80] Thus, Clinton embraced HIC's dialogue method because it occupied a middle ground between action and inaction.

This middle ground was not neutral, however, because Clinton desperately tried to make the Democratic Party attractive to White suburbanites.

Racially divided communities became even more divided after the passage of Clinton's crime legislation.[81] The '94 Crime Bill increased the incarceration of Black men across the nation. The law's impact was mostly seen every day by militarized, mostly White police departments arresting Black people in their communities.[82] Clinton's hijacking of the national reconciliation movement, symbolized by his call for "forgiveness" for past racism, juxtaposed what many saw as the continuation of racism through "broken windows" policing (a theory that visible signs of crime create an environment conducive to further crime), which heightened the awareness that inner cities were still Black and poor while suburbs were mostly White and affluent. Thus, as HIC found in their national project, it became harder to foster meaningful dialog between the wealthy and poor, urban and suburban, as well as Black and White about ways to improve society. The irony of the Clinton years, as well as HIC's noble efforts, was that nationally they calcified divisions that had resulted from historical injustices. Thus, in this climate, Richmond's dialogue culture was not equipped to handle hard-hitting racial issues. Meaningful discussions about racial inequity had to wait another generation.[83]

"I Think We Achieved a Balance"

As the twenty-first century drew nearer, HIC maintained their loosely connected national network from their offices in West End Richmond. At that time, corporate and museum leaders were completing the Canal Walk Project. Representing the collective interests of the business and museum communities, the Canal Walk was a mile-long path along the recently restored Kanawha Canal next to the James River.[84] Displayed along the path were twenty-nine murals showing Richmond's historical transition from a rural frontier to a postindustrial city. Plans for this project went surprisingly uncontested. City leaders and many residents wanted this rebuilt area to attract newer retail, restaurant, and real estate investment.[85] The Canal Walk also differed from the "Main to the James" development plans that perpetuated the notion that infrastructural and economic progress in Richmond required expressways and highways connecting the inner city to the suburbs. But more importantly, this rebuilt area would show the new commitment from business interests, elected officials, and the museum community to the notion that inner city space with historical value better reflected the city's evolving antiracist identity.[86]

Richmond leadership erected the Canal Walk during a southern urban shift toward a newer form of racial capitalism. Southern city leaders worked with their local museums to make their heritage tourism industry more racially inclusive.[87] Tours that normally interpreted plantations and the property of wealthy slaveholders now included stories about slavery and Jim Crow from the perspective of Black people. This shift was not so much about morality. Rather, inclusive heritage tourism functioned as a commodifiable form of reconciliation, marketing southern cities as great places to live, work, and visit. Or in the words of a prominent historian, southern cities engaged in the "commercialization of Black history as a gesture of [racial] reconciliation."[88] Richmond fell neatly within this regional development. The Canal Walk appeared to be the perfect combination of capitalist investment and public history, which reflected the progressive racial attitudes and programs actively taking place both within and outside of city borders.[89]

Although billed by the local media to be a racially inclusive addition to the city's landscape and culture, the juxtaposition between Confederate and civil rights imagery proved problematic. The *Times-Dispatch* gave its readers a peek of the mural in honor of Robert E. Lee. The next day, Councilman Saad El Amin vocalized his dissent and called for a Black boycott of the Canal Walk's grand opening.[90] "We got what we wanted. The mural's coming down," he said confidently after speaking with members of the museum and business communities.[91]

The local SCV chapter protested the grand opening by draping a large Confederate flag over the canal and chanting "We want Lee." White and Black public officials shared the SCV's desire for Lee's image along the Canal Walk. While they were not open Lost Cause apologists, they saw Richmond's progressive identity as rooted in a balancing of contested histories. Richmond mayor Tim Kaine told the *Times-Dispatch*, "Much of our history is not pleasant, [but] you can't Whitewash it."[92] Former Virginia governor L. Douglas Wilder agreed with Kaine, saying, "There is a place for Robert E. Lee on the Wall." One of the most memorable and controversial scenes from the grand opening was not the SCV protest; rather, it was Wilder sailing down the canal with invited guests and saluting the Confederate flag they hung. "The majority of Richmonders are not [yet] interested in obliterating [Confederate] history," said Wilder.[93] While Wilder's actions received criticism, his words reflected the opinion of many locals.

Richmonders further demystified and disempowered the Lost Cause by making a balanced public history narrative a part of their progressive identity. When asked if a Confederate mural should represent Richmond on a new public project, a Black resident told the *Times-Dispatch* that "the mural is about Richmond and the Civil War. How can you talk about the Civil War without Lee?"[94] While the newspaper openly platformed dissent to the Arthur Ashe statue years prior, interviews with those closest to the situation confirmed that Black Richmonders were, in general, not opposed to the Lee mural. Thus, the museum and business communities organized a nineteen-member biracial committee to reevaluate the murals and ensure that they represented Richmond's history in a way that reflected its current understanding of racial reconciliation.[95]

HIC helped the committee organize citywide dialogues to gauge public opinion about which murals should represent Richmond. With overwhelming public and committee support, the city council placed the Lee mural back on the floodwall in September 1999. "I think we needed balance and I think we achieved a balance," a Black committee member said after the decision. This episode shows that Richmonders, by and large, saw no reconciliation in shunning Confederate memory. By balancing it with Black history, however, the city collectively disempowered it.[96] Whereas Lost Cause memory once dominated Richmond's public history and collective identity, it now only existed as a part of the city's past. This showed that many Richmonders no longer revered their Confederate memory, as it served only an honorary role in attracting tourism and reflecting how far the collective mind moved beyond the days of slavery and Jim Crow.

After the Canal Walk controversy, the museum community and HIC began a campaign "to put the Civil War in its place in Richmond."[97] Grounding this decision was the collective acknowledgement that Richmond, for its decades-long efforts, had not gone far enough to unshackle itself from the reputational blight of the Lost Cause. State official H. Alexander Wise Jr. told the *Times-Dispatch* that "Richmond always seems to trip over itself in matters of race and the Civil War, in controversies ranging from the placement of the Arthur Ashe statue on Monument Avenue to hanging Robert E. Lee's mural on the flood wall."[98] The reality was that balancing the city's history through public art was not enough; local institutions felt compelled to take more control. The main issue was that Richmond had several historical institutions that in their individual ways dealt with the city's identity. There was no one place that interpreted the Civil War, the Confederacy, and White supremacy as a part of, and not the central theme of, Richmond's identity. This reality was not lost on locals: "Is Richmond's Civil War history holding us back? No, but our approach to it is."[99]

The newest approach to using public history to reform the collective identity resulted in the Tredegar National Civil War Museum—later named the American Civil War Museum. Located at the former Tredegar Iron Works factory along the James River, near the Canal Walk, the museum's mission to be *the* place to interpret the Civil War from a non–Lost Cause perspective was intentionally designed "to remove blight from the city's reputation," the future director said upon its inception.[100] Popular support for this project proved that Richmonders no longer wanted their city to be the Lost Cause sanctuary.[101] Rather, the American Civil War Museum was Richmond's counter to the long-held myths it had perpetuated with the coronation of Monument Avenue in 1890.[102]

Richmond's White and Black communities, as well as the long-despised Museum of the Confederacy, worked with HIC to donate money and artifacts for the Civil War Museum. Upon the museum's completion on October 7, 2006, a local minister prayed that it would be "a place of hope" and reconciliation for the city, the South, and the nation.[103] After opening, the museum helped exorcise Lost Cause memory from Richmond's identity by housing and reinterpreting the Civil War for the city. From here on, Richmond's Civil War history was not the bullhorn for White supremacy. This really hit home when the American Civil War Museum rejected a $100,000 statue of Jefferson Davis holding a mixed-race child that was commissioned and donated by the SCV.[104]

The American Civil War Museum precipitated a public revaluation of racial reconciliation in twenty-first-century Richmond. "I ... have interest in racial reconciliation, which I think is a major focus and underlying motivation for all of us who are involved," the museum director said in 2006. He accurately described the agenda to convert the "Civil War from an open wound into a community asset and healing opportunity."[105] In modern Richmond, reconciliation no longer meant balancing Confederate memory with civil rights history, nor did it require confining and reinterpreting Confederate history within designer institutions. Racial reconciliation meant littering the landscape with relics to drown out the remaining Lost Cause symbolism and its supporters.[106]

The American Civil War museum and United States Historical Society ignored SVC protests and erected the statue of Abraham Lincoln and his son Tad along the Canal Walk in 2003.[107] The city spoke again when five thousand residents watched the Slavery Reconciliation Statue be placed along the James River in 2007, a project opposed by Lost Cause advocates and completed with the efforts of Black councilwoman Delores McQuinn and HIC.[108] Richmonders supported the Virginia Civil Rights Memorial in 2008, a privately financed ($2.6 million) work featuring the statues of Black attorneys Oliver White Hill and Spottswood W. Robinson III along with the Prince Edward children who boycotted segregated schools in 1951.[109] In 2011 the city council commissioned a statue in honor of Black businesswoman Maggie Lena Walker along downtown's East Broad and North Adams Streets, which was completed in 2017.[110] The upliftment of civil rights monuments at the expense of Confederate memory effectively put Richmond in line with other southern cities that, as was said about Richmond specifically, erected "public expressions of reconciliation" in the new century.[111] More than expressions, however, Richmonders said with their actions what many did not seem to hear: the city *was* the *former* Confederate capital.

Black grassroots organizations cemented Richmond's shift away from Confederate history and more toward venerating the formerly enslaved. After the Canal Walk controversy, the Elegba Folklore Society worked with Mayor Tim Kaine's fifteen-member ad hoc committee on creating "a process to determine how history should be interpreted throughout the city."[112] This led to the Sacred Ground Historical Reclamation Project of Defenders of Freedom, Justice, and Equality. Their goal was to "reclaim" spaces where racism was introduced, fermented, solidified, and resisted within the city.[113] Specifically, they wanted to consolidate a nine-acre lot in Shockoe Bottom that encompassed an African burial ground, the Lumpkin Slave Jail, the existing Richmond Slave Trail, and a site of Gabriel's Rebellion into the Shockoe Bottom Memorial Park. This proposed "site of consciousness [is] where," in the words of Ana Edwards of Sacred Ground, "people [will] interact with the past" through public art and a museum dedicated to interpreting the history of slavery.[114] Sacred Ground's dedication to memorializing Black spaces in Richmond and shifting the city's public history narrative more toward its Black history, placed the organization in opposition to government-sponsored commercial interests.

Local businesspeople and the city council wanted to turn the Bottom into a shopping and restaurant district anchored by a new baseball park. Black women such as Edwards of Sacred Ground, Monica Esparaza of the African Ancestral Chamber, Christy Coleman of the American Civil War Museum, Delegate Deloris McQuinn, as well as other local politicians and academics, rose in opposition to every development project in the area. The competing visions for the Bottom exposed the fractures in Richmond's newer antiracist identity, as Black history now conflicted with the "city's need for economic development," said Rob Nieweg, field director for the National Trust for Historic Preservation.[115] The Black female activists made it clear that, as was said by Coleman, they were "not opposed to growth ... but not if the cost is so high it allows us to forget our past, even the most painful elements of it." In 2013 opponents gathered over 1,600 signatures on a petition to prevent the ballpark from coming into fruition.[116] Edwards mobilized others to block development into the area, all the while drawing detailed plans for the Memorial Park.[117] Their efforts, which began in 2004, paid off as the ballpark agenda failed in 2015 and the city and Commonwealth agreed, as of July 2021, to construct the Shockoe Bottom Memorial Park.[118]

The efforts of Black history activists and the influx of newer monuments devoted to racial equality helped attract newer, more progressive Richmond residents who made the balance between Confederate and civil rights history unreconcilable in the public arena.[119] Between 2000 and 2020, over 32,000 new residents settled in the city, thanks in large part to VCU expansion (from 7,000 to 32,000 students), the in-migration of over seventy biotech firms, regressive local and state tax policies, as well as the antisuburban yuppies and real estate investors they all attract.[120] The influx of more liberal professionals added to the existing resentment against Confederate memory. The most blatant example of this was the rise and almost routine vandalism against Confederate relics from 2000 to 2020.[121] Other forms of dissent were not so criminal, as Richmonders, both new and old, began expressing that Confederate history belonged in textbooks and museums, not in public spaces.[122]

In 2010 the Virginia Museum of Fine Arts (VMFA) removed Confederate flags from the restored Confederate chapel on their campus. This began yet another battle in the war between Richmond and the SCV, the group that had rented the chapel since 1993. They resisted the decision by spawning the Virginia Flaggers, who opposed flag removal and protested (with Confederate flags) in front of the VMFA on a weekly basis. They also purchased private property around the borders of Richmond and erected enormous Confederate flags that no visitor or resident could ignore.[123] Still, Richmond's Confederate identity was a thing of the past; a fact that was driven home when the American Civil War Museum subsumed the Museum of the Confederacy in 2018.

The *Virginia Mercury* comically questioned how "in the former Confederate Capital, there's no longer a Museum of the Confederacy." The last museum director made it clear how the times made it difficult to turn the "museum for the Confederacy [in]to being a museum about the Confederacy." Thus, the merger represented a major milestone in the museum community's long trek toward reconciling Richmond's public history. As was said by local director Christy Coleman: "We want to get away from the mythmaking and back to history."[124] In the process, the museum community was fulfilling its mission to form, as stated in the *Times-Dispatch*, "a common history its citizenry can rally behind."[125]

Richmond's efforts happened alongside a state, regional, and national fight to dissociate from Confederate symbolism. "This is a battle that is going on all over the country," nationally known white supremacist David Duke stated in a parking lot rally at Chesterfield Towne Center in 2000.[126] While directly responding to Richmond's refusal to acknowledge Confederate History Month, his words addressed the current and future efforts to banish Confederate imagery from the public sphere. A major articulation for this was the close association between Confederate symbols and hate crimes against Black people.[127] The public and corporations pressured state and local governments between Maryland and Texas to rename schools and roads, as well as ban Confederate flags from public property.[128] Seismic changes in Virginia began with the General Assembly following the lead of Florida and changing the official state song in 1997.[129] Virginia cities such as Arlington and Lexington removed Confederate flags and names from public property in 2013 and 2014 to spite "Confederate reminiscers and mythologizers." These moves implied that, as the *Times-Dispatch* hypothesized in 2014, "those statues [along Monument Avenue] should all be torn down" to "repudiate not only everything bad about the Confederacy but also everything good as well."[130] By the 2010s it was clear that Richmonders, and many Virginians for that matter, generally did not revere their Confederate past like the generations before them.

National tragedies forced Richmond to capstone its stand against Lost Cause symbolism: a stand the city had long taken; a stand that the nation often forgot and ignored. The murder of Black people and antiracism protestors in Charleston (2015), Charlottesville (2017), and Minneapolis (2020) compelled Richmond mayor Levar Stoney to remove the Confederate statues from Monument Avenue and other parts of the city beginning on July 1, 2020.[131] This decision resulted from years of commissions (filled with academics and residents) designed to reinterpret them.[132] Yet Stoney risked a felony charge and ordered their removal under the guise of public safety, a common tactic used by fellow southern leaders between Virginia and Texas.[133] His decision, and the tremendous public support for it, reflected Richmond's answer to the question about whether "racial reconciliation can take place as long as they [Confederate monuments] stand."[134] Many Richmonders, both lifelong and recent residents, believed that systemic changes to racial disparities could not take place until the relics of White supremacy were physically torn from the landscape.[135] A local Black historical reenactor said it best when he claimed: "If we can dismantle the symbols of White supremacy, it means we can dismantle the legacy of White supremacy."[136] With this mentality being developed over decades of social and political changes, and now still alive and well, it is safe to say that Richmond is many things, but the capital of the Confederacy is no longer one of them.

Epilogue

"CAPITAL OF RECONCILIATION?"

> By doing this, how exactly do the people of Richmond benefit? Will the city's crumbling infrastructure and failing schools miraculously improve after this is done? Will the tens of thousands of dollars required for removals ensure that a better life for the city's citizens will follow?
>
> —Stuart Butler, Letter to the Editor, *Times-Dispatch,* June 20, 2020

> Does removal of statues mean that more or less attention will be paid in the future to the major work that is undone? These are public monuments to the hidden artifacts that still hold our metropolitan city in bondage to the scandal of the Confederacy. The gravestones will be removed, but the buried bodies will continue to haunt us. The national media will shift their attention somewhere else. But the hidden, destructive divisions will remain.
>
> —Reverend Dr. Benjamin Campbell, "Remove Real Artifacts of the Confederacy," *Richmond Times-Dispatch,* August 27, 2017

WELL BEFORE the Covid-19 pandemic and removal of Confederate statues in 2020, Richmond residents fully acknowledged that systemic racial poverty plagued the area. Yet they ignored the prospect that the ground-level action they used to alter the city's identity could help solve it. Rather, they saw—and still see—disparate racial poverty as an issue that city government, first and foremost, should remedy. For most of my lifetime, Richmond was, economically, a municipality for the poor—the white-collar salt mines where suburbanites earned the salaries that protected their coveted places in Henrico and Chesterfield Counties and West End Richmond. That all changed in the 2010s when corporate influx made Richmond a "millennial magnet," ranking it in the top five of up-and-coming southern cities. This newfound wealth did not improve the lives of most Richmonders, as nearly 50 percent of the metro area's impoverished residents—mostly Black—lived meager lives within the city limits.[1] Because of the focus on history and identity, Richmond's racial reconciliation movement has long ignored the dreadful realities that truly plague Richmond life.

Mayor Levar Stoney (first elected in 2016 and reelected in 2020) responded to this crisis with a new budget proposal during his 2019 reelection campaign. Stoney culminated a series of citizen demands into a $758 million budget proposal that would use surplus tax revenue—cultivated from slight tax increases—to flood the city's dire transportation, education, and housing departments with enough cash to lower the rising costs of being a poor minority in Richmond. In all, Stoney sought to do what the first majority Black city council of 1977 could only dream of: use the power of local government to correct economic disparities in perpetuity. Stoney's historic budget and reformation of city government succumbed to the Covid-19 pandemic and unrest of summer 2020.[2]

Stoney won widespread support among the activist community with his proposal despite being the usual target of their dissent. "We can't talk about racial reconciliation without doing the work," a trio of activists said in support of the mayor's budget.[3] However, the costs of the pandemic and protests turned the city's slight surplus into major deficits after Stoney won a tough reelection campaign, built largely on his promise to deliver the new budget.[4] "This budget is not the budget we first proposed, nor is it the budget we wanted, but it's the budget we have to live with in light of these most difficult and challenging times," Stoney disappointingly said after it became clear that his campaign promises would be unkept.[5] The failed budget signaled that even as the statues came down and Richmond's millennial stock ascended higher, the inequitable ecosystem of working poverty, housing instability, and underperforming public schools remain firmly rooted beneath the surface, suppressing the potential of Richmond's human capital.[6]

Modern Richmonders need to make what began on July 1, 2020, a watershed moment where reconciliation involves fixing "the real issues of race in Richmond." Gross disparities in wealth, housing, and education have ironically gotten worse while the city has become expressively and aesthetically antiracist. This is because the spirit of reconciliation that flourished in the late twentieth century was not that of the Richmond Urban Institute but rather that of Hope in the Cities. Thus, racial disparities worsened as too many people saw Black monuments going up and racist relics coming down as the zenith, and not starting point, for fixing racial issues. Too many area residents rested on the laurels of public history and identity, ignoring their personal responsibility in helping racially reconcile Richmond. The downstream result is the contemporary city: one where antiracist attitudes and the cosmetic improvements that accompany them, play cover for the bigoted personal choices of individuals to not live among the Black Richmond working class as equals.

When disparities became too great to ignore, as I argue, area residents predictably deferred to government what they should have done themselves—namely, live out the antiracist attitude they embrace by making homes among the working and underclasses and sending their children to inner-city schools from kindergarten through twelfth grade. Many area residents will not personally invest in a more wholistic city, one where race and class do not dictate one's future outcomes. Richmond is a better city to live in now than ever. However, if area residents do not, themselves, break the cycle of race-based poverty, "Richmond's makeover," said longtime activist Benjamin Campbell, runs the risk of being "more cosmetic than substantive."[7]

"The Change Has to Do with Our Problems Getting Larger"

"There has been a change, no mistake about it," said longtime political scientist John V. Moeser about Richmond in the twenty-first century. However, he lamented that "the change has to do with our problems getting larger."[8]

Framing Mayor Stoney's budget was Richmond's unforeseen and inequitable economic and populational boom in the 2000s. For the first time since Henry Marsh ran for elected office in 1965, the city was and is trending both White and wealthy, with nearly 233,000 residents, neatly split between Whites and Blacks in 2020.[9] Much of this has to do with both phases of racial reconciliation, when city leadership came together and committed to rebuilding inner city infrastructure in the 1980s, and neighborhood organizations and academic and public history groups changed the city's identity in the 1990s and 2000s. By the 2020s Richmond had become a city both physically and identifiably open for businesses that furthered the existing and unresolved issues with race-based urban poverty.

Corporate influx exacerbated existing racial disparities among the city's poor. Between 2000 and 2020, ten Fortune 1000 companies called Richmond home because of its corporate tax rate of 6 percent. City government also committed to invest in infrastructure while residents created the antiracist climate that modern firms need to attract highly skilled, knowledge-based labor. At the same time, the poverty rate increased from 20 to 25 percent, with Blacks going from 61 percent of people living in poverty to a full two-thirds. Whites decreased to under 25 percent of those in poverty. Rates of poverty among Black people increased from 30 to 34 percent, whereas poverty among Whites decreased from 17 to 15 percent.[10] The paradox Richmond experienced was the fulfillment of urban America's skills mismatch, where firms dependent on knowledge-based workers relocate to former industrial manufacturing centers where public education lags far behind industry demands. Thus, when industry comes in, they recruit labor from across the country, leaving many underskilled locals (often minorities) trapped in service, retail, and fast-food labor markets that do not pay a living wage. This is a trend happening across the South and the nation.

The reinforcement of Black urban poverty by corporate influx is more a product of history than sinister design. As biotech, banking, insurance, education, and healthcare firms came to Richmond and recruited highly educated and skilled administrative and managerial labor, they ended up with mostly White workers ($128,000 yearly earnings on average), many of whom benefitted from systemic educational advantages provided for middle-class suburban Americans after World War II.[11] Adversely, the local Blacks who were locked out of quality education filled the ranks of the often nonsalaried, low-wage laborers ($27,000 annually).[12] For the Black working class, wages did not keep up with inflation. The average impoverished family of four in Richmond earns around $25,000 a year, while a single poor person regardless of race makes around $12,000; these 2020 numbers are almost identical to those seen twenty years prior.[13] It also has not helped that Blacks now share space (both physically and financially) with an increasing number of low-skilled migrants from south of the US border.[14] While the corporate influx to Richmond is the crowning achievement of both phases of racial reconciliation, it is also the result of national economic trends that block urban Blacks from the economic spoils surrounding them.

Residents have taken a more passive, less socially responsible approach to Black urban poverty. While contributing to systemic racial poverty, local employers are not as much to blame as Richmonders, both past and present, who divested from local schools and neighborhoods. By doing that, they left working- and underclass Blacks with a resource-poor city government that felt compelled to do the impossible: tax and redevelop the city out of poverty. The belief that city government was primarily responsible for fixing urban poverty persisted since the Marsh Revolution and well into the 1980s.[15] After John V. Moeser's groundbreaking 2011 study, entitled "Unpacking the Census," interested residents, political leaders, and academics pressured local government to actively fix the systemic racial poverty they oversaw but did not create.[16] This report was supported and distributed by over eighty community organizations, one of them being Initiatives of Change. A year later, Mayor Dwight C. Jones created, and the subsequent Stoney administration strengthened, the

Office of Community Wealth Building (OCWB). The OCWB works as a liaison between local legislators (city council) and businesspeople to pipeline low-skilled Black and brown residents to livable-wage employment.[17]

If Richmonders insist on city government correcting the historical sins of White middle- and upper-class divestment, then compulsory community investment is required. The neoliberal OCWB forms partnerships with nonprofits to provide underclass families with private forms of welfare and job access.[18] This antipoverty apparatus is innovative, garnering much praise from academics and city elites around the nation.[19] However, Richmond cannot nonprofit or welfare its way out of systemic poverty issues. Rather, stable government-sponsored pipelines out of poverty require strong policies, such as requiring, not asking, major corporations to reinvest surplus capital into the city's many job training programs that help make up for the skills gap created by historical divestment in urban education.

What cannot happen is what has been happening: mainly relying on controversial public-private, taxpayer subsidized economic crapshoots. In the past, these get-rich-quick schemes included the Richmond Coliseum, Project One, and the Sixth Street Marketplace. More recent "silver bullet strategies"—in the words of Richmond historian and political insider Julian Hayter—were the proposed Black sports hall of fame in downtown and the baseball park in Shockoe Bottom in the late 1990s and early 2000s; the city *paying* to host the Washington Redskins (now Washington Commanders) training camp from 2013 to 2021; the Sixth Street Marketplace-esque Navy Hill Project in 2018; and the recently defeated casino proposal.[20] Placing the burden on city government to correct the sins of residential divestment compels its representatives to be more speculative with the meager tax revenue needed to serve the urban poor. Residents must acknowledge that they are (knowingly or unknowingly) a part of the problem plaguing poor Black Richmonders. By doing so, they can make the logical step toward converting the past reconciliatory efforts into meaningful action towards equity.

"It's Called the Food Chain, Isn't It!"

The unrest of the summer of 2020 was not just about police misconduct. Rather, some argued tearing down monuments was also deconstructing the mindsets that allowed for a racial reconciliation movement that left the city's abhorrent housing situation largely unaddressed. Between 2000 and 2020, home prices ballooned, lowering Black inner-city residency. This was no coincidence, as gentrification in Richmond recently ranked among the worst in the nation, going by inclusionary housing metrics that calculated the ease by which people of all income levels and races accessed stable housing situations.[21] As city government demolished public housing and developers and urban pioneers raised the cost of living, evictions have soared and access to affordable housing has decreased to an all-time low.[22]

The failure of Stoney's 2019 budget proposal reflected the limits of relying on city government to correct past sins. The pandemic ensured that Virginia's first-ever publicly run eviction diversion program (created in 2019) could not keep up with demand.[23] The budget failure, and mounting evictions of poor Blacks, compelled protesters to use the national unrest over the deaths of George Floyd and Breonna Taylor at the hands of police officers as a platform to highlight the housing crisis. "For far too long," a *Times-Dispatch* editorial said about Richmond's housing crisis, "city residents have endured the traumatic domino effect of homelessness, resulting in part from being evicted or not being able to afford decent housing in the first place."[24] Instead of marching downtown, they took their homemade signs and megaphones to the Windsor Farms neighborhood—the traditional bedroom of Richmond powerbrokers and a symbol of Richmond's top-down housing market that privileges the few at the expense of many.[25] The 2020 protesters had it right by protesting inequitable housing in class-exclusive neighborhoods and not at city hall. After all, it was the long uninterrupted class-based housing segregation that confined working-class Blacks into substandard dwellings. Residents must take collective responsibility for this trend, as history shows that when city government is left fixing the results of de facto class segregation and residential flight, it only makes things worse.

In 1998 the Richmond Redevelopment and Housing Authority accepted a $26.9 million federal grant to replace Blackwell's (Southside) 440 public housing units with 800 market-rate and Section 8 units.[26] This was a stark reversal to the 1950s and 1960s, when city government eagerly demolished single-family units and crammed Blacks into public housing. This new mission was to increase city real estate values and reverse the historical impact of urban renewal by transitioning the city's 97 percent Black public housing occupants to affordable, mixed-income housing.[27] As of 2013 the city *had* demolished the 440 units, but it had replaced them with only 200 mixed-income dwellings. Most of Blackwell's four thousand impoverished residents were subsequently priced out of the area by new rental companies and homeowners who were not forced by the city to accept Section 8 vouchers.[28] Former Blackwell residents turned into activists. They petitioned city leaders to mandate the construction of one new public housing unit for every one demolished.[29] Believing that this policy would scare off private real estate investors, city leaders bitterly denounced the proposal. The city council later partnered with a nonprofit development firm to demolish East End's Creighton Court and build three hundred mixed-income units. Even with Blackwell and Creighton gone, Richmond still has the most concentrated public housing situation and affordable housing deficit between Philadelphia and Atlanta.[30] As of 2020 the city stares at an affordable housing deficit of thirty thousand units; Virginia as a whole needs around three hundred thousand.[31] While originally argued as a benefit to the Black poor and the city at large, Richmond's war on public housing has exacerbated a problem that has, while changing in nature, remained unanswered since World War II.[32]

City government has also spurred private-sector speculation that undercuts its mission to provide housing stability for working- and underclass Blacks. The city council's fifteen-year tax abatements (enacted in 1995) on capital improvements to "slum" or dilapidated properties unleashed a monsoon of White real estate investment in the majority Black Northside, East End, Jackson Ward, Carver, and Oregon Hill.[33] Paying for much of these abatements were working-class Blacks whose rents, property taxes, and utilities increase beyond their means to pay.[34] Blacks accounted for 90 percent of Church Hill homeowners in 2000. This dropped 30 percent by 2015, while White homeownership in the area increased 160 percent.[35] When asked about how she afforded the higher cost of living on a working-class salary, a Black Church Hill woman once joked that she was "just holding on. Tax bill going up. Water bill going up. Everything going up—but your income." A local White developer unabashedly responded by saying, "It's called the food chain, isn't it!"[36] Public pressure compelled the city council to mostly end the unprecedented fifteen-year tax abatements in January 2020, which "allowed for this city to be gentrified with [Black] taxpayer dollars," Councilman Mike Jones said critically. As of 2023, only firms that set aside at least 30 percent of their developments for affordable housing will receive fifteen-year abatements.[37] This will exacerbate the lingering problem few have been discussing. That is, as of fiscal year 2020, Richmond only collected $1 million for every $84 million in assessed taxable real estate, the chickens of over two decades of progentrification abatements that will, one day, come to roost.[38]

Although the abatements are gone, middle-class and affluent speculation and Black dislocation are ironically in Richmond to stay. The speculation often begins with VCU graduates or lower-middle-class Whites buying cheap residential or commercial property in majority Black areas. Then, investors purchase, rehabilitate, and resell or rent older properties with ironclad screening processes to prevent "undesirable" occupancy. "This is the cycle we've seen in Richmond for years now," a White woman once said about gentrification in the capital city.[39] Contributing to the housing crisis are elevated rates of Black foreclosures and evictions. Since the 2008 economic crash, longtime Black homeowners and renters in Northside, Southside, and East End have accounted for more than half of the city's foreclosures and evictions.[40] Richmond's eviction epidemic exists within a statewide problem. Virginia currently holds five of the nation's top ten eviction-heavy cities—Richmond, Hampton, Newport News, Norfolk, and Chesapeake, all of which have large or majority working-class Black populations.[41] Grounding this eviction epidemic are the nation's strongest prolandlord and antitenant state laws.[42] This situation has swelled affordable housing waiting lists beyond the levels that Henry Marsh saw in the late 1960s.[43] Richmond ranks among cities nearly three times its size—such as Baltimore, Atlanta, Houston, Dallas, and Virginia Beach—in rates of Black displacement. Nearly four hundred Black families on average were relocated during every gentrification project in Richmond from 1990 to 2020.[44]

Richmond area residents themselves must collectively decide to break the housing cycle that has trapped poor Blacks in substandard living conditions. The clustering of middle- and upper-class people into class-exclusive neighborhoods is not new or unique to Richmond, but now it has worsened housing affordability in this new age of gentrification, where urban pioneers have more disposable income than ever. Average home prices in Richmond have increased from $150,000 in 2000 to just over $250,000 in 2021.[45] Prices will climb even higher because the increased use of telework is slowly turning Richmond into a suburb of Washington, DC, ensuring that high-income earners will be the only people who can afford homes in the city.[46] City government's latest plans involve affordable housing construction through the Affordable Housing Trust Fund (2004); promoting working-class homeownership with the Maggie Walker Community Land Trust (2018); and Mayor Stoney's Eviction Diversion Program (2019).[47] City leadership, however, cannot keep up the double tap dance of attracting wealthier residents without sponsoring the removal of the working class. To combat this, residents should refuse to live in class-homogenous clusters. It is the clustered influx of investment that creates the tsunami of gentrification that washes away the Black poor. If monied residents refused to change their housing patterns, racially inequitable

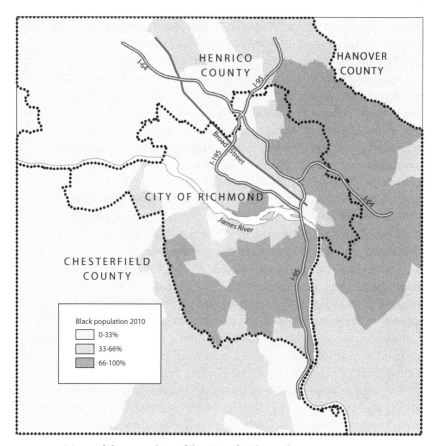

FIGURE 7. Map and demographics of the City of Richmond, 2010

housing access will remain unreconciled and inconsistent with the racial progress made over the last six decades.

"Real Artifacts of the Confederacy"

The meat of Levar Stoney's budget battle in 2019 was dedicated to reforming Richmond Public Schools (RPS). His proposed tax increases involved dumping tens of millions into shuttering academic programs and increasing fiscal and disciplinary accountability among RPS bureaucrats. In all, his proposal would have attempted to make RPS what it is currently not among most residents: a trusted, legitimate pillar and valuable contributor to Richmond life.[48] Unfortunately for Stoney, increased funding could not hide the fact that reforming RPS is, without a doubt, the most challenging (and probably impossible) proposition that residents can task city government with. Administrations before Stoney admitted this much.

City officials in 2000 assessed the high poverty rate (then 21 percent) and substandard housing situation and predicted that Richmond's school-age population would continue its decades-long decline well into the twenty-first century. By 2020 city officials were optimistic about every aspect of city life except public schools. Justifying this pessimism was the fact that school enrollment remained largely stagnant despite the city's population increase.[49] This meant that the newer and affluent residents intentionally bypassed city schools for private options. Both 2000 and 2020 city plans made clear that the "quality and perception of Richmond Public Schools" would not improve along with other aspects of city life, a reality that Stoney's budget proposal had to combat in 2019.[50]

Both city plans and the mayor did not say what many residents make plain in casual conversations: schools in the City of Richmond are in shambles because middle-class families of both races have long condemned them to being the underfunded repositories for the metro area's poorest, underperforming Black and brown students. Richmond's iron triangle of oppression is grounded by a failing school system that, despite some diligent instructors, parents, and administrators, rarely provides a pathway out of the systemic racial poverty that impacts other aspects of city life, such as employment and housing. In most cases, RPS absorbs, solidifies, and perpetuates the city's issues with poverty.[51] Like employment and housing access, the city school system remains as unreconciled as it did during the modern civil rights movement.

RPS is still defined by racial segregation nearly seventy years after *Brown*. Whites of all classes, and later the Black middle class, fled RPS between the 1960s and 1980s. By the 1990s Black school officials recruited some middle-class (mostly White) families back to the district by ending crosstown busing and implementing neighborhood zoning, school choice options, and magnet schools.[52] These plans initially convinced some White families to stay in RPS, but only for their neighborhood elementary schools.[53] Once their children reached middle and high school, and would likely attend classes with the Black Richmond lower middle and working classes, White parents transitioned them to suburban public or private schools. This was openly practiced during my childhood, and the *Times-Dispatch* finally admitted to Richmond's "long-discussed but little-documented phenomenon" in 2018 called "playground talk."[54]

Residents' school choices compelled RPS (a wing of city government) to undermine the spirit of *Brown*. The increase in non-Black students came with a Faustian bargain to allow middle-class Black and White families to segregate schools within the district. As of 2020, around 75 percent of RPS schools have fewer than 10 percent non-Black students; this is the worst rate of intradistrict segregation in the Commonwealth.[55] As of 2019, RPS put almost all of its federal Title I funding (around $20 million annually) into elementary education—the Whitest and most affluent part of city schools. The overwhelmingly Black middle and high schools have poverty rates as high as 80 percent per school.[56] In spite of the slight influx of non-White students, RPS remains home to the metro areas poorest students because middle-class families of every race still flee the district.[57] By 2020, nearly 19,000 of the nearly 30,000 students (66 percent) qualified for free and reduced lunches, while the state average was around 30 percent per district.[58] RPS ranked second in the Commonwealth with the highest percentage of student poverty, and seventh with the sheer number of poor children.[59] Still, RPS remains the only district in the metro area that enrolls significantly fewer children (around 70 percent) into school than are born within its jurisdiction. Chesterfield enrolls more than 90 percent, and Henrico enrolls above 115 percent, many of them being from families who fled RPS by the middle school years.[60]

RPS's student makeup has led to a culture of failure, corruption, and ineffectiveness that is downright embarrassing. The high concentration of poor Black students has solidified a culture where low grades, high disciplinary issues, and teacher apathy not only lead the Commonwealth but comprise the functional norm.[61] RPS officials have lowered the minimal value of their graduates' diplomas by implementing severely relaxed graduation requirements to keep up with the Commonwealth average. Some teachers delegitimized RPS even further by coaxing students to cheat on state-sponsored standardized tests. Superintendent Jason Karmas noted that discovery of the scandal was not that difficult because "to be blunt: too many people thought how could Carver [Elementary School], which serves nearly 100% low-income students and students of color, have such high scores? There must be something going on."[62] Compounding corruption issues were the "sloppy accounting, poor communication and misused money" discovered by the mayor's office during Stoney's 2019 budget initiative.[63]

As many city schools hover around provisional or unaccredited status, state and local legislators have soured on RPS, regularly lowering their percentage of funding since 2009.[64] Chesterfield's and Henrico's higher enrollment, better test scores, and smaller corporate revenue bases annually net them more state funding than RPS.[65] While many have spoken out about the inequitable funding calculator that ensures that students who have keep getting, the Virginia legislature makes plain with taxpayers' money what Richmond area residents have said with their feet for years. RPS remains an illegitimate, bastard institution that must prove itself *worthy* of significant financial investment.[66]

RPS's struggles are best seen, however, in the very public issues of teacher retention, facility dilapidation, and city efforts to remedy them. RPS operates on the opposite end of the spectrum, where schools with economically stable, high-performing students tend to have low teacher turnover rates, regardless of starting salary and midcareer pay.[67] RPS annually loses around 20–25 percent of its teachers to resignations, more than twice the state and national average.[68] Retention rates have gotten so bad that RPS administration engaged in another scandal to hide retention statistics from public inquiry as recent as 2020.[69] VCU, parent groups, and the city council have partnered to remedy this issue, but for dedicated teachers, retention rates are a reflection of facility management, as many school buildings were once deemed "borderline criminal" by a longtime teacher and "functionally obsolete" by local government.[70] RPS worked with city government to open the Patrick Henry School of Sciences and Art in 2010, and renovated Southside's Huguenot High School, Elkhart and Thompson middle schools, and E. S. H. Greene Elementary School, as well as East End's George Mason Elementary School and Martin Luther King Jr. Middle School (formerly Mosby Middle School) by 2019.[71] The mayor has even promised more renovations in the years to come.[72] Antithetical to recent governmental progress was the unanimous vote to keep RPS virtual for the 2020–21 school year.[73] Not only have RPS teachers informed me privately that the learning gap between their students and suburban counterparts is widening, but local private schools used RPS's closure, and overall incompetence, as a marketing tool to tighten their stranglehold on some of the metro area's best students and most involved families.[74]

Public education remains at the heart of Richmond's racial reconciliation dilemma in the twenty-first century. Even more than the statues that no longer sit on Monument Avenue, the "real artifacts of the Confederacy," as Benjamin Campbell wrote in the aftermath of the mass shooting of Blacks at a church in Charleston, are Richmond Public Schools. Public schools are meant to cultivate economic prosperity and social harmony by developing human capital from every corner of a community. Yet by providing separate and unequal education, the Richmond area confines the children of the less fortunate to the dark carousel of low-wage labor, which ensures they will struggle to earn livable incomes and maintain stable housing situations. In sum: residents ensure that RPS reproduces the White supremacy and Black inferiority that slavery and Jim Crow were known for. The area residents who intentionally abandon RPS and thus confine them to a meager function for poor Blacks, should know that they are, in a twenty-first-century context, in line with the fallen Confederates who would be proud to know that in spite of their surrender on April 9, 1865, the citadel of their racist rebellion still maintains a functional system of racial inequity in spite of the more recent efforts to end it.

"If Richmond is truly to become the 'Capital of Reconciliation,'" wrote Campbell, then human investment and sacrifice on the part of the area populace are desperately needed.[75] Middle- and upper-class families must invest their children, money, and time to rehabilitate city schools and end the skills gap and live among the working and underclass to dissuade gentrification. Richmond undoubtedly has the courage to change, but it is up to residents to lead leadership by enacting change in their everyday lives. Sacrificing the privileges of a racist history and culture is harder than sacrificing that history itself. The recent past indicates that no city is more equipped to do that than Richmond. America's original sin of racism, in many ways, began in Richmond. It is this author's belief that, as was said by Campbell, "here where racism started in this country is where it should end."[76]

NOTES

Abbreviations

BTA	Black Teens for Advancement
CAB	Citizens Against Busing
CCA	Carillon Civic Association
CCCA	Creighton Court Civic Association
CRA	Community Reinvestment Act of 1977
DDU	Downtown Development Unlimited
FHA	Federal Housing Authority
GRTC	Greater Richmond Transit Co.
HIC	Hope in the Cities
HMCA	Home Mortgage Disclosure Act of 1975
IoC	Initiatives of Change
MRA	Moral Re-Armament
OCWB	Office of Community Wealth Building
OEO	Office of Economic Opportunity
RAA	*Richmond Afro-American*
RCAP	Richmond Community Action Program
RITA	Richmond Independent Taxpayer Association
RPS	Richmond Public Schools
RRHA	Richmond Redevelopment and Housing Authority
RTD	*Richmond Times-Dispatch*
RUI	Richmond Urban Institute
SCV	Sons of Confederate Veterans
UR	University of Richmond
VCU	Virginia Commonwealth University
VEPCO	Virginia Electric and Power Co.
VM	Valentine Museum
VMFA	Virginia Museum of Fine Arts
VMHC	Virginia Museum of History and Culture
WP	*Washington Post*

Prologue

1. William Julius Wilson, *The Declining Significance of Race* (Chicago: University of Chicago Press, 1980); Eduardo Bonilla-Silla, *Racism Without Racists: Color-Blind Racism and the Persistence of Racial Inequality in Contemporary America* (Lanham, MD: Rowman & Littlefield, 2003); and Tim

Wise, *Colorblind: The Rise of Post Racial Politics and the Retreat from Racial Equity* (San Francisco: City Lights, 2010).
2. "Richmond, Va., Mayor Orders Emergency Removal of Confederate Statues," *NPR*, July 1, 2020, https://www.npr.org/sections/live-updates-protests-for-racial-justice/2020/07/01/886204604/richmond-va-mayor-orders-emergency-removal-of-confederate-statues; "Celebrating July Fourth Amid an Ongoing Struggle for Equality," *Richmond Times-Dispatch*, July 5, 2020, 4A. (Hereafter cited as *RTD*.)
3. "Proposal Addresses RVA's Historical Inequities," *RTD*, April 5, 2019, A9; "Richmond 300: A Guide For Growth, Designing an Equitable, Sustainable, and Beautiful Richmond for its 300th Birthday in 2037," September 29, 2020, https://www.rva.gov/sites/default/files/2021-03/R300_Adopted_210331_0.pdf.
4. "Statues vs. Systemic Change," *Boston Globe*, July 18, 2020, https://www.bostonglobe.com/2020/07/18/metro/amid-renewed-calls-racial-justice-how-meaningful-is-symbolic-change/.
5. John V. Moeser and Rutledge M. Dennis, *The Politics of Annexation: Oligarchic Power in a Southern City* (Boston, MA: Shenkman Publishing, 1982); Christopher Silver, *Twentieth-Century Richmond: Planning, Politics, and Race* (Knoxville, TN: University of Tennessee Press, 1984); Lewis A. Randolph and Gayle T. Tate, *Rights for a Season: The Politics of Race, Class, and Gender in Richmond, Virginia* (Knoxville: University of Tennessee Press, 2003); Julian Maxwell Hayter, *The Dream Is Lost: Voting Rights and the Politics of Race in Richmond, Virginia* (Lexington: University of Kentucky Press, 2017).
6. Benjamin Muse, *Virginia's Massive Resistance* (Bloomington: University of Indiana Press, 1961); Robbins L. Gates, *The Making of Massive Resistance: Virginia's Politics of Public School Desegregation, 1954–1956* (Chapel Hill: University of North Carolina Press, 1964), 1–24; Robert A. Pratt, *The Color of Their Skin: Education and Race in Richmond, Virginia, 1954–89* (Charlottesville: University of Virginia Press, 1992); Matthew D. Lassiter and Andrew B. Lewis, eds., *The Moderates' Dilemma: Massive Resistance to School Desegregation in Virginia* (Charlottesville: University of Virginia Press, 1998); Alexander S. Leidholdt, *Standing Before the Shouting Mob: Lenoir Chambers and Virginia's Massive Resistance to Public School Integration* (Tuscaloosa: University of Alabama Press, 1997); William P. Hustwit, *James J. Kilpatrick: Salesman for Segregation* (Chapel Hill: University of North Carolina Press, 2013); Jeffrey E. Littlejohn and Charles H. Ford, *Elusive Equality: Desegregation and Resegregation in Norfolk's Public Schools* (Charlottesville: University of Virginia Press, 2012); Brian J. Daugherity, *Keep On Keeping On: The NAACP and the Implementation of Brown v. Board of Education in Virginia* (Charlottesville: University of Virginia Press, 2016); Jill Ogline Titus, *Brown's Battleground: Students, Segregationists, and

the Struggle for Justice in Prince Edward County, Virginia *(Chapel Hill: University of North Carolina Press, 2011).*
7. Here, I see "modern" as post-1968, which is generally seen as the final year of the traditional civil rights movement, marked by the passage of the Fair Housing Act of 1968—the last piece of civil rights legislation dealing directly with Black people.
8. Kevin M. Kruse, *White Flight: Atlanta and the Making of Modern Conservatism* (Princeton, NJ: Princeton University Press, 2005); Matthew D. Lassiter, *The Silent Majority: Suburban Politics in the Sunbelt South* (Princeton, NJ: Princeton University Press, 2007); Joseph Crespino, *In Search of Another County: Mississippi and the Conservative Counterrevolution* (Princeton, NJ: Princeton University Press, 2007); Tracy E. K'Meyer, *Civil Rights in the Gateway to the South: Louisville, Kentucky, 1945–1980* (Lexington: University of Kentucky Press, 2009); Leonard N. Moore, *Black Rage in New Orleans: Police Brutality and African American Activism from World War II to Hurricane Katrina* (Baton Rouge: Louisiana State University Press, 2011); Steven Estes, *Charleston in Black and White: Race and Power in the South after the Civil Rights Movement* (Chapel Hill, NC: University of North Carolina Press, 2015); Maurice J. Hobson, *The Legend of the Black Mecca: Politics and Class in the Making of Modern Atlanta* (Chapel Hill: University of North Carolina Press, 2017).
9. Clarence N. Stone, *Regime Politics: Governing Atlanta, 1946–1988* (Lawrence: University Press of Kansas, 1989); Larry Keating, *Atlanta: Race, Class, and Urban Expansion* (Philadelphia: Temple University Press, 2001); Ronald H. Bayor, *Race and the Shaping of Twentieth-Century Atlanta* (Chapel Hill: University of North Carolina Press, 2000); Alton Hornsby Jr., *Black Power in Dixie: A Political History of African Americans in Atlanta* (Gainesville: University of Florida Press, 2009); Tomiko Brown-Nagin, *Courage to Dissent: Atlanta and the Long Civil Rights Movement* (New York: Oxford University Press, 2011); Hobson, *Legend of the Black Mecca*, 7.
10. John B. Hatch, *Race and Reconciliation: Redressing Wounds of Injustice* (Lanham, MD: Lexington Book, 2008).
11. Charles P. Henry, *The Politics of Racial Reparations* (New York: NYU Press, 2007); Ronald W. Walter, *The Price of Reconciliation* (Ann Arbor: University of Michigan Press, 2010).

1. The Marsh Revolution

1. The chapter opening epigraph is from Henry L. Marsh III, *The Memoirs of Honorable Henry L. Marsh, III: Civil Rights Champion, Public Servant, Lawyer* (Hampton Falls, NH: Grant House Publishers, 2018), 3.
2. "RF Majority of Six Wins; Carwile, Bagley Lead Vote," *RTD*, June 12, 1968, 1–2.

3. William Waller Hening, ed., *The Statutes at large; Being a Collection of All the Laws of Virginia* (Richmond, 1810).
4. Ira Berlin, *Slaves without Masters: The Free Negro in the Antebellum South* (New York: New Press, 1974).
5. "Disorder on the Railroad," *Richmond Planet*, December 30, 1899, 1.
6. John Egerton, *Speak Now Against the Day: The Generation before the Civil Rights Movement in the South* (Chapel Hill: University of North Carolina Press, 1995), 29–30.
7. W. J. Cash, *Mind of the South* (New York: Vintage Books, 1941), 378; Egerton, *Speak Now Against the Day*, 19–25.
8. Certificate of birth for Henry Levander Marsh III, December 10, 1933, Virginia Department of Health, Richmond, Births, 1864–2016; Richmond City Directory, 1933, US City Directories, 1822–1995 (ancestry.com); Marsh, *Memoirs*, 19.
9. US Census, 1940, St. Johns, Hertford, NC, Roll m-t0627-02929, Page 6A, Enumeration District 46-12; US Census, 1940, Newport, Isle of Wight, VA, Roll m-t0627-04271, Page 2B, Enumeration District 47-5; Marsh, *Memoirs*, 19.
10. Julian Bond interview with Henry Marsh, Explorations in Black Leadership Online Archive, University of Virginia Institute for Public History, August 31, 2000; Richmond City Directory, 1959, US City Directory (ancestry.com).
11. Julian Bond interview with Marsh, August 31, 2000.
12. Richmond City Directory, 1954, US City Directories, 1822–1995, ancestry.com; Marsh, *Memoirs*, 29–35.
13. Marsh, *Memoirs*, 27; Richmond City Directory, 1944, US City Directories, 1822–1995, ancestry.com; Francis Earle Lutz, *Richmond in World War II* (Richmond, VA: Dietz, 1951), 67–74.
14. Marie Tyler-McGraw, *At the Falls: Richmond, Virginia, and Its People* (Chapel Hill: University of North Carolina Press, 1994), 273–77; Bond interview with Marsh, August 31, 2000.
15. Author interview with Viola Baskerville, June 28, 2019; with William Mason, July 22, 2019.
16. Adah L. Ward Randolph, "It Is Better to Light a Candle Than to Curse the Darkness: Ethel Thompson Overby and Democratic Schooling in Richmond, Virginia, 1910-1958," *Educational Studies* 48, no.1 (2010): 220–43; Margaret Edds, *We Faced the Dawn: Oliver Hill, Spottswood Robinson, and the Legal Team That Dismantled Jim Crow* (Charlottesville: University of Virginia Press, 2018), 31.
17. Richmond City Directory, 1954, US City Directories, 1822–1995, ancestry.com; Marsh, *Memoirs*, 29–35.
18. "Alumni Notes," *Virginia Union Bulletin* 32, nos. 2–3 (January–February 1932): 10–12; "Alumni Campaign Progress," *Virginia Union Bulletin* 38, no. 3

(February 1938): 5–7; "Alumni Corner," *Virginia Union Bulletin* 40, no.1 (November 1939): 13–97, Virginia Union University (hereafter cited as VUU) Archives, Richmond; Raymond Gavins, *The Perils and Prospects of Southern Black Leadership* (Durham, NC: Duke University Press, 1977), 22–26.

19. Thomas L. Dabney, "The Study of the Negro," *Journal of Negro History* 19, no. 3 (July 1934): 288; Raymond Gavins, "Gordon Blaine Hancock: An Appraisal," *New South* (Fall 1970), Miscellaneous and Other Writings, 1937–70, Box 2; Gordon Hancock Speech at the Francis J. Torrance School of Race Relations, VUU, January 27, 1932, Correspondences, Box 1, both in Gordon Blaine Hancock Papers, Duke University Libraries, Durham, NC.
20. Henry L. Marsh, undated profile, Alumni: Archives Vertical File, VUU Archives.
21. "Assembly Agrees to Limit Action to Referendum," *RTD*, December 1, 1955, A1.
22. Ibid., A3.
23. "Tax Funds Denied Virginia Schools for Whites Only," *New York Times*, August 25, 1961, 1.
24. "Court Ruling Uncontested by Negroes," *Washington Post*, July 4, 1959, D3 (hereafter cited as *WP*); Marsh, *Memoirs*, 6.
25. Marsh, *Memoirs*, 4–8; Bond interview with Marsh, August 31, 2000.
26. Edds, *We Faced the Dawn*, 194; "U.S. Courts Opens Va. U. Law School," *Richmond Afro-American*, September 9, 1950, 1. (Hereafter cited as *RAA*.)
27. Edds, *We Faced the Dawn*, 33.
28. Ibid., 47–91; "Negroes Plan New Virginia Court Actions," *WP*, September 11, 1948, B3.
29. Jill Ogline Titus, *Brown's Battleground: Segregationists and the Struggle for Justice in Prince Edward County, Virginia* (Chapel Hill: University of North Carolina Press, 2011), 63–130; "Commission Weighs Segregation Ideas," *Richmond News Leader*, November 16, 1954, 1; Edds, *We Faced the Dawn*, 265–66.
30. "Sharp Debate Held on Referendum" *RTD*, December 1, 1955, A1; Marsh, *Memoirs*, 4–7; Bond interview with Marsh, August 31, 2000.
31. Marsh, *Memoirs*, 14–15; Henry L. Marsh and Dianne Harris Certificate of Marriage, August 11, 1962, Virginia Department of Health, Richmond, Marriages, 1936–2014, Roll 101144780; "School Closings Argued in Court," *New York Times*, July 25, 1961, 24.
32. "34 Are Arrested in Sitdowns Here," *RTD*, February 23, 1960, 1; "Hill Blast Va. State Legislature," *RAA*, March 5, 1960, 1–2; "Student Sentenced: Fined in Farmville Appeals Are Noted," *RTD*, April 27, 1963, 3; "Trial Date Set for Demonstrators," *RTD*, September 18, 1963, 2; "Judge Withdraws from Racial Trials," *RTD*, November 20, 1963, 4; "Wounding Case Sent Back Prince Edward," *RTD*, April 11, 1964, 5; "Racial Cases' Transfer from Danville Opposed," *RTD*, January 12, 1965, 5; "Federal Courts Refuse to Hear Danville

Racial Demonstrators," *RTD*, January 22, 1966, 2; "Lawyer for NAACP Convicted, Fined in Prince Edward," *RTD*, April 28, 1967, 19.
33. "Negro Pupils' Side Presented to Court: Before Judge Lewis No Desegregation Plan," *WP*, July 26, 1961, C1; "White School Denied to Negro Scoring IQ of 160," *WP*, August 19, 1961, C1.
34. Bradley v. the School Board of the City of Richmond, US Court of Appeals, Fourth Circuit 317 F 2d 429.41 (1963).
35. Marsh, *Memoirs*, 51–53.
36. "Biracial Committee of 12 Named by City," *Richmond News Leader*, August 8, 1960, clipping, Box 3, M183, Richmond Annexation Files, Virginia Commonwealth University, Richmond. (Hereafter cited as VCU.)
37. "Richmond Quietly Leads Way in Race Relations," *WP*, July 29, 1962, E1.
38. Matthew D. Lassiter, *The Silent Majority: Suburban Politics in the Sunbelt South* (Princeton, NJ: Princeton University Press, 2006), 12, 48–51, 125–26.
39. Gloster B. Current, Director of Branches, to Dr. J. M. Tinsley, September 25, 1947, Folder 3, Richmond, Virginia, 1947–48, Box 1 C209, NAACP Papers, Library of Congress; Marvin T. Chiles, "A Period of Misunderstanding: Reforming Jim Crow in Richmond, Virginia, 1930–1954," *Virginia Magazine of History and Biography* 129, no. 3 (Fall 2021): 244–78.
40. "Oliver W. Hill Elected to Council by 9,097 Votes," *RAA*, June 12, 1948, 1–2; "He's Richmond's First Councilman in Sixty Long Years," *RAA*, June 19, 1948, 1–2; "Meet Richmond's New City Fathers after Hours," and "Richmond Makes History," *RTD*, June 14, 1948, 1, 8; Edds, *We Faced the Dawn*, 192–93, 272–73.
41. Crusade Memo, April 2, 1966, Historian Binder, 1953–68 (4 of 11), Box 1, M306, Crusade for Voters Papers, VCU; "The Crusade for Voters Story," undated, Historian Binder 1, 1953–88 (2–11), ibid.; "Council Approves Resolution for Fair Employment," *RAA*, June 2, 1962, 1; "Letters to the Forum: Mr. Carwile Comments on Councilmanic Election," *Richmond News Leader*, June 18, 1964; "Keep Our Vote Solid," *RAA*, June 6, 1964, 1, 3; "Pannell's Quitting Confirms Suspicions, Carwile Says," *Richmond News Leader*, July, 2, 1965; "Keep Vote Solid" and "Cephas Cites City Needs in Safety, Recreation," *RAA*, June 6, 1964, 3; "Carwile Deplored 'Vote Manipulators,'" *RTD*, June 15, 1964, 18.
42. "Councilman Cephas Pledges No Mistakes from the Heart," *RAA*, June 20, 1964, 1–2; Councilmanic Elections, June 10, 1964, Exhibits 3 and 4, Box 3, M183, Richmond Annexation Files, VCU.
43. Autobiography of B. Addison Cephas Jr., People: Biographies, Box 1, M277, Eleanor P. Sheppard Papers, VCU. (Hereafter cited as Sheppard Papers, VCU.)
44. Crusade Memo, April 2, 1966, Historian Binder, 1953–68 (4 of 11), Box 1, M306, Crusade Papers, VCU; "Marsh to Run for Council," *RAA*, April 16, 1966, 1–2; Hayter, *Dream Is Lost*, 40.

45. Report of the Historian William Armestead Thornton, Historian Binder 1, 1953–88 (1 of 11), Box 1, M306, Crusade Papers, VCU; Bond interview with Marsh, August 31, 2000.
46. Crusade Memo, April 2, 1966, Historian Binder, 1953–68 (4 of 11), Box 1, M306, Crusade Papers, VCU; "Marsh to Run for Council," *RAA,* April 16, 1966, 1–2; Marsh, *Memoirs,* 4–7.
47. Sunday Night Meeting, May 29, 1966, Folder 69, Mss1 W5603b FA2, Wheat Papers, VMHC, Virginia Museum of History and Culture. (Hereafter cited as Wheat Papers, VMHC.)
48. "Confusion Grips Council Election," *Richmond News Leader,* June 13, 1966, 1.
49. "Endorsement Seen a Big Vote Boost," *RAA,* May 14, 1966, 1–2; Bond interview with Marsh, August 31, 2000; "What's Your Excuse for Not Voting," May 1966; "Go to the Polls Early This Tuesday," June 14, 1966, Crusade Memo, Historian Binder 1, 1953–88 (2–11), Box 1, M306, Crusade Papers, VCU.
50. Richardson Dilworth, "American Way Is Urban Way," *WP,* January 20, 1961, C4; James K. Sanford, ed., *Richmond: Her Triumphs, Tragedies, and Growth* (Richmond, VA: Metropolitan Richmond Chamber of Commerce, 1975), 214; "DuPont to Expand," *WP, Times Herald,* June 9, 1960, B10.
51. "A Southern Moderate Predicts Victory," *New York Times,* January 11, 1959, SM17; Virginia H. Hein, "The Image of 'A City Too Busy to Hate': Atlanta in the 1960s," *Phylon* 33, no. 3 (3rd Quarter, 1972): 205–22; Kevin Kruse, *White Flight: Atlanta and the Making of Modern Conservatism* (Princeton, NJ: Princeton University Press, 2005), 41; Lassiter, *Silent Majority,* 11; "Race Issue Won't Stymie Industry, Hartsfield Says," *Atlanta Constitution,* March 30, 1959, 7.
52. "Richmond Quietly Leads Way in Race Relations," *WP,* July 29, 1962, E1.
53. "Congregationalists Report 49% Ready to Accept Negroes: 49% in Congregationalist Survey Willing to Take Negro Members," *New York Times,* January 5, 1959, 1; "New Voices in the South," *Atlanta Constitution,* February 23, 1959, 1.
54. "State Grows Steadily Away from Deep South Tradition," *Atlanta Journal and the Atlanta Constitution,* July 30, 1961, B5; "Virginia Opposes Integration Now," *New York Times,* April 10, 1955, 36.
55. Lassiter, *Silent Majority,* 35–43; "Stanley Supports Park Segregation," *WP,* March 19, 1955, 6; "Court Bars Bias at Public Parks," *New York Times,* March 15, 1955, 14; "8 of Virginia's 9 State-Owned Parks to Remain Segregated this Summer," *WP,* March 24, 1955, 1; "Virginia Urged to Sell Its Parks," *WP,* April 21, 1956, 22; "Dixie Cities Fight Integration Plans of 13 Bus Lines: Montgomery Will Enforce Segregation," *Atlanta Constitution,* April 25, 1956, 1, 7; "300 Richmond Parents Defy Placement Rule, Lawyer Says," *WP,* May 24, 1957, B1.
56. Steven F. Lawson, *Running for Freedom: Civil Rights and Black Politics since 1941* (New York: Wiley, 2014), 45–50; "From the Virginia Board of Elections

to John M. Brooks of the NAACP," State Board of Elections, Bulletin No. 2, May 22, 1958, John Brooks Papers, VCU; "Hub of Integration Move," *Atlanta Journal and Atlanta Constitution*, April 24, 1960, 5E.

57. Carl T. Rowan, "Crisis in Civil Rights Leadership," *Ebony*, November 1966, 27–37.
58. Hayter, *Dream Is Lost*, 86–89; Silver, *Twentieth-Century Richmond*, 317.
59. Silver, *Twentieth-Century Richmond*, 213–30, quote 230.
60. "Richmond District," *Virginia Road Builder*, April 26, 1965; Robert L. Horn, Executive Director to the Richmond Regional Planning Commission to the Richmond City Council, June 1, 1965, Folder 11, Mss1 W5603b FA2, Wheat Papers, VMHC.
61. Urban Renewal in Richmond, May 26, 1962, A Research Project Conducted by H.O.M.E of Richmond, Virginia, Racial Steering by Real Estate Sales Agents in Metropolitan Richmond, Virginia, March 1980, Box 20, M258, Richmond Urban Institute Papers, VCU; "U.S. Aid Urged in Urban Decay Fight," *WP*, May 18, 1960, B7; "90 Cities in 1960 Enter Urban Renewal Program," *WP*, August 10, 1960, B5; "Slum Owners Reaped Millions, Chamber Says," *WP*, June 5, 1961, A22; "Urban Renewal Hit at NAACP Rally," *WP*, August 15, 1960, B6; "'Deal' to Bar Low Rents Laid to RLA," *WP*, August 28, 1959, D1; "Renewal Plans Backed for NE," *WP*, September 10, 1959, B2; "Baltimore Slum Fight Recertified," *WP*, December 12, 1959, B7; "Redeveloper Cites Problems of 'Slum Image,'" *WP*, March 15, 1960, A16; "Atlanta Surges Ahead with Record Building," *Atlanta Constitution*, January 3, 1959, 4; "Must Speed Slum Projects for both Races, Mayor Says," *Atlanta Constitution*, January 5, 1960, 11; "Savannah Slum Shift Speeded," *Atlanta Constitution*, January 13, 1961, 25; "Civic Groups Rally to Aid in 'Fight Blight' Campaign," *Atlanta Constitution*, January 20, 1961, 36; "War on Slums Fills a Need, Maddox Says," *Atlanta Constitution*, January 24, 1963, 8; "Skyscraper to Go on Renewal Site," *Atlanta Constitution*, March 16, 1961, 1; "Negro Needs in Housing Discussed," *WP*, April 22, 1960, B8; "Kennedy Asks Congress for $3.2 Billion Housing," *Atlanta Constitution*, March 30, 1961, 1.
62. "Portsmouth Fights Blight," *WP*, August 29, 1959, C3; "Alexandria Gets Funds for Pilot Renewal Project," *WP*, November 7, 1959, B4; "Roanoke Blight Fight Recertified," *WP*, June 11, 1960, B10; "Harrisonburg Gets Funds to Plan Downtown Renewal," *WP*, June 18, 1960, B11; "Lynchburg Gets Urban Renewal Funds," *WP*, January 27, 1961, A6; "Charlottesville Gets U.S. Help," *WP*, May 13, 1961, B9; "$2 Million Renewal Sped in Bristol Business Area," *WP*, July 3, 1964, C11; "Urban Renewal Plan 'Autocratic,'" *WP*, May 4, 1960, C3; "Speeding Urban Renewal," *WP, Times Herald*, September 20, 1960, A14; "Yes, You Can Still Fight City Hall," *WP*, January 1, 1961, E8; "Slum Moves Send Negroes to Others," *WP*, July 6, 1961, A2; "Aldermen Must Face City's Housing Problem," *Atlanta Constitution*, March 3, 1960, 4;

Ed Grimsley, "Downtown Virginia," 23–29, *Commonwealth Magazine* 34, no. 5 (May 1967), in Wheat Papers, VMHC; "Continuous Transportation Planning Process, Richmond Regional Area," Mss1 W5603b FA2, Series 1 Expressways (1 of 2), Wheat Papers, VMHC.
63. Author interview with Reverend Dr. Benjamin Campbell, March 14, 2019.
64. An Analysis of Negro Employment in the City Government by the Research Committee for the Crusade for Voters, 1963, Richmond City Council, NAACP, 1963, Box 6, M277, Sheppard Papers, VCU. For more on the small role blacks played in city government and committee work, see Folder 6, entitled "Personnel," ibid.
65. "Negro Colleges Lack Job Placement Staffs," *WP*, July 24, 1964, C2; Lerone Bennett Jr., "Old Illusions and New Souths," *Ebony*, August 1971, 35.
66. Herman P. Miller, "Progress and Prospects for the Negro Worker," *Challenge*, February 1966, found in a letter from W. Kent Carter Jr. to Mr. James C. Wheat, Wheat and Co., Inc., May 20, 1966, Folder 40, Mss1 W5603b FA2, Wheat Papers, VMHC.
67. Silver, *Twentieth-Century Richmond*, 218–19. For more, see ibid., chapter 7.
68. Robert Nelson, "University of Richmond Digital Scholarship Lab Unveils New Mapping Project Focusing on Urban Renewal, Family Displacements, Race," University of Richmond Newsroom, 2017; Grimsley, "Downtown Virginia," 26; "Richmond Gets Grant," *WP*, November 20, 1964, B3.
69. Resolution No. 66-R90, October 25, 1966, City Council Minutes 1966–67, Richmond City Journal, Library of Virginia, Richmond, 88–89; Silver, *Twentieth-Century Richmond*, 159–97, 270–330; "Henry Marsh Refuses to Sin by Silence," Editorial by Howard Carwile, *RAA*, November 12, 1966, 3.
70. "Statement to the Newspapers," November 23, 1966, Resolution No. 66-R99, Mss1 W5603b FA2, Series 1, Housing Committee, Wheat Papers, VMHC.
71. "Marsh Says His Stand No Threat to Housing," *RTD*, November 26, 1966, 1, 4; "Expressway View Restated by Marsh," *RTD*, November 28, 1966, 2.
72. "Bagley, Wheat Charge Housing Interference," *RTD*, November 25, 1966, 1; "Marsh Will Press Expressway Plea," *RTD*, November 27, 1966, 1, 25.
73. "Marsh Says Expressway Plan Anti-Colored," *RAA*, November 12, 1966, 1; "Idlewood Ave. Residents Urged to Pack City Hall" and "Marsh Leads Drive to Save Homes," *RAA*, November 19, 1966, 1, 2, 18; "Marsh Questions $$ Angle," *RAA*, November 26, 1–2; "Idlewood Express Route Is Again Criticized by Marsh," *RTD*, November 28, 1966, 1–2; "Mundle's Popularity Continues to Drop," *RAA*, December 31, 1966, 1–2.
74. David E. Longley, Manager of Jefferson Townhouse Apartments to Mr. J. C. Wheat Jr., March 5, 1969; Alan Kiepper to Mr. Richard J. Mase, Assistant Vice-President of F.C.H Service, Inc., April 1, 1968, Mss1 W5603b FA2, Series 1, Housing Committee, Wheat Papers, VMHC; J. R. Pattills, Chief of Environmental Health to City Manager, September 14, 1967; Fredric A.

Fay, Executive Director to Alan Kiepper and Vice Mayor Winfred Mundle, September 14, 1967; Alan F. Kiepper, City Manager to Eleanor P. Sheppard, September 25, 1967, "Richmond City Council Housing, 1967," Box 5, M277, all in Sheppard Papers, VCU; "City Council Sidesteps Marsh's Resolution," *RTD*, November 29, 1966, 1–2; "RF Block Sinks Marsh's Effort to Save Homes," *RAA*, December 3, 1966, 1–2; "Picket Lines Loom as Bulldozers Zero In on Homeowners," *RAA*, December 10, 1966, 1–2; "West End Residents Renew Fights against Expressway," *RAA*, December 17, 1966, 1–2; "Expressway Foes Sleeping," *RTD*, February 27, 1967, 13; "All-America Award Target of Criticism," *RAA*, April 1, 1967, 1–2; "Delay Coliseum to Free Money for Poor: Marsh," *RAA*, May 18, 1968, 1–2; Ed Grimsley, "The New Coliseums," *Commonwealth Magazine* 34, no. 2 (February 1967): 19–26; "All-American Richmond? City Councilman Says No," *New York Times*, April 11, 1967, 27, clipping found in a letter from A. J. Brent to James C. Wheat, April 14, 1967, Mss1 W5603b FA2, Series 1, Racial Problems (1 of 2), 40, Wheat Papers, VMHC.

75. "Henry Marsh to Nominate W. T. Kenney," *RAA*, November 18, 1967, 1–2; "Cephas, Mundle Mum on Issue," *RAA*, November 25, 1967, 1.
76. "Cephas, Mundle Votes Help Defeat Kenney," *RAA*, December 2, 1967, 1–2; "Crusade to Endorse Fully Integrated Slate," *RAA*, May 25, 1968, 1 and 22; "Mundle, Cephas Defeated; Marsh, Carpenter Win," *RAA*, June 15, 1968, 1–7; "What Happened in Tuesday's Vote," *RTD*, June 14, 1968, 1; Councilmanic Election, June 10, 1968, results found in Phil J. Bagley Jr., Deposition 1971, Box 2, M183, Richmond Annexation Files, VCU.
77. Tracy E. K'Meyer, *Civil Rights in the Gateway to the South: Louisville, Kentucky, 1945-1980* (Lexington: University Press of Kentucky, 2009), 179–215.
78. Rowan, "Crisis in Civil Rights Leadership," 27–37; Hasan Kwame Jeffries, *Bloody Lowndes: Civil Rights and Black Power in Alabama's Black Belt* (New York: New York University Press, 2009), 143–79; Joshua Bloom and Waldo E. Martin Jr., *Black against Empire: The History and Politics of the Black Panther Party* (Berkley: University of California Press, 2016), 1–15.
79. "Rebellion in Ohio," *Wall Street Journal*, July 13, 1967, clipping found in the letter from John S. Battle, Partner of McGuire, Woods, & Battle Law Firm, July 14, 1967, Mss1 W5603b FA2, Series 1, Housing Committee, Wheat Papers, VMHC.
80. W. Avon Drake and Robert D. Holsworth, *Affirmative Action and the Stalled Quest for Black Progress* (Urbana: University of Illinois Press, 1996); "Photo Review of Headline Events in '66," *RAA*, January 7, 1967, no page number; "R. F. Must Go!," *RAA*, June 8, 1968, 1–3.
81. Thomas Sugrue, *Sweet Land of Liberty: The Forgotten Civil Rights Movement in the North* (New York: Random House, 2008), 45–67.
82. "Carmichael Visits Protesters at VU," *RTD*, April 3, 1968, 1.
83. "Richmond: A Changing City," *WP*, June 26, 1967, 2.

84. "A Hand Up—Not Head Out," *RTD,* January 7, 1968, F1, F4.
85. The Kiplinger Washington Letter, Circulated Privately to Businessmen, August 4, 1967, Mss1 W5603b FA2, Series 1, Racial Problems (1 of 2), 40, Wheat Papers, VMHC.
86. Council Crime Report, Conducted by Councilman Phil J. Bagley, B. A. Cephas, and Mayor Morrill M. Crowe, January 21, 1968, Mss1 W5603b FA2, Series 1, Racial Problems (1 of 2), 40, Wheat Papers, VMHC.
87. Alfonso J. Cervantes, "To Prevent a Chain of Super-Watts," *Harvard Business Review,* September–October 1967, 55–65, Mss1 W5603b FA2, Series 1, Racial Problems (1 of 2), 41, Folder 22, Wheat Papers, VMHC; Frank R. Barnett, President of the National Strategy Information Center, to Mr. J. C. Wheat Jr., February 21, 1968, (2 of 2), ibid.; "The Negro Veteran, Urban Stability and the National Purpose," National Strategy Information Center Third Draft, February 14, 1968, 1, ibid.; "Urban Coalition Formed to Meet Crisis in Cities," *United States Municipal News* 34, no.16 (August 15, 1967), found in ibid.
88. Director of Public Safety to City Manager, December 14, 1964, Folder 22, Mss1 W5603b FA2, Wheat Papers, VMHC.
89. Meeting of School-Community Coordinators, April 16, 1968, Mss1S4772a, James A. Sartain Papers, Virginia Museum of History and Culture, Richmond. (Hereafter cited as Sartain Papers, VMHC.)
90. "Richmond: A Changing City," *WP,* June 26, 1967, 2.
91. "Uneasy Peace Grips Six Ghettos," "Black Power: What the Term Means to Richmonders," and "Cleveland, N.Y. Hardest Hit by Wave of Wave of Violent Unrest," *RAA,* July 30, 1966, 1–2.
92. "Richmond: A Changing City," *WP,* June 26, 1967, 2.
93. Moeser and Dennis, *Politics of Annexation,* 50–73; Drake and Holsworth, *Affirmative Action,* 50; Hayter, *Dream Is Lost,* 81.

2. Annexation

1. "Richmond: A Changing City," *WP,* June 26, 1967, 2.
2. An Analysis of the Voting in the Councilmanic Election, June 11, 1968, Mss1 W5603b FA2 ca. 4500, Wheat Papers, VMHC.
3. Matthew Mace Barbee, "White Supremacy and the Landscapes of Memory in Richmond, Virginia in the 1960s," *Activist History Review,* October 27, 2017, https://activisthistory.com/2017/10/27/white-supremacy-and-the-landscapes-of-memory-in-richmond-virginia-in-the-1960s/; "Fifty Years Ago, Richmond Took Over Part of Chesterfield," *Chesterfield Observer,* April 28, 2020, https://www.chesterfieldobserver.com/articles/fifty-years-ago-richmond-took-over-part-of-chesterfield-the-politics-of-annexation-explores-why/; "Richmond's Controversial Chesterfield Annexation, 50 Years Later," *NPR,* May 20, 2020, https://vpm.org/news/articles/13596

/richmonds-controversial-chesterfield-annexation-50-years-later; Hayter, *Dream Is Lost*, chapter 2.
4. Lassiter, *Silent Majority*, 13, 128.
5. "Old Virginia Seeks to Learn How to Run a Modern City," *WP*, April 2, 1967, G1.
6. "More Negroes Vie in Virginia City Elections," *WP*, June 9, 1968, 2, D1.
7. "State Senate Endorses Annexation Power for Richmond," *WP*, April 3, 1969, 1.
8. "A History of Virginia State Capitol and Capitol Square," https://virginiacapitol.gov/wp-content/uploads/2016/04/English-both-sides.pdf.
9. "State Senate Endorses Annexation Power for Richmond," *WP*, April 3, 1969, 1.
10. "Old Leadership Not Swayed," *RTD*, September 22, 1981, 1, 6.
11. Team of Progress, undated biographies of white leadership; the Honorable Morrill M. Crowe, Mayor, City of Richmond, Virginia, undated biography; Clipping of James C. Wheat, Jr., Editorial Page of the *Richmond News-Leader*, June 7, 1968; Biography of Thomas P. Bryan, Chairman of the *RTD*; Biography of Edward Grimsley, Editor of the *Richmond News-Leader*, all in People: Biographies, Box 1, M277, Sheppard Papers, VCU; History of Richmond, Prepared by the Office of the City Clerk, January 10, 2019, 1–20, Richmond City Hall; List of Contributors and Prospect List to the Virginia Municipal League, April 21, 1969, Richmond, Box 5, M246, Horace H. Edwards Papers, VCU; author interview with Terry Drumheller, July 23, 2019.
12. Richmond Forward Breakfast Meeting at the Commonwealth Club, August 26, 1963; Edwin P. Conquest, Executive of Miller & Rhoads to Members of "The Group," October 22, 1963; Edwin Hyde to "The Group," October 30, 1963; Edwin P. Conquest to Members of "The Group," October 31, 1963; Invitation to Richmond Forward Dinner at the John Marshall Hotel, undated, 1966 Campaign-Platform and Campaign Literature, Mss1 W5603b FA2, Series 2, Box 11, Wheat Papers, VMHC.
13. RF: Vote for Sound Government Brochure, undated, Folder 68; Revised List of Richmond Forward Trustees, February 24, 1964; Articles of Incorporation of Richmond Forward, undated, 1966 Campaign-Platform and Campaign Literature, Mss1 W5603b FA2, Series 2, Box 11, Wheat Papers, VMHC.
14. "Old Leadership Not Swayed," *RTD*, September 22, 1981, 1, 6.
15. Author interview with Dr. John Moeser, March 11, 2019.
16. Edward H. Peeples, *Scalawag: A White Southerner's Journey through Segregation to Human Rights Activism* (Charlottesville: University of Virginia Press, 2014), 15.
17. Author interviews with Benjamin Campbell, March 14, 2019; with Terry Drumheller, July 23, 2019; with John Moeser, March 11, 2019.
18. Richmond City Directory, 1900–1950, in US City Directories, 1822–1995 database; Virginia, Death Records, 1912–2014, in Virginia Department

of Health Records; Virginia, Select Marriages, 1785–1940, film number 2048498, 70, ancestry.com.
19. University of Richmond 1925 Yearbook, US School Yearbooks, 1880–2012, ancestry.com.
20. Author interview with Terry Drumheller, July 23, 2019.
21. US Federal Census, 1900–1970; Richmond City Directory, 1900–1950, US City Directories, 1822–1995 database, ancestry.com.
22. "Five More Enter Race for Council," *RTD,* April 12, 1952, 1, 4.
23. Philip J. Bagley Jr., Social Security Application, number: 223-10-1923, Issue State: Virginia, Issue Date: Before 1951, in US Social Security Death Index, 1935–2014, ancestry.com; Daniel J. Arkin, "Regime Politics Surrounding Desegregation Decision-Making during Massive Resistance in Richmond, Virginia" (PhD. diss. Virginia Commonwealth University, 1991), 50–55.
24. Robert L. Hill, Planning Consultant, to the Mayor and Council of the City of Richmond, February 26, 1969, Mss1 W5603b FA2, Series 1, Housing Committee (1 of 2), 40, Wheat Papers, VMHC.
25. "Richmond Summer '68-Hot or Cool," memo sent to James Wheat, March 6, 1968, Mss1 W5603b FA2, Series 1, Racial Problems (1 of 2), 40, Wheat Papers, VMHC.
26. Thomas Sugrue, *Origins of the Urban Crisis: Race and Inequality in Postwar Detroit* (Princeton, NJ: Princeton University Press, 1998).
27. "The Urban Crisis," *WP,* September 14, 1967, A20.
28. "A Policy of Economic and Human Resources," Speech delivered at the Annual Convention of National League Cities in Boston, Massachusetts, July 31, 1967, Mss1 W5603b FA2, Series 1, Racial Problems (2 of 2), 41, Wheat Papers, VMHC.
29. Richmond Bill Sauder, "Jim Wheat: Stocks and Civic Enterprise," *Commonwealth Magazine* 34, no.1 (January 1967): 32–34; Ed Grimsley, "Downtown Virginia," *Commonwealth Magazine* 34, no. 5 (May 1967): 23–29.
30. "Virginia City Debts Near Quarter Billion," *WP,* January 7, 1955, 22.
31. Richard A. Chandler, Assessor of Real Estate to the City Council of Richmond, December 22, 1966, Folder 15, Mss1 W5603b FA2, Wheat Papers, VHMC.
32. Assessor of Real Estate Annual Report, 1964–1965; District Comparisons of Average Assessed Value in Relation to Sales Price, 1965; Changes Made against 1965 Real Estate Land Book, Folder 15, Mss1 W5603b FA2, Wheat Papers, VMHC.
33. 1960 Family Income Comparison for Richmond City-Henrico County; Increase in Welfare Costs City of Richmond, 1950–1968; Foster Care & Aid to Dependent Children, Number Served and Cost 1960 and 1967; Changes in Richmond's Population, 1950–1967; additional tables found in a packet from George R. Talcott, Boundary Expansion Coordinator of Chesterfield County to Mr. Nathan Forb, Councilman for the City of Richmond,

February 26, 1968, Exhibit Px. 14, 1968, Annex, Box 3, M183, Richmond Annexation Files, VCU.
34. "Richmond: A Changing City," *WP*, June 26, 1967, 2.
35. Alan F. Kiepper, City Manager to the City Council, August 22, 1968; "Richmond," National Real Estate Investor, June 1968, Folder, 15, Mss1 W5603b FA2, Wheat Papers, VMHC.
36. Annual Message by Horace H. Edwards, President of the Virginia Municipal League Assembled in Convention in Richmond, September 19, 1966, Significant Developments Facing the City of Richmond, 1960, Box 5, M246, Horace H. Edward Papers, VCU (hereafter cited as Edward Papers, VCU); "A Policy of Economic and Human Resources," Speech delivered at the Annual Convention of National League Cities in Boston, Massachusetts, July 31, 1967, Mss1 W5603b FA2, Series 1, Racial Problems (2 of 2), 41, Wheat Papers, VMHC.
37. Robert D. Zeinemann, "Overlooked Linkages between Municipal Incorporation and Annexation Laws: An In-Depth Look at Wisconsin's Experience," *Urban Lawyer* 39, no. 2 (2007): 257–318.
38. "The Development of a County: Chesterfield's Past Present, & Future," *Richmond Surroundings New City Magazine* (Fall 1982), Library of Virginia.
39. Report of Chesterfield County to the Virginia Metropolitan Area Study Commission, June 14, 1967, Chesterfield Annexation (Burnett Statement), 1969, Box 1, M246, Edward Papers, VCU.
40. "The Urban Crisis," *WP*, September 14, 1967, A20.
41. "Urban Crisis Is Talent," *WP*, February 2, 1968, C1.
42. A. F. Weber, "Suburban Annexations," *North American Review* 166 (May 1899): 610–14.
43. Kenneth T. Jackson and Stanley K. Shultz, *Cities in American History* (New York: Knopf, 1972); Alfred J. Watkins and Arnold Fleischmann, "Annexation, Migration and Central City Population Growth," *Social Science Quarterly* 61, no. 3 (December 1980): 612–22.
44. "Cities Had Big Annexation Year," *WP*, April 16, 1960, B3.
45. "City Growth High in '60," *New York Times*, July 09, 1961, 39.
46. Arnold Fleischmann, "The Territorial Expansion of Milwaukee: Historical Lessons for Contemporary Urban Policy and Research," *Journal of Urban History* 14, no.2 (February 1988): 147–70.
47. Watkins and Fleischmann, "Annexation, Migration and Central City," 619.
48. Ibid., 620.
49. "1952 Annexation Doubled the Size of Atlanta," *Atlanta Constitution*, January 18, 1970, 12J.
50. "New Legislature to Get Tax Bills," *Atlanta Journal*, January 10, 1960, E5; "5 Committees Consider Joint Planning Unit," *Atlanta Constitution*, February 05, 1960, 1.

51. "Atlanta-Hapeville Feud Threatens Airport Road," *Atlanta Constitution,* February 12, 1960, 1, 6; "House Votes Road Annexing, Okays 'Unfit' Signs for Slums," *Atlanta Constitution,* February 17, 1960, 12; "Annexation Is Illegal, East Point Believes," *Atlanta Constitution,* Feb 26, 1960, 7; "Annexation School Plan Wins Handily in Fulton," *Atlanta Constitution,* November 9, 1960, 1.
52. "58 Georgia Cities Used Annexation to Grow Since '50," *Atlanta Journal,* May 28, 1961, 34.
53. "Race: The Phony Issue," *Atlanta Constitution,* April 4, 1966, 4.
54. "Hartsfield Says City Must Annex Leadership as It Goes to Suburbs," *Atlanta Constitution,* May 20, 1964, 10.
55. "Negro Majority Seen for Atlanta by '75," *Atlanta Constitution,* December 14, 1963, 8.
56. "Atlanta in the Throes of Growing Pains," *Wall Street Journal,* March 27, 1969, 16.
57. "Discord Veils the Urban Crisis," *Atlanta Constitution,* December 8, 1968, A1, A16.
58. "It's Time to Move toward Annexation," *Atlanta Constitution,* December 8, 1965, 4; "A Ruling for Progress," *Atlanta Constitution,* September 28, 1968, 4; "Atlanta Accepts Change, Moves Ahead," *Atlanta Constitution,* January 18, 1970, 14J.
59. David G. Temple, *Merger Politics: Local Government Consolidation in Tidewater Virginia* (Charlottesville: University of Virginia Press 1966), 1.
60. "Expanding Cities," *Wall Street Journal,* December 9, 1960, 1.
61. A. J. Watkins and Arnold Fleischmann, "Annexation and Population Growth in Texas Cities," *Texas Business Review* 52, no. 9 (September 1978): 173–78; "Houston—Booming Even by Sunbelt Standards," *New York Times,* January 9, 1977, 41; Virginia Marion Perrnod, *Special Districts, Special Purposes: Fringe Governments and Urban Problems in the Houston Area* (College Station: Texas A&M University Press, 1984).
62. "Annexation Sometimes Risky Task," *Atlanta Journal,* February 7, 1960, 15B.
63. "Land Annexed before Census," *WP,* April 2, 1960, A6; "Rockville Asked to Annex Area," *WP,* March 16, 1960, C11.
64. "Hub of Integration Move," *Atlanta Journal,* April 24, 1960, E5; "No More Nashville," *Wall Street Journal,* September 4, 1963, 12.
65. "Cities Land in Court for Applying Annexation to Their Growing Pains," *Atlanta Journal,* May 8, 1960, E9.
66. "Mayors in South Confer on Cities," *New York Times,* November 17, 1968, 42.
67. Chester W. Bain, *A Body Incorporate: The Evolution of City-County Separation in Virginia* (Charlottesville: University of Virginia Press, 1967), 23–53.

68. J. Harvey Wilkerson III, *Harry Byrd and the Changing face of Virginia Politics* (Charlottesville: University of Virginia Press, 1984), 9–11, 24–61; "'Little Fellow' Often Overlooked in Virginia," *WP,* June 12, 1957, A1; Temple, *Merger Politics,* 19–20.
69. "Executive Outlines Conditions Required to Attract Industries," *WP,* November 14, 1961, B4.
70. Nelson Wikstrom, *City Manager Government in Henrico, Virginia: Implementation, Evolution, and Evaluation* (Henrico, VA: N.p., 2002), 111–28.
71. "Virginians Flooding to 5 City Areas," *WP,* September 1, 1960, B5; Wilkerson, *Harry Byrd,* 158–63.
72. Wilkerson, *Harry Byrd,* 170; Marshall W. Fishwick, *Virginia: A New Look at the Old Dominion* (New York: Harper and Brothers, 1959), 257–60; "New Census Look at Cities and Race," *WP,* March 26, 1961, E3; "Falls Church Heads Vote to Restudy Annexation," *WP,* February 24, 1960, B1.
73. "Can Afford Tax Rise, Fairfax Citizens Say," *WP,* January 7, 1960, B5; "Alexandria Plans Annexation Study," *WP,* January 7, 1960, B5; "Alexandria Mayor, 6 Candidates Give Stand on City Issues," *WP,* March 21, 1961, B2; "Counter-Attack to Annexation Endorsed by Fairfax Heads," *WP,* February 4, 1960, A3.
74. Bain, *A Body Incorporated,* 96–97.
75. "North Virginia Bills Get New Help in Richmond," *WP,* February 27, 1966, B4; "Bill to Stall Annexation by Alexandria Blocked," *WP,* January 30, 1968, 1.
76. Wilkerson, *Harry Byrd,* 187; "Norfolk Area Plans Metropolitan Talks," *WP,* April 17, 1960, B3.
77. Temple, *Merger Politics,* 48.
78. "Tidewater Calls Merger Parley," *WP,* December 14, 1961, D2; Temple, *Merger Politics,* 3.
79. "Norfolk Area Plans Metropolitan Talks," *WP,* April 17, 1960, B3; "Consolidation Urged in Portsmouth Area," *WP,* December 13, 1961, B15.
80. "Merger Bill Passes over Stern Protest," *WP,* February 2, 1962, B2; "2 New Virginia Cities to be Born on Jan. 1," *WP,* December 28, 1962, A8.
81. "Plans for Expanding Municipal Borders Gaining in Virginia," *New York Times,* February 18, 1962, 57; "Urban Annexation Rights Are Asked in Virginia," *WP,* April 6, 1963, C2; Lassiter, *Silent Majority,* 281–83.
82. "A Third Possibility," *WP,* February 19, 1962, A14; "High Court to Study Pleas in Annexation," *WP,* December 8, 1960, B6; "Developer Sues to Get Annexation," *WP,* September 19, 1962, B3; "Va.-Md. Briefs: Williamsburg Annexation Area Sliced," *WP,* March 14, 1962, B6; "Annexation Suit Goes to State Court," *WP,* April 19, 1963, C10; "Williamsburg Annexation Suit Upheld," *WP,* December 3, 1963, C6.
83. "Merger Bill Passes over Stern Protest," *WP,* February 2, 1962, B2; "Va. Constitution: Revise or Replace?," *WP,* April 27, 1967, B1.

84. "Annexation Threat Seen as Brewing Discord in Virginia," *WP,* May 10, 1967, 1; D. Andrew Austin, "Politics vs Economics: Evidence from Municipal Annexation," *Journal of Urban Economics* 45, no. 3 (May 1999): 501–32.
85. "Counties Emerging from Jungle," *WP,* July 15, 1962, E7.
86. "D.C. among Cities Losing Population," *WP,* June 8, 1960, B4.
87. "Census Disappoints Cities as People Go Suburban," *Atlanta Journal,* May 22, 1960, 13D; "Floundering U.S. Cities Place Hopes in Annexation," *WP,* August 17, 1960, B2.
88. "Suburbs Shun City Interests," *WP,* January 2, 1960, B2; "Negroes Spurn Annexing Deal," *Atlanta Constitution,* January 21, 1969, 7; "Negro Entrapment May Begin Fading," *Atlanta Constitution,* February 9, 1969, 27A.
89. "New Census Look at Cities and Race," *WP,* March 26, 1961, E3; "S.C. Annex Law Stifles Change, Official Claims," *Atlanta Constitution,* November 16, 1969, 20A.
90. "Old Virginia Seeks to Learn How to Run a Modern City," *WP,* April 2, 1967, G1.
91. Silver, *Twentieth-Century Richmond,* 233–37.
92. "Flight to the Suburbs, Southern-Style," *WP,* March 13, 1960, E2.
93. "The Important Facts about the Proposed Merger of Henrico and Richmond," Brochure found in Consolidation 1961–1972, Box 1 M283, Virginia Crockford Papers, VCU; "Proposed City Budget Might Pass Untrimmed," *RTD,* March 9, 1961, 2; "2 in Council Ask Merger Change," *RTD,* August 29, 1961, 1, 4.
94. "Merger Urged for Richmond," *WP,* August 1, 1961, B8; "Plan to Merge Richmond, Va., and Adjacent County Is Filed: Project Would Create City Having Area Fifth Largest of Any in the Nation," *New York Times,* August 6, 1961, 66; "Richmond Merger Plan Seen Key to Problem Facing Large Cities: Would Be 36th Largest," *WP,* August 6, 1961, B2; Silver, *Twentieth-Century Richmond,* 245.
95. Moeser and Dennis, *Politics of Annexation,* 34–40.
96. Ibid., 38–40.
97. Silver, *Twentieth-Century Richmond,* 238–45; Lassiter, *Silent Majority,* 281.
98. "Richmond Merger Rejected in Vote," *New York Times,* December 13, 1961, 46.
99. Moeser and Dennis, *Politics of Annexation,* 34–38, 80–85; City of Richmond v. United States of America, No. 74–201, U.S. Supreme Court (1974) Appendix 1, 16–18; "Annexation Will Meet Resistance," *RTD,* December 14, 1961, 1; "Annexation Suit Time Predicted," *RTD,* December 15, 1961, 1; "Precedent Challenged by Annexation Move," *RTD,* December 24, 1961, 1; "Hopes Differ on Annexation Suit as New Year Arrives," *Richmond News Leader,* January 1, 1962, 1.
100. The Report by the Virginia Metropolitan Areas Study Commission, November 15, 1967, Mss1 W5603b FA2, Series 1, Racial Problems (1 of 2), 40, Wheat Papers, VMHC.

101. An Act to Create a Virginia Metropolitan Area Study Commission, to Provide Its Composition to Prescribe Its Powers and Duties, Acts of the General Assembly of the Commonwealth of Virginia, April 4, 1966, Regular Session 1966, 1–50; Report by the Virginia Metropolitan Areas Study Commission, Wheat Papers, VMHC.
102. A Bill to Provide for the Merger of the City of Richmond and the County of Henrico and to Create a Commission to be known as the Richmond-Henrico Merger Commission: providing Composition, Terms, Powers, and Duties, and to Appropriate Funds, February 1968, Senate Bill No.441; Proceedings and Debates of the Virginia House of Delegates pertaining to Amendment of the Constitution, Extra Session 1969, 515–30, General Assembly Archives, Richmond.
103. "Regional Plan too Innovative to Digest," *WP,* February 22, 1968, 1; "State Senate Endorses Annexation Power for Richmond," *WP,* April 3, 1969, 1.
104. Report of Chesterfield County to the Virginia Metropolitan Area Study Commission, June 14, 1967, Chesterfield Annexation (Burnett Statement), 1969, Box 1, M246, Edward Papers, VCU.
105. Author interview with Wayland Rennie, July 17, 2015.
106. Deposition of Irving G. Horner, July 13, 1971; Deposition of Alan F. Kiepper, July 15, 1971; Holt I Drafts of Arguments, 1969: Curtis Holt, Sr., v. City of Richmond, No.151-71-R, November 20, 1971, Box 2, M183, Annexation Files, VCU.
107. The Report by the Virginia Metropolitan Areas Study Commission, November 15, 1967, Mss1 W5603b FA2, Series 1, Racial Problems (1 of 2), 40, Wheat Papers, VMHC.
108. *Holt v. Richmond* (1971), 168.
109. The City of Richmond and Annexation, Undated Memo sent to Councilman James C. Wheat Jr., Folder 154, Mss1 W5603b FA2, Wheat Papers, VMHC.
110. Lassiter, *Silent Majority,* 283.
111. "They're Still Ahead, 6–3," *RAA,* June 13, 1970, 1.

3. Dogtown

1. Lerone Bennett Jr., "Old Illusions and New Souths," *Ebony* 10, no. 3 (August 1971): 73; "1,000 Cheer Anti-Busing Talks; Rain Sends Rally Indoors," *RTD,* February 25, 1972, 17.
2. Kenneth T. Jackson, *Crabgrass Frontier: The Suburbanization of the United States* (Oxford: Oxford University Press, 1987); Robert O. Self, *American Babylon: Race and the Struggle for Postwar Oakland* (Princeton, NJ: Princeton University Press, 2005); Lassiter, *Silent Majority,* 31–33.
3. Model Cities Grant and Code Enforcement Program for the Blackwell Area of South Richmond, November 21, 1968, letter from Alan Kiepper,

City Manager, to James C. Wheat Jr., November 21, 1968, Mss1 W5603b FA2, Series 1, Housing Committee, Folder 40, Wheat Papers, VMHC.
4. Proposed Southside Concentrated Code Enforcement Project, December 11, 1967, Mss1 W5603b FA2, Series 1, Housing Committee, Folder 40, Wheat Papers, VMHC.
5. Author interviews with Viola Baskerville, June 28, 2019; with William Mason, July 23, 2019; with Dr. Edward Peeples, June 24, 2019; "NAACP Rips Gov. Godwin," *RAA,* October 22, 1966, 1; "Photo Review of Headline Events in '66," *RAA,* January 7, 1967, n.p.; "The Tragedy of Governor Godwin," *RAA,* November 11, 1967, 1; "Ministers Urge Patience," *RTD,* August 1, 1970, B3; Reverend Robin D. Mines Testimony, Growing Up in Civil Rights Richmond: A Community Remembers, University of Richmond Museum, 2019, 62; author interview with Terry Drumheller, July 23, 2019.
6. Author interviews with William Mason, July 23, 2019; with Dr. Edward Peeples, June 24, 2019.
7. Bradley v. School Board of the City of Richmond, Virginia, 317 F. Supp. 555 (1970), 5–8.
8. Ibid., 8.
9. Roscoe E. Reeve, "Freedom of Choice," Section Four, Miscellaneous Writings and Papers, Mss1 SA 772a, Sections 134–38, Sartain Papers, VMHC.
10. "New Moves to Speed School Desegregation Readied in Government," *Wall Street Journal,* January 24, 1966, 1.
11. Racial Change Enrollments for North, East, West, and South Sides of City, April 16, 1970, Plan III Revised, 1970, Box 1, M283, Crockford Papers, VCU.
12. The City of Richmond and Annexation, Undated Memo sent to Councilman James C. Wheat Jr., Folder 154, Mss1 W5603b FA2, Wheat Papers, VMHC.
13. Lassiter, *Silent Majority,* 225–50.
14. Alexander v. Holmes County Board of Education, 396 U.S. 1218 (1969).
15. June Shagaloff, "A Review of Public School Desegregation in the North and West," *Journal of Educational Sociology* 36, no. 6 (February 1963): 292–96; David Douglas, *Jim Crow Moves North: The Battle over Northern School Segregation, 1865–1954* (Cambridge: Cambridge University Press, 2005); Sugrue, *Sweet Land of Liberty;* Ronnie A. Dunn, et al., *Boycotts, Busing, and Beyond: The History and Implications of School Desegregation in the Urban North* (Dubuque, IA: Kendall Hunt, 2016); "Integration in North Still Faces Big Obstacles," *New York Times,* May 8, 1966, 1; "Integration Plan Is Issue in Denver School Election Tomorrow," *New York Times,* May 19, 1969, 20; "Smooth Riding," *Wall Street Journal,* April 27, 1970, 1.
16. "Governors in the South Promise to Battle Busing," *New York Times,* January 22, 1970, 18; "Gov. Kirk Tells a Federal Judge He'll Fight Early Desegregation," *New York Times,* January 23, 1970, 15; "Bill Planned to Bar Busing for Integration," *WP,* January 23, 1970, E7; "Fla. Schools Must Obey

Court Edict," *WP*, February 1, 1970, A10; "Governors Lose Bid to Sue on Schools," *New York Times*, February 3, 1970, 14; "Court Bars 2 Southern School Suits," *WP*, February 3, 1971, A1; "South Moves to Copy N.Y. Law on Schools," *WP*, February 12, 1970, A15; "Integration Bar Passes Md., Test," *WP*, March 13, 1970 C1; "Integration Comes to Mississippi," *WP*, February 15, 1970, A1; "Judge Bids Defiant Kirk Pay $10,000-a-Day Fine," *New York Times*, April 12, 1970, 1.

17. Author interview with Viola Baskerville, June 28, 2019.
18. "The Schools, Annexing Tie Seen," *Richmond News Leader*, November 22, 1968, 1, 10.
19. Sartain Meeting with Milton Randolph, undated, Mss1S4772a, Sartain Papers, VMHC.
20. Author interview with Reginald Gordon, June 27, 2019.
21. Carmen Francine Foster, "Tension, Resistance, and Transition: School Desegregation in Richmond's Northside, 1960–1963" (PhD diss., University of Virginia, 2014), 78–103, 111.
22. Sartain, "The Northside—Negro Suburbia?," undated, Mss1S4772a, Sartain Papers, VMHC.
23. Dr. C. M. Achilles to Mr. Nathaniel Lee, June 17, 1968, ibid.
24. Sartain Meeting with Milton Randolph, undated, ibid.; "Scare Tactics Cited in Area House Sales," *Richmond News Leader*, November 23, 1968, 9.
25. Foster, "Tensions, Resistance, and Transition," 104–32.
26. Ibid., 111, 125, 134.
27. Sartain Meeting with Milton Randolph, undated, Mss1S4772a, Sartain Papers, VMHC.
28. Minutes for the Meeting of the Urban Specialist Team, March 26, 1968, ibid.
29. Roscoe E. Reeves, to Urban Team Members, July 25, 1968; Tentative Interview Guide: Parents Living in Northside Who Sends Children Outside to School, undated, both in Mss1S4772a, Sartain Papers, VMHC.
30. Minutes for the Meeting of the Urban Specialist Team, March 26, 1968, ibid.
31. Roscoe E. Reeve Notes on John Marshall High School, May 2, 1968, Mss1S4772a, Sartain Papers, VMHC; Foster, "Tensions, Resistance, and Transition," 109, 140–45.
32. Foster, "Tensions, Resistance, and Transition," 139–40.
33. Dr. C. M. Achilles to Mr. Nathaniel Lee, June 17, 1968, Mss1S4772a, Sartain Papers, VMHC.
34. Quote from Foster, "Tension, Resistance, and Transition," 106.
35. Robert K. Roney, Member of the Urban Team to H. I. Willet, Superintendent, June 12, 1968, Mss1S4772a, Sartain Papers, VMHC.
36. Minutes for the Meeting of the Urban Specialist Team, April 24, 1968, ibid.

37. Foster, "Tensions, Resistance, and Transition," 108.
38. Minutes for the Meeting of the Urban Specialist Team, March 26 and April 24, 1968, Mss1S4772a, Sartain Papers, VMHC.
39. Minutes for the Meeting of the Urban Specialist Team, March 26, 1968, ibid.
40. Minutes for the Meeting of the Urban Specialist Team, March 15, 1968, ibid.
41. Workshop Evaluation, undated; Roscoe E. Reeves to Urban Team Members, July 25, 1968, both in Mss1S4772a, Sartain Papers, VMHC.
42. Roscoe E. Reeves to Urban Team Members, July 25, 1968, ibid.
43. Minutes for the Meeting of the Urban Specialist Team, April 24, 1968, ibid.
44. Minutes for the Meeting of the Urban Specialist Team, March 15, 1968, ibid.
45. Dr. C. M. Achilles to Mr. Nathaniel Lee, June 17, 1968, ibid.
46. Roscoe E. Reeve Notes on John Marshall High School, May 2, 1968, ibid.
47. Tentative Interview Guide: Parents Living in Northside Who Sends Children Outside to School, undated, Mss1S4772a, Sartain Papers, VMHC.
48. James A. Sartain, "The Push-Pull Theory of Migration," undated, and Tentative Interview Guide: Parents Living in Northside Who Sends Children Outside to School, undated, both in ibid.
49. Minutes for the Meeting of the Urban Specialist Team, March 13 and March 22, 1968, Mss1S4772a, Sartain Papers, VMHC.
50. Notes of Robert K. Roney, March 25, 1968, ibid.
51. James A. Sartain, "Implications and Recommendations of Urban Team Study on Northside Schools," Report Done for the City Council of Richmond, Virginia, November 28, 1968, Folder 30, Mss1 W5603b FA2, Wheat Papers, VMHC.
52. Minutes for the Meeting of the Urban Specialist Team, March 26, 1968, Mss1S4772a, Sartain Papers, VMHC.
53. Jim Sartain to Nat Lee, undated, and Minutes for the Meeting of the Urban Specialist Team, March 20–21, 1968, both Mss1S4772a, Sartain Papers, VMHC.
54. Sartain, "Push-Pull Theory of Migration," undated, ibid.
55. Bill Leftwich, Ginter Park Data, undated, Sections 54–106; and the Views of a Former White Liberal, Sections 110–16, both Mss1SA772a, Sartain Papers, VMHC. For more on the extensive studies done to examine White comfort levels with integrated schools, see Mss1SA772a, Sections 1–106 of the Sartain Papers, VMHC.
56. For more information about Crockford's civic activities, see folders entitled Committee on Youth, 1962–66, Richmond Council of Women Organizations, 1965–68, Richmond Federation of PTA, 1955–1972, and Citizens for Excellent Public Schools, 1970–72, in Box 1, M283, Crockford Papers, VCU.
57. Citizens for Excellent Public Schools, 1970–72; and National Congress of Parents and Teachers Biographical Data, Personal Information, Box 1, M283, Crockford Papers, VCU.

58. "Guidelines for School Desegregation: A Summary Explanation of the Revised Statement of Policies for School Desegregation Plans under Title VI of the Civil Rights Act of 1964," pamphlet published by US Department of Health, Education, and Welfare, undated, Desegregation 1966–71, Box 1, M283, Crockford Papers, VCU.
59. Concerned Parents Association of West Hampton School to School Board, City of Richmond, May 4, 1970, Desegregation 1966–71, Box 1, M283, Crockford Papers, VCU.
60. Mrs. Anne Glenn Tinsley to Mrs. W. H. Crockford, Chairman, May 5, 1970; Mr. and Mrs. Wythe Kelly III to Mrs. W. H. Crockford, May 8, 1970; and Mrs. Philip Frederick Jr. to Mrs. W. H. Crockford, August 8, 1970, Desegregation 1966–71, Box 1, M283, Crockford Papers, VCU.
61. Mr. and Mrs. Wythe Kelly III to Mrs. W. H. Crockford, May 8, 1970, ibid.
62. Albert S. Katz to Mrs. W. H. Crockford, May 5, 1970, Busing 1970–72, ibid. For more examples of White parental discontent with busing, see the Minutes of the Regular Meeting of the School Board of the City of Richmond, March 19–December 31, 1970, 149–325, Box 2, M283, ibid.; Susan M. Corbell to Judge Robert Merhige, August 27, 1970, August 1970–December 1970, Box 4, Judge Robert Merhige Collection, Special Collections, School of Law, University of Richmond (hereafter cited as Merhige Collection, UR).
63. West End Concerned Parents and Friends Newsletter, July 1970, Busing 1970–72, Box 283, Crockford Papers, VCU; and William H. Fowlkes to W. H. Crockford, III, July 13, 1970, Desegregation, 1966–71, Box 1, M283, Crockford Papers, VCU.
64. "Busing-Never," political ad for Citizens Against Busing, *RTD*, July 23, 1970, 8.
65. "West End Parents Protest Busing Move," *RTD*, July 3, 1970, 15, B4; "Cary School Plan Suggested," *RTD*, July 9, 1970, 1–2; Petition Opposing Busing, newspaper ad for West End Concerned Parents and Friends, *RTD*, July 19, 1970, 70; "Richmond Eyes Second School of Cary Type," *RTD*, July 10, 1970, 4; "1,700 Hear Ways to Fight Busing," *RTD*, July, 24, 1970, 17.
66. "3 Area Groups Hold Antibusing Rallies," *RTD*, July 31, 1970, 23; "No Role for Assembly in Busing Issue Seen," *RTD*, August 1, 1970, 1, 13.
67. "Busing Foes Will Petition Congress," *RTD*, July 11, 1970, 11; "Busing Possibility Spurs Home Sales," *RTD*, July 12, 1970, 41; "West End Group Eyes Suit Against Busing," *RTD*, July 16, 1970, 35; "Anti-Busing Federation Is Sought," *RTD*, August 4, 1970, 13; "Holton Receives Busing Opponents," *RTD*, August 6, 1970, 67, 70.
68. James L. Doherty to the *RTD*, August 6, 1970, Folder 9, Box 18; "Urban Team Study on Northside Schools," Richmond School Board Grant Proposal to the US Department of Health, Education, and Welfare, June 1970, August 1970–December 1970, Box 1, Merhige Collection, UR.
69. Mrs. Mattie Lee Simmons to Judge Robert Merhige, August 9, 1970, ibid.

70. Plaintiffs' Proposed Plan of Desegregation, undated, Undated Memo sent to Councilman James C. Wheat Jr., Folder 154, Mss1 W5603b FA2, Wheat Papers, VMHC.
71. HEW Plan, undated, Undated Memo sent to Councilman James C. Wheat Jr., ibid.
72. Wanner v. Arlington County, VA., 357 F.2d 452 (4th Cir. 1966); Green v. School Board of New Kent County, 391 U.S. 430, 437 (1968); Brewer v. School Board of Norfolk, 397 F. 2d 37 (4th. Cir. 1968); United States v. School Board of Franklin City (4th Cir. June 11, 1970) No. 14, 276; and Green v. School Board of Roanoke, Virginia, No. 14, 335 (4th Cir. June 17, 1970).
73. Clark v. Board of Education of Little Rock, No. 19,795 (8th Cir. 1970); Swann v. Charlotte-Mecklenburg Board of Education, et al., No. 14, 517, 14, 518 (4th Cir. May 26, 1970); Northcross v. Board of Education of Memphis, 397, 397 U.S. 232 (1970); Alexander v. Holmes County Board of Education, 396 U.S. 19 (1969); United States v. Montgomery County Board of Education, 395 U.S. 225 (1965); United States v. Indianola Municipal Separate School District, 410 F. 2d. 626 (5th Cir.) cert. den. 396. U.S. 1011 (1969); Carter v. West Feliciana Parish School Board, 396 U.S. 297 (1970); Valley v. Rapides Parish School Board, 423 F. 2d 1132 (5th Cir. 1970).
74. Open Letter to the Richmond School Board and the United States District Court by the Summer Hill Concerned Parents and Friends, August 12, 1970, August 1970–December 1970, Box 4, Merhige Collection, UR.
75. "Both Sides Dislike Ruling," *RTD,* August 18, 1970, 15–16; "School Plan Given Interim Approval," *RTD,* August 18, 1970, 1, 4.
76. Laurie Lulman to Judge Robert Merhige, undated, August 1970–December 1970, Box 4, Merhige Collection, UR.
77. Robert F. Harman, DDS, to Judge Earl Abbot, Judge Clifton Forge, August 24, 1970, August 1970–December 1970, Box 4, Merhige Collection, UR; see also George Mader to Mr. L. D. Adams, Superintendent, August 29, 1970; James L. Doherty to Mrs. W. H. Crockford, September 21, 1970, Desegregation, 1966–71; Mrs. D. H. Welchons to Mrs. W. H. Crockford, III, November 11, 1970; A. Prescott Rowe to Mrs. W. Hamilton Crockford, III, November 12, 1970, Consolidation, 1961–72, Box 1, M283, all in Crockford Papers, VCU.
78. Author interview with Dr. Ed Peeples, June 24, 2019.
79. Author interview with Rob Corcoran, March 11, 2019.
80. Transportation Report to the City Council, undated; T. Steven Daugherty to Mayor T. W. Bliley, Mrs. Hamilton Crockford III, Gov. A. L. Holton, and others, August 20, 1970, Consolidation, 1961–72, Box 2, M283, Crockford Papers, VCU.
81. J. Claiborne Mills Jr. to Judge Robert Merhige and Mrs. W. Hamilton Crockford, September 6, 1970; T. L. Pickle to Judge Robert R. Merhige., September 7, 1970; Paul T. Bassett to Dr. L. D. Adams, Superintendent and

Mrs. W. Hamilton Crockford, September 10, 1970, August 1970–December 1970, Box 4, Merhige Collection, UR; "Integration Not Going as Planned," *RTD*, September 13, 1970, 1, 41; John A. Gunn to Mrs. Crockford, October 14, 1970, Busing 1970–72, Box 1, M283, Crockford Papers, VCU; William G. Colby Jr. to Mrs. W. Hamilton Crockford, November 18, 1970; Urchie B. Ellis to Honorable Thomas J. Bliley Jr., Mayor of Richmond, November 20, 1970; Johnie Lu Morgan to Mrs. W. H. Crockford, *Richmond News-Leader*, *RTD*, and WRVA Mailbag, November 20, 1970, Consolidation, 1961–72, Box 2, M283, Crockford Papers, VCU.

82. CEPS Executive Board to Ad Hoc Committee on Public Schools, Greater Richmond Chamber of Commerce, August 9, 1971; CEPS Convening Committee, undated, both Folder 154, Mss1 W5603b FA2, Wheat Papers, VMHC.
83. Recommendation from Henrico County Council Executive Committee, March 2, 1971, Consolidation, 1961–72, Box 2, M283, Crockford Papers, VCU.
84. Mrs. Harold E. Greer Jr., Chamber of Commerce, to Mr. James C. Wheat Jr., September 11, 1971, Folder 154, Mss1 W5603b FA2, Wheat Papers, VMHC.
85. Author interview with Dr. Ed Peeples, June 24, 2019.
86. Ibid.; Rob Corcoran, *Trustbuilding: An Honest Conversation on Race, Reconciliation, and Responsibility.* (Charlottesville: University of Virginia Press, 2010), 124–31; author interviews with Rob Corcoran, March 11, 2019; with Benjamin Campbell, March 12, 2019.
87. Testimonies of Valerie P. Perkins, Mark Person, Phillip H Brunson III, and Yolanda Burrell Taylor in N. Elizabeth Schlatter and Ashley Kistler, eds., *Growing Up in Civil Rights Richmond: A Community Remembers* (Richmond, VA: University of Richmond Museums, 2019), 52, 55, 64, 86.
88. Memorandum to File . . . Confidential—Not for Publication: Notes from meeting with Richmond School Board, September 24, 1971, Folder 154, Wheat Papers, VMHC.
89. "Police Deny School Violence," *RTD*, September 4, 1970, B1, B4.
90. Author interview with Abner Linwood Holton III., September 29, 2020.
91. "Nerve Centers Here Dissect Rumors," *RTD*, September 13, 1970, C1, C11.
92. "Parents Charge Cover-ups," *RTD*, September 18, 1970, B1, B6.
93. "Wait-and-See Approach Advised by Holton," *RTD*, September 25, 1970, 1–2.
94. Memorandum to File . . . Confidential—Not for Publication: Notes from meeting with Richmond School Board, September 24, 1971, Folder 154, Wheat Papers, VMHC.
95. "Youngsters Respond to Freedom," *RTD*, June 21, 1970, D1, D9.
96. For Critical Minds and Compassionate Hearts: Richmond Citizen's Elementary School Proposal, undated, Folder 30, Mss1 W5603b FA2, Wheat Papers, VMHC.

97. Author interview with Rob Corcoran, March 11, 2019.
98. Elizabeth L. O'Leary, *The Carillon Neighborhood: A History* (Richmond, VA: Carillon Civic Association, 2013), 32–35; author interviews with Dr. Elizabeth O'Leary, June 26, 2019; with Rob Corcoran, March 11, 2019; with Susan Corcoran, May 7, 2019; with Dr. Rutledge B. Dennis, July 26, 2019.
99. Edward E. Fowler, Major USAF, to Judge Robert Merhige, August 30, 1971, August 1970–December 1970, Box 4, Merhige Collection, UR.
100. Motion for Joinder, Nov. 4, 1970, 90a–98a; Amended Complaint, December, 14, 1970; Motion to Recuse, *Bradley v. Richmond School Board,* Folder 9, Box 18, Merhige Collection, UR; see also Richard D. Obenshain, Counsel West End Concerned Parent and Friends to Mrs. W. H. Crockford, November 15, 1970; Professor Isabel Rogers to Mrs. W. Hamilton Crockford, January 26, 1972; Bill Watts WLEE News to Mrs. Hamilton Crockford III, March 17, 1972, Consolidation, 1961–72; Sub-Division Boundary Descriptions, April 30, 1971, Desegregation, 1966–71; Ron Hill WLEE News to Mrs. W. Hamilton Crockford, March 24, 1972, all in Folder Busing 1970–72, Box 1, M283, Crockford Papers, VCU.
101. "The Richmond Decision," WRIC TV4 Editorial, January 26 and 27, 1972, Box 4, January 28–March 7, 1972, Merhige Collection, UR; Mrs. Thomas C. Sanders, President of the Federation to the Richmond Area News Media, January 10, 1972, Consolidation, 1961–72, Box 1, M283, Crockford Papers, VCU.
102. Resolution of the Chesterfield County Council of PTAs, undated; Resolution of the Providence Junior High PTA, February 14, 1972; A. M. Davis Elementary PTA to Judge Robert R. Merhige, January 21, 1972; Nathaniel W. Holland Jr. to Judge Robert R. Merhige, August 12, 1970; Carlton Boyer to Judge Robert R. Merhige, January 19, 1972, all in Box 4, January 1–20, 1972, January 28–March 7, 1972, August 1970–December 1970, Merhige Collection, UR; Vivian S. Easterling, Secretary of the Chesterfield Education Association to Mrs. W. H. Crockford III, January 26, 1971; "To All State Association Presidents, Executive Secretaries and Urban Association Presidents," Hilda S. Morano, President Henrico Education Association, April 7, 1972, Consolidation, 1961–72, Box 1, M283, Crockford Papers, VCU.
103. Harold M. Ratcliffe to Mrs. W. Hamilton Crockford III, February 24, 1971, Consolidation, 1961–72, Box 1, M283, Crockford Papers, VCU.
104. "Mr. Green's Jerry-Built Rig," *RTD,* November 22, 1971, 12; "Wilder, Duval, Gartlan Oppose Anti-Busing Bill," *RAA,* February 19, 1972, 1, 24; "Massive Resistance Mood Pervades General Assembly," *RAA,* February 26, 1972, 1, 24.
105. Andrew W. Coates Jr. to Judge Robert Merhige, February 2, 1972, Box 4, January 28–March 7, 1972, Merhige Collection, UR; Richmond Area Cooperation Committee, ad for "Anti-Busing Rally!," *RTD,* April 18, 1972, 15.
106. Sick of Hypocrite Judges to Judge Robert Merhige, February 20, 1972, Box 4, January 28–March 7, 1972, Merhige Collection, UR.

107. Author interviews with Wayland Rennie, July 17, 2015; with Benjamin Campbell, March 12, 2019.
108. Unnamed Letter to Judge Robert R. Merhige, January 11, 1972; Mr. and Mrs. Johnson to Mr. Bullshit (So-called Judge Merhige), January 19, 1972; Untitled Letter to Judge Robert Merhige, January 24, 1972, all in Box 4, Merhige Collection, UR.
109. "Protest Motorcade May Extend 50 Miles," *RTD*, February 17, 1972, 1–2; "3,261 Cars Make Trip to Washington," *RTD*, February 13, 1972, 1, 5; and "Protest Reactions Is [*sic*] Varied in Area," *RTD*, February 19, 1972, 17.
110. "Protest Reactions Is [*sic*] Varied in Area," *RTD*, February 19, 1972, 17; "1,000 Cheer Anti-Busing Talks; Rain Sends Rally Indoors," *RTD*, February 25, 1972, 17.
111. Interim Report by the Greater Richmond Chamber of Commerce Committee on Public Education, January 14, 1972, Desegregation 1966–71; "Reversal of the Richmond Busing Decision," Education Summary, June 23, 1972, Box 1, M283, Crockford Papers, VCU.
112. Progress Report on Planning the Consolidation of the Richmond, Chesterfield, and Henrico School Divisions, April 7, 1972, Consolidation, 1961–72; "Reversal of the Richmond Busing Decision," Education Summary, June 23, 1972, 1–3, Busing 1970–72; Bradley v. Richmond School Board, 834–75; CEPS Newsletter, January 1972, all in Box 2, M283, Crockford Papers, VCU; "In Richmond Politics: It's a New Ball Game," *RAA*, April 29, 1972, 1–2; "De-Annex Decision Not 'The Last Word,'" *Richmond News Leader*, May 4, 1972, 1.
113. "Some Progress—But Virginia Continues to Resist," *RAA*, May 14–18, 1974, 5.
114. Clara Silverstein, *White Girl: A Story of School Desegregation* (Athens: University of Georgia Press, 2004), 123–26.
115. Author interview with Reginald Gordon, June 27, 2019.
116. Testimony from Mark Person in Schlatter and Kistler, *Growing Up in Civil Rights Richmond*, 55, 97.

4. Richmond Community Action Program

1. The chapter epigraph is from "Self-Help Employment Effort," Plan to Reduce Poverty by Winfred Mundle, Vice Mayor to City Council, May 31, 1968, Folder 40, Box 3, Mss1 W5603b FA2, Series 1, Race Problems, Wheat, Papers, VMHC; Stone, *Regime Politics*; Brown-Nagin, *Courage to Dissent*; Lawson, *Running for Freedom*.
2. "Officials, Residents Disagree on Project," *RTD*, July 6, 1970, B4.
3. Cervantes, "To Prevent a Chain of Super-Watts," *Harvard Business Review* (September–October 1967): 55–65, copy found in Folder 40, Race Problems, Mss1 W5603b FA2, Series 1, Box3, Wheat Papers, VMHC.
4. "Housing Residents Comment," *RTD*, July 25, 1971, D1.

5. Lyndon B. Johnson, Annual Message to the Congress on the State of the Union, January 8, 1964, American Presidency Project Online, https://www.presidency.ucsb.edu/documents/annual-message-the-congress-the-state-the-union-25; and Martha J. Bailey and Nicolas J. Duquette, "How Johnson Fought the War on Poverty: The Economic and Politics of Funding at the Office of Economic Opportunity," *Journal of Economic History* 74, no. 2 (June 2014): 351–88.
6. "Cleveland's Antipoverty Plan Called Nation's Worst," *Pittsburgh Courier,* January 2, 1965, 16; "Mayor Denies Charges on Antipoverty Plan," *Chicago Daily Defender,* April 22, 1965, 8; "War on Poverty Becoming Hot War," *Michigan Chronicle,* May 1, 1965, B4; "Antipoverty Program: For Whom? By Whom?," *Los Angeles Sentinel,* May 13, 1965, A6.
7. Kent B. Germany, *New Orleans after the Promises: Poverty, Citizenship, and the Search for the Great Society.* (Athens: University of Georgia Press, 2007), 2–11; William S. Clayson, *Freedom Is Not Enough: The War on Poverty and the Civil Rights Movement in Texas* (Austin: University of Texas Press, 2010); Lisa Gayle Hazirjian and Annelise Orleck, eds., *The War on Poverty: A New Grassroots History, 1964–1980* (Athens: University of Georgia Press, 2011), 359–62.
8. Susan Abrams Beck, "The Limits of Presidential Activism: Lyndon Johnson and the Implementation of the Community Action Program," *Presidential Studies Quarterly* 17, no. 3 (Summer 1987): 541–57.
9. "Hawkins' Aide Tells Poverty Meet Aims," *Los Angeles Sentinel,* January 28, 1965, A2; "Shriver Solicits Aid of Churches in Poverty Fight," *Chicago Defender,* January 30, 1965, 14; "Officials Hear Aide: Antipoverty War Chief for Area-Wide Attacks," *New Journal and Guide,* January 30, 1965, B2; "Hutchins Launches Antipoverty War," *Michigan Chronicle,* February 13, 1965, 2; "Ohio's War on Poverty to Be Examined in Dayton Meeting," *Call and Post,* May 29, 29, 12B; "Shriver Cautions Church on Poverty War Dangers," *Baltimore Afro-American,* June 5, 1965, 3; and "Form New Group to Push War on Poverty," *Chicago Defender,* June 5, 1965, 4.
10. "Who's Soaking the Poor?," *Baltimore Afro-American,* May 1965, 15, A4; Madelyn L. Kafoglis, "Participatory Democracy in the Community Action Program," *Public Choice* 5 (Fall,1968): 73–85; Richard K. Fenn, "The Community Action Program: An American Gospel?," *Science and Society* 33, no. 2 (Spring 1969): 209–22; Melvin B. Mogulof, "A Developmental Approach to the Community Action Program Idea," *Social Work* 12, no. 2 (April 1967): 12–20; Sar A. Levitan, "The Community Action Program: A Strategy to Fight Poverty," *Annals of the American Academy of Political and Social Science* 385 (September 1969): 63–75; Jerome S. Sloan, "The Community Action Program and the Social Responsibility of the Local Lawyer," *Virginia Law Review* 51, no. 8 (December 1965): 1545–85; John A. Perrotta, "Machine Influence on a Community Action Program:

The Case of Providence, Rhode Island," *Polity* 9, no. 4 (Summer 1977): 481–502.
11. "36 Member Group Formed to Develop Antipoverty Plans," *RTD*, June 2, 1965, 1, 4.
12. "U.S. Says Poor Must Have Voice in Poverty War," *Norfolk Journal and Guide*, December 11, 1965, 7.
13. "Poverty Unit Submits $44,282 Budget," *RTD*, June 25, 1965, 2; "City Given Poverty Fund Rules," *RTD*, September 24, 1965, 2; "Plan to Aid Family Life Is Proposed," *RTD*, December 30, 1965, 1, 5.
14. "Antipoverty Tactics Argued," *RTD*, January 30, 1967, 1, 2.
15. "Nell Barnes Pusey," *Richmond News Leader*, June 7, 1968, 14.
16. "They Must Help Themselves," *RTD*, June 3, 1965, 16.
17. "Hare Resigns RCAP Post, Back Chiles as Successor," *RTD*, August 29, 1969, C1.
18. "Plea Made on Routing of Process," *RTD*, April 22, 1966, 1, 2; and "Two Officials Named by Antipoverty Group," *RTD*, January 21, 1966, 2; "Thornton Is Endorsed for Relations Director," *RTD*, June 5, 1969, C2; John T. Kneebone and Eugene P. Trani, *Fulfilling the Promise: Virginia Commonwealth University and the City of Richmond, 1968–2009* (Charlottesville: University of Virginia Press, 2020), 200.
19. "Antipoverty Tactics Argued; Session Votes Fund Appeals," *RTD*, January 30, 1967, 1–2; "Plea Made on Routing of Protests," *RTD*, April 22, 1966, 1–2; "Vernelle 'Nell' Barnes Pusey Dies at 92," *RTD*, November 24, 2008; "Attention Voters with Professional Men," Paid Political Advertisement in the *RTD*, November 1, 1964, 30-A; and https://www.legacy.com/us/obituaries/timesdispatch/name/paul-pusey-obituary?pid=18824437.
20. "Chiles Pilots RCAP, Seeks Broader Help," *RTD*, December 11, 1977, K1; and A Day in the Life of a Neighborhood Worker, Folder 40, Box 3, Mss1 W5603b FA2, Series 1, Race Problems, Wheat Papers, VMHC.
21. "Plea Made on Routing of Protest," *RTD*, April 22, 1966, 1–2.
22. John Chiles's father, John Sr., was a longtime civil rights advocate and NAACP member in the Richmond area. For more on his support of Black advancement, see Richmond Branch of the National Association for the Advancement of Colored People, a list of Richmond Negro Physicians, October 4, 1930, in the NAACP Branch Files, Folder 23, Box G210, NAACP Papers, Library of Congress.
23. "Hare Resigns RCAP Post, Back Chiles as Successor," *RTD*, August 29, 1969, C1; "RCAP Post Filled at Stormy Meeting," *RTD*, October 23, 1969, A1, A6.
24. "Program to Aid Young Women Is Considered," *RTD*, February 5, 1966, 3; "Neighborhood Centers Backed for Five Areas," *RTD*, August 18, 1966, 2; "They Must Help Themselves," *RTD*, June 3, 1966, 16.

25. "Antipoverty Officials Expect to Meet Federal Objections," *RTD*, May 27, 1966, 2; "Survey of City Neighborhoods Shows Varying Personalities," *RTD*, May 28, 1966, 5.
26. "Antipoverty Workers' Rent Said Raised," *RTD*, October 20, 1966, 1, 6.
27. "Antipoverty Tactics Argued," *RTD*, January 30, 1967, 1, 2.
28. "Neighborhood Centers Backed for Five Areas," *RTD*, August 18, 1966, 2; ad "Action Program to Open Center," *RTD*, October 30, 1966, B17.
29. "Three Antipoverty Projects Costing $216,923 Approved," *RTD*, April 5, 1966, 2; "Richmond Activities," *RTD*, January 7, 1968, F4.
30. Supportive Explanatory Data Relative to R-CAP Project Cutbacks, October 1968, Folder 40, Box 3, Mss1 W5603b FA2, Series 1, Race Problems, Wheat Papers, VMHC.
31. A Day in the Life of a Neighborhood Worker, Folder 40, Box 3, Mss1 W5603b FA2, Series 1, Race Problems, Wheat Papers, VMHC.
32. "Creighton Court Tenant Wins Eviction Stay," *RTD*, April 30, 1966, 2; "Marsh Pledges Reforms Here in Housing," *RTD*, September 2, 1966, 2.
33. "Housing Chief Concern in City's Poverty Areas," *RTD*, September 9, 1966, 1.
34. S. S. Wurtzel, President of the Richmond Areas Community Council to James C. Wheat, November 24, 1967; Fitzgerald Bemis to James C. Wheat, November 8, 1967, both in Folder 41, Race Problems, Mss1 W5603b FA2, Series 1, Box 3, Wheat Papers, VMHC.
35. "Antipoverty Workers' Rent Said Raised," *RTD*, October 20, 1966, 1, 6.
36. "Creighton Court Suit Here Is Dismissed by Merhige," *RTD*, August 27, 1969, B5.
37. "Antipoverty Workers' Rent Said Raised," *RTD*, October 20, 1966, 1, 6.
38. "Curtis Holt: Man Who Fought City Hall and Won," *RAA*, January 29, 1983, 2–3; "Project Residents Organize To Fight 'Injustices,'" *RAA*, July 2, 1966, 1–2; "Mothers Fight Public Housing," *RAA*, January 7, 1967, 1; "Black, White Tenants Unite in Protest," *RAA*, May 4, 1968, 1–2; "Housing Unit Denies Charges in Suit," *RTD*, May 17, 1966, 2.
39. "Virginians Lean Toward Skepticism," *WP*, January 3, 1965, B1; "The Antipoverty Program," *Norfolk Journal and Guide*, February 20, 1965, 6; "Antipoverty Warfare," *Norfolk Journal and Guide*, March 27, 1965, A12; "Poverty Assault Stymied in Some Localities," *RTD*, November 6, 1966, 37; "Hearing on Poverty Is Scheduled Jan. 29," *RTD*, January 10, 1967, 13; "Virginia Candidates Shy at Great Society Issue," *WP*, October 27, 1966, B1.
40. "Poll of Congress Opposes Tax Rise," *New York Times*, December 23, 1966, 13.
41. "Urge 'Poor War' Boycott," *Chicago Daily Defender*, July 7, 1965, 1; "Another Battle in 'War' on Poverty," *Philadelphia Tribune*, June 29, 1965, 20; "Two Sets March," *Chicago Daily Defender*, July 22, 1965, 3; "U.S. Inspects Poverty War Here," *Pittsburgh Courier*, July 31, 1965, 1; "Poverty Council Scored by

Dailey," *New York Times,* January 2, 1966, 49; "Oakland Is Split on Poverty Plans," *New York Times,* January 17, 1966, 20; "Facing the Inflation Problem," *New York Times,* January 5, 1966, 30; "Slowdown in Poverty War Urged," *WP,* December 20, 1966, A4.
42. "To Produce a Creative Disorder," *New York Times,* February 27, 1966, SM6.
43. For the lawsuit, see "Richmond: Former Confederate Capital Finally Falls to Blacks," *Ebony,* June 1980, 34–39. For previous treatments of Holt's accomplishments, see Hayter, *Dream Is Lost,* 125–26, 130; and Moeser and Dennis, *Politics of Annexation,* 141–43.
44. Richmond City 1948 Directory, US City Directories, 1822–1995; Virginia, Marriage Records, 1936–2014, Roll 101167677, Virginia Department of Health; and US WWII Draft Cards Young Men, 1940–47, Records of the Selective Service System, 147, Box 357, National Archives, all at ancestry.com.
45. "Housing Chief Concern in City's Poverty Areas," *RTD,* September 9, 1966, 1; S. S. Wurtzel, President of the Richmond Areas Community Council to James C. Wheat, November 24, 1967; Fitzgerald Bemiss to James C. Wheat, November 8, 1967, both in Folder 41, Race Problems, Mss1 W5603b FA2, Series 1, Box 3, Wheat Papers, VMHC.
46. "Suitable Public Housing Sites Will Be Sought Here," *RTD,* September 1, 1966, 26.
47. "Creighton Court Tenant Wins Injunction to Prevent Eviction," *RTD,* September 7, 1966, 2; "Curtis Holt: Man Who Fought City Hall and Won," *RAA,* January 29, 1983, 2–3; "Creighton Court Tenant Wins Eviction Stay," *RTD,* April 30, 1966, 2.
48. "36 Member Group Formed to Develop Antipoverty Plans," *RTD,* June 2, 1965, 1, 4; Supportive Explanatory Data Relative to R-CAP Project Cutbacks, October 1968, Folder 40, Box 3, Mss1 W5603b FA2, Series 1, Race Problems, Wheat Papers, VMHC.
49. Mrs. Richard Soulen, Secretary to Mayor Phil Bagley, October 8, 1968, ibid.
50. "Antipoverty Workers' Rent Said Raised," *RTD,* October 20, 1966, 1, 6.
51. Alan Kiepper, City Manager of Richmond, to the City Council of Richmond, August 12, 1968, Human Relations Commission, Box 3, Mss1 W5603b FA2, Series 1, Race Problems, Wheat Papers, VMHC.
52. Richmond Summer 1968—Hot or Cool, speech delivered by Mayor Morrill Crowe to James C. Wheat, March 6, 1968, Folder 40, Box 3, Mss1 W5603b FA2, Series 1, Race Problems, Wheat Papers, VMHC.
53. "Poverty Fighters Chart Programs," *RTD,* March 20, 1966, 1, 14; "Antipoverty Programs Here Likely to Be Sharply Curtailed," *RTD,* July 19, 1966, 2; "Changes Gives Assurance Poor Will Be Represented," *RTD,* June 1, 1966, 2.
54. Ernest E. Mayo Sr., of Ernest E. Mayo, Inc., General Contractors to James Wheat, October 29, 1968, Folder 40, Box 3, Mss1 W5603b FA2, Series 1, Race Problems, Wheat Papers, VMHC.

55. "'Poor Man's Meal' Called Cheap Politics," *RTD,* August 8, 1969, B1.
56. "Business Is Urged to Heighten Its Activity in War on Poverty," *New York Times,* March 5, 1966, 46; "Self-Help Employment Effort," Plan to Reduce Poverty by Winfred Mundle, Vice Mayor to City Council, May 31, 1968; Charles A. Burtner, Executive Manager of the Richmond Chamber of Commerce to the Executive Committee to the Chamber of Commerce, July 7, 1968, both in Folder 40, Box3, Mss1 W5603b FA2, Series 1, Race Problems, Wheat Papers, VMHC.
57. C. W. Pinnell Jr., Owner of Pinnell's Incorporated, to James C. Wheat, November 5, 1968, ibid.; Emergency Convocation: The Urban Coalition in DC, August 24, 1967, Folder 41, ibid.
58. "Crowe Asks Report on Needed Workers," *RTD,* October 29, 1968, 1, 3.
59. "Antipoverty Tactics Argued; Session Votes Fund Appeals," *RTD,* January 30, 1967, 1, 2.
60. Robert J. Habenicht, President of the Urban League to James Wheat, October 10, 1968; Mary Auginteanu to Members of the City Council, October 15, 1968, both in Folder 40, Box 3, Mss1 W5603b FA2, Series 1, Race Problems, Wheat Papers, VMHC.
61. Weston A. Hare, R-CAP Executive Director to Phil J. Bagley, Mayor of Richmond, November 8, 1968, ibid.
62. Mrs. William Selden, President of the Richmond Federation of Parent-Teacher Associations, to James Wheat, October 21, 1968, Folder 40, Box 3, Mss1 W5603b FA2, Series 1, Race Problems, Wheat Papers, VMHC.
63. "Crowe Asks Report on Needed Workers," *RTD,* October 29, 1968, 1, 3.
64. Gay Henderson, President of the Hillside Civic Association, to Mayor Phil J. Bagley, October 27, 1968, Folder 40, Box 3, Mss1 W5603b FA2, Series 1, Race Problems, Wheat Papers, VMHC.
65. Author interview with Viola Baskerville, June 28, 2019; Church Hill Revitalization Plan Draft, 1–3, found in undated folder, Box 21, M293, Clarence L. Townes Jr. Papers, VCU. (Hereafter cited as Townes Papers, VCU.) A copy of the revitalization draft is also in the possession of the author. Procedural Plan Appraisal and Acquisition for the Richmond Expressway System, March 21, 1967, Folder 41, Box 3, Mss1 W5603b FA2, Series 1, Race Problems, Wheat Papers, VMHC.
66. Meeting of School-Community Coordinators, April 16, 1968, Mss1S4772a, Sartain Papers, VMHC.
67. Mrs. Mary W. Wyche, Organizer of the Southside Home Owners Protective League, October 9, 1968, Folder 40, Box 3, Mss1 W5603b FA2, Series 1, Race Problems, Wheat Papers, VMHC.
68. Curtis Holt, Creighton Court Civic Association, to Phil Bagley, October 27, 1968, ibid.
69. "Negro Uprisings More Serious Than Imagined: Efforts Futile to Blame Outside Agitation," *Dallas Times Herald,* August 9, 1967, clipping found

in Folder 41, Box 3, Mss1 W5603b FA2, Series 1, Race Problems, Wheat Papers, VMHC.
70. Allix B. James to James C. Wheat, August 11, 1967, ibid.
71. "The VCHR Observer," vol 1, no.1 (September 1967), found in ibid.
72. Executive Director-Commission on Human Relations, undated, Folder 43, Box 3, Mss1 W5603b FA2, Human Relations Commission, Series 1, Race Problems, Wheat Papers, VMHC.
73. An Ordinance to Establish a Commission on Community Relations, 88–221, July 19, 1968; Virginia State NAACP Conference of Branches to James C. Wheat, August 21, 1968, ibid.
74. Samuel Clark, Calvin Faison, L. L. Henderson, Mrs. Elizabeth Mallory, and Evelyn E. Fields, to the city council, August 22, 1968; Basic Provisions Human Relations Commission Ordinance, November 6, 1968, both in Folder 43, Human Relations Commission, Box 3, Mss1 W5603b FA2, Series 1, Race Problems, Wheat Papers, VMHC.
75. Recommendations to the City Council from Citizen Member of the Voice of Poverty, Linwood Corbett, January 13, 1969; Recommendation List for Human Relations, April 15, 1969, Executive Director-Commission on Human Relations, undated, both in ibid.
76. "Council Names 15 to Relations Unit," *RTD*, January 14, 1969, 1.
77. Gay Henderson, President of the Hillside Civic Association to Mayor Phil J. Bagley, October 27, 1968, Folder 40, Box 3, Mss1 W5603b FA2, Series 1, Race Problems, Wheat Papers, VMHC.
78. Curtis Holt, Creighton Court Civic Association, to Phil Bagley, October 27, 1968, ibid.; "Picketing Starts at City Hall," *RTD*, October 16, 1968, B3.
79. "Holt to Seek City Council Position," *RTD*, December 27, 1969, B2; Curtis Holt, Creighton Court Civic Association, to Phil Bagley, October 27, 1968, Folder 40, Box 3, Mss1 W5603b FA2, Series 1, Race Problems, Wheat Papers, VMHC.
80. Hayter, *Dream Is Lost*, 125–27.
81. Author interviews with John Moeser, March 11, 2019; with Benjamin Campbell, March 14, 2019; with Rutledge Dennis, July 26, 2019. Dennis is Professor of Political Science at George Mason University and longtime Richmond resident. He interviewed Curtis Holt in the 1980s. Many of Holt's motivations and goals described here come from Dennis's interview with Holt.
82. Councilmanic Election, June 10, 1970, tabulation found in the Box 3, M183, Annexation Files, VCU.
83. "Fulton Renewal Plans Held Step to Disaster," *RTD*, March 11, 1968, 1–2.
84. Author interview with John Moeser, March 11, 2019.
85. Moeser and Rutledge, *Politics of Annexation*, 144–71.
86. De-Annexation Fund, paid advertisement in the *RTD*, March 24, 1971, 11; "Quick De-Annexation Is Forecast," *RTD*, March 19, 1974, 17; author interview with Rutledge Dennis, July 26, 2019.

87. Moeser and Dennis, *Politics of Annexation*, 15.
88. "Crusade to Enter Annexation Suit," *RTD*, October 17, 1972, 34; "Crusade Annexation Plea Filed," *RTD*, October 20, 1972, 23.
89. "Crusade Undecided about Position as Intervener in Annexation Case," *RAA*, October 28, 1972, 20; "Crusade Leader Explains Goals in Effort to Enter Annex Suit," *RAA*, November 11, 1972, 3.
90. Author interview with Rutledge Dennis, July 26, 2019.
91. "Holt Raps Crusade Plan to Intervene," *RTD*, October 18, 1972, B3.
92. "Conduct of Fans at Games Praised" and "Credit Should be Given only Where It Is Due," *RAA*, November 25, 1972, 5; "Marsh Welcomes Holt," *RAA*, April 16–20, 1974, 7; "Crusade Reacts to Annex Ruling," *RAA*, June 4–8, 1974, 5.
93. "Curtis Holt, Sr., Faces Charges," *RTD*, October 16, 1972, 20; "Bail Bond Study Slated for Release in January," *RTD*, November 15, 1972, 15–16; "Blacks Have No Chance in City, State Courts" and "Reference to Crusade Hit by Another Reader," *RAA*, November 18, 1972, 5.
94. Author interview with Benjamin Campbell, March 14, 2019.
95. "Thornton Appointment Makes Job Outlook Brighter in City," *RAA*, March 4, 1972, 1, 5; "Holt Case Before Supreme Court," *RAA*, May 13, 1972, 1, 26; "Intern in City Manager's Office Sees Pressure as Key to Progress," *RAA*, May 27, 1972, 6; "Whites Keep Edge on School Board but Blacks Seen Becoming Its Head," *RAA*, June 10, 1972, 3; "Rev. Jones Heads Richmond Schools," *RAA*, July 29, 1972, 1–2; "Blacks in Running for 6 Top Positions," *RAA*, June 2, 1973, 1–2; "Mrs. Dell Continues to Gain Support," *RAA*, June 23, 1973, 6; "Richmond's First Chief of Welfare Bares Plans," *RAA*, January 5, 1974, 3; "Push for Full-Time Black Judge Sparks Political Moves," *RAA*, January 12, 1974, 7; "RRHA Has Another Chance to Pick Black for Position," *RAA*, January 26, 1974, 8; "Morris, Wilder Scored Big Triumph in the Making of First Black Judge," *RAA*, February 9, 1974, 1–2; "The Sheffield Appointment: A Significant Breakthrough," *RAA*, October 12, 1974, 1–2; "New City School Chief Given a Big Sendoff," *RAA*, February 14, 1976, 12.
96. "Marsh Wants Fair Shot for City Hopefuls," *RAA*, October 16, 1976, 1–2.
97. "Black Political Power Is Appraised in Session at VCU," *RAA*, November 6, 1976, 11; and "Crusade Calls Meeting" and "Political Tempo Picks Up in City," *RAA*, November 20, 1976, 1.
98. "Afro Backs 6 Candidates" and "Crusade Action in 5th District Seen Aiding TOP-Backed Hopeful," *RAA*, February 26, 1, 8; "Curtis Holt, Sr., District System Praised," *RAA*, March 12, 1977, 5; "Marsh Eyeing Mayorship, Befriends Richardson," *RAA*, March 5, 1977, 1, 11; "City's Black 5th District Really Has Toss-Up Status," *RAA*, January 8, 1977, 7.
99. "Crusade Discusses Voter Registration," *RAA*, February 21, 1976, 13; "Ward System Would Produce New Black Faces," *RAA*, June 5, 1976, 9; "New City Crusade President: Do Battle with the Vote," January 22, 1977, 7; "The

Meaning of Our 5–4 Victory," *RAA*, March 5, 1977, 1; "Holt vs. Marsh: Political Battle Shaping Up," *RAA*, October 26–30, 1976, 7; "City Crusade Tells Endorsement Plans under District System," *RAA*, December 4, 1976, 14.

5. Project One

1. Katharine C. Lyall, "Public-Private Partnerships in the Carter Years," *Proceedings of the Academy of Political Science* 36, no. 2 (1986): 4–13.
2. "Hotel Issue Dominated Session Here," *RTD*, October 8, 1982, B3.
3. Stone, *Regime Politics*, x–xi.
4. "Faith in South Proved to be Right," *Atlanta Constitution*, January 9, 1977, 19A; Melissa Dean, *Desegregating Private Higher Education in the South: Duke, Emory, Rice, Tulane, and Vanderbilt* (Baton Rouge: Louisiana State University Press, 2013).
5. "Sunbelt and Suburbia Still Strong Magnets for Migrating Americans during Decade," *Wall Street Journal*, July 2, 1980, 17.
6. "4 Manking on the Inner City," *WP*, April 29, 1978, E11.
7. Table 21: Population of the 100 Largest Urban Places, 1980, US Bureau of the Census, https://www.census.gov/population/www/documentation/twps0027/tab21.txt.
8. "Sleepy Richmond Wakes Up, and Now Struggles to Adjust," *Wall Street Journal*, December 22, 1981, 23.
9. "Richmond: Former Confederate Capital Finally Falls to Blacks," *Ebony*, June 1980, 34–39.
10. "Sleepy Richmond Wakes Up," *Wall Street Journal*, December 22, 1981, 23.
11. Amy Shanker and Len Rodman, "Public-Private Partnerships," *Journal (American Water Works Association)*, 88, no. 4 (1996): 102–7; Thea Hoeth, "Public-Private Partnerships in State Government," *Public Productivity and Management Review* 15, no. 2 (Winter 1991): 147–50; Dominique Custos and John Reitz, "Public-Private Partnerships," *American Journal of Comparative Law* 58 (2010): 555–84.
12. Andrew V. Sorrell and Bruce A. Vlk, "Virginia's Never-ending Moratorium on City-County Annexations," *Virginia News Letter* 88, no. 1 (January 2012): 1–4.
13. Author interview with Benjamin Campbell, March 12, 2019.
14. "Captains in War on Poverty," *RTD*, December 11, 1977, K1.
15. "Board Spends Much Time Disproving Myths on Growth," *RTD*, December 11, 1977, D1; David R. Godschalk, "New Community Development Partnerships in America," *Community Development Journal* 8, no. 2 (April 1973): 60–69; William H. Frey, "Central City White Flight: Racial and Nonracial Causes," *American Sociological Review* 44, no. 3 (June 1979): 425–48; Frey, "Black In-Migration, White Flight, and the Changing Economic Base of the Central City," *American Journal of Sociology* 85, no. 6 (1980):

1396–417; Rachel A. Woldoff, *White Flight/Black Flight: The Dynamics of Racial Change in an American Neighborhood* (Ithaca, NY: Cornell University Press, 2011).
16. "Black Mayors Conference Claims Leadership Role," *WP,* October 30, 1977, A3.
17. "Carter Losing Black Support, Caucus Warns," *RTD,* July 30, 1977, A11; "Carter Pledges Jobs Action to Blacks," *Facts on File World News Digest,* September 17, 1977, 1; "Carter Tells Black Caucus to Expect Job Bill Accord," *RTD,* September 26, 1977, A6; "Black Caucus, Rights Panel Support Action Programs," *RTD,* October 12, 1977, A3.
18. Jon C. Teaford, *The Road to Renaissance: Urban Revitalization in America, 1940–1985* (Baltimore: Johns Hopkins University Press, 1990); Christa A. Smith, "Predicting Success or Failure on Main Street: Urban Revitalization and the Kentucky Main Street Program, 1979–1999," *Southeastern Geographer* 42, no.2 (November 2002): 248–61.
19. Katharine C. Lyall, "Public-Private Partnerships in the Carter Years," *Proceedings of the Academy of Political Science* 36, no. 2 (1986): 4–13.
20. "Notes on Realty," *WP,* February 19, 1977, E10; "Freshman Year on the Job," *U.S. News & World Report,* December 26, 1977, 22; "Geno Baroni to Get HUD Housing Post," *WP,* March 2, 1977, A3; "EDA Funds to Increase," *WP,* June 16, 1977, D1.
21. "Newark—$19.8 Million to Improve Downtown," *New York Times,* February 6, 1977, 2; "With Spring, Downtown Starts to Stir," *New York Times,* March 20, 1977, 264; "Detroiters Lift Sights from Mire: Renaissance Center," *Christian Science Monitor,* April 14, 1977, 4; "U.S. Downtowns Get Back on Their Feet," *Christian Science Monitor,* December 21, 1977, 11.
22. "Southwest Residents Seek Faster Metro Cleanup at Waterside Mall," *WP,* May 12, 1977, DC1; "Rezoning to Revitalize Georgetown Area," *WP,* November 15, 1977, A2; "U.S. Giving Cities $150 Million for Redevelopment Projects," *WP,* April 7, 1978 1; "Memphis Seeks to Restore Its Status," *New York Times,* November 19, 1977, 48; "Baltimore Boosts 'Shopsteading' for City Neighborhoods," *WP,* January 4, 1978, A1; "Miami Beach Will Seek Larger Convention Business," *Atlanta Constitution,* February 14, 1978, 6D; "New Plaza in Downtown New Orleans Is A Wild and Mad Vision," *WP,* February 9, 1979, B8; "Pipelines to Neighborhoods," *New York Times,* March 24, 1978, A26; "4 Manking on the Inner City," *WP,* April 29, 1978, E11.
23. "Give Senators, Congressmen Time to Think," *New World News,* June 9, 1979, 3, Richmond 1977–91, File Cabinet 1, Moral Re-Armament/Initiatives of Change Papers, Richmond. (Hereafter cited as IoC Papers.)
24. Joint Letter to the Honorable Henry L. Marsh III., Mayor of the City of Richmond, Virginia, March 14, 1977, Richmond 1977–91, File Cabinet 1, IoC Papers; Randy Ruffin to Rob Corcoran, December 6, 1978, ibid.; author

interviews with Rob Corcoran, May 11, 2019; with John Moeser, May 10, 2019.
25. Author interview with Benjamin Campbell, March 12, 2019.
26. Joint Letter to the Honorable Henry L. Marsh III., Mayor of the City of Richmond, March 14, 1977, Richmond 1977–91, File Cabinet 1, IoC Papers; "Give Senators, Congressmen Time to Think," *New World News,* June 9, 1979, 3.
27. "Richmond-A Model City?," *New World News,* January 7, 1978, 1–7.
28. Richmond Expressway System Engineering Report by the Committee on Trafficways, October 1966; Planning Considerations Regarding Expressway System as Proposed by Richmond Metropolitan Authority, 1967, Richmond Expressway System Engineering Report, 1966, Box 9, M277, Sheppard Papers, VCU; author interviews with Robert Corcoran, March 11, 2019; with Benjamin Campbell, May 12, 2019.
29. Minutes of a Regular Meeting of the Executive Committee of the Board of Directors of Downtown Development Unlimited Held on April 22, 1977, DDU General and Correspondences 1977, Box 1:18, M281, A. J. Brent Papers, VCU. (Hereafter cited as Brent Papers, VCU.)
30. Howard Gillette Jr., *Camden after the Fall: Decline and Renewal in a Post-Industrial City* (Philadelphia: University of Pennsylvania Press, 2009), 122–44.
31. Annual Report to the State Corporation Commission of Virginia, January 1, 1977, DDU General and Correspondences 1977, Box 1:18, M281, Brent Papers, VCU.
32. A. J. Brent to Mr. B. A. Soyars, Vice President of Philip Morris, Inc., November 28, 1977; Lee F. Davis Jr. to Mr. Benjamin A. Soyars, Vice President of Philip Morris, Inc., December 9, 1977, both in ibid.
33. "U.S. Giving Cities $150 Million for Redevelopment Projects," *WP,* April 7, 1978, 1; "Dayton Diversifies Downtown—and People Return," *Christian Science Monitor,* October 19, 1977, 14.
34. Agreement Between DDU, A Virginia non-Stock Corporation, and Gerald D. Hines Interests, February 28, 1977; Informal Meeting of the Council of the City of Richmond, Project One, October 18, 1977, Downtown Development Unlimited General and Correspondences 1977; Office Memorandum, Downtown Development Unlimited Hotel Meeting on December 7, 1977, all in Box 1:18, M281, Brent Papers, VCU.
35. "Project I Approved, but Cloud Remains," *RTD,* November 29, 1977, Press Clippings, Project One Collection, Valentine Museum, Richmond (hereafter cited as VM).
36. RITA did not leave archival records behind. Most information about them in the subsequent pages comes from other organizational and personal papers archived at VCU's Special Collections Library.

37. "Project Creates Some Unlikely Bedfellows Here," *RTD*, December 20, 1977, Press Clippings, Project One Collection, VM; "Bond Sale Referendum Petitions Are Presented," *Richmond News Leader*, December 27, 1977; "The Authority of Municipal Bonds, 1978," *Daily Bond Buyer*, a culmination of news clippings from either the *RTD* or *Richmond News Leader* found in DDU General and Correspondences 1978, Box 1:19, M281, Brent Papers, VCU; "Competition Feared for Hotel Plan," *Richmond News Leader*, January 25, 1978; "Merhige Clears Way for Project in Suit Dismissal," *RTD*, April 4, 1978; "Project One," *RTD*, April 23, 1978, Press Clippings, Project One Collection, VM.
38. "Radical Tax Cuts Will Cost You Money," ad against RITA, November 2, 1981, Tensions in the Richmond Community, Drafts, Questionnaires, 1980–81, Box 16, M258, Richmond Urban Institute Papers (hereafter cited as RUI Papers), VCU.
39. Emerging Sources of Tension, Undated 1981, ibid.
40. Author interviews with Benjamin Campbell, May 12, 2019; with Dr. Ed Peeples, June 24, 2019.
41. Financial Executives of DDU to Executive Board and City Council, December 18, 1979; Public Hearing Comments on Richmond Independent Taxpayer Association, undated; A Report on Eight Propositions to Amend Richmond's City Charter Scheduled for Referendum on January 22, 1980; Brochure of the History and Purpose of Richmond Urban Institute, Race Relations in Richmond, 1980–1984, Boxes 11 and 12, M240, George Stevenson Kemp Papers, VCU.
42. "Center Foes Clear Hurdle, But Another Is Raised," *RTD*, December 31, 1977; "Bids Opening Slate Today on Coliseum," *RTD*, April 24, 1968, B1; "Claude Ritter Is a Worrier," *RTD*, December 29, 1968, E1, E2; "Delay Coliseum to Free Money for Poor: Marsh," *RAA*, May 18, 1968, 1–2; Ed Grimsley, "The New Coliseums," *Commonwealth Magazine* 34, no. 2 (February 1967): 19–26.
43. "Downtown Procedure Is Reversed," *RTD*, October 15, 1978, copy sent to Brent by RITA on October 23, 1978, found in DDU General and Correspondences 1978, Box 1:19, M281, Brent Papers, VCU.
44. "A City Revival?," *Newsweek*, January 15, 1979, 28; "Pittsburgh 'Renaissance' Meets Modern Resistance," *New York Times*, June 13, 1980, A12.
45. "The Charleston Flap," *WP*, March 3, 1979, B1; "Urban Rebirth May Be Myth, Studies Show," *Atlanta Constitution*, June 15, 1980, 1B.
46. "U.S. Giving Cities $150 Million for Redevelopment Projects," *WP*, April 7, 1978, 1.
47. "4 Manking on the Inner City," *WP*, April 29, 1978, E11.
48. "Study Says Old Cities Continue to Decline Despite Rejuvenation," *New York Times*, July 7, 1980, A1.

49. "'Revitalization' Held to Be Spotty," *New York Times,* June 1, 1980, R1.
50. "Neighborhood Movement Seeking Clout, Strategy," *WP,* June 24, 1978, E25.
51. "Southwest Residents Seek Faster Metro Cleanup at Waterside Mall," *WP,* May 12, 1977, DC1.
52. "A Towering Rise in Downtown Construction," *Business Week,* March 5, 1979, clipping found in DDU General and Correspondences, 1979, Box 1:18 M281, Brent Papers, VCU.
53. "A Low Blow," *RTD,* January 4, 1979; "Richmond Sues to Sell Bonds," *RTD,* March 14, 1979; "Property Acquisition to Continue," *RTD,* March 31, 1979; "Project I Foes Seeking to Block Land Acquisition," *Richmond News Leader,* August 7, 1979, Press Clippings, Project One Collection, VM; A. J. Brent to Honorable Henry L. Marsh III, April 18, 1979, DDU General and Correspondences, 1979, Box 1:18 M281, Brent Papers, VCU.
54. Brent to Marsh, April 18, 1979; A. J. Brent to Honorable Manuel Deese, January 11, 1979; Memo to Members of the Executive Committee DDU, January 18, 1979, ibid.
55. "The New Elite and an Urban Renaissance," *New York Times,* January 14, 1979, SM4.
56. Lassiter, *Silent Majority,* 13–27.
57. "Probable Cut in U.S. Aid Termed Threat to Revitalization of Cities," *New York Times,* January 21, 1979, 1.
58. "Two Tales of the Cities," *WP,* February 19, 1979, A27.
59. "Cities Feel Effects of U.S. Fund Cuts," *WP,* January 4, 1982, A1.
60. "Carter Trims Plans on Funds for Cities," *New York Times,* January 4, 1979, A13; "City Gets $3.2 Million Grant to Aid New Shopping Center," *WP,* January 4, 1979, C10; "New Rochelle Battles to Brighten Its Image," *New York Times,* January 12, 1979, B1; "New York Waterfront Project Set," *New York Times,* January 28, 1979, 45; "Baltimore: An Urban Winner," *WP,* February 3, 1979, E8; "Shopping Back in the Center," *WP,* April 7, 1979, B1.
61. "Battle Lines Drawn over Plan to End City Grant Program," *WP,* February 10, 1981, A2.
62. "Marriott Opening Was Quite a Bash," *Atlanta Constitution,* February 19, 1981, 6F; "New Marriott Seeking to Blend Convention Trade, Island Grace," *Atlanta Constitution,* August 9, 1981, 4G.
63. "New Hotel in NYC Has Unusual Site," *Atlanta Constitution,* July 19, 1981, 8G.
64. "Convention Center Plan Divides Yonkers Leaders," *New York Times,* September 23, 1979, WC1.
65. "Richmond Hotel Owners Returning Federal Grant," *WP,* August 22, 1981, E26.
66. "The Great Quest for Hotel Guests: Hotels," *New York Times,* April 28, 1985, SM28; "Major Portion of Mayflower Project Done," *WP,* November 1, 1982,

WB13; "Renovation Planned to Restore Former Glory of Imperial Hotel," *Atlanta Constitution,* June 18, 1982, 1D.
67. "Green Light for Project One Given by State Supreme Court," *RTD,* January 12, 1980, Press Clippings, Project One, VM.
68. "Green Light for Project One Given by State Supreme Court," *RTD,* January 12, 1980; "On Their Way Out," *RTD,* February 16, 1980; "Some Still Seek New Store Sites," *RTD,* February 24, 1980; "Downtown Addition," *RTD,* April 30, 1982; "Girding for Project One," *RTD,* June 24, 1981; "City Council Sets First Bond Sales in over Two Years," March 4, 1980; "Razing Continues on Broad Street," February 6, 1981; "New Beginning for Richmond," February 18, 1981; "Project One Hotel Site Cleared," April, 14, 1982; "Downtown Demolition Continues," April 20, 1981; "They're Working on the Project," June 23, 1981, all in *Richmond News Leader;* articles found in Press Clippings, Project One, VM.
69. "Racial Tensions in Richmond," Richmond First Club Bulletin, February 26, 1981, Race Relations in Richmond, 1980–84, Box 11, M240, George Stevenson Kemp Papers, VCU.
70. Memorandum for Mr. Brent from Lee F. Davis Jr., July 28, 1980, DDU General and Correspondences, 1980; Memorandum for File from Lee F. Davis Jr., Project One Hotel, March 1, 1982, DDU General and Correspondences, 1982, Brent Papers, VCU.
71. "Marriott Hotels Come Home," *WP,* March 9, 1981, WB1.
72. Memorandum for File from Lee F. Davis Jr., Project One Hotel, March 1, 1982, DDU General and Correspondences, 1982, Brent Papers, VCU.
73. Author interview with Benjamin Campbell, January 6, 2016.
74. "Hotel Start Is Set for Oct. 19," *RTD,* October 7, 1982, B1.
75. Ibid.; "City, Marriott Set Project One Deal," *RTD,* February 13, 1982, A1–A2; "Marsh's Role Is Point of Contention," *RTD,* September 24, 1984, A1, A5.
76. Missioner's Report, August 24, 1981, Co-Missioner Benjamin Campbell Reports, 1980–82, Box 3, M258, RUI Papers, VCU.
77. "Richmond Project May Heal Black-White Rift," *New York Times,* October 24, 1982, 25.
78. Author interview with John Moeser, March 11, 2019.
79. "Market May Boost Richmond Harmony," *WP,* July 6, 1985, F3.
80. Organizational History of the Richmond Renaissance, Inc., Sixth Street Marketplace Project, undated, A New Cooperative Spirit, Notes and Revisions, Box 21, M293, Townes Papers, VCU.
81. Author interview with Benjamin Campbell, January 6, 2019.
82. Ibid.; author interview with John Moeser, March 11, 2019.
83. Author interview with Benjamin Campbell, January 6, 2016.
84. Bond interview with Marsh, August 30, 2000.
85. "Leininger Dismissed," *RTD,* August 29, 1978, A1, A5.

86. "U.S. Backs Richmond Ward Setup," *WP*, September 1, 1981, C1.
87. Tensions in the Richmond Community, August 1980, Drafts, Questionnaires, 1980–81, Boxes 1 and 16, M258, RUI Papers, VCU.
88. Author interview with Benjamin Campbell, March 12, 2019; Hayter, *Dream Is Lost*, 170–74; "Council Seeks Alternative on Budget," *RTD*, April 19, 1981, C3.
89. "Richmond Project May Heal Black-White Rift," *New York Times*, October 24, 1982, 25.
90. "U.S. Backs Richmond Ward Setup: U.S. Rejects Challenge to Richmond Districts," *WP*, September 1, 1981, C1.
91. "Virginia National Plans New Hotel for Richmond," *WP*, July 27, 1981, WB9.
92. Honorable Henry L. Marsh III to James C. Barstow, reprinted in *RTD*, August 1, 1981, Press Clippings, Project One Collection, VM.
93. "Marsh Fears New Hotel Is Peril to Project One," *RTD*, August 1, 1981, 1.
94. Resolution 81-R132-125, November 9, 1981, p. 452, Minutes of the City Council of the City of Richmond, Virginia, October 8, 1979–June 3, 1982, City Hall Archives, Richmond.
95. "Allow Second Hotel, Panel Urged," *RTD*, August 3, 1982, 1.
96. "Hotel Issue Dominated Session Here," *RTD*, October 8, 1982, B3.
97. "Richmond Settles Suit Blocking Hilton Hotel Project," *WP*, June 6, 1983, WB22.
98. "Hilton Site Owner Sues City," *RTD*, December 30, 1981, B1; "City Officials File Answers to Claims in Hilton Lawsuit," *RTD*, February 20, 1982, B8.
99. "Council Votes to Settle Last Hilton Suit," *RTD*, September 27, 1983, B1.
100. "Injunction to Permit Hilton Hotel Denied," *RTD*, January 15, 1982, B1; "Efforts to Build Richmond Hilton Set Back in Court," *WP*, January 18, 1982, 5.
101. "Sept.1 Trial Set for 2 Hilton Suits," *RTD*, February 19, 1982, B1.
102. "Judge Says Hilton Group Can Sue City," *RTD*, February 26, 1982, A3.
103. "Was the Hilton Wrangle Worth It," *RTD*, July 3, 1983, C1.
104. "City Put Hilton Case Behind It," *RTD*, February 15, 1987, H1.
105. "City's Ramada to Open Next Year on Tight Location," *RTD*, April 7, 1985, E1.
106. "Hilton Planned for Chesterfield," *RTD*, November 15, 1984, B1.
107. "Hilton Is Still Feasible," *RTD*, July 13, 2005, B1; "A Hilton Rises," *RTD*, May 7, 2006, F2; "Arise Miller & Rhodes," *RTD*, February 9, 2009, E8.
108. Hayter, *Dream Is Lost*, 174–94; Marvin T. Chiles, "Tough on Conduct: Punitive Leadership in Urban Public Schools, A Case Study of Angry Principal Dr. Roy A. West, 1986–1991," *Spectrum: A Journal on Black Men* 8, no.1 (Fall 2020): 55–85.
109. "Council Considers Repeal of Law that Halted Hilton," *RTD*, September 29, 1983, B7; "State Growth in 1985 May Slow a Little Bit," *RTD*, January 13, 1985, B1.
110. "Downtown Boom in Trouble," *RTD*, March 13, 1988, B1.

111. "Richmond Project May Heal Black-White Rift," *New York Times,* October 24, 1982, 25.
112. "Marsh Drops Developer of Hotel for Project I," *Richmond News Leader,* August 26, 1981; Hayter, *Dream Is Lost,* 173.

6. Richmond Renaissance and Sixth Street Marketplace

1. "Where's the Party? Tenth Anniversary of 6th Street Marketplace Goes Uncelebrated," *RTD,* September 18, 1995, D16.
2. "Hooping It Up in Heart of City: Streetball Tourney Scene of Fun, Fights," *RTD,* April 14, 1996, B1.
3. Frederick Chiriboga to the *RTD,* April 16, 2015; Patricia D. Fishback, League of Women Voters, to the *RTD,* May 17, 2018, 7A.
4. Racial capitalism is described by urban and economic scholars as the commodification of race and race relations for profit. In the Richmond context, this means projecting the notion of racial harmony as a means of recruiting industry and consumers to buy and sell within city limits.
5. Cedric Robinson, *Black Marxism: The Making of the Black Radical Tradition* (Chapel Hill: University of North Carolina Press, 1983); Nancy Leong, "Racial Capitalism," *Harvard Law Review* 126, no. 8 (June 2013): 2151–226; Jodi Melamed, "Racial Capitalism," *Critical Ethnic Studies* 1, no.1 (Spring 2015): 76–85. A variation of this phrase ("elite racial reconciliation") was first used by political scientists Willie Avon Drake and Robert D. Holsworth in their monograph *Affirmative Action and the Stalled Quest for Black Progress* (Urbana: University of Illinois Press, 1996), 71, 87, 90. Drake and Holsworth used "elite racial reconciliation" to describe the process of wealthy whites cutting a few blacks in on lucrative projects to secure their political allegiance. I, on the other hand, use "elite reconciliation" to describe the process of black and white leaders forming interpersonal political bonds and using them to fund projects to facilitate racial harmony among the populace.
6. "Sleepy Richmond Wakes Up, and Now Struggles to Adjust," *Wall Street Journal,* December 22, 1981, 23.
7. Tyler-McGraw, *At the Falls,* 305.
8. "Homeless Use Doorways," *RTD,* January 14, 1981, B11.
9. "A Brief History" of St. Paul's Episcopal Church, https://www.stpaulsrva.org/alittlemorehistory.
10. Author interview with Benjamin Campbell, March 12, 2019.
11. Undated and Untitled Meeting Notes of the Richmond Black and White Club, February 18, 1981, Richmond Urban Forum, 1981–82, Box 37, M302, Mary Tyler Cheek McClenahan Papers, VCU. (Hereafter cited as McClenahan Papers, VCU.)

12. Ibid. A list of women who formed the Richmond Urban Forum does not exist. Their earliest meetings omitted the names of members in an effort to maintain secrecy. Later membership lists included the names of members; however, it is not certain which socialites participated in the initial group. The only known member was a famous socialite, Mary Tyler Cheek McClenahan—the daughter of Douglas Southall Freeman and the wife of a local elite—who archived the collection.
13. Forum Committee Meeting, April 2, 1981; Suggested Names for Forum Members, undated; Resume for Melvin D. Law Application for Admission to the Richmond Urban Forum, undated; T. S. Ellis III to Benjamin Campbell, April 23, 1981; Meeting of Richmond Urban Forum, May 14, 1981; Edgar J. Diermeier to A. C. Epps, June 26, 1981, Richmond Urban Forum, 1981–82, Box 37, M302, McClenahan Papers, VCU.
14. Opening Remarks, First Richmond Urban Forum, September 29, 1981, Richmond Urban Forum, 1981–82, ibid.
15. Author interviews with John Moeser, March 11, 2019; with Benjamin Campbell, March 12, 2019; "Sleepy Richmond Wakes Up, and Now Struggles to Adjust," *Wall Street Journal*, December 22, 1981, 23.
16. Meeting of Richmond Urban Forum, May 14, 1981, Richmond Urban Forum, 1981–82, Box 37, M302, McClenahan Papers, VCU.
17. Untitled and Unsigned Letter to Rob Corcoran, November 26, 1984, Richmond 1977–91, File Cabinet 1, IoC Papers.
18. Additions to Forum Dinner List, undated, Richmond Urban Forum, 1982–83, Box 37, M302, McClenahan Papers, VCU.
19. Author interview with William J. "Bill" Martin, July 23, 2019.
20. "Office of the City Manager to Mr. Clarence Townes," September 25, 1981, Richmond Renaissance: Capital City Government Commission, 1981, Box 16; Richmond Renaissance Organizational History, Folder entitled "A New Cooperative Spirit," Box 21, M283, Townes Papers, VCU; "The Renaissance Story," Richmond Renaissance Festival Marketplace, undated brochure, HT, 168. R5 R55 1900z, VMHC.
21. "City Renaissance Plan Unveiled," *RTD*, March 25, 1982, 1.
22. Howard Gillette Jr., *Civitas by Design, Building Better Communities, from the Garden City to the New Urbanism* (Philadelphia: University of Pennsylvania Press, 2010), 78–84.
23. "Tales of Two (Convention) Cities," *Atlanta Constitution*, August 19, 1980, 4A; "Reviewing the Urban Renaissance," *Christian Science Monitor*, September 16, 1980, 12.
24. David Wilson, "Urban Revitalization on the Upper West Side of Manhattan," *Economic Geography* 63, no. 1 (January 1987): 35–47; "Mall Stands Alone in Brooklyn 'Renaissance,'" *New York Times*, April 9, 1982, B1; "D.C. Planners Ponder What to Do about Doldrums Downtown," *WP*, March 30, 1981, WB1; "The 'New Washington' and the Old," *WP*, November 16, 1980, L1.

25. General Population Characteristics for the 1980 US Census, Vol. 1, Part 48, Virginia PC80-1-B48, August 1982, https://www2.census.gov/prod2/decennial/documents/1980/1980censusofpopu80148uns_bw.pdf.
26. "How James Rouse Shapes Cities," *Christian Science Monitor,* August 31, 1984, 18.
27. "Norfolk Opens Complex with a Big Splash," *WP,* June 2, 1983, B1.
28. WAVY Archive: Norfolk Granby Mall, 1979, https://www.youtube.com/watch?v=8xUt83wwXSc.
29. "Inner-City Sharing in Norfolk Revitalization," *Atlanta Constitution,* May 22, 1983, 29A.
30. "New Rouse Firm to Aid Low-Income Housing," *WP,* April 8, 1981, D7.
31. "Citizens Respond to the Call," *Norfolk Journal and Guide,* April 21, 1982, 1.
32. "Norfolk Opens Complex with a Big Splash: Norfolk Opens Waterside Marketplace with a Celebration, and High Hopes," *WP,* June 2, 1983, B1; "Citizens Respond to the Call," *Norfolk Journal and Guide,* April 21, 1982, 1.
33. "Waterside Lags behind Schedule," *Norfolk Journal and Guide,* March 24, 1982, 3; "NAACP Gears Up for Jobs," *Norfolk Journal and Guide,* April 7, 1982, 1.
34. "Norfolk Cancels Waterside Plan, Delay Blamed," *WP,* March 27, 1982, E28.
35. "Norfolk Opens Complex with a Big Splash," *WP,* June 2, 1983, B1.
36. "Richmond Wants to Try the Rouse Touch," *WP,* April 12, 1982, WB43.
37. Honorable Henry L. Marsh III, Mayor of Richmond, Draft of Speech, April 14, 1982, Richmond Renaissance Correspondences, Notes, and Misc., March–April 1982, Box 17, M283, Townes Papers, VCU.
38. "Rouse Plan Links Downtown," *RAA,* April 16, 1983, 1; "Richmond Conference for Unity in Diversity," *New World News,* December 22, 1984, Richmond 1977–91, File Cabinet 1, IoC Papers; Gillette, *Civitas by Design,* 80–90.
39. Richmond Renaissance Newsletter to Potential Tenants, April 11, 1982, Richmond Renaissance Correspondences, Notes, and Misc., March–April 1982, Box 17, M283, Townes Papers, VCU.
40. T. Justin Moore to the Honorable Henry L. Marsh III, March 16, 1982; T. Justin Moore to Frederick Deane Jr., March 24, 1982; Xerox Customer Credit Information Form, Issue Date April 1, 1982, Richmond Renaissance, Inc., Correspondences, Notes, Misc., March–April 1982, Box 17, M283, Townes Papers, VCU.
41. T. Justin Moore to Clarence L. Townes, March 19, 1982, ibid.
42. "Townes Gets New GOP Post, Gives Formula," *RAA,* March 5, 1966, 1; "Proud to Be Black," Editorial, *RAA,* March 12, 1966, 8; "There's Good News," *RAA,* October 19–23, 1976, 3.
43. "Dedicating a Dormitory," *RTD,* May 18, 1969, B8.
44. "Anti-Integration Laws Are Explained," *RTD,* B10; "T. Justin Moore [Sr.], 67, Dies Here," *RTD,* March 11, 1958, 1; Legal Notices 8-A, *RTD,* November 27, 1958, 20.

45. "T. Justin Moore Jr. Named 1962 UGF Drive Chairman," *RTD,* April 11, 1962, 2; "UGF Passes $2,000,000 in Donations," *RTD,* November 9, 1962, 7; "United Way Kicks Off Campaign With 18% of $8.7 Million Goal," *RTD,* September 14, 1982, B1.
46. "Memorial Thomas Justin Moore, Jr., '46," *Princeton Alumni Weekly,* undated, https://paw.princeton.edu/memorial/thomas-justin-moore-jr-%E2%80%9946; "T. Justin Moore, Jr., 74, Ex Chief of the Virginia Power Company," *New York Times,* May 3, 1999; "VEPCO Team Helped Westinghouse Choose South Boston," *RTD,* July 23, 1967, 47; "Management Realigned by VEPCO," *RTD,* November 29, 1977, A6.
47. Remarks of T. Justin Moore Jr., Chairman of the Board, VEPCO, before the Richmond First Club, April 8, 1982, Richmond Renaissance Correspondences, Notes, and Misc., March–April 1982, Box 17, M283, Townes Papers, VCU.
48. Author interview with Bill Martin, July 23, 2019.
49. Memorandum: Potential Board Members, April 5, 1982; Mayor Henry Marsh III to T. Justin Moore, April 9, 1982, Richmond Renaissance Correspondences, Notes, and Misc., March–April 1982, Box 17, M283, Townes Papers, VCU.
50. "Cooperation from Area Sought by City Boosters," *RTD,* April 9, 1982, B8; "Issues Involved in Establishment of 'Renaissance' A Public Private Partnership," Richmond Renaissance, Inc., Correspondences, Notes, Misc., March–April 1982, Box 17, M283 Townes Papers, VCU.
51. "How James Rouse Shapes Cities," *Christian Science Monitor,* August 31, 1984, 18.
52. Joshua Olsen, *Better Places, Better Lives: A Biography of James Rouse* (New York: Urban Land Institute, 2003); "James Rouse Sets Talk on Social Responsibility," *WP,* May 20, 1978, E19; "It's Hard for Wealthy to Aid Poor—Rouse," *WP,* June 3, 1978, E27.
53. Olsen, *Better Places,* 34; and Robert Fishman, "The Garden City Tradition in the Post-Suburban Age," *Built Environment* 17, No. ¾ (1991): 232–41.
54. "James W. Rouse, 81, Dies," *New York Times,* April 10, 1996, A17.
55. "Detroiters Lift Sights from Mire," *Christian Science Monitor,* April 14, 1977, 4; "Philadelphia Mall Opened," *WP,* August 20, 1977, D13; "Municipal Mall," *Wall Street Journal,* March 30, 1978, 1.
56. Henry G. Cisneros, "Preserving Everybody's History," *Cityscape* (December 1996): 85–97; "Preserving the Heart of an Old City," *WP,* August 16, 1978, A15; "Peachtree Expansion Plans in High Gear: Portman's Plans Concern Forces on the Southside," *Atlanta Constitution,* August 20, 1978, 19C.
57. "How James Rouse Shapes Cities," *Christian Science Monitor,* August 31, 1984, 18.
58. "Rouse in Business Hall of Fame," *WP,* March 16, 1981, WB30; Summary Description All Requests, Community Development Block Grant, 1982–83,

Richmond Renaissance Correspondences, Notes, Misc., March–April 1982, Box 17, M283, Townes Papers, VCU.

59. "Is Baltimore Truly Back?," *WP,* November 24, 1984, A1; "The Rise and Fall of the Greater Baltimore Committee: The Elite Organization That Started Solving Baltimore's Problems in the '50s Seems to Have Few Answers for Them Today," *Baltimore,* May 1982, 85–89; "Baltimore," *WP,* July 2, 1980, B1; "Is Baltimore Truly Back?," *WP,* November 24, 1984, A1.

60. "New Rouse Firm to Aid Low-Income Housing," *WP,* April 8, 1981, D7; "Welcoming Waterfront," *WP,* July 5, 1980, B1; "For Baltimore, a High Tide of Success," *New York Times,* August 9, 1981, 20; "Rouse Bullish on River Mall in Norfolk," *WP,* February 15, 1982, 40; "Norfolk Opens Complex with a Big Splash," *WP,* June 2, 1983, B1; "How James Rouse Shapes Cities," *Christian Science Monitor,* August 31, 1984, 18; Charles Robb to William B. Thalhimers Jr. and Philip H. Hawley, undated letter found in Richmond Renaissance Correspondences, Memo from Moore to Deane and Townes Regarding Jim Rouse's Ideas on Richmond Renaissance's Executive Director, 1982, Box 17, M283, Townes Papers, VCU.

61. "Richmond Wants to Try the Rouse Touch," *WP,* April 12, 1982, WB43; "Wonderful Things Seen for Richmond," *Richmond News Leader* April 16, 1982; "Rouse: Richmond's Urban Moses," *Richmond News Leader,* April 19, 1982; "Marketplace Bet Is $23 Million," *RTD,* undated press clipping found in City Planning, Sixth Street Marketplace Collection, VM; T. Justin Moore to Frederick Dean Jr, and Clarence L. Townes, May 5, 1982; memo from Moore to Deane and Townes Regarding Jim Rouse's Ideas on Richmond Renaissance's Executive Director, 1982; T. Justin Moore to Mr. James Rouse, April 19, 1982, all in Box 17, Richmond Renaissance Correspondences, Notes, and Misc., March–April 1982, Box 17, M283, Townes Papers, VCU.

62. Richmond Renaissance Inc., Minutes of the Executive Committee, May 3–October 15, 1982; Elizabeth C. Rothberg to Clarence L. Townes Jr., September 2, 1982; Louis Harrison Jones to Clarence L. Townes Jr., September 7, 1982; Roland Turpin to Clarence L. Townes Jr., September 23, 1982; Richmond Renaissance Inc., Financial Statement as of June 15, 1982, Box 16, M283, Townes Papers, VCU; G. Timothy Oksman to T. Justin Moore, undated, found in the Richmond Renaissance Correspondences, Notes, Misc., May–December, 1982, M283, Townes Papers, VCU.

63. Southeastern Institute of Research, Inc., Market and Opinion Research, "City-wide Survey of Attitudes and Opinions Regarding Downtown," May 31, 1983, Research Prepared for Richmond Renaissance, Townes Papers, VCU.

64. "4th Street Shooting Is Fatal," *RTD,* August 31, 1982, B1.

65. "Jackson Ward Man Is Slain," *RTD,* December 26, 1982, B7.

66. "City Man Is Slain," *RTD,* June 16, 1983, D3.

67. "Richmonder Found Not Guilty in Jackson Ward Man's Death," *RTD*, October 12, 1983, B4.
68. Application for Jackson Ward to be Admitted to the National Register of Historic Places, July 30, 1976; Jackson Ward, Summary Tape File 3G, Neighborhood Revitalization Division of the Department of Planning and Community Development, City of Richmond Neighborhood Statistics, November 1985, Box 5, M303, Richmond Renaissance Papers, VCU.
69. For more on crime and perceptions of crime in Jackson Ward, see Table 1, Reported Offenses: 1976–80, Second Street Study Area, Richmond, Virginia, 1980, Economic and Market Analysis, 1–10; A Commercial Revitalization Plan for the Second Street Commercial Area, 3–7, 2nd Street Commercial Revitalization, 1981, Box 4, M303, Richmond Renaissance Papers, VCU.
70. "Jackson Ward," Paper Presented at the Liaison Committee of Richmond Renaissance, Box 16, M283, Townes Papers, VCU.
71. Jackson Ward, Summary Tape File 3G, Neighborhood Revitalization Division of the Department of Planning and Community Development, November 1985; Economic and Market Analysis: Second Street Commercial Revitalization Study, by John E. Scott and Associates, January 19, 1981, 2nd Street Commercial Revitalization, 1981, Boxes 4 and 5, M303, Richmond Renaissance Papers, VCU.
72. For more on crime and perceptions of crime in Jackson Ward, see Table 1, Reported Offenses: 1976–80, Second Street Study Area, Richmond, Virginia, 1980, Economic and Market Analysis, 1–10; A Commercial Revitalization Plan for the Second Street Commercial Area, 3–7, 2nd Street Commercial Revitalization, 1981, Box 4, M303, Richmond Renaissance Papers, VCU.
73. Economic and Market Analysis, 1–10; A Commercial Revitalization Plan, 3–7, ibid.
74. Ibid.
75. Economic and Market Analysis: Second Street Commercial Revitalization Study, January 19, 1981, ibid.; A Revitalization Plan for the Second Street Business District Area, Prepared by Albert G. Dobbins III, December 1983, Second Street Business District Revitalization, 1983, Box 4, M303, Richmond Renaissance Papers, VCU; Minutes of the Liaison Committee Meeting, January 26, 1983; Richmond Renaissance Inc., Minutes of the Executive Committee, January 7, 1983; Executive Committee Agenda Meeting, January 21, 1983; Richmond Renaissance Incorporate Minutes of the Executive Committee, January 21, 1983; Richmond Renaissance, Board of Directors, Executive Committee, Liaison Committee, Minutes and Agenda, 1983, Boxes 16 and 17, M283, Townes Papers, VCU.
76. S. Buford Scott to Clarence L. Townes Jr., January 13, 1983, Richmond Renaissance, Correspondences, Notes, Misc., January, 1983, Box 16, M283,

Townes Papers, VCU; Economic and Market Analysis: Second Street Commercial Revitalization Study, Richmond, Virginia, by John E. Scott and Associates, January 19, 1981; A Commercial Revitalization Plan for the Second Street Commercial Area, Richmond, Virginia, Urban Services, March 1981, 2nd Street Commercial Revitalization, 1981; Diane P. Hayes, Third Street Project: Developing Our Own Feature, January 1982, 48, Third Street Project, 1982; A Revitalization Plan for the Second Street Business District Area, Richmond, Virginia, Prepared by Albert G. Dobbins III, December 1983, Second Street Business District Revitalization, 1983, Box 4, M303, Richmond Renaissance Papers, VCU; "Image Is Key to Successful Tourism Marketing Plan," *Newsline* 8, no. 6 (June 1982); Manuel Deese to Clarence L. Townes Jr., June 16, 1982, Richmond Renaissance, Correspondences, Notes, Misc., May–December, 1982, Box 17, M283, Townes Papers, VCU.

77. Revitalization Plan for the Second Street Business District Area, December 1983, Second Street Business District Revitalization, 1983, Box 4, M303, Richmond Renaissance Papers, VCU; Richmond Renaissance Inc., Minutes of the Executive Committee, January 21, 1983, Richmond Renaissance Board of Directors, Executive Committee, Liaison Committee, Minutes and Agenda, 1983, Boxes 16 and 17, M283, Townes Papers, VCU.
78. *Baltimore*, May 1982, clipping found in Clarence L. Townes to Laurie Naismith, June 25, 1982, Annual Meeting of the Board of Directors, September 12, 1983, Box 16, Townes Papers, VCU.
79. Roland R. Wesley, Esq., to Manuel Deese, City Manager, April 9, 1984, Affirmative Action and Minority Business Tenant Opportunity, 1984, Box 10, M303, Richmond Renaissance Papers, VCU.
80. Report to the Executive Committee, February–May 1984; Richmond Renaissance Inc., Annual Meeting of the Board of Directors, September 12, 1983; Annual Meeting of the Board of Directors, September 27, 1984, Richmond Renaissance, Board of Directors, Executive Committee Minutes and Agendas, 1984, Box 16, M283, Townes Papers, VCU.
81. "Marketplace Details Are Released," *RTD,* April 17, 1984; Richmond Renaissance Inc., Annual Meeting of the Board of Directors, September 27, 1984; Richmond Renaissance Minutes of the Executive Committee, April 20 and May 4, 1984, Box 16, M283, Townes Papers, VCU.
82. "Opera Group Said Ready to Accept Theaters," *RTD,* May 9, 1984, B1; "New Side Design Gets Mixed Reviews," June 19, 1984; "Council Authorizes 6th Street Marketplace Pact," June 12, 1984; "Redesign Settles Dispute over Marketplace Access," July 31, 1984, all from *Richmond News Leader;* found in Press Clippings, Sixth Street Marketplace Collection, VM.
83. Minority Entrepreneur Training Proposal, June 1, 1984, Affirmative Action and Minority Business Tenant Opportunity, 1984, Boxes 10 and 13, M303, Richmond Renaissance Papers, VCU.

84. Manny Deese, City Manager for the City of Richmond, to Jim Rouse, November 11, 1983; Manuel Deese, City Manager, to Mr. T. Justin Moore Jr., Chairman of the Board Richmond Renaissance, April 9, 1984, Boxes 10 and 13, M303, Richmond Renaissance Papers, VCU; "Black Business in Richmond Get Major Piece of Downtown Rebuilding Action," *Minorities and Women in Business,* January–December 1985, Box 21, M283, Townes Papers, VCU.

85. Minority Entrepreneur Training Proposal, June 1, 1984, Affirmative Action and Minority Business Tenant Opportunity, 1984; City of Richmond Minority Business and Tenant Opportunity Program 6th Street Marketplace, undated; "Plan to Assist Minority Businesses Which May Be Interested in Operating Businesses in the Sixth Street Festival Marketplace Upon Its Commencement," Resolution 83-R269, December 5, 1983; 6th Street Market Minority Tenant Program; 6th Street Festival Community Interests: Impacts on Black Community Interests, March 15, 1984; Minority Entrepreneur Training Proposal, June 1, 1984, Affirmative Action and Minority Business Tenant Opportunity, 1984, all found in Box 10, M303, Richmond Renaissance Papers, VCU.

86. "Old Confederate Capital Builds Racial Harmony," *New York Times,* November 18, 1985, A16.

87. "Black Business in Richmond Get Major Piece of Downtown Rebuilding Action," *Minorities and Women in Business,* January–December 1985, found in Box 21, M283, Townes Papers, VCU.

88. "A Tale of Two Marketplaces," *Urban Reporter,* June 15–27, 1986, found in Box 21, M283, Townes Papers, VCU.

89. Clarence L. Townes to Jeff Nowakowski, November 13, 1984, Media-Negative TV Reporting, 1984, Box 13, M303, Richmond Renaissance Papers, VCU; "Candidates Blame News Media for Downtown's Image Problem," *RTD,* April 5, 1990, 27.

90. Author interview with Benjamin Campbell, March 14, 2019.

91. Thomas C. Boushall to Andrew J. Brent, May 4, 1981, Box 1:18, M281, Brent Papers, VCU.

92. "Merchant Is Counting the Empties," *RTD,* May 16, 1991, 18.

93. Author interview with Viola Baskerville, June 28, 2019.

94. Phil Bagley Jr., former Richmond Mayor, to the *RTD,* September 26, 1991, 12.

95. "The Development of Henrico: Growth into the 80s" *Richmond Surroundings* magazine (Spring 1982); "The Development of a County: Chesterfield's Past Present, and Future," ibid. (Fall 1982); and State of the City Report, Richmond, Department of Community Development Division of Comprehensive Planning, 1989, found in Second Street Business District Revitalization, 1983, Box 4, M303, Richmond Renaissance Papers, VCU.

96. Ronald Wilson, "Richmond's 6th Street Marketplace: Assessment of a Failed Festival Market" (MA thesis, Massachusetts Institute of Technology,

September 1989); RR 6th Street Marketplace Assessment, September 1989, Box 37, M308, McClenahan Papers, VCU.
97. "Crime Takes Over Church Hill," *RAA,* December 1, 1984, 1; Report from the Secretary of Public Safety to the General Assembly on the Status of Neighborhood Watch in Virginia, House Joint Resolution No. 50, *House and Senate Documents in the Virginia 1984 Session, vol.1, House 1–15,* Virginia General Assembly Archives, Richmond, H-10; "Deese Warns Crooks," *RAA,* February 18, 1984, 1; "Issues Forcing Community Action," *RAA,* April 6, 1985, 1; "Mayor West Wants More Use of Electric Chair," *RAA,* August 3, 1985, 1; "Crime in Virginia 1985," Compiled by Uniform Crime Reporting Section, Department of Police, Richmond, 54; "Violent Crime Total for Virginia, 1985," Uniform Crime Reporting Statistics, FBI Crime Data Explorer, https://cde.ucr.cjis.gov/LATEST/webapp/#/pages/home; "Wilder Calls for All-Out War on Crime," *RAA,* November 21, 1987, 1; "Prince of the City," *RTD,* March 5, 1991, 12.
98. Chiles, "Tough on Conduct," 55–85.
99. "Marketplace Ripple Effect Regarded as Slight So Far," *RTD,* June 29, 1986, G1.
100. "A Year Later, Marketplace Still Working Out Kinks," *RTD,* September 11, 1986, 1.
101. "Sixth Tenant Is Sued by Marketplace," *RTD,* March 10, 1987, 8.
102. "Bobb's Team Facing Tough Choices in 1988," *RTD,* January 4, 1988, B1.
103. "Downtown Direction," *RTD,* January 26, 1989, A14.
104. "Cokesbury Joins Downtown Exodus," *RTD,* July 27, 1989, 1.
105. "With Miller & Rhoads Goes Friend, Supporter," *RTD,* December 21, 1989, F1.
106. "A Tradition Ends," *RTD,* November 13, 1991, 14.
107. "Downtown Merchants Seek Action," *RTD,* September 19, 1989, A8; "Don't Count Out Richmond in the Development Picture," *RTD,* October 24, 1989, B15; "Miller & Rhoads Closing Downtown Store Today," *RTD,* January 6, 1990, A1; "The R-Word Hit Home in Area in 1990," *RTD,* December 31, 1990, B3.
108. "6th Street Marketplace Loses Two Harris Stores," *RTD,* July 21, 1990, B5; "The R-Word Hit Home," *RTD,* December 31, 1990, B3.
109. Dr. Eugene P. Trani, "Richmond at the Crossroads: The Greater Richmond Metropolitan Area and the Knowledge Based Technology Economy of the 21st Century," Report delivered at St. John's College, Cambridge, England, Easter Term, 1998, Eugene P. Trani Papers, VCU; and Virginia Biotechnology Research Park Project Overview & Current Status, June 1993, Virginia Technology Research Park, 1992–94, Box 108, M302, McClenahan Papers, VCU.
110. "Marketplace Risks," *RTD,* April 10, 1990, 12.
111. "Tomorrow's Election," *RTD,* April 30, 1990, 14.

112. "Improving Richmond Ideas Flow," *RTD*, June 7, 1990, 17; "6th Street Bill," *RTD*, October 13, 1990, A10.
113. "Demolition of 6th Street Bridge," *RTD*, June 14, 1991, 1.
114. "Raze It?," *RTD*, June 19, 1991, 10; "Duh," *RTD*, August 8, 1991, 14; Phil Bagley Jr., "City's Decline Began Years Ago," editorial, *RTD*, September 26, 1991, 12; and Phil Bagley Jr., "Richmond Deserves More Than Current Council," editorial, *RTD*, March 4, 1992, 12.
115. "Where's the Party," *RTD*, September 18, 1995, D16.
116. "Council Endorses Downtown Hotel Project," *RTD*, September 25, 2001; "Remaking Downtown," *RTD*, September 26, 2001, Press Clippings, Sixth Street Marketplace Collection, VM.
117. "Marketplace Plan Saddens Tenants," *RTD*, September 27, 2001; "City Offers $30,000 to Stores," *RTD*, October 18, 2002, ibid.

7. Richmond Urban Institute

1. Benjamin Campbell, *Richmond's Unhealed History* (Richmond, VA: Brandylane, 2012), 210.
2. Grassroots Economic Development Proposal, March 13, 1983, Grassroots Economic Development, Box 7, M258, RUI Papers, VCU.
3. Undated Annual Report, 1982, Annual/Semi-Annual Meetings, 1980–83, 1985, Box 1, M258, RUI Papers, VCU.
4. RUI 1985 Council, Officers, and Staff, Administrative Officers, 1984–86, Box 1, M258, RUI Papers, VCU; Undated Annual Report, 1982, Annual/Semi-Annual Meetings, 1980–83, 1985, ibid. For more on the interest VCU professors took in researching and engaging with civic groups in 1980s Richmond, see Kneebone and Trani, *Fulfilling the Promise*, .102–68.
5. By-Laws of RUI, undated, By-Laws, Certificate of Incorporation, 1980–85, Box 2, M258, RUI Papers, VCU.
6. "A Lifetime of Starts, She's Just Getting Started," *RTD*, April 11, 1982, H1, H21.
7. Author interview with Benjamin Campbell, March 12, 2019.
8. "A Lifetime of Starts," *RTD*, April 11, 1982, H1, H21; and Edyth Roger Application for Commissioner of the RUI, July 1980, Co-Missioner, Edythe Rogers, Resume and Records, 1979–83, Box 3, M258, RUI Papers, VCU.
9. "A Lifetime of Starts," *RTD*, April 11, 1982, H1, H21.
10. Potential Churches for Life in the Cities Seminar, Urban Consultations, Tensions Report Notes, 1981–82, Box 16, M258, RUI Papers, VCU.
11. Missioner's Report, April 27, 1981, Edythe Rogers, Resume and Records, 1979–83, Box 3, M258, RUI Papers, VCU.
12. RUI Annual Meeting, January 25, 1982, Annual/Semi-Annual Meetings, 1980–83, 1985, Box 1, M258; Report of Urban Missioner Edythe Rodgers, January 31, 1981, Edythe Rogers, Resume and Records, 1979–83, Box 3, M258; Problems & Possibilities for Interracial Strategies, undated

memo, Co-Missioner, Edythe Rogers, Resume and Records, 1979–83, Box 3, M258; RUI Administrative/Finance Committee Meeting Agenda, March 24, 1981, Administration/Finance Committee Agenda Minutes, 1980–82, Box 1, M258; Edythe M. Rodgers to the Council of RUI, February 18, 1981, Edythe Rogers, Resume and Records, 1979–83, Box 3, M258, all found at RUI Papers, VCU.
13. Workshop on the Effective Use of Power and Community Building, September 24, 1983, Announcements 1982–83, Box 1, M258; RUI Financial Statement, December 31, 1980, Administration/Finance Committee Agenda Minutes, 1980–82, Box 1, M258; Report of the Administrative/Finance Committee of the RUI, May 1980–February 23, 1981, Administration/Finance Committee Agenda Minutes, 1980–82, Box 1, M258; Report of Administration Committee, December 22, 1980, Administration/Finance Committee Agenda Minutes, 1980–82, Box 1, M258; Racism/Racial Polarization Committee of the Richmond Urban League Annual Report February, 17, 1980, Racism/Polarization Committee, 1980–81, Box 10, M258; List of Proposed Participants in Conferences, July 22, August 26, September 23, October 28, 1981, Tensions in the Richmond Community, Drafts, Questionnaires, 1980–81, Box 16, M258; Recommendations to the RUI, undated, Tensions in the Richmond Community, Drafts, Questionnaires, 1980–81, Box 16, M258; Missioner's Report April 19, 1982, Tensions Report Notes, 1981–82, Box 16, M258, all found at RUI Papers, VCU.
14. Minutes of Racial/Ethnic Issues Committee, April 10, 1984, Racial Ethnic Issues Committee, 1984–85, Box 10, M258; Racial Tensions Report II, Potential Key Leaders to be Interviewed July 1984, Racial Ethnic Issues Committee, 1984–85, Box 10, M258, all found at RUI Papers, VCU.
15. Silver, *Twentieth-Century Richmond*; Pratt, *Color of Their Skin*, 33.
16. Chiles, "Down Where the South Begins," 61–4.
17. Sartain Meeting with Milton Randolph, undated, Mss1S4772a, Sartain Papers, VMHC; "Scare Tactics Cited in Area House Sales," *Richmond News Leader*, November 23, 1968, 9.
18. Beryl Satter, *Family Properties: How the Struggle Over Race and Real Estate Transformed Chicago and Urban America* (New York: Picador, 2010); Richard Rothstein, *The Color of Law: A Forgotten History of How Our Government Segregated America* (New York: W.W. Norton, 2017); Luke Ritter, "The Discriminating Priority of Integration: Open Housing Activism in St. Louis County, 1968–1977," *Journal of the Illinois State Historical Society* 106, no. 2 (Summer 2013): 224–44.
19. T. B. Benson, "Segregation Ordinances," *Virginia Law Register* 1, no. 5 (September 1915): 330–56; "Municipal Segregation Ordinances," *Virginia Law Review* 3, no. 4 (January 1916): 304–9; Richard Rothstein, "From Ferguson to Baltimore: The Fruits of Government-Sponsored Segregation," *Journal of Affordable Housing and Community Development Law* 24, no. 2 (2015): 205–10.

20. "Unconstitutionality of Segregation Ordinances," *Yale Law Journal* 27, no. 3 (January 1918), 393–97; Hurd v. Hodge, 334 U.S. 24, 68 S. Ct. 847; 92 L. Ed. 2d 1187 (1948); Joe T. Darden, "Black Residential Segregation since the 1948 *Shelley v. Kraemer* Decision," *Journal of Black Studies* 25, no. 6 (July 1995): 680–91.
21. Lily Greismer, "Good Neighbors for Fair Housing: Suburban Liberalism and Racial Inequality in Metropolitan Boston," *Journal of Urban History* 39, no.3 (May 2013): 454–77.
22. Nicholas Dragen Bloom, *Suburban Alchemy: 1960s New Towns and the Transformation of the American Dream* (Columbus: Ohio State University Press, 2001); Anny Forsyth, *Reforming Suburbia: The Planned Communities of Irvine, Columbia, and the Woodlands* (Berkley: University of California Press, 2005); Ocean Howell, "The Merchant Crusaders: Eichler Homes and Fair Housing," *Pacific Historical Review* 85, no. 3 (August 2016): 379–407; "Proxmire Bill Would Require Lenders to Open Their Books on Mortgages," *WP,* April 26, 1975, E14.
23. Proposed Neighborhood Assistance Act of 1979, summary, Neighborhood Assistance Act, Box 26, M258, RUI Papers, VCU; "Fed Issues Lender 'Redlining' Rules," *WP,* June 2, 1976, E2.
24. Patricia A. McCoy, "The Home Mortgage Disclosure Act: A Synopsis and Recent Legislative History," *Journal of Real Estate Research* 29, no. 4 (2007): 381–98.
25. "To Stop Redlining," *New York Times,* June 14, 1976, 30; "Some Banks Accused of Ignoring U.S. Law on Mortgage Disclosure," *New York Times,* October 9, 1976, 22.
26. "Mortgage Lenders Apply to Avoid Revealing Information on Redlining," *New York Times,* September 27, 1976, 19; "Urban Parley Acts to Halt Redlining and Blockbusting," *New York Times,* April 21, 1975, 23; "'Redlining' by Lenders Is Called Cause of Old Communities' Decay," *New York Times,* May 26, 1975, 20; "Some Banks Accused of Ignoring U.S. Law," *New York Times,* October 9, 1976, 22; "Washington & Business: Redlining Fight," *New York Times,* October 21, 1976, 67; "Mixed Results Seen for Loan Disclosures," *WP,* March 5, 1977; "'Redlining'—Byrne vs. Banks," *New York Times,* January 28, 1978, NJ1.
27. Rebecca F. Guy, Louis G. Pol, and Randy E. Ryker, "Discrimination in Mortgage Lending: The Home Mortgage Disclosure Act," *Population Research and Policy Review* 1, no. 3 (October 1982): 283–96; "Redlining Data Is Criticized," *Atlanta Constitution,* June 18, 1976, 13D; "S&Ls Change Lending Pattern: Mortgage Lenders Putting More Cash in Once 'Redlined' Area of D.C.," *WP,* October 3, 1976, 1.
28. Missioner's Report, August 24, 1981, Co-Missioner Benjamin Campbell Reports, 1980–82, Box 3, M258, RUI Papers, VCU.

29. Racial Steering by Real Estate Sales Agents in Metropolitan Richmond, Virginia, A Research Project Conducted by HOME, March 1980, Housing Opportunities Made Equal, 1979–80, Box 20, M258, RUI Papers, VCU.
30. Benjamin Campbell Testimony before Representatives of the Federal Reserve Board, December 5, 1981, Federal Reserve Board, Housing Issue, 1981–82, Box 12, M258, RUI Papers, VCU.
31. Racial Steering by Real Estate Sales Agents in Metropolitan Richmond, Virginia, A Research project Conducted by HOME, March 1980, Housing Opportunities Made Equal, 1979–80, Box 20, M258, RUI Papers, VCU.
32. Home's Marketing Program to Let Consumers Choose, December 1979, Housing Opportunities Made Equal, 1979–80, Box 20, M258, RUI Papers, VCU.
33. Author interview with Benjamin Campbell, March 12, 2019.
34. Racial Steering by Real Estate Sales Agents in Metropolitan Richmond, Virginia, A Research project Conducted by HOME, March 1980, Housing Opportunities Made Equal, 1979–80, Box 20, M258, RUI Papers, VCU.
35. Investment Patterns in Richmond, 1979, Published May 9, 1981, Home Mortgage Patterns in Richmond, 1979, Box 19, M258, RUI Papers, VCU.
36. Community Reinvestment Agreement, October 1, 1983, Community Reinvestment Act, Box 19, M258, RUI Papers, VCU; "Lenders Discover Advantages and New Market with Community Reinvestment Act," *Journal of Housing,* March 1980; "Community Groups and CRA: Case Studies of Action Strategies," *Neighborhood Revitalization Project* 1, no. 1 (July 1980), Community Reinvestment Act, Box 19, M258, RUI Papers, VCU; and Community Reinvestment Act Statement of Community Services: Central Fidelity Bank, August 1, 1985, ibid.
37. Average Income Necessary to Purchase an Average House in Richmond, undated chart made by RUI, Federal Reserve Board, Housing Issue, 1981–82, Box 12, M258, RUI Papers, VCU.
38. Community Reinvestment Agreement, October 1, 1983, Community Reinvestment Act, Box 19, M258, RUI Papers, VCU.
39. "Average Income Necessary to Purchase an Average House in Richmond," Federal Reserve Board, Housing Issue, 1981–82, Box 12, M258, RUI Papers, VCU; Community Reinvestment Act Statement of Community Services: Central Fidelity Bank, August 1, 1985, Community Reinvestment Act, Box 19, ibid.
40. "Laws Against Redlining Force Lenders to Make Some Shifts," *Wall Street Journal,* December 29, 1982, 9; Community Reinvestment Act Statement of Community Services, undated; and "Community Groups and CRA: Case Studies of Action Strategies," *CRA Reporter,* July 1980, Community Reinvestment Act, 1983–85, Box 19, M258, RUI Papers, VCU.

41. "Blacks in the N.J. Suburbs," *New York Times*, June 24, 1979, E6; "Black Flight," *Wall Street Journal*, August 20, 1979, 1; "The Changing Suburbs," *WP*, April 9, 1981, MD1; "Black Flight from District Upset P.G. School Guidelines, Trial Told," *WP*, May 14, 1982, 14; "Black Flight/White Flight," *Atlanta Constitution*, September 26, 1979, 1C; "Moving On Out," *WP*, April 23, 1984, A13; "Black Flight—From the Inner City," *WP*, May 12, 1985, B8.
42. "Gentrification in London," *WP*, November 5, 1977.
43. Lance S. Freeman, "Commentary: 21st Century Gentrification," *Cityscape* 18, no. 3, Gentrification (2016): 163–68.
44. "Bringing It All Back Home," *Christian Science Monitor*, November 18, 1977, 17; "San Francisco Hippie Haunt Undergoes 'Gentrification' and House Prices Soar," *Wall Street Journal*, July 1978, 1; "There Are Always Losers," *Atlanta Constitution*, January 1, 1979, 3C; "The New Elite and an Urban Renaissance," *New York Times*, January 14, 1979, SM4; "Gentrification," *New York Times*, February 11, 1979, SM 26; "Denver Activist Fight for Tenants Displaced by Urban Gentrification," *WP*, March 21, 1981, E24; "Urban Uplift," *New York Times*, February 1, 1982, 1.
45. "Gentrification Means Moving the Poor," *WP*, October 27, 1979, E4; "Hoboken Gentrification and the City's Poor," *New York Times*, December 13, 1981, NJ50; "Stop Forced Removal of Residential and Commercial Tenants," *New York Times*, June 25, 1983, 23.
46. Kneebone and Trani, *Fulfilling the Promise*, 133.
47. "The New City Dwellers," February 22, 1981, H1, H9; "Gentrification Exacts Toll, Speaker Says," September 25, 1986, C14; "Clay Street Projects Splits City Planners," June 4, 1985, B1, B3; "Group Success Rate Is Study in Contrasts," May 13, 1986, A1, A7; "Marketplace Ripple Effect Is Regarded as Slights So Far," June 29, 1986, G1, G5; Preddy D. Ray, "Task Force for Historic Preservation and Minority Taskforce," editorial, January 23, 1984, 10, all from *RTD*.
48. Kneebone and Trani, *Fulfilling the Promise*, 141.
49. Home Base, Inc., January 1983, Box 19, M258, RUI Papers, VCU.
50. Proposal to Establish a Richmond Non-Profit Housing Corporation, March 1982, Proposal to Allstate, November 28, 1984; Julia Seward to Rayford Harris, March 14, 1983, Home Base, Inc., Box 19, M258, RUI Papers, VCU.
51. Contributors, March 1983–December 1985, Home Base, Inc., Box 19, M258, RUI Papers, VCU.
52. Services Offered by Home Base, Inc., August 1, 1985, ibid.
53. Home Base Proposal 1986, Home Base, Inc., Box 19, M258, RUI Papers, VCU; "Local Housing Group Shows How its Done," *RAA*, April 13, 1985; "Banks to Start Low Income Housing programs," *RTD*, June 2, 1985, E1 "Look Before You Wield a Mallet," *Richmond News Leader*, September 7, 1984, A12; "Richmond Housing Program Approved for State Tax Credits,"

Richmond News Leader, August 7, 1985, A26; "Housing Counseling Office Opens," *RAA,* August 10, 1985, 2.

54. "The Home Mortgage Disclosure Act" and "Mortgage Disclosure Still Contested," both *WP,* January 29, 1979, E29.
55. Gerald S. McDougall and Harold Bunce, "Urban Services and the Suburbanization of Blacks," *Social Science Quarterly* 67, no. 3 (September 1986): 596–603; Mark Schneider and Thomas Phelan, "Black Suburbanization in the 1980s," *Demography* 30, no. 2 (May 1993): 269–79; "Theory of Black Middle-Class Flight Challenged," *WP,* March 29, 1990, A12; Marcus D. Casey and Bradley L. Hardy, "The Evolution of Black Neighborhoods since Kerner," *Journal of the Social Sciences* 4, no. 6, Fiftieth Anniversary of the Kerner Commission Report (September 2018): 185–205.
56. "The New Black Flight," *Wall Street Journal,* April 25, 2002; "County Faces Black Flight, Polls Shows," *WP,* September 19, 2002; John Iceland, Gregory Sharp, and Jeffrey M. Timberlake, "Sun Belt Rising: Regional Population Change and the Decline in Black Residential Segregation, 1970–2009," *Demography* 50, no. 1 (February 2013): 97–123; Dan Holland, "Forging a Consistent Vision: The People Who Shaped Manchester's Renewal, 1964–2014," *Pennsylvania History: A Journal of Mid-Atlantic Studies* 86, no. 2 (Spring 2019): 254–86; "White Flight Is Not Black Fright," *Christian Science Monitor,* March 11, 1994, 4.
57. Mary Pattillo, "Black Middle-Class Neighborhoods," *Annual Review of Sociology* 31 (2005): 305–29; Mary J. Fischer and Travis Scott Lowe, "Homebuyer Neighborhood Attainment in Black and White: Housing Outcomes during the Housing Boom and Bust," *Social Forces* 93, no. 4 (June 2015): 1481–512.
58. Official Application for Use of Capitol Square Grounds, August 26, 1983, Announcements 1982–83, Box 1, M258, RUI Papers, VCU.
59. What We've Been Doing!, undated; Annual Meeting of the RUI, January 25, 1982, Annual/Semi-Annual Meetings, 1980–83, 1985, both in Box 1, M258, RUI Papers, VCU.
60. Untitled memo, Wednesday's Child Originals, 1982, Box 16, ibid.
61. Undated Camp Schedule, Master Schedule, undated, Wednesday's Child Originals, 1982, ibid.; RUI to the Richmond Public Library, July 1982, ibid.
62. Undated and unattributed speech, Grassroots Economic Development Correspondence, 1983–85, Box 8, ibid.
63. Wednesday's Child Summer Camp, undated memo, Wednesday's Child Originals, 1982, ibid.
64. Missioner's Report, April 27, 1981, Edythe Rogers, Resume and Records, 1979–83, Box 3, ibid.
65. Ann Field Alexander, *Race Man: The Rise and Fall of the "Fighting Editor" John Mitchell Jr.* (Charlottesville: University of Virginia Press, 2002); L. M. Blair Kelley, *Right to Ride: Streetcar Boycotts and African American*

Citizenship in the Era of Plessy v. Ferguson (Chapel Hill: University of North Carolina Press, 2010); "The Not-So-Guilded Age of Jim Crow," Maymont Foundation, https://maymont.org/explore/historic-estate/african-american-voices/jim-crow.

66. Chiles, "A Period of Misunderstanding," 264–66.
67. "NAACP Sets Segregation Court Tests," *RTD*, July 2, 1951, 1–2; "1952 to See More Attacks on Segregation," *RTD*, December 27, 1952, 1–2; "VTC Ends Enforcement of Segregation on Buses," *RTD*, April 25, 1956, 1; "Mixed Seating Not New Here," *RTD*, November 14, 1956, 1.
68. Basic Information about the Greater Richmond Transit Company, March 1982, Bus Riders Committee Meeting, 1981–83, Box 1, M258, RUI Papers, VCU.
69. Junfeng Jiao, "Identifying Transit Deserts in Major Texas Cities Where the Supplies Missed the Demands," *Journal of Transport and Land Use* 10, no. 1 (2017): 529–40.
70. GRTC Bus Riders Committee, Bus Riders Committee Meeting, 1981–83, Box 1, M258, RUI Papers, VCU.
71. Report on the Electric Trolley Route Location Committee, April 7, 1981, at Reynolds Metal, Bus Riders Committee Meeting, 1981–83, ibid.
72. Larry D. Schroeder and David L. Sjoquist, "The Rational Voter: An Analysis of Two Atlanta Referenda on Rapid Transit," *Public Choice* 33, no. 3 (1978): 27–44.
73. Steven Dornfeld, "1969 Bus Strike: Twin Cities Mass Transit Turning Point," *Minnesota History* 66, no. 7 (Fall 2019): 274–89; Mark Gallimore, "Coordination or Competition? State Regulation of Motor Buses under Private Ownership and the Decline of Mass Transit in Pittsburgh," *Pennsylvania Magazine of History and Biography* 138, no. 1 (January 2014), 39–71.
74. "Seamless Transit: How to Make Bay Area Public Transit Function Like One Rational, Easy-to-Use System," Report Published by San Francisco Bay Area Planning and Urban Research Association, April 1, 2015, 51.
75. "Caution Signal for America's Mass Transit," *U.S. News & World Report*, September 5, 1983, 53–54; Keith R. Ihlanfeldt, "Rail Transit and Neighborhood Crime: The Case of Atlanta, Georgia," *Southern Economic Journal* 70, no. 2 (October 2003): 273–94; William Patty Jordan, "Crime on the Bus: Bus Driver Safety in Postwar Washington, D.C.," *Washington History* 25 (Summer 2013): 36–51; Amy A. Helling and David S. Sawicki, "Disparate Trends: Metropolitan Atlanta Since 1960," *Built Environment* 20, no. 1 (1994): 9–24; Jeffrey R. Brown and Gregory L. Thompson, "The Relationship between Transit Ridership and Urban Decentralization: Insights from Atlanta," *Urban Studies* 45, nos. 5/6 (May 2008): 1119–39; Gregory Thompson, Jeffrey Brown, and Torsha Bhattacharya, "What Really Matters for Increasing Transit Ridership: Understanding the Determinants of Transit Ridership Demand in Broward County, Florida," *Urban Studies*

49, no. 15 (November 2012): 3327–45; Transportation Council Minutes, September 17, 1983, Bus Riders Committee Meeting, 1981–83, Box 1, M258, RUI Papers, VCU.
76. Ibid.
77. Ibid.
78. Benjamin Campbell, Urban Missioner, to James W. Rouse, April 7, 1982; "Richmond's Third Century: Rebirth of Cities," speech given by James W. Rouse, April 15, 1982; "Rouse: Richmond's Urban Moses," *Richmond News Leader*, April 14, 1982, 19, clippings in James Rouse Developer File, 1981–82, Box 14, M258, RUI Papers, VCU.
79. Campbell to Rouse, April 7, 1982; "Richmond's Third Century," Rouse speech April 15, 1982; "Rouse: Richmond's Urban Moses," Rouse file, ibid.
80. Author interview with Benjamin Campbell, March 14, 2019.
81. GRTC Citizens Committee to Brick Rider, Chairman of the Board of GRTC, April 14, 1982, Bus Riders Committee Meeting, 1981–83, Box 1, M258, RUI Papers, VCU.
82. Minutes of the Bus Riders Committee, December 7, 1982, February 14, 1983, and April 11, 1983, ibid.
83. Frederick S. Fisher, Chairman of Citizens Transportation Council, September 1, 1983, Bus Riders Committee Meeting, 1981–83, Box 1, M258, RUI Papers, VCU.
84. Grassroots Economic Development Proposal, March 13, 1983, Grassroots Economic Development, Box 7, ibid.
85. Undated and unattributed speech, Grassroots Economic Development Correspondence, 1983–85, Box 8, ibid.
86. Charles A. Hosay to Center for Community Change, January 27, 1984, Grassroots Economic Development, Box 7, M258, RUI Papers, VCU; Grassroots Economic Development Committee, October 18, 1983, ibid.; Sheila Crowley to Rutledge Dennis, January 18, 1984, ibid.
87. Possible Criteria for Grassroots Business, undated, Grassroots Economic Development, Box 7, M258, RUI Papers, VCU; Youth Employment Work Plan, 1984, Summer Youth Employment, 1981–85, Box 14, ibid.; and Sheila Crowley to Mayor Roy West, June 29, 1984, Grassroots Economic Development Correspondence, 1983–85, Box 8, ibid.
88. New Horizons, undated, Summer Youth Employment, 1981–85, Box 14, M258, RUI Papers, VCU.
89. Summer Jobs '85 Directory, ibid.
90. Undated and unattributed speech, Grassroots Economic Development Correspondence, 1983–85, Box 8, ibid.
91. RUI Officers and Council Members, 1984, Administrative Officers, 1984–86, Box 1, M258, RUI Papers, VCU.
92. Citizens Transportation Council, November 1983, Bus Riders Committee Meeting, 1981–83, Box 1, ibid.

93. 1985 Proposed Program Summary, Racial Ethnic Issues Committee, 1984–85, Box 10, ibid.; Invitation for RUI Annual Meeting, January 31, 1983, Announcements 1982–83, Box 1, ibid.
94. Internal Memo from Theresa T. Caldwell, Moderator, undated, Administrative Officers, 1984–86, Box 1, M258, RUI Papers, VCU.

8. Moral Re-Armament and Hope in the Cities

1. Oregon Hill Summary Tape File 1G, Neighborhood Revitalization Division, Department of Planning and Community Development, City of Richmond Neighborhood Statistics, November 1985, Box 5, M303, Richmond Renaissance Papers, VCU; Richmond's Vacant Housing Catalog: A Partial Listing of Vacant Houses Available for Purchase in Richmond, VA, Winter/Spring 1989; undated memo, "RBHC, Abandoned Property Project, 1989–1990," Box 18, M302, all in McClenahan Papers, VCU.
2. Author interview with Reginald Gordon, June 27, 2019.
3. Phillip H. Brunson III, Testimony in Fleming, *Growing Up in Civil Rights Richmond*, 64; author interview with Rutledge Dennis, July 26, 2019.
4. "Oregon Hill Resident Believes Vandalism Had No Racial Bias," *RTD*, August 22, 1990, B4; "Terrorism Hits Blacks in Oregon Hill," *RAA*, August 25, 1990, 1.
5. "Oregon Hill Resident Believes No Racial Bias," *RTD*, August 22, 1990, B4; "Not All in Neighborhood Are Racist," *RAA*, August 25, 1990, 1; "Terrorism Hits Blacks in Oregon Hill" and "Rebel Flag Flies Defiantly," *RAA*, August 25, 1990, 1.
6. "Battle of Historic Status Turns Racial in Richmond," *WP*, October 22, 1990, D5.
7. "Oregon Hill Resident Believes No Racial Bias," *RTD*, August 22, 1990, B4.
8. "Terrorism Hits Blacks in Oregon Hill" and "Rebel Flag Flies Defiantly," *RAA*, August 25, 1990, 1.
9. "Richmond Historic District Rejected," *WP*, October 24, 1990, B5a.
10. "City Nears Adoption of New Rebeless Flag," *RAA*, September 22, 1990, 1; "Creation of a New City Flag," Resolution 91-R183-170, July 22, 1991; "Designating an Official Flag for the City of Richmond," Ordinance 1993-048-29, February 22, 1993, all in Richmond City Hall Archives; "Unfurling the History of the Flag," *RVA News*, February 24, 2014.
11. O'Leary, *Carillon Neighborhood*, 1–29; author interview with Dr. Elizabeth L. O'Leary, June 26, 2019; Carillon Neighborhood Historic District, National Register of Historic Places Registration Form, National Park Service, https://npgallery.nps.gov/NRHP/AssetDetail/407171d0-e004-4fb2-9479-cfc9781233ff.
12. O'Leary, *Carillon Neighborhood*, 20–28.

13. Author interviews with Rob Corcoran, March 11, 2019; with Susan Corcoran, May 7, 2019; O'Leary, *Carillon Neighborhood*, 26.
14. Irish Jesuit Province, "Catholics and Moral Rearmament," *Irish Monthly* 67, no. 796 (October 1939): 722–26.
15. Every ordinance and resolution cited henceforth comes from the Richmond City Hall Archives; "Richmond-A Model City?," *New World News*, January 7, 1978, 1–7; Dialog at City Hall, June 9, 1989; Notes from the Monthly Meeting & Potluck Supper, January 5, April 6, May 4, June 1, July 6, September 15, 19, Richmond, 1977–91, File Cabinet 1, IoC Papers; author interviews with Benjamin Campbell, March 12, 2019; with Rob Corcoran, March 11, 2019; with Susan Corcoran, May 7, 2019.
16. Monthly Meeting & Potluck Supper, September 15, 1990, Richmond 1977–91, File Cabinet 1, IoC Papers.
17. Author interviews with Rob Corcoran, March 11, 2019; with Benjamin Campbell, March 12, 2019.
18. Author interview with Rob Corcoran, March 11, 2019.
19. Richmond Group to Caux and Liverpool 1983, Richmond 1977–91, File Cabinet 1, IoC Papers.
20. Author interview with Paige Chargois, May 17, 2019.
21. Author interviews with Rob Corcoran, March 11, 2019; with Susan Corcoran, May 7, 2019.
22. Author interview with Rob Corcoran, March 11, 2019.
23. "Are We Free Enough to Care?," *New World News*, March 13, 1982, 18; "Robert and Susan Corcoran," *New World News*, March 17, 1983, 3; To Mr. and Mrs. C. Burton and the Citizens of Richmond, Virginia, U.S.A., 1983; "Richmonders to Deliver Message to English City," *RTD*, July 30, 1983, A9; "Fact Finding Americans Arrive in City," *Daily Post*, August 22, 1983; "Caux 1983," *News of Moral Re-Armament*, September 1983; "Richmond in Liverpool," *New World News*, September 17, 1983, 20; "A New Concept of Leadership," *News of Moral Re-Armament*, October 1983; "A New Leadership," Speech Delivered in Liverpool, November 1983; "US Conference, Who Leads the Leaders," *New World News*, December 24, 1983, 1–20, Richmond 1977–91, all in File Cabinet 1, IoC Papers; Zimbabwe 1984, folder, ibid.
24. Author interview with Rob Corcoran, March 11, 2019; unpublished internal memo, Susan Corcoran, January 9, 1984; unpublished internal memo, R. L. Corcoran, February 13, 1984; "Unity in Diversity, Will Richmond Lead the Way," October 1984; Program for Moral Re-Armament Conference, Unity in Diversity, November 16–18, 1984; untitled and unsigned letter to Rob Corcoran, November 26, 1984; "Richmond Conference for Unity in Diversity," *New World News*, December 22, 1984, all in Richmond 1977–91, File Cabinet 1, IoC Papers; Zimbabwe 1984, folder, ibid.; *The Courage to Change* (Documentary, 1987), 15:53–18:07, ibid.

25. Author interview with Paige Chargois, May 17, 2019.
26. Unpublished memo, R. L. Corcoran, February 13, 1984, Richmond 1977–91, File Cabinet 1, IoC Papers.
27. 1103 Sunset Avenue Guest Book, found in the Richmond home of Rob and Susan Corcoran, May 7, 2019.
28. Letter to Friends, March 4, 1986; Rob and Susan Corcoran to Ben Trotter, Virginia Brinton, Collie Burton, Terry Blair, and Betty Clarke, April 11, 1986; Operating Expenses for Richmond Center for Year 1985; Rob and Susan Corcoran to Friends, July 10, 1986; "Richmond Launches Out," *MRA Newsletter*, December 1986; Brochure for "Open House to Meet a Multi-racial Group from Richmond," October 11, 1987; Richmonders Visit Program, October 9–14, 1987; Brochure for *The Courage to Change,* October 25, 1987; unpublished letter from Rob Corcoran, October 26, 1987; Invitation to Lunch Dialogue with European Visitors, May 10, 1989; Dialog at City Hall, June 9, 1989, all in Richmond 1977–91 folder, File Cabinet 1, IoC Papers; City-Wide Workshop/Dialog, March 27, 1990, Reports, 92–94, ibid.; author interview with Paige Chargois, May 17, 2019.
29. Kneebone and Trani, *Fulfilling the Promise*, 35–53.
30. Mary K. Kinnick and Mary F. Ricks, "The Urban Public University in the United States: An Analysis of Change, 1977–1987," *Research in Higher Education* 31, no. 1 (February 1990): 20–35.
31. Kneebone and Trani, *Fulfilling the Promise*, 187–92.
32. Minutes, Regular Meeting of the Board of VCU, July 19, 1990; July 18, 1991; November 1, 1991; January 17, 1991; May 21, 1993; November 18, 1993, VCU Archives.
33. Author interviews with Christy Coleman, June 25, 2019; with Bill Martin, July 23, 2019.
34. Valentine Museum Strategic Plan for the 1990s, December 17, 1990, VM Archives.
35. "A Terrain of Conflict," Project Overview, 1993, ibid.
36. Ibid.; Valentine Museum Strategic Plan for the 1990s, December 17, 1990, VM Archives.
37. "To Celebrate African Presence in the Americas," Valentine Museum News Release, August 20, 1993, VM Archives.
38. "Same Spaces, Separate Lives" Gallery Guide, September 23, 1993, ibid.
39. "A Terrain of Conflict," Project Overview, 1993, ibid.
40. Second Street: Business and Entertainment in Jackson Ward, 1900–1965, Exhibition Exploring Black Entrepreneurs and Entertainers Opens at Valentine, January/February 1990, ibid.
41. Frank Jewel, President and Director of the Valentine Museum, to Marsha Semmell, Acting Director, Division of Public Programs, August 31, 1993; Malcolm X: Man, Ideal and Icon, July 31, 1989, both VM Archives.
42. Valentine Museum Strategic Plan for the 1990s, December 17, 1990, 5, ibid.

43. Virginia Historical Society: Fifth Century Fund, undated memo; Jan Aldrich, Resident Campaign Director, to Robert S. Jepson Jr., July 24, 1990, both in Folder 158, Mss1 W5603b FA2, Wheat Papers, VMHC.
44. "Wilder Statue Proposed," *RAA*, April 27, 1991, 1; "Officials Reaffirm Commitment to Jackson Ward," *RAA*, May 11, 1991, 1; "Civil Rights Heroes: Monuments Proposed," *RAA*, June 8, 1991, 1; "African American Heritage Development Plan," September 3, 1991, African American Heritage Development Plan Pact, M303 Box 1, Richmond Renaissance Papers, VCU; "Chamber Fights Its White Image," *RAA*, September 7, 1991; Melvin L. Urofsky, "The Virginia Historical Society: The First 175 Years, 1831–2006," *Virginia Magazine of History and Biography* 114, no.1 (Winter 2006): 185–200; author interviews with Christy Coleman, June 25, 2019; with Bill Martin, July 23, 2019.
45. Interview with Dr. Elizabeth L. O'Leary, June 26, 2019; "Virginia Museum of Fine Arts: Charges of Racism Accelerate," *RAA*, June 8, 1991, 8; "Events Will Commemorate Walker," *RAA*, June 27, 1992, 3; "Museum Omits Black Artifacts" and "Valentine Museum Presents Free Film," *RAA*, July 11, 1992, 1.
46. "Jackson Ward Reunion Set," *RTD*, August 16, 1991, D3; and quotes found in Valerie Hubbard, "Get Ready for This Really Big Reunion," *RTD*, August 13, 1992, D27.
47. Roy Proctor, "Dance," *RTD*, August 1, 1993, S5; "Programs for Disabled Set," *RTD*, January 24, 1992, D5; "The Tradition Continues," *RTD*, July 1, 1992, C4.
48. "Dogwood Dell, 1993," *RTD*, May 23, 1993, J6; ad quotes found in Jessica Ronky Haddad, "Janine Bell Has a Mission," *Style Weekly*, August 13, 2001, https://www.styleweekly.com/richmond/janine-bell-has-a-mission-to-make-sure-richmond-embraces-its-african-roots/Content?oid=1360533.
49. Author interview with Benjamin Campbell, March 14, 2019.
50. Ibid.; Route Taken by the Richmond Unity Walk, June 1993, Unity Walk 1993, File Cabinet 1, IoC Papers.
51. Author interview with Sylvester Turner, March 13, 2019.
52. Ibid.
53. Rob Corcoran to Board, June 1, 1990, Reports 1992–94, File Cabinet 1; Minutes of Monthly Meeting & Potluck Supper, July 6, September 15, October 5, November 9, and December 14, 1990, Richmond 1977–91, File Cabinet 1, IoC Papers; author interview with Sylvester Turner, March 13, 2019.
54. "Tension Grows over Shelter for Homeless on Resurgent Ponce de Leon," *Atlanta Journal-Constitution*, July 20, 1986, E1; "Prostitutes Could Do Better off Ponce, Advocate Says," *Atlanta Journal-Constitution*, August 2, 1990, E3; "A Shady Lane," *Atlanta Journal-Constitution*, September 5, 1990, C1.
55. "A Brief History of BTA," undated, BTA Folder, File Cabinet 1, IoC Papers.
56. Black Teens for Advancement Overview Brief, 1991–92, BTA Folder, File Cabinet 1, IoC Papers.

57. Rob Corcoran to MRA Board, October 29, 1990; letter from BTA to Dr. W. Foster, Director of Pupil Personnel Services Department, Atlanta public schools, undated; "There for the Young Black Male," *For a Change*, October, 1991, 12–13; "Black Teens Who Fight Violence," *Cincinnati Enquirer*, December 3, 1992; "Brothers with an Attitude," *Urban Family* (Fall 1993); "Anti-Hate Message Taken Abroad," *Atlanta Journal/The Atlanta Constitution*, September 24, 1993; Thomas E. Ager, Assistant Superintendent of Secondary Education in Atlanta Public Schools, to Edward Johnson, January 18, 1994; BTA Leadership Conference, February 19, 1994, clippings all found in BTA Folder, File Cabinet 1, IoC Papers.
58. Private letter to Board of Moral Re-Armament, April 26, 1990, Hope in the Cities National Folder 1990, File Cabinet 1, IoC Papers.
59. Auhtor interview with Paige Chargois, May 17, 2019; Believers Take Action Memo from MRA Hope in Atlanta, undated, HIC National 1990, File Cabinet 1, IoC Papers.
60. "Black Teens Visit in Hope of Healing," *News-Press*, March 27, 1994; Dr. Ed and Harmon Johnson to Mayor Bill Campbell of Atlanta, Georgia, July 9, 1994. For more on the BTA, see the BTA Atlanta, File Cabinet 1, IoC Papers; author interview with Sylvester Turner, March 13, 2019; private letter to Board, April 26, 1990, HIC National 1990, File Cabinet 1, IoC Papers.
61. Author interview with Sylvester Turner, March 13, 2019.
62. Rob Corcoran to Board, January 10, 1991; internal memo, January 28, 1991; Invitation to St. Paul's Episcopal Church Parish Hall, May 1, 1991; notes from the National Urban Ministers meeting in Chicago, January 14, 1991, HIC National 1990; To Participants in Hope in the Cities Forums, June 6, 1991; Rob Corcoran to HIC Board, June 21, 1991; Hope in the Cities: A Citizens' Initiative, undated; Proposal for Conferences/Retreats for Community Leaders, undated; minutes of HIC Working Group, November 20, 1991, Reports 92–94, File Cabinet 4; and Hope in the Cities, A Discussion Paper, Leesburg, October 1991, all in HIC National 1991, File Cabinet 1, IoC Papers.
63. Author interview with Benjamin Campbell, March 14, 2019.
64. Author interview with Paige Chargois, May 17, 2019.
65. Ibid.; "Community Activists Aim to Curb Exodus from Inner City Areas," *Richmond News Leader*, March 13, 1992, 8; HIC Lunch Forum, March 12, 1992, Richmond 1977–91, File Cabinet 1, IoC Papers.
66. Agenda for Healing the Heart of America: An Honest Conversation on Race, Reconciliation, and Responsibility, Conference, June 16–20, 1993, File Cabinet 1, IoC Papers.
67. Richmond Sponsoring Committee and Corporate Sponsors, found in a bound book of miscellaneous conference materials, File Cabinet 1, IoC Papers; Mayor Walter T. Kenney to Moral Re-Armament, July 20, 1992; Kenney to Harry Jacobs of the Martin Agency and Grace Harris, VCU Provost, February 24, 1993, File Cabinet 1, IoC Papers.

68. Author interview with Sylvester Turner, March 13, 2019.
69. Conference update, May 17, 1993; Agenda for Healing the Heart of America Conference, June 16–20, 1993, File Cabinet 1, IoC Papers.
70. Author interviews with Rob Corcoran, March 11, 2019; with Susan Corcoran, May 7, 2019; with Benjamin Campbell, March 14, 2019.
71. Author interviews with Benjamin Campbell, March 14, 2019; with Rob Corcoran, March 11, 2019.
72. *Healing the Hearts of America Conference* (Documentary), 3:50–3:54, 4:25–4:40, Initiatives of Change Video Archives, https://www.youtube.com/watch?v=4QJZRjPnwoI.
73. Author interviews with Rob Corcoran, March 11, 2019; with Benjamin Campbell, March 14, 2019; Corcoran, *Trustbuilding*, 209–12; "International Panel to Target Racism in Richmond," *RTD*, April 23, 1993, B6; "Conference Call, Richmonders Invite the World Here to Try to Heal the Hurt of Racism," *Style Weekly*, June 1, 1993, 14; "City's History All but Dictated That It Be Conference Site," *RTD*, May 30, 1993, B1, B6; Rob Corcoran, "Honest Conversation Can Heal a City," editorial, *RTD*, June 12, 1993, F7; "Unity Walk to Take Positive Steps," *RTD*, June 14, 1993, B1, B7; "Unity Walk Was Emotional, Spiritual, Dramatic for Many," *RTD*, June 19, 1993, A1, A3; "Walk for Unite," *Richmond Free Press*, June 14–26, 1993, 1; "Ability to Compete Globally Linked to Solving Racism," *RTD*, June 17, 1993, 1; "Healing of American Cities Can Start in Richmond" *RTD*, June 13, 1993, F7.
74. HIC Special Report from Richmond, June 1993, Newsletters and Releases Scrapbook, File Cabinet 4, IoC Papers.
75. Author interview with Benjamin Campbell, March 14, 2019; Healing the Heart of America, conference flyer, June 1993; HIC Special Report from Richmond, June 1993; 1993 pre-conference, File Cabinet 1, IoC Papers.
76. Author interviews with Paige Chargois, May 17, 2019; with Benjamin Campbell, March 14, 2019.
77. Rob Corcoran to Ben Campbell and Janine Bell, June 1993; Richmond Unity Walk Program, June 1993, 1–4; Healing the Heart of America conference brochure and program found in a bound book of miscellaneous conference materials, File Cabinet 1; National HIC Coalition, December 1993, Newsletters and Releases Scrapbook, File Cabinet 4, IoC Papers. For the positive responses about the conference, see folder entitled, 1993 Conference, File Cabinet 1, HIC Archives, IoC Papers. For more on the conference, see the bound book of miscellaneous conference materials in File Cabinet 1, IoC Papers.
78. Author interview with Paige Chargois, May 17, 2019.
79. Notes from Breakfast Meeting with Sponsoring Committee, September 16, 1993, Some Ideas for Future Directions, 1993, Reports 92–94, File Cabinet 1, IoC Papers; author interviews with Rob Corcoran, March 11, 2019; with Benjamin Campbell, March 12, 2019.

80. Author interviews with Benjamin Campbell, March 14, 2019; with Rob Corcoran, March 11, 2019.
81. Author interview with Benjamin Campbell, March 14, 2019.
82. "In Search of Forgiveness," *RTD*, clipping found in the IoC Papers, A1, A10.
83. Working Committee Memo for the Richmond Unity Walk, May 14, 1997, Unity Walk/Slave Walk, File Cabinet 1, IoC Papers; author interview with Paige Chargois, May 17, 2019.

9. Monument Avenue

1. Virginia 2000: Population and Housing Unit Counts, 2000 Census of Population and Housing, October 2003, US Census Bureau, https://www.census.gov/prod/cen2000/phc-3-48.pdf; "Mural Lights Discussion," *RTD*, February 4, 2000, E5.
2. "Monument Led to Avenue Gem," *RTD*, March 27, 1977, C1, C3.
3. "How Much Do You Know about Monument Avenue," *RTD*, February 23, 1981, B4; "Celebrations Set for Series of Historic Birthdays," *RTD*, December 28, 1986, J5; "Appomattox Was Lee's Greatest Victory," *RTD*, January 17, 1991, 15.
4. "Community's Displeasure," *RTD*, March 23, 2000, B1.
5. "Confederate History Resolution Draws Near," *RTD*, March 15, 2000.
6. "Community's Displeasure," *RTD*, March 23, 2000, B1.
7. "Powhatan Ponders Confederate Issue," *RTD*, March 8, 2004, B1; "Henrico Chairman Opposes Commemoration," *RTD*, March 29, 2000, A7.
8. "Mall Crowd Rallies with Duke," *RTD*, April 2, 2000, A1; "Community's Displeasure," *RTD*, March 23, 2000, B1; "Pastor, NAACP Call for Boycott of Malls," *RTD*, March 28, 2000, A1; "Former Klan Chief to Go to Malls," *RTD*, March 30, 2000, B5; "Community's Displeasure," *RTD*, March 23, 2000, B1; "Eight Suspended for Confederate Attire," *RTD*, April 13, 2000, B7; "Henrico Expunges Flag Suspensions," *RTD*, January 7, 2001, A1; "DuPont Workers Staging Protests," *RTD*, November 3, 2000, B8.
9. "At Virginia's Capitol, Politics of History Is Unavoidable," *RTD*, May 14, 2000, F2; "Gilmore's Outreach in Danger," *RTD*, May 7, 2000, A1; "Blacks Set to Denounce Gilmore Proclamation," *RTD*, April 5, 2000, B1; "A Vision of Virginia's History," *RTD*, April 9, 2000, F2; "Va. Scraps Tribute to Confederacy," *WP*, March 21, 2001, A1.
10. "Warner Won't Issue Proclamation," *RTD*, March 15, 2002, B1.
11. Margaret Edds, "Focusing a New Lens on Confederate History," *Norfolk-Virginia Pilot*, March 24, 2002, J5.
12. "S.C. Lowers Its Disputed Flag," *WP*, July 2, 2000, A4; "Ole Miss Can Ban Rebel Flag," *WP*, August 20, 2000, D10; "Ga. Senate Backs New Flag, Muting Confederate Symbol," *WP*, February 4, 2001, A3A; "In New Orleans, a Rebel Last Stand," *WP*, July 8, 2001, A11A; "Signs of Confederacy Vanishing

in the South," *New York Times,* December 25, 2004, A24; "Bastion of Confederacy Finds Its Future May Hinge on Rejecting the Past," *New York Times,* December 5, 1999, 29.
13. "What Richmond Has Gotten Right about Interpreting Its History," *Smithsonian,* May 18, 2017, https://www.smithsonianmag.com/history/what-richmond-has-gotten-right-about-interpreting-its-confederate-history-180963354/.
14. "Colorblindness Has Become a Conservative Shield for Racial Inequality," *WP,* August 7, 2020, https://www.washingtonpost.com/outlook/2020/08/07/colorblindness-has-become-conservative-shield-racial-inequality/; "Color-Blindness Is Counterproductive," *Atlantic,* September 13, 2015, https://www.theatlantic.com/politics/archive/2015/09/color-blindness-is-counterproductive/405037/.
15. "Richmond Leaders Want Confederate Monuments Removed," *RTD,* June 3, 2020, 1.
16. W. Fitzhugh Brundage, *The Southern Past: A Clash of Race and Memory* (Cambridge, MA: Harvard University Press, 2005), 316–18.
17. Raymond Arsenault, *Arthur Ashe: A Life* (New York: Simon & Schuster, 2018), 1–20.
18. Author interview with Tom Chewning, May 10, 2019; Eric Allen Hall, *Arthur Ashe: Tennis and Justice in the Civil Rights Era* (Baltimore: Johns Hopkins University Press, 2014), 1–33; Arthur Ashe and Arnold Rampersad, *Days of Grace, A Memoir* (New York: Knopf, 1993), 61; author interview with William Mason, July 22, 2019.
19. "Richmond's Rare Opportunity," *RTD,* February 2, 1966, 16.
20. Hall, *Arthur Ashe,* 6; author interview with Tom Chewning, May 10, 2019; Ashe and Rampersad, *Days of Grace,* 100–112.
21. Author interview with Tom Chewning, May 10, 2019.
22. Quote taken from "Tennis Champ Arthur Ashe Dies," *RTD,* February 7, 1993, A1; "Ashe Returns to the City Disowned in Youth," *New York Times,* May 7, 1992, A18.
23. Plan for Follow-Through? Mentoring Phase, Virginia Heroes, Inc., undated; Proposal Continued Support of the Virginia Heroes, Inc., Project: An Anti-Drug and Drop-Out Prevention Program Relating to High Risk, Inner-City Youth, 1992–1993, Virginia Heroes 1992–1996, Box 108, M302, McClenahan Papers, VCU; "Heroes Will Foster Staying in School," *Richmond News Leader,* April 18, 1991, 15; "Sixth Graders to Head Heroes Success Stories," *RTD,* November 12, 1991, B3.
24. "Tennis Champ Arthur Ashe Dies," *RTD,* February 7, 1993, A1.
25. "Thousands Pay Tribute to Arthur Ashe," *RAA,* February 20, 1993, 1; Commending Various State and City Officials for Their Roles in Arranging the Memorial Service for Arthur R. Ashe, Jr., Resolution 93-R45-40, February 22, 1993; Tribute to Arthur Ashe, Jr., February 10, 1993, Arthur Ashe Folder

Series 11, Box 3, Governor Wilder's General Files, L. Douglas Wilder Library, VU; "Thousands Pay Respects to Ashe," *RTD*, February 10, 1993, A6.
26. Expressing Appreciation for the Life of Arthur Robert Ashe, Jr., and Sorrow at His Passing, Resolution 93-R17A-30, February 8, 1993. For more resolutions detailing the various appointments to the Appropriate Memorial Committee, see RVA.com, https://richmondva.legistar.com/Legislation.aspx; "Bobb to Proceed with Plans for Hall," *RTD*, February 8, 1993, D3.
27. Creating a Committee to Study an Appropriate Memorial for the Life of Arthur Ashe, Jr., Resolution 93-R38-81, April 13, 1993.
28. Author interview with Tom Chewning, May 10, 2019.
29. "Ashe Due Spot Among Heroes," *RTD*, June 13, 1995, 1, A8; and "Landmark Decision in Richmond: Statue to Honor Tennis Great Ashe," *WP*, June 20, 1995, B7.
30. James M. Lindgren, *Preserving the Old Dominion: Historic Preservation and Virginia Traditionalism* (Charlottesville: University of Virginia Press, 1993); Odell R. Byrd, *Richmond: A City of Monuments and Statues* (Richmond, VA: Tambuzi, 1989); Robert P. Winthrop, *Richmond's Monument Avenue* (Chapel Hill: University of North Carolina Press, 2001), 13–35, 97–138.
31. "Monument Site for Ashe Put in Doubt," *RTD*, June 27, 1995, A1; "The Statue," *RTD*, June 28, 1995, A10.
32. Driggs, Wilson, and Winthrop, *Richmond's Monument Avenue*, 55–93; Matthew Mace Barbee, *Race and Masculinity in Southern Memory: A History of Richmond, Virginia's Monument Avenue* (Lanham, MD: Lexington Books, 2014), 19–36; "Stand Firm," *Richmond Planet*, June 7, 1890, 2.
33. "'Clustering' of White Students Divides Richmond Again," *WP*, December 4, 1992, D1; "Judge Grants Delay of Class Integration at Richmond School," *New York Times*, February 7, 1993, 2; "Richmond: In Search of Southern Comforts," *WP*, March 14, 1993, BB43.
34. "Monument Site for Ashe Put in Doubt," *RTD*, June 27, 1995, A1.
35. "Ashe Due Spot among Heroes," *RTD*, June 13, 1995, 1, A8.
36. Author interview with Tom Chewning, May 10, 2019; "Monument Issue Divides Old Dominion," *WP*, September 29, 1991, B3; "No Mixed Icons," *WP*, July 6, 1995, VA1.
37. "Ashe Monument Could Be Symbol of Reconciliation," *RTD*, June 26, 1995, B1.
38. Lawrence T. Vetter to Timothy G. Oaskman, Esquire, Re: Committee to Study an Appropriate Memorial for the Life of Arthur Ashe, Jr., May 31, 1994; minutes of Virginia Heroes, Inc., Board of Directors Meeting, June 27, 1994, Virginia Heroes, 1992–96, Box 108, McClenahan Papers, VCU; Tim Kaine to Virginia Heroes Site Selection Committee for the Arthur Ashe Monument, February 14, 1995, ibid.; Paul DiPasquale to Committee

Members Virginia Heroes Site Selection Committee for the Arthur Ashe Monument, February 17, 1995, ibid.

39. "World Watches City Struggle," *RTD*, July 11, 1995, 1, A6, A8; "City OKs Monument Site for Ashe," *RTD*, June 20, 1995, 1, A5; "Debate on Location for Ashe Statue Continues," *RTD*, July 6, 1995, A12; "Sculptor Cites Statue Claim," *RTD*, July 8, 1995, 1, A6, A8; minutes of the City Council of Richmond, Virginia, March 27–September 25, 1995, 303, 308, 338, Richmond City Hall; "City Was Split over Memorial to Tennis Great," *WP*, July 18, 1995, A1.

40. "Someone of Ashe's Statue Should Be in Historic District," *RTD*, June 25, 1995, D4.

41. "Raising a Racket," *RTD*, June 21, 1995, D1; "Return to Square One," *RTD*, June 28, 1995, A1.

42. "Monument Issue Divides Old Dominion," *WP*, September 29, 1991, B3.

43. Author interview with Tom Chewning, May 10, 2019.

44. "Mayor Young on CBS," *RTD*, June 28, 1995, A6; "Ashe Family Has Diverse Views on Statue," *RTD*, June 29, 1995, A1; "Richmond Ex-Mayor Is Indicted," *WP*, September 22, 1998, B4.

45. Author interview with Tom Chewning, May 10, 2019; "Monument Site for Ashe Put in Doubt," *RTD*, June 27, 1995, A1; "Ashe Statue without a Home," *RAA*, June 29–July 5, 1995, 1–2; Creating a Citizen Commission to Advise Council and the City Manager Concerning the Development of an Arthur Ashe Park in Downtown Richmond and Making It the Home of an African-American Sports Hall of Fame, Resolution 95-R236–208, September 11, 1995, Richmond City Hall; "Mayor Offers a Compromise," *RTD*, July 17, 1995, 1, A7, A8.

46. Author interviews with Tom Chewning, May 10, 2019; with Viola Baskerville, July 28, 2019.

47. "City Was Split over Memorial to Tennis Great," *WP*, July 18, 1995, A1; Public Hearing on the Appropriate Location for the Arthur Ashe Jr. Memorial Statue, minutes of the City Council of the City of Richmond, March 27–September 25, 1995, 341–51, Richmond City Hall; To Approve the Intersection of Roseneath Avenue and Monument Avenue as the Location for the Arthur Ashe Memorial Statue and Monument, Resolution 95-R225–175, July 17, 1995, 303, 308, 338; "We Rose to Ashe's Level," *RAA*, July 20–26; "Ashe Statue Will Go on Monument: National Embarrassment Avoided in Our Finest Hour," "Hearing Puts Focus on City," and "Statue Placement: A Monumental Site," *Richmond-Times-Dispatch*, July 18, 1995, A1, A10; "Richmond Approves Monument to Ashe," *WP*, July 19, 1995, B5; author interviews with Tom Chewning, May 10, 2019; with Paige Chargois, May 17, 2019; with Viola Baskerville, July 28, 2019.

48. Author interview with Tom Chewning, May 10, 2019.

49. "Richmond's Civil War Monuments Need More Context," *RTD,* June 24, 2010.
50. M. Belinda Tucker and Claudia Mitchell-Kernan, "New Trends in Black American Interracial Marriage: The Social Structural Context," *Journal of Marriage and Family* 52, no. 1 (February 1990): 209–18; Matthijs Kalmijn, "Trends in Black/White Intermarriage," *Social Forces* 72, no.1 (September 1993): 119–46; Steven A. Tuch et al., "Trends: Race Relations and American Youth, 1976–1995," *Public Opinion Quarterly* 63, no. 1 (Spring 1999): 109–48.
51. Lee Sigelman et al., "Making Contact? Black-White Social Interaction in an Urban Setting," *American Journal of Sociology* 101, no. 5 (March 1996): 1306–22; Tuch, "Trends," 113; Scott L. Feld and William C. Carter, "When Desegregation Reduces Interracial Contact: A Class Size Paradox for Weak Ties," *American Journal of Sociology* 103, no. 5 (March 1998): 1165–86.
52. Lee Sigelman and Susan Welch, *Black Americans' Views of Racial Inequality: The Dream Deferred* (Cambridge: Cambridge University Press, 1991); David Sears, Jim Sidanius, and Lawrence Bobo, eds., *Racialized Politics: The Debate about Racism in America* (Chicago: University of Chicago Press, 2000); Howard Schuman, Charlotte Steeh, Lawrence D. Bobo, and Maria Krysan, *Racial Attitudes in America: Trends and Interpretations* (Cambridge, MA: Harvard University Press, 1997); David A. Strauss, "The Myth of Colorblindness," *Supreme Court Review* (1986): 99–134; Richard Lowry, "Yuppie Racism: Race Relations in the 1980s," *Journal of Black Studies* 21, no. 4 (June 1991): 445–64; Charles Taylor, "The Politics of Recognition," in Amy Gutmann, ed., *Multiculturalism: Examining the Politics of Recognition* (Princeton, NJ: Princeton University Press, 1994).
53. Sheila Flemming-Hunter, "Conversations about Reparations for Blacks in America: A Twenty-first-Century Model in Civic Responsibility and Engagement," *Phylon* 53, no. 2 (Winter 2016): 100–25; "Black-White Scoring Gap Widens on the SAT II Test," *Journal of Blacks in Higher Education* 27 (Spring 2000): 41–43.
54. "Many in Poll See Worsening in Race Relations," *New York Times,* June 27, 1990, 2.
55. Victor A. Matheson and Robert A. Baade, "Race and Riots: A Note on the Economic Impact of the Rodney King Riots," *Urban Studies* 41, no. 13 (December 2004): 2691–96; "From Riots of 60s to Riots of the 90s, a Frustrating Search to Heal a Nation," *New York Times,* May 8, 1992, A19; "Charles Murray: White America's Deadly Seducer," *Journal of Blacks in Higher Education* 6 (Winter 1994–95), 72–73; Shelby Steele, *The Content of Our Character: A New Vision of Race in America* (New York: St. Martin's Press, 1990); Howard Winant, "Race and Race Theory," *Annual Review of Sociology* 26 (2000): 169–85; John McWhorter, *Losing the Race: Self-Sabotage in Black America* (New York: Perennial, 2001), 12–30.

56. Timothy J. Minchkin, "One America? Church Burnings and Perceptions of Race Relations in the Clinton Years," *Australasian Journal of American Studies* 27, no. 2 (December 2008): 1–28.
57. "Many in Poll See Worsening in Race Relations," *New York Times*, June 27, 1990, 2.
58. Rob Corcoran to Professor John Charles Thomas, January 5, 1995, Call to Community, File Cabinet 1, IoC Papers.
59. Rob Corcoran to Thomas, January 5, 1995; Rob Corcoran to Melvin Law, Chair of Richmond School Board, undated letter, Call to Community, File Cabinet 1, IoC Papers.
60. Rob Corcoran to Joyce Hamilton, African American Studies at the University of Hartford [CT], March 11, 1998; Rob Corcoran to Randy Ross-Ganguly, September 16 and 22, 1998, Camden, NJ, File Cabinet 1, IoC Papers.
61. Rob Corcoran to HIC Steering Committee, February 9, 1995, "Call to Community" and WCVE Channel 23, File Cabinet 1, IoC Papers.
62. Robert E. Jones to HIC, April 15, 1994, Dayton, OH; Robert Webb to Rob Corcoran, November 3, 1994, Cincinnati, OH; Robert E. Jones, Senior Pastor of College Hill Community Church, to Donald Loughman, June 9, 1994; A Call to Community position paper, February 22, 1996; Ruth Messinger, Borough President of Manhattan, New York, to Rob Corcoran, May 10, 1996; Jerry E. Abramson, Mayor of Louisville, to Walter T. Kenney, May 23, 1996; Henry Louis Gates Jr., Professor of the Humanities at Harvard University, to Karen Greisdorf, July 24, 1996; *National Launch of A Call to Community*, undated booklet; Call to Community National Endorsers & Partners, September 19, 1996, all found in File Cabinet 1, IoC Papers; Kurt Schmoke, Mayor of City of Baltimore, to Fellow Mayors, January, 1996, Call to Community, ibid.
63. HIC final report to W. K. Kellogg Foundation, June 2000, File Cabinet 3, IoC Papers.
64. Author interviews with Rob Corcoran, March 11, 2019; with Benjamin Campbell, March 14, 2019; with Sylvester Turner, March 13, 2019; with Susan Corcoran, May 7, 2019; with Paige Chargois, May 17, 2019.
65. Author interview with Paige Chargois, May 17, 2019.
66. HHH Press Release, October 13, 1996, Hartford, CT; Ian Mayo to Rob Corcoran, September 4, 1995, Hartford, CT; Hope in the Cities meeting, March 31, 1999, Camden City Hall; Randy Ganguly to Rob Corcoran, August 14, 1999; HIC organization meeting, August 12, 1999, Philadelphia; "Forum Tries to Close Groups' Differences," *Courier-Post*, October 3, 1999; Honest Conversation, Spring 2000, Publication of Hope in the Cities, Camden, NJ; Philadelphia's Hope in the Cities/Healing the Heart of America Conference, June 1–4, 1995, Philadelphia; "Hope in the Cities Conference Focuses on Violence," *North Philly Matters* 1, no.10 (May 1995):

1; Ada Montrae, US Justice Department and Conciliation Specialist, to Rob Corcoran, December 23, 1996, Philadelphia; Rob Corcoran to Ada Montrae, June 8, 1998, Philadelphia, all found in File Cabinet 1, IoC Papers; *Sheff v. O'Neill*, 678 A.2d 1267 (1996); HIC Twin Cities report, November 10, 1999; Youth Alienation and Violence Dialogue Series Project, September 1999, Twin Cities, MN; John B. Hirt, PhD, to Rob Corcoran, October 16, 1998, Pittsburg; Michael A Olson to Rob Corcoran, November 22, 1993, Twin Cities, MN, File Cabinet 1, IoC Papers; "Ethnic Change Tests Mettle of Minneapolis Liberalism," *New York Times*, October 18, 1997, 2.

67. Rob Corcoran to Geoffrey Pugh, December 20, 1994, Cincinnati, OH, File Cabinet 1, IoC Papers.
68. Patrick McNamara to Rob Corcoran, January 24, 1999, Oregon 1997–98, ibid.
69. Ian Mayo to Rob Corcoran, June 5, 1995, Hartford, CT, ibid.
70. Cricket White to Rob Corcoran, October 17, 1999, Selma, AL, ibid.
71. Author interview with Paige Chargois, May 17, 2019.
72. Jon F. Hale, "The Making of the New Democrats," *Political Science Quarterly* 110, no. 2 (Summer 1995), 207–32.
73. Darren Wheelock and Douglas Hartmann, "Midnight Basketball and the 1994 Crime Bill Debates: The Operation of a Racial Code," *Sociological Quarterly* 48, no. 2 (Spring 2007): 315–42; "Bill Clinton's Treatment of Lani Guinier," *WP*, June 6, 1993; Claire Jean Kim, "Managing the Racial Breach: Clinton, Black-White Polarization, and the Race Initiative," *Political Science Quarterly* 117, no.1 (Spring 2002): 55–79.
74. Minchkin, "One America?," 15.
75. Rob Corcoran to Patrick McNamara, November 3, 1998, Call to Community, File Cabinet 1, IoC Papers.
76. Martín Carcasson and Mitchell F. Rice, "The Promise and Failure of President Clinton's Race Initiative of 1997–1998: A Rhetorical Perspective," *Rhetoric and Public Affairs* 2, no. 2 (Summer 1999): 243–74.
77. Renée M. Smith, "The Public Presidency Hits the Wall: Clinton's Presidential Initiative on Race," *Presidential Studies Quarterly* 28, no. 4 (Fall 1998): 780–85.
78. "Clinton Sees Fairfax as Racial Model for U.S.: President Wants Panel to Study County's Varied Population for Clues to the Future," *WP*, October 01, 1997, A1; "Alexandria Plans Program of Racial Dialogue," *WP*, February 19, 1998, VA1A; "President Nudges His Race Panel to Take Action: A Panel Lacking Clear Direction from the President," *New York Times*, October 01, 1997, A23; Flemming-Hunter, "Conversations about Reparations for Blacks in America," 100–25.
79. Carcasson and Rice, "Promise and Failure of Clinton's Race Initiative," 243–74; "The Politics of Reconciliation," *New York Times*, January 21, 1997, A22; "President Nudges Hist Race Panel to Take Action," *New York Times*,

October 1, 1997, 23; "Why Talk about Race? Welfare and Crime Demand More Than Feel-Good Chat," *WP,* December 7, 1997; "Where Image Prevails, Talk about Race Turns Bland," *New York Times,* December 9, 1997, E2; "A Renewed Sense of Purpose for Clinton's Panel on Race," *New York Times,* March 20, 1998, 21.

80. Project Summary for the W. K. Kellogg Foundation, October 5, 2000, found in the Kellogg Funding Proposal 2000 binder; Elizabeth Furse, Member of U.S. Congress, to Michael D. Henderson, January 15, 1997, Call to Community; Call to Community list of national endorsers and partners, September, 19, 1996; Rob Corcoran to John Springer, June 1, 1997, Baltimore MD; Rob Corcoran to Mr. Philip Freeman, June 9, 1998, Camden, NJ, all in File Cabinet 1, IoC Papers; Corcoran, *Trustbuilding,* 89–92; *One America in the 21st Century: America Dialogue Guide, Conducting a Discussion on Race* (Washington, D.C., March 1998), 1–31.

81. "The Controversial 1994 Crime Law That Joe Biden Helped Write, Explained," *Vox,* September 29, 2020, https://www.vox.com/policy-and-politics/2019/6/20/18677998/joe-biden-1994-crime-bill-law-mass-incarceration.

82. National Research Council, *The Growth of Incarceration in the United States: Exploring Causes and Consequences* (Washington, DC: National Academies Press, 2014), 83; "Biden Defends Crime Bill Amid Criticism from Democratic Foes and Trump," *CNN,* June 6, 2019, https://www.cnn.com/2019/06/06/politics/joe-biden-crime-bill-2020-campaign/index.html.

83. "Conversations about Race," *WP,* June 14, 1998, A2; Theda Skocpol, Claire Jean Kim, "Clinton's Race Initiative: Recasting the American Dilemma," *Polity* 33, no. 2 (Winter 2000): 175–97; "African American Voters Standing by Clinton," *WP,* September 17, 1998.

84. Richmond Canal Dedication brochure, June 4, 1999; Richmond Canal Dedication brochure, June 4, 1999, Richmond Riverfront Development Corp., Box 115, M303, McClenahan Papers, VCU.

85. Report of the Advisory Committee to the Historic Riverfront Foundation, September 20, 1999, Box 115, M303, McClenahan Papers, VCU; "A New Vision for City Canals," *RTD,* June 1, 1999, A1, D1, D16.

86. Richmond Historic Riverfront Foundation, 1999; Committee Meets to Review Floodwall Images, June 14, 1999, Box 115, M303, McClenahan Papers, VCU.

87. Marie Tyler-McGraw, "Southern Comfort Levels: Race, Heritage Tourism, and the Civil War in Richmond," in James Oliver Horton and Lois E. Horton, eds., *Slavery and Public History: The Tough Stuff of American Memory* (Chapel Hill: University of North Carolina Press, 2006), 150–67; Anne Farrisee, "Heritage Tourism: Telling the Rest of the Story," *Georgia Historical Quarterly* 83, no.1 (Spring 1999): 101–7; Kathleen Brown, "Tourism Trends

284 NOTES TO PAGES 191–193

for the 90s," *History News* 48, no. 3 (May–June 1993): 4–7; Brundage, *Southern Past*, 300–305.
88. Brundage, *Southern Past*, 303–11.
89. Tyler-McGraw, "Southern Comfort Levels," 150–67.
90. "A New Vision for City Canals," *RTD*, June 1, 1999, A1, D1, D16.
91. "R. E. Lee Portrait Removed from Wall," *RTD*, June 3, 1999, A1, A8; "Ex-Council Member Had Contentious Career," *Washington Times*, July 26, 2003.
92. "Lee Absent for Canal Walk's Opening" and "Many Say Put the Portrait Back," *RTD*, June 4, 1999, A1, A17; "Mayor: Congratulations to Us," *RTD*, June 5, 1999, A1; "About 250 Protest Removal of Lee," *RTD*, June 14, 1999, B1.
93. "Praise, Protest at Waterway Ribbon-Cutting," *RTD*, June 5, 1999; "Five Council Members Back Lee," *RTD*, June 11, 1999, A1; "El-Amin Reasserts Stance on Mural," *RTD*, June 7, 1999, B1; "Group Starts Lee Discussion," *RTD*, June 15, 1999, B1.
94. "Lee Absent for Canal Walk's Opening" and "Many Say Put the Portrait Back," *RTD*, June 4, 1999, A1, A17.
95. "Group Starts Lee Discussion," *RTD*, June 15, 1999, B1.
96. "Put Lee on Floodwall, Panel Says," *RTD*, July 1, 1999, A1; "Talking about the Walk," *RTD*, July 7, 1999, A1; Directing the Removal of the Image of All Twenty-Nine (29) Images Which are not Displayed or Are Contemplated to Be Displayed on the Richmond Floodwall or Any Other Public Property Connected with the Richmond Canal Walk, Res. 99-R155, City Council of Richmond, July 12, 1999, Richmond City Hall.
97. Alex Wise Speech, undated [February 1999?]; H. Alexander Wise Jr, to the Honorable Bobby Scott, November 2, 1999, American Civil War Museum, File Cabinet 1, IoC Papers.
98. "Making History," *RTD*, September 3, 2000, B1.
99. Clipping of "Center Offers a New Approach to Civil War History," *RTD*, October 29, 2003, American Civil War Museum, File Cabinet 1, IoC Papers.
100. H. Alexander Wise to Bobby Scott, November 2, 1999, American Civil War Museum, ibid.
101. H. Alexander Wise to Rob Corcoran, February 12, 2000; H. Alexander Wise to Reverend Paige Chargois, April 14, 2000; *Tredegar National Civil War Center Sources Key African-American Collection* newsletter, September 12, 2000; Vice Admiral Samuel L. Gravely Jr., First African-American Admiral in the United States Navy, Will Chair Foundation, September 19, 2000; Carmen Foster to Alex Wise and Rob Corcoran, November 6, 2000; Tredegar National Civil War Center Foundation agenda, January 9, 2001, American Civil War Museum, File Cabinet 1, IoC Papers. Any newspaper citations cited hereafter without page numbers were found in clipping form in the IoC Papers.

102. Tredegar National Civil War Foundation, Board of Directors, National Advisory Board, and Community Advisory Board, undated, American Civil War Museum, File Cabinet 1, IoC Papers.
103. "Civil War Site: A Place of Hope," *RTD*, October 7, 2006, B3; author interview with Christy Coleman, June 25, 2019.
104. "Davis Statue May Be Moving On," *RTD*, November 19, 2008, B1; "Mississippi Considers Taking Statue of Jefferson Davis," *RTD*, February 7, 2009, A2.
105. "New Civil War Center Stresses Healing Process," *RTD*, October 5, 2006, B1; "Civil War Site: A Place of Hope," *RTD*, October 7, 2006, B3, clippings found in Lincoln Statue, File Cabinet 3, IoC Papers.
106. "Monumental Problem in Richmond," *RTD*, March 7, 2005, B1; "African American Monuments Catching on in Richmond," *RTD*, February 13, 2012.
107. Charles F. Bryan, President and CEO of the Virginia Historical Society, to Mr. and Mrs. Cowles, undated, Lincoln Statue, File Cabinet 3, IoC Papers; To Modify the Composition of the Slave Trail Commission and to Establish a Quorum for Meetings, Res. 2000-R111-109, July 24, 2000; To Support and Encourage the Placement and Dedication by the United States Historical Society of a Life-Size Bronze Statue of Abraham Lincoln Sitting on a Bench Beside His Son Tad, Res. 2003-04255, February 24, 2003; Res. 2007-R057-38; "Lincoln Statue Unveiled: Reaction Mixed among Residents," *RTD*, April 6, 2003, B1; Monument Avenue Commission Report, Prepared for the Office of the Mayor and City Council, City of Richmond, July 2, 2018, copy in the possession of the author.
108. Email from Cricket White to Rob Corcoran, November 9, 1999, Reconciliation Statue, File Cabinet 1, IoC Papers; "A Monument to Reconciliation," *RTD*, March 31, 2007, A1; "An Opportunity to Move Forward," *RTD*, June 24, 2007, E1; To Recognize the Historic Significance of the Richmond Slavery Reconciliation Statue Unveiling, March 12, 2007, Res. 2010-R171-180, Richmond City Hall.
109. "Monumental Problem in Richmond," *RTD*, March 7, 2005, B1; "Hill Statue Belongs on Monument," *RTD*, August 7, 2007, B1; "Statue a First for Virginia: Monument Will Bring Some Racial Parity to Capitol Square," *RTD*, July 19, 2008, A1; "Memorial Brings Needed Progress to Past Ignorance," *RTD*, July 22, 2008, B1.
110. To Support the Erection of a Statue Honoring Maggie L. Walker, Res. 2010-R171-180, November 22, 2010, Richmond City Hall; "The First Woman to Start a Bank—A Black Woman—Finally Gets Her Due in the Confederacy's Capital," *WP*, July 14, 2017.
111. "Statue a First for Virginia," *RTD*, July 19, 2008, A1; To Support the Erection of a Statue Honoring Maggie L. Walker, November 22, 2010, Richmond City Hall; "The First Woman to Start a Bank," *WP*, July 14, 2017.
112. Carrie Johnson, "Struggling to Tell All Sides Story," *RTD*, March 3, 2000, A1.

113. Althea Fung, "Juneteenth an 'Opportunity to Uncover History,'" *RTD*, June 20, 2010; and Zachary Reid, "Group Talks Strategy," *RTD*, October 10, 2010.
114. Quote found in K. Burnell Evans, "Group's Alternatives to Mayor's Shockoe Bottom Stadium Plan Take Shape," *RTD*, March 26, 2015; Ana Edwards and Phil Wilayto, "Governor's Proposal Misses Mark," *RTD*, December 15, 2020, 17A; Shockoe Alliance, Shockoe Small Area Plan: A Guide for Growth and Commemoration, July 19, 2021, 10, https://www.rva.gov/sites/default/files/2021-07/ShockoePlanDraft_210719_reduced.pdf.
115. K. Burnell Evans, "Group's Alternatives to Mayor's Plan Take Shape," *RTD*, March 26, 2015.
116. Michael Martz, "Coalition Takes States against Ballpark in Bottom," *RTD*, October 15, 2013.
117. A Community Proposal for Shockoe Bottom: Historic Place, Sacred Ground, Site of Consciousness, August 15, 2015, https://drive.google.com/file/d/0B7R6niR8W-yfQ1VtQVNsVmlTeTFueTMwTHZIZ3Nac3pzWTMo/view?resourcekey=0-FuhxAahfTBZ_8mhCQhU9qA; A Community Proposal for Shockoe Bottom Memorial Park, August 2017, https://drive.google.com/file/d/0ByGRw5JOG3LPOGV1MzRMS24zeXh3d1VGd2g4Rzdnck5tTohz/view?resourcekey=0-Ofv42aFFp32bAaVShbon2A; Edwards and Wilayto, "Governor's Proposal Misses Mark," *RTD*, December 15, 2020, 17A.
118. Shockoe Alliance, Shockoe Small Area Plan, July 19, 2021; C. Suarez Rojas, "City's Shockoe Bottom Plan Centers on Memorial Site," *RTD*, July 20, 2021, 1A.
119. "Monumental Problem in Richmond," *RTD*, March 7, 2005, B1.
120. "Richmond 300: A Guide for Growth: Designing an Equitable, Sustainable, and Beautiful Richmond for its 300th Birthday in 2037," September 29, 2020, 142, https://www.rva.gov/sites/default/files/2021-03/R300_AdoptedES_210226.pdf; Jason Richardson, Bruce Mitchell, and Juan Franco, "Shifting Neighborhoods: Gentrification and Cultural Displacement in American Cities," a report published by the National Community Reinvestment Coalition, March 2019; Shekinah Mitchell, "In Richmond, Virginia, Gentrification Is Colonization," report published by the National Community Reinvestment Coalition, March 18, 2019; "Oregon Hill Showing Kinder, Gentler Side Development, Gentrification Pushing Out Old Ways," *RTD*, January 16, 2005, B1; "Suburban Poverty and No Place to Go," *RTD*, December 20, 2009; "A Decade of Change for Region, but More Is Needed," *RTD*, December 31, 2009; "Life on Richmond's Boulevard Is Looking Up," *RTD*, April 18, 2010; "Public Square Explores Segregation in Richmond," *RTD*, April 24, 2015, 1A; "Church Hill Meeting an Open Door to Dialogue," *RTD*, April 15, 2016, 1B; "As Mosby Court Goes, So Goes City," *RTD*, April 11, 2017, 1B; "Gentrification Threatens RVA's Black History," *RTD*, June 17, 2018, 1E.

121. "Lee Monument Spray Painted with Graffiti," *RTD*, January 7, 2000, B3; "Debated Portrait of Lee Is Burned off Floodwall," *RTD*, January 18, 2000, A1; "Davis Monument Is Vandalized," *RTD*, April 9, 2002, B5; "Thousands Sound Off," *RTD*, March 24, 2003, B1; "Robert E. Monument Defaced," *RTD*, January 18, 2004, B4; "Unauthorized Plaques Placed on Monument Avenue Statues," *RTD*, December 17, 2011; "Lee Monument Vandalized," *RTD*, January 28, 2012; "Graffiti Shows Up on Stuart Monument," *RTD*, September 1, 2014; "Monument Avenue's Jefferson Davis Statue Is Vandalized, Creating a Stir," *RTD*, June 26, 2015, 1A; "Richmond Sculptor Gets Call to Repair City Statues," *RTD*, July 16, 2016, 1B; "Columbus Statue in Byrd Park Vandalized," *RTD*, October 14, 2015, 2b; "Pine Tar Splattered on Base of Statue of JEB Stuart on Monument Avenue," *RTD*, August 27, 2017, 2b; "'Racist' Painted on Base of Jefferson Davis Statue," *RTD*, October 18, 2017, 7B; "Statue Found Vandalized Twice in a Day: Richmond Spends $16,000 Cleaning Monuments in Last Two Years," *RTD*, October 19, 2017, 1B; "Robert E. Lee Statue on Monument Avenue Vandalized," *RTD*, August 5, 2018, 3A; "Richmond AP Hill Statue Vandalized," *RTD*, August 23, 2018, 3A.
122. "Poll Finds Richmond Region Optimistic about Race," *RTD*, June 20, 2010.
123. Author interview with Elizabeth O'Leary, May 17, 2019; "Rebel Flag Not a Sight to Show a Passer-by," *RTD*, September 27, 2013.
124. "In the Former Confederate Capital, There's No Longer a Museum of the Confederacy," *Virginia Mercury*, October 2, 2018; "A New Way to Tell the Civil War Narrative," *WP*, April 16, 2018, A1, A13; "Richmond's New Civil War Museum Aims to Shatter Conventional Views of Conflict," *WP*, April 26, 2019.
125. "Monumental Problem in Richmond," *RTD*, March 7, 2005, B1.
126. "Mall Crowd Rallies with Duke," *RTD*, April 2, 2000, A1.
127. "Confederate Flag-Waving Disserves the South," *New York Times*, February 13, 1997, A32; "Symbol of the Old South Divides the New South," *New York Times*, January 21, 1996, E5; "Time to Lower Rebel Flag, A Southern Governor Says," *New York Times*, November 27, 1996, A1.
128. "Maryland to Recall Flag License Plates," *New York Times*, January 3, 1997, A14; "Texas Removes Confederate Symbol from Court," *WP*, June 13, 2000, A21; "Suit Filed over Confederate Flag Display," *WP*, September 22, 2000, B3A; "Confederate Flag Pulled at Historic Sites in Mo.," *WP*, January 15, 2003, A3; "VA Beach May Stand to Gain," *RTD*, February 5, 2005, B5; "Court Upholds Ban on Confederate Flag," *New York Times*, August 20, 2000, 22; "Ga. State Flag Choice Raises Flap," *WP*, April 30, 2003, A3; "Signs of Confederacy Vanishing in the South," *New York Times*, December 25, 2004, A24; "The South Ain't Just Whistlin' Dixie," *New York Times*, September 18, 2011, SR14; "Supreme Court Upholds Texas Ban on License Plates with Confederate Flags," *New York Times*, June 19, 2015, A12; "NASCAR Racetracks Ask Fans to Put Away Confederate Flags," *New York Times*, July 3,

2015, B12; "Southern Bands, Progressive and Proud," *New York Times*, October 9, 2016, AR1.
129. "In Symbols of Old South, New Bitterness," *New York Times*, February 8, 1997, 1.
130. *Sons of Confederate Veterans v. City of Lexington* (2013); "Monumental Questions," *RTD*, January 9, 2014, B3.
131. "Crews Take Confederate Statue from Libby Hill," *RTD*, July 9, 2020, 1A.
132. Author interviews with Sylvester Turner, March 13, 2019; with Johnathan Zur, March 13, 2019; with Benjamin Campbell, March 14, 2019; with Reginald E. Gordon, June 27, 2019; Office of Community Wealth Building Flyer, undated; "Mayor Stoney: Richmond's Confederate Monuments Can Stay, but 'Whole Story' Must Be Told," *RTD*, June 22, 2017, A1; Monument Avenue Commission New Monuments working group meeting notes, August 2, 2017, Monument Avenue Commission Collection, City and County of Richmond Archives; "Confederate Monuments Are about Maintaining White Supremacy," Editorial, *WP*, July 27, 2017.
133. "Racist Monuments Need to Be Gone," *RTD*, June 14, 2020, 1D; "Va. Leads in Removing Confederate Symbols," *RTD*, September 5, 2020, 1A; Whose Heritage master sheet, data on Confederate Monuments collected by the Southern Poverty Law Center; and Monument Avenue Commission Report, July 2, 2018, Monument Avenue Commission Collection, City and County of Richmond Archives.
134. "Richmond's Civil War Monuments Need More Context," *RTD*, June 24, 2010.
135. "Apologies for Police Misconduct are Not Enough," *RTD*, June 3, 2020.
136. "'The Lost Cause Is Dead.' Let's Dismantle Its Legacy beyond the Symbols," *RTD*, June 3, 2020.

Epilogue

1. "The City of Richmond: Report to our Citizens, FY2017," http://www.rva.gov/sites/default/files/2019-04/2017%20Report%20to%20Our%20Citizens.pdf; Business Facilities' 2019 Metro Rankins Report, July–August 2019, https://businessfacilities.com/2019/07/business-facilities-2019-metro-rankings-report/; "Richmond's Concentrated Poverty Rate Is the Highest in Virginia," *Center Square*, September 25, 2019, https://www.thecentersquare.com/virginia/richmond-s-concentrated-poverty-rate-is-the-highest-in-virginia/article_0ecacfb0-dff4-11e9-960f-dbb0b1013f68.html.
2. "Stoney Defends Budget and Tax Plan," *RTD*, March 20, 2019, A1; "Proposal Addresses RVA's Historical Inequities," *RTD*, April 5, 2019, A9.
3. "Richmond Mayor Stoney Marches with Demonstrators after Apology," *WAVY*, June 2, 2020, https://www.wavy.com/news/virginia/richmond

/richmond-mayor-stoney-marches-with-demonstrators-after-apology-over-tear-gas-tuesday-afternoon/; "Protestors Demand Mayor Stoney's Resignation," *WTVR,* June 2, 2020, https://www.wtvr.com/news/local-news/protestors-demand-mayor-stoneys-resignation; "State Senator Joe Morrisey Calls for Levar Stoney to Resign," *WRVA Radio,* June 19, 2020, https://www.audacy.com/newsradiowrva/blogs/jeff-katz/va-state-sen-joe-morrissey-wants-levar-stoney-to-resign; "A Decade of Change for Region, but More Is Needed," *RTD,* December 31, 2009; "Q&A Mayor Levar Stoney," *RTD,* January 2, 2020, A1, A7; "Proposal Addresses RVA's Historical Inequities," *RTD,* April 5, 2019, A9.

4. "What Will 2021 Hold for Cities? With No Help Coming from the Federal Government, Can Richmond's Mayor Still Execute an Equity Agenda?" *Atlantic,* December 30, 2020; "Richmond Ends Budget Year with Surplus Despite Pandemic," *Virginia Public Media,* August 18, 2020; "Richmond Unrest Saw Nearly $4M in Fire Damage during Initial Unrest," *US News and World Report,* September 7, 2020.
5. "Richmond City Council Passes Adjusted FY2021 Budget," *WWBT,* May 11, 2020, https://www.nbc12.com/2020/05/11/richmond-city-council-passes-adjusted-fy-budget/.
6. "Richmond 300: A Guide for Growth," 82.
7. "A Decade of Change for Region, but More Is Needed," *RTD,* December 31, 2009; "In Richmond, Old-Fashioned Charm and Newfound Aplomb," *WP,* March 6, 2016, EZ.
8. "Poverty in Richmond: How Long Must We Wait?," *RTD,* July 1, 2012.
9. "Richmond 300: A Guide for Growth."
10. John V. Moeser et al., "Unpacking the Census: 2017 Updates—Master Copy," Poverty in Metropolitan Richmond, Bonner Center for Civic Engagement, 2019, https://scholarship.richmond.edu/cgi/viewcontent.cgi?article=1038&context=poverty.
11. Industries by Neighborhood in Richmond, Statistical Atlas, https://statisticalatlas.com/place/Virginia/Richmond/Industries.
12. "Richmond Lands 7 Fortune 500 Companies," *Bizsense,* May 17, 2019, https://richmondbizsense.com/2019/05/17/richmond-lands-7-fortune-500-list/; "35 Virginia Companies Make 2020 Fortune 1000 List," *Virginia Business,* May 18, 2020. The Fortune 1000 companies are Altria, CarMax, Performance Food Group, Dominion Energy, Owens & Minor, and Genworth Financial. City of Richmond, Greater Richmond Partnership, https://www.grpva.com; Capital Improvement Plan for Richmond, Virginia, FY 2020–24, 2, http://www.richmondgov.com/budget/documents/CapitalImprovementPlans/2020-2024_AdoptedCapitolImprovementPlan.pdf; Quick Facts for Richmond, Virginia, 2019, US Census Bureau, https://www.census.gov/quickfacts/fact/table/richmondcityvirginia,VA/PST045219.

13. Moeser, "Unpacking the Census: 2017 Updates."
14. Julie M. Weise, *Corazon de Dixie: Mexicanos in the US South Since 1910* (Chapel Hill: University of North Carolina Press, 2015); Katherine Schaeffer, "In a Rising Number of U.S. Counties, Hispanic and Black Americans Are the Majority," Pew Research Center, November 20, 2019; H. B. Cavalcanti and Debra Schaleef, "The Case for Secular Assimilation? The Latino Experience in Richmond, Virginia," *Journal for the Scientific Study of Religion* 44, no.4 (December 2005): 473–83; "Richmond's Population Expected to Become One-Third Hispanic, Top 250,000 by 2040," *Church Hill People's News*, July 3, 2017, https://chpn.net/2017/07/03/richmond-population-expected-to-become-13-hispanic-top-250000-by-2040/; Laura Goren and Michael Cassidy, "A Closer Look: The Contribution of Hispanic and Latino Immigrants to Virginia's Economy," *Commonwealth Institute*, June 2015, 1–4; Debra J. Schleef and H. B. Cavalcanti, *Latinos in Dixie: Class and Assimilation in Richmond, Virginia* (Albany, NY: State University of New York Press, 2009).
15. "Richmond's Poor: Why are 77% Women and Children 1984," Box 14, M258, RUI Papers, VCU.
16. Ibid.
17. Office of Community Wealth Building flyer, undated; Office of Community Wealth Building brochure, undated; and Annual Report 2018 from the Office of Community Wealth Building to the Mayor of the City of Richmond, March 2019, 1–32, copy in the possession of author; Steve Dubb and Alex Rudzinski, "Richmond, Virginia, Social Enterprise Feasibility Enterprise Analysis: Reducing Poverty and Building Community Wealth Through Social Enterprise," Final Report Submitted to the City of Richmond, June 2016, https://www.rva.gov/sites/default/files/2019-10/SocialEnterprise_6-16.pdf; author interview with Reginald Gordon, June 27, 2019.
18. Stoney Administration to Launch Richmond Resilience Initiative, Guaranteed Income Pilot Program, press release by the Office of Mayor of the City of Richmond, October 29, 2020.
19. Marjorie Kelly and Sarah McKinley, "Cities Building Community Wealth," *Democratic Collaborative*, November 2015, 66, https://democracycollaborative.org/sites/default/files/downloads/CitiesBuildingCommunityWealth-Web.pdf; Lawrence T. Brown, *The Black Butterfly: The Harmful Politics of Race and Space in America* (Baltimore: Johns Hopkins University Press, 2021).
20. Julian Maxwell Hayter, "City Profile of Richmond, Virginia," *Thriving Cities*, University of Virginia Institute for Advanced Studies in Culture, 2015, https://static1.squarespace.com/static/5a0f45fad74cff16c9f6e45e/t/5b4fab87f950b72639899c00/1531947915667/City-Profile-Richmond.pdf; "Richmond Casino Race," *WRIC*, February 23, 2021; Economic Impact of Casinos on Home Prices Literature Survey and Issue Analysis,

NAR Research, July 2014, https://stoppredatorygambling.org/wp-content/uploads/2014/07/2013-Realtor-study-NAR-Casino-Research.pdf; Alan Mallach, "Economic and Social Impact of Introducing Casino Gambling: A Review and Assessment of the Literature," Federal Reserve Bank of Philadelphia, March 2010, 15–23.

21. Erika C. Poethig et al., "Inclusive Recovery in US Cities," *Urban Institute,* April 25, 2018, https://www.urban.org/sites/default/files/publication/97981/inclusive_recovery_in_us_cities_0.pdf.
22. "Protests Turn Focus to Gentrification, Evictions," *RTD,* June 12, 2020, A6.
23. "Richmond to Create Va's First Eviction Diversion Program," *RTD,* February 1, 2019, A1.
24. "Proposal Addresses RVA's Historical Inequities," *RTD,* April 5, 2019, A9.
25. "Hundreds March in Carytown Demanding Racial Equality," *CBS News 6,* June 11, 2020.
26. *Hope VI Program Authority and Funding,* published by the US Department of Housing and Urban Development, March 2007, https://www.hud.gov/sites/documents/DOC_9838.PDF; Lallen T. Johnson-Hart, "Residential Outcomes of HOPE VI Relocates in Richmond, VA" (MA thesis, VCU, Richmond, May 2007).
27. Richmond Master Plan, 2000–2020, Department of Community Development, January 8, 2001, 20–96.
28. Thad Williamson and Amy L. Howard, "Reframing Public Housing in Richmond, Virginia: Resident, Resistance, and the Future of Redevelopment," *Cities: The International Journal of Urban Policy* 55, no. 1 (December 2016): 33–39, https://static1.squarespace.com/static/5ab4249136099bed55e0f45f/t/5b92b053352f537f39ed1f60/1536340051747/Refrming+Public+Housig.pdf; "Blackwell: Neighborhoods in Bloom Retrospective," Federal Reserve Bank of Richmond, Community Development, 2017, https://www.richmondfed.ws/-/media/richmondfedorg/publications/community_development/neighborhoods_in_bloom/2017/nib_blackwell.pdf.
29. "Exploring the Health Implication of Mixed-Income Communities," Center for the Study of Social Policy, January 2019, https://cssp.org/wp-content/uploads/2019/03/MISA-East-End-Church-Hill-North-Richmond.pdf; "Steve Markel Says Church Hill Project, Which Includes Grocery Store, 'Is Truly A Philanthropic Operation,'" *RTD,* May 21, 2019; "Project Snapshot: Church Hill North Rising," *Richmond Bizsense,* February 26, 2020; "RRHA Board Approves Demolition of Creighton Court," *WWBT,* January 16, 2020; "Richmond Residents Move into New Affordable Housing," *Richmond 6 News,* October 27, 2020; "Private Home at 20th and R Included Income Qualified Home," *Church Hill People's News,* November 2, 2020.
30. Richardson, Mitchell, and Franco, "Shifting Neighborhoods: Gentrification and Cultural Displacement in American Cities"; Mitchell, "In Richmond,

Virginia, Gentrification is Colonization"; Lea Whitehurst-Gibson and Bruce Mitchell, "Gentrification: A Mixed Bag in Historic Richmond, Virginia, Neighborhood," an essay from the NCRC's Gentrification and Cultural Displacement, April 9, 2019.

31. Kathryn Howell, "Eviction and Rental Housing Market," RVA Evictions Lab, https://rampages.us/rvaevictionlab/.
32. Proposed Capital Fund Program: Five Year Action Plan for Fiscal Years 2020–2024, Richmond Redevelopment & Housing Authority, August 2020, https://www.rrha.com/wp-content/uploads/2020/08/Proposed-CFP_Five-Year-Action-Plan-2020_24.pdf; "Creighton Court Plan Raises Questions about Richmond's Housing Project," *VADogwood*, April 19, 2021, https://vadogwood.com/2021/04/18/creighton-court-plans-raise-questions-about-richmonds-housing-projects/.
33. Whitehurst-Gibson and Mitchell, "Gentrification."
34. "Gentrification: Greater Fulton is Changing," Newsletter for the Greater Fulton Civic Association 33, no. 2 (Fall 2018): 201, http://www.nrccafe.org/wp-content/uploads/2018/10/FULTONNewsletter-106969.pdf.
35. "Gentrification: The 'Negro Removal Program' Is Displacing Black People, Culture," *Richmond Free Press*, December 28, 2018.
36. "There Goes the Hood," *Style Weekly*, April 11, 2007.
37. "Richmond Makes Changes to Tax Program, Pushes for More Affordable Housing," *WWBT*, January 30, 2020.
38. "Richmond 300: A Guide for Growth," 135, 181.
39. "Where Will We Live When the Entire City's Been Gentrified?" *RVAMag*, July 31, 2018; "Community Advocates Discuss Race, Gentrification," *APNews*, February 11, 2019.
40. Richmond Land Bank Annual Plan, Maggie Walker Community Land Trust, July 2018–June 2019, https://www.richmondlandbank.com/_files/ugd/19392a_68b56cd1b6ca42c9864867fcbf92aaf2.pdf; "Richmond to Create Va's First Eviction Diversion Program," *RTD*, February 1, 2019, A1.
41. Top Evicting Large Cities in the United States, 2000–2016, Princeton University Eviction Lab Database, https://evictionlab.org/rankings//evictions?r=United%20States&a=0&d=evictionRate&l=6.
42. Woody Rogers and Leah Demarest, "Comparative Law and Policy Analysis for Addressing Evictions in Richmond, Virginia," RVA Evictions Lab, L. Douglas Wilder School of Government at Virginia Commonwealth University, October 2019; Howell, "Eviction and Rental Housing Market," RVA Eviction Lab, undated; Benjamin F. Teresa, "The Geography of Eviction in Richmond: Beyond Poverty," RVA Eviction Lab, undated; and Woody Rogers, "The Connections between Evictions and Foreclosures in Richmond," RVA Eviction Lab, May 2019.
43. "Northam, Bogged Down by Blackface Scandal, Seeks to Link Affordable Housing Efforts to Racial Equity," *Washington Business Journal*, June 5,

2019; "Richmond Residents, Activists Question Stoney's Second Term Promises," *VADogwood,* January 13, 2021; and "Mayor Stoney Asks for Feedback on Draft Equity Agenda," *WWBT,* February 23, 2021.
44. Richardson, Mitchell, and Franco, "Shifting Neighborhoods"; Mitchell, "In Richmond, Virginia, Gentrification Is Colonization"; Whitehurst-Gibson and Bruce Mitchell, "Gentrification."
45. "Richmond 300: A Guide for Growth."
46. "Homes for Sale in Richmond Are Hard to Find—Here's Why," *Richmond Bizsense,* March 22, 2021, https://richmondbizsense.com/2021/03/22/homes-for-sale-in-richmond-are-hard-to-find-because-theyre-selling-faster/.
47. "How Some Cities Are Planning to Revive Neighborhoods without Displacement," *WP,* August 29, 2019; "The Bedrock of Wealth Inequality," *Virginia Mercury,* July 21, 2020; "Rent-to-Own Program Offers Bridge for Area Families," *RTD,* November 26, 2020 A6; Affordable Housing Trust Fund, Year End Report for Richmond, Virginia, December 2020; "Richmond 300: A Guide for Growth"; Richmond Equity Agenda, City of Richmond, Virginia's Mayor's Office, February 2021, https://www.rva.gov/rvaequity.
48. "How Can We Best Meet RVA's Needs," *RTD,* April 7, 2019, E1.
49. "Richmond 300: A Guide for Growth," 90.
50. Richmond Master Plan, 2000–2020, Department of Community Development, January 8, 2001.
51. Kathryn Howell, "Eviction and Educational Instability in Richmond, Virginia," RVA Eviction Lab, https://rampages.us/rvaevictionlab/.
52. Chiles, "Tough on Conduct," 55–85.
53. "'Clustering' of White Students Divides Richmond Again," *WP,* December 4, 1992, D1.
54. "Officials Work to End Migration of Kids Born in City to Other Districts," *RTD,* March 11, 2018, 1A.
55. "Richmond Schools Must Break Cycle of Segregation," *RTD,* August 28, 2019, 13A; Genevieve Siegel-Hawley et al., "School Segregation by Boundary Line in Virginia: Scope, Significance, and State Policy Solutions," Center for Education and Civil Rights, VCU, November 2020, 7–10, https://scholarscompass.vcu.edu/cgi/viewcontent.cgi?article=1013&context=edlp_pubs.
56. "Nearing the 90th Anniversary of Thomas Jefferson High School, Parents Still Search for Solutions to Basic Problems," *Style Weekly,* February 26, 2019.
57. Moeser, "Children under 18 Living in Poverty, 2000–2015," Poverty in Metropolitan Richmond, Bonner Center of Civic Engagement, 2017, https://scholarship.richmond.edu/cgi/viewcontent.cgi?article=1028&context=poverty.
58. Richmond Public Schools Approved Budget, FY2019–2020, https://www.rvaschools.net/operating-office/budget.

59. "On the Road to Glory," Richmond Public Schools Newsletter, 2015; Chris Duncombe and Michael Cassidy, "Mapping Opportunity: Examining the K–12 Policy Landscape in Greater Richmond," Commonwealth Institute, April 2017, 1–15, https://thecommonwealthinstitute.org.
60. Genevieve Seigel Hawley, "Mitigating Milliken? School District Boundary Lines and Desegregation Policy in Four Southern Metropolitans Areas, 1990–2010," *American Journal of Education* 120, no. 3 (May 2014), 391–433; Enrollment Figures from Richmond City Public School State Report Card, February 2021, https://schoolquality.virginia.gov/divisions/richmond-city-public-schoolsdesktopTabs-3.
61. "Va. Education Disparities—Report," *RTD*, October 31, 2017, 2B; Duncombe and Cassidy, "Mapping Opportunity," 1–15; "One in Three Richmond Seniors Missed Too Many Classes—They'll Still Graduate," *RTD*, May 1, 2018.
62. Superintendent Jason Kamas Statement on VDOE Report Regarding SOL Testing at Carver Elementary School, Richmond City Public Schools, undated memo; Report on George Washington Carver Elementary School Spring 2018 Standards of Learning Test Investigation, conducted by the Virginia Department of Education, July 30, 2018, https://www.wric.com/wp-content/uploads/sites/74/2018/07/G.W.20Carver20SOLs20report_1532983461807_50163797_ver1.0.pdf.
63. "Richmond Systemic Confusion over Money Is Unacceptable," *RTD*, March 30, 2019, A12.
64. Duncombe and Cassidy, "Mapping Opportunity," 1–15; "How Can We Best Meet RVA's Needs," *RTD*, April 7, 2019, E1; "RPS Superintendent Talks Poverty Rates, Ways to Improve after SOL Scores Released," *WRIC*, August 13, 2019; "Richmond Public Schools Approve Budget, FY2019–2020; Richmond City Council Passes Adjusted FY2021 Budget," *WWBT*, May 11, 2020, https://www.nbc12.com/2020/05/11/richmond-city-council-passes-adjusted-fy-budget/.
65. "Richmond Schools Wrestle with Low Graduation Rates," *RVAMag*, May 24, 2019; Duncombe and Cassidy, "Mapping Opportunity," 1–15.
66. Author interviews with Benjamin Campbell, May 14, 2019; with Patrick Graham, July 9, 2019; Andreas D. Addison, City Councilman for the City of Richmond, "Improving Richmond Public Schools," *Medium*, July 27, 2018.
67. Nicole Simon and Susan Moore Johnson, "Teacher Turnover in High-Poverty Schools: What We Know and Can Do," *Teachers College Record* 117, no. 3 (2015): 1–36.
68. Phoebe M. Brannock, "Ready, Set, Teach: Reducing Teacher Turnover in Richmond," *College of William and Mary News & Media*, June 5, 2018, https://www.wm.edu/news/stories/2018/ready,-set,-teach-reducing-teacher-turnover-in-richmond.php; Annual Report on the Condition and Needs of Public Schools in Virginia, 2018, presented to the Governor of

Virginia and General Assembly by the Virginia Board on Education, December 1, 2018; Instructional Personnel Turnover Rate by Virginia Public School Division, Annual Instructional Personnel Data Collection, Virginia Department of Education, March 12, 2020, https://www.doe.virginia.gov/teaching-learning-assessment/teaching-in-virginia/education-workforce-data-reports.

69. "Richmond Public Schools Must Provide Turnover Data," *RTD,* June 24, 2020, 4.
70. "Mice, Mold, Decrepitude," *WP,* May 26, 2019, C1, C6; Richmond Master Plan, 2000–2020, Department of Community Development, January 8, 2001; "Unequal Opportunities: Fewer Resources, Worse Outcomes for Students with Concentrated Poverty," Commonwealth Institute, December 11, 2017; Teacher Retention Study, Metropolitan Educational Research Consortium, VCU School of Education, May 20, 2020, https://drive.google.com/file/d/14SYGHlxhqapIgLCa3N3hqPPiFoztTRfH/view.
71. "Richmond Officials Want School Facilities Upgrades," *RTD,* February 7, 2018, 1A; "RPS School Construction Costs, Process Criticized," *Richmond Free Press,* November 8, 2019, http://richmondfreepress.com/news/2019/nov/08/rps-school-construction-costs-process-criticized/.
72. "George Wythe High Selected as Next School Construction Site," *WTVR,* October 22, 2020, https://www.wtvr.com/news/local-news/richmond/george-wythe-high-school-selected-as-next-school-construction-project.
73. "Richmond Public School Board Votes to Stay Virtual for Second Semester," *WRIC,* December 8, 2020.
74. "Local Private School Enrollment Spikes as Parents Avoid Virtual-Only Classes," *Richmond Bizsense,* September 4, 2020, https://richmondbizsense.com/2020/09/04/local-private-school-enrollment-spikes-as-parents-avoid-virtual-only-classes/.
75. "Remove Real Artifacts of the Confederacy," *RTD,* August 27, 2017, 6E; "Richmond Won't Keep Growing Unless Its Schools Improve," *RTD,* March 6, 2019, 9A; "Richmond Public Schools Needs More Than Money," *RTD,* April 24, 2019, 9A.
76. Benjamin Campbell, Opinion Editorial, "The Sickness of Our Heart," *Style Weekly,* June 8, 1993, clipping found in the HIC Press Book, File Cabinet 1, IoC Papers.

BIBLIOGRAPHY

AUTHOR INTERVIEWS

Baskerville, Viola, June 28, 2019
Campbell, Rev. Benjamin, March 12, 2019
Chargois, Dr. Paige, May 17, 2019
Chewning, Tom, May 10, 2019
Coleman, Christy, June 25, 2019
Corcoran, Rob, March 11, 2019
Corcoran, Susan, May 7, 2019
Dennis, Dr. Rutledge, July 26, 2019
Drumheller, Terry, July 23, 2019
Gordon, Reginald, June 27, 2019
Graham, Dr. Patrick, July 2, 2019
Holton, Abner Linwood III, September 29, 2020
Martin, William (Bill) J., July 23, 2019
Mason, William, July 22, 2019
Moeser, Dr. John, March 11, 2019
O'Leary, Dr. Elizabeth L., June 26, 2019
Peeples, Dr. Edward, June 24, 2019
Rennie, Wayland, July 17, 2015
Turner, Rev. Sylvester, March 13, 2019
Zur, Jonathan, March 13, 2019

ARCHIVAL COLLECTIONS

City and County of Richmond

Monument Avenue Commission Collection
Richmond City Council Minutes
Richmond School Board Minutes

Duke University Libraries, Archives and Manuscripts

Gordon Blaine Hancock Papers

Initiatives of Change Papers, Richmond

Hope in the Cities Papers

Library of Congress

NAACP Papers

University of Georgia
Walter J. Brown Media Archives and Peabody Awards Collection

University of Richmond, Special Collections, School of Law
Judge Robert Merhige Collection

University of Virginia, Albert and Shirley Small Special Collections Library
Explorations in Black Leadership Project Papers

Valentine Museum, Richmond
Project One Collection
Sixth Street Marketplace Collection

Virginia Commonwealth University, Special Collections Library, Richmond
Andrew Brent Papers
Clarence L. Townes Jr. Papers
Collie Burton Papers
Crusade for Voters Papers
Downtown Development Unlimited Collection
Eleanor P. Sheppard Papers
George Stephenson Kemp Papers
Henry I. Willett Papers
Horace H. Edward Papers
Howard Carwile Papers
John Mitchell Brooks Papers
L. Douglas Wilder Papers
Mary Tyler Cheek McClenahan Papers
Richmond Annexation Files
Richmond Incorporation Papers
Richmond Renaissance Inc. Papers
Richmond Urban Institute Papers
Willie Dell Papers
Virginia Crockford Papers, James Branch Cabell Library

Virginia Museum of History and Culture, Richmond, Museum Collections Catalogue
James C. Wheat Jr. Papers, 1922–92
James A. Sartain Papers

Virginia Union University
L. Douglas Wilder Library and Learning Resource Center
Virginia Union Alumni Bulletins

Newspapers and Magazines

Activist History Review
Atlanta Journal and Constitution
Atlantic
Baltimore Afro-American
Baltimore
Boston Globe
Business Facilities
Call and Post
Chesterfield Observer
Chicago Daily Defender
Christian Science Monitor
Church Hill People's News
City Square
Ebony magazine
Jet magazine
Los Angeles Sentinel
Michigan Chronicle
Norfolk Guide and Journal
New York Times
Norfolk-Virginia Pilot
Philadelphia Tribune
Pittsburg Courier
Smithsonian magazine
Richmond Bizsense
Richmond Dispatch
Richmond Free Press
RichmondMag
Richmond Planet/Afro American
Richmond Times-Dispatch
Richmond News-Leader
Richmond Surroundings, New City magazine
RVA News
Style Weekly
US News & World Report
VADogwood
Virginia Business
Wall Street Journal

Washington Business Journal
Washington Post
William and Mary News Media

PRIMARY SOURCE DOCUMENTS AND PUBLIC REPORTS

"Blackwell: Neighborhoods in Bloom Retrospective." Federal Reserve Bank of Richmond, Community Development, 2017. Accessed February 23, 2023 https://www.richmondfed.ws/-/media/richmondfedorg/publications/community_development/neighborhoods_in_bloom/2017/nib_blackwell.pdf.
"City of Richmond: Report to our Citizens: FY 2017." http://www.rva.gov/sites/default/files/2019-04/2017%20Report%20to%20Our%20Citizens.pdf.
Corona, Rosalie, Tanya Gonzalez, Robert Cohen, Charlene Edwards, and Torey Edmonds. "Richmond Latino Needs Assessment: Health and Safety Needs of Latino Children and Families Living in Richmond, Virginia." Report prepared for the City Council of Richmond, Virginia, December 2006.
Dubb, Steve, and Alex Rudzinski. "Richmond, Virginia: Social Enterprise Feasibility Enterprise Analysis: Reducing Poverty and Building Community Wealth through Social Enterprise." Final Report Submitted to the City of Richmond, June 2016. https://www.rva.gov/sites/default/files/2019-10/SocialEnterprise_6-16.pdf.
Duncombe, Chris, and Michael Cassidy. "Mapping Opportunity: Examining the K–12 Policy Landscape in Greater Richmond." Commonwealth Institute, April 2017, 1–15. https://thecommonwealthinstitute.org.
"Economic Impact of Casinos on Home Prices Literature Survey and Issue Analysis." NAR Research, July 2014. https://stoppredatorygambling.org/wp-content/uploads/2014/07/2013-Realtor-study-NAR-Casino-Research.pdf.
"Exploring the Health Implication of Mixed-Income Communities." Center for the Study of Social Policy, January 2019. https://cssp.org/wp-content/uploads/2019/03/MISA-East-End-Church-Hill-North-Richmond.pdf.
Greater Fulton Civic Association. "Gentrification: Greater Fulton Is Changing." *Community Newsletter* 33,2 (Fall 2018): 201. http://www.nrccafe.org/wp-content/uploads/2018/10/FULTONNewsletter-106969.pdf.
Hayter, Julian Maxwell. "City Profile of Richmond." *Thriving Cities*. University of Virginia Institute for Advanced Studies in Culture, 2015. https://static1.squarespace.com/static/5a0f45fad74cff16c9f6e45e/t/5b4fab87f950b72639899c00/1531947915667/City-Profile-Richmond.pdf.
"Hope VI Program Authority and Funding." US Department of Housing and Urban Development, March 2007. https://www.hud.gov/sites/documents/DOC_9838.PDF.
Howell, Katherine. "Eviction and Rental Housing Market." RVA Eviction Lab, L. Douglas Wilder School of Government, Virginia Commonwealth University, undated. https://rampages.us/rvaevictionlab/.

"Industries by Neighborhood in Richmond." Statistical Atlas.com. Accessed February 21, 2023. https://statisticalatlas.com/place/Virginia/Richmond/Industries.

Johnson, Lyndon B. Annual Message to the Congress on the State of the Union, January 8, 1964. http://www.lbjlibrary.net/collections/selected-speeches/november-1963-1964/01-08-1964.html.

Kelly, Marjorie, and Sarah McKinley. "Cities Building Community Wealth." *Democratic Collaborative,* November 2015. https://democracycollaborative.org/sites/default/files/downloads/CitiesBuildingCommunityWealth-Web.pdf.

Mallach, Alan. "Economic and Social Impact of Introducing Casino Gambling: A Review and Assessment of the Literature." Federal Reserve Bank of Philadelphia, Community Affairs Discussion Paper,10–01, 2010. https://www.researchgate.net/publication/46451697_Economic_and_social_impact_of_introducing_casino_gambling_a_review_and_assessment_of_the_literature.

Metropolitan Educational Research Consortium and VCU School of Education. Teacher Retention Study, May 20, 2020. https://drive.google.com/file/d/14SYGHlxhqapIgLCa3N3hqPPiFoztTRfH/view.

Mitchell, Shekinah. "In Richmond, Virginia, Gentrification Is Colonization." National Community Reinvestment Coalition, March 18, 2019. https://ncrc.org/gentrification-richmondva/.

Moeser, John V., Nina Mauney, Evelyn Jeong, and Emily Routman. "Unpacking the Census: 2017 Updates—Master Copy, Poverty in Metropolitan Richmond." Bonner Center for Civic Engagement, University of Richmond, 2019. https://scholarship.richmond.edu/cgi/viewcontent.cgi?article=1038&context=poverty.

Nelson, Robert. "University of Richmond Digital Scholarship Lab Unveils New Mapping Project Focusing on Urban Renewal, Family Displacements, and Race." University of Richmond Newsroom, 2017. https://news.richmond.edu/releases/article/-/14939/university-of-richmond-digital-scholarship-lab-unveils-new-mapping-project-focusing-on-urban-renewal-family-displacements-and-race.html.

Poethig Erika C., Solomon Greene, Christina Plerhoples Stacy, Tanaya Srini, and Brady Meixell. "Inclusive Recovery in US Cities." Urban Institute, April 25, 2018. https://www.urban.org/sites/default/files/publication/97981/inclusive_recovery_in_us_cities_0.pdf.

"Proposed Capital Fund Program: Five-Year Action Plan for Fiscal Years 2020–2024." Richmond Redevelopment & Housing Authority, August 2020. https://www.rrha.com/wp-content/uploads/2020/08/Proposed-CFP_Five-Year-Action-Plan-2020_24.pdf.

"Proposed FY 20–FY24 Capital Improvement Plan." http://www.richmondgov.com/budget/documents/CapitalImprovementPlans/2020-2024_Adopted CapitolImprovementPlan.pdf.

Richardson, Jason, Bruce Mitchell, and Juan Franco. "Shifting Neighborhoods: Gentrification and Cultural Displacement in American Cities." National Community Reinvestment Coalition, March 2019. https://ncrc.org/gentrification/.

"Richmond 300: A Guide for Growth." Master Plan, City of Richmond, September 29, 2020. https://www.rva.gov/sites/default/files/2021-03/R300_Adopted_210331_0.pdf.

Schaeffer, Katherine. "In a Rising Number of U.S. Counties, Hispanic and Black Americans Are the Majority." Pew Research Center, November 20, 2019. https://www.pewresearch.org/fact-tank/2019/11/20/in-a-rising-number-of-u-s-counties-hispanic-and-black-americans-are-the-majority/.

Siegel-Hawley, Genevieve, et al. "School Segregation by Boundary Line in Virginia: Scope, Significance and State Policy Solutions." Center for Education and Civil Rights, November 2020. https://scholarscompass.vcu.edu/cgi/viewcontent.cgi?article=1013&context=edlp_pubs.

"Unequal Opportunities: Fewer Resources, Worse Outcomes for Students with Concentrated Poverty." Commonwealth Institute, December 11, 2017.

Uniform Crime Reporting Statistics, U.S. Department of Justice Online Database. https://www.bjs.gov/ucrdata/Search/Crime/Local/RunCrimeTrendsInOneVar.cfm.

US Census Bureau. Quick Facts for Richmond, Virginia, 2019. https://www.census.gov/quickfacts/fact/table/richmondcityvirginia,VA/PST045219.

"Virginia State Capitol and Capitol Square." Virginia Capitol.gov. Accessed February 21, 2023. https://virginiacapitol.gov/wp-content/uploads/2016/04/English-both-sides.pdf.

Secondary Sources

Alexander, Ann Field. *Race Man: The Rise and Fall of the "Fighting Editor," John Mitchell, Jr.* Charlottesville: University of Virginia Press, 2002.

Alexander, Michele. *The New Jim Crow: Mass Incarceration in the Era of Colorblindness.* New York: New Press, 2010.

Anderson, Alan, and George W. Pickering. *Confronting the Color Line: The Broken Promises of the Civil Rights Movement in Chicago.* Athens: University of Georgia Press, 2008.

Arkin, Daniel J. "Regime Politics Surrounding Desegregation Decision-Making during Massive Resistance in Richmond, Virginia." PhD diss., Virginia Commonwealth University, 1991.

Arsenault, Raymond. *Arthur Ashe: A Life.* New York: Simon & Shuster, 2018.

Ashe, Arthur, and Arnold Rampersad. *Days of Grace: A Memoir.* New York: Knopf, 1993.

Austin, D. Andrew. "Politics vs Economics: Evidence from Municipal Annexation." *Journal of Urban Economics* 45, no. 3 (May 1999): 501–32.

Avery, Myrta Lockett. *Dixie after the War: Social Conditions in the South during Reconstruction*. New York: Doubleday, 1906.
Ayers, Edward L. *The Promise of the New South: Life After Reconstruction*. 15th Anniversary Edition. Oxford: Oxford University Press, 2007.
Bacigal, Ron. *May It Please the Court: A Biography of Judge Robert R. Merhige, Jr.* Lanham, MD: University Press of America, 1992.
Bailey, Martha J., and Nicolas J. Duquette. "How Johnson Fought the War on Poverty: The Economic and Politics of Funding at the Office of Economic Opportunity." *Journal of Economic History* 74, no. 2 (June 2014): 351–88.
Bain, Chester W. *A Body Incorporate: The Evolution of City-County Separation in Virginia*. Charlottesville: University of Virginia Press, 1967.
Barbee, Matthew Mace. *Race and Masculinity in Southern Memory: A History of Richmond, Virginia's Monument Avenue*. Lanham, MD: Lexington Books, 2014.
Bauman, Robert. *Race and War on Poverty from Watts to East L.A.* Norman: University of Oklahoma Press, 2008.
Bayor, Ronald. *Race and the Shaping of Twentieth-Century Atlanta*. Chapel Hill: University of North Carolina Press, 1996.
Beck, Susan Abrams. "The Limits of Presidential Activism: Lyndon Johnson and the Implementation of the Community Action Program." *Presidential Studies Quarterly* 17, no. 3 (Summer 1987): 541–57.
Benson, T. B. "Segregation Ordinances." *Virginia Law Register,* New Series, 1, no. 5 (September 1915): 330–56.
Berlin, Ira. *Slaves without Masters: The Free Negro in the Antebellum South*. New York: New Press, 1974.
"Black-White Scoring Gap Widens on the SAT II Test." *Journal of Blacks in Higher Education* 27 (Spring 2000): 41–43.
Bloom, Joshua, and Waldo E. Martin Jr. *Black against Empire: The History and Politics of the Black Panther Party*. Berkeley: University of California Press, 2016.
Bloom, Nicholas Dragen. *Suburban Alchemy: 1960s New Towns and the Transformation of the American Dream*. Columbus: Ohio State University Press, 2001.
Bonilla-Silla, Eduardo. *Racism without Racists: Color-Blind Racism and the Persistence of Racial Inequality in Contemporary America*. Lanham, MD: Rowman & Littlefield, 2003.
Bowen, Dawn S. "The Transformation of Richmond's Historic African American Commercial Corridor." *Southeastern Geographer* 43, no. 2 (November 2003): 260–78.
Brooks, Clayton McClure. *The Uplift Generation: Corporation across the Color Line in Early Twentieth-Century Virginia*. Charlottesville: University of Virginia Press, 2017.
Brown-Nagin, Tomiko. *Courage to Dissent: Atlanta and the Long Civil Rights Movement*. New York: Oxford University Press, 2011.

Brown, Elsa Barkley, and Gregg D. Kimball. "Mapping the Terrain of Black Richmond." *Journal of Urban History* 21, no. 3 (March 1995): 309–12.
Brown, Jeffrey R., and Gregory L. Thompson. "The Relationship between Transit Ridership and Urban Decentralization: Insights from Atlanta." *Urban Studies* 45, nos. 5/6. (May 2008): 1119–39.
Brown, Kathleen. "Tourism Trends for the 90s." *History News* 48, no. 3 (May–June 1993): 4–7.
Brown, Lawrence T. *The Black Butterfly: The Harmful Politics of Race and Space in America*. Baltimore: Johns Hopkins University Press, 2021.
Brown, Leslie. *Upbuilding Black Durham: Gender, Class, and Black Community in the Jim Crow South*. Chapel Hill: University of North Carolina Press, 2008.
Bruce, Philip Alexander, et al. *History of Virginia*. 6 vols. Chicago: American Historical Society, 1924.
Bruce, Mildred Davis. "The Richmond School Board and the Desegregation of Richmond Public Schools." PhD diss., College of William and Mary, 1988.
Brundage, W. Fitzhugh. *The Southern Past: A Clash of Race and Memory*. Cambridge, MA: Harvard University Press, 2005.
Buni, Andrew. *The Negro in Virginia Politics, 1902–67*. Charlottesville: University of Virginia Press, 1967.
Byrd, Odell R. *Richmond: A City of Monuments and Statues*. Richmond, VA: Tambuzi, 1989.
Cabell, James Branch. *Let Me Lie: Being in the Main an Ethnological Account of the Remarkable Commonwealth of Virginia and the Making of Its History*. New York: Farrar, Straus, 1947.
Cable, George Washington. *The Negro Question*. New York: Charles Scribner's Sons, 1898.
———. *The Silent South: Together with the Freedman's Case in Equity and the Convict Lease System*. New York: Charles Scribner's Sons, 1899.
Calihan, Shirley L. *A Mini History of the Richmond Public Schools, 1869–1992*. [Richmond, VA?]: [Unknown], 1992. [Found at the Richmond City Public Schools office in city hall.]
Carcasson, Martín, and Mitchell F. Rice. "The Promise and Failure of President Clinton's Race Initiative of 1997–1998: A Rhetorical Perspective." *Rhetoric and Public Affairs* 2, no. 2, Special Issue on Civil Rights in the Postmodern Era (Summer 1999): 243–74.
Carey, Hampton D. "New Voices in the Old Dominion: Black Politics in Richmond and the Virginia Southside, 1867–1902." PhD diss., Columbia University, 2000.
Casey, Marcus D., and Bradley L. Hardy. "The Evolution of Black Neighborhoods since Kerner." *Journal of the Social Sciences* 4, no. 6, Fiftieth Anniversary of the Kerner Commission Report (September 2018): 185–205.
Cash, W. J. *Mind of the South*. New York: Vintage Books, 1941.

Cashin, Sheryll. *The Failures of Integration: How Race and Class Are Undermining the American Dream*. New York: Public Affairs Council, 2004.
Cavalcanti, H. B., and Debra Schaleef. "The Case for Secular Assimilation? The Latino Experience in Richmond, Virginia." *Journal for the Scientific Study of Religion* 44, no. 4 (December 2005): 473–83.
"Charles Murray: White America's Deadly Seducer." *Journal of Blacks in Higher Education* 6 (Winter 1994–95): 72–73.
Chesson, Michael. *Richmond after the War: 1865–1890*. Richmond: Virginia State Library, 1981.
Chiles, Marvin T. "Black Richmond Activism before the Modern Civil Rights Movement." *Journal of African American History* 105, no. 1 (Winter 2020): 56–82.
———. "A Period of Misunderstanding: Reforming Jim Crow in Richmond, Virginia, 1930–1954." *Virginia Magazine of History and Biography* 129, no. 3 (Fall 2021): 244–78.
———. "Richmond's Urban Crisis: Racial Transition during the Civil Rights Era, 1960–1977." MA thesis, James Madison University, 2016.
———. "Tough on Conduct: Punitive Leadership in Urban Public Schools, A Case Study of Angry Principal Dr. Roy A. West, 1986–1991." *Spectrum: A Journal on Black Men* 8, no. 1 (Fall 2020): 55–85.
Cie, Louis Bernard. "Law Enforcement in Richmond: A History of Police-Community Relations, 1737–1974." PhD diss., Florida State University, 1975.
Cimbala, Paul A., and Barton C. Shaw, eds. *Making A New South: Race, Leadership, and Community after the Civil War*. Gainesville: University of Florida Press, 2007.
Cisneros, Henry G. "Preserving Everybody's History." *Cityscape* (December 1996): 85–97.
Clayson, William S. *Freedom Is Not Enough: The War on Poverty and the Civil Rights Movement in Texas*. Austin: University of Texas Press, 2010.
Clayton, Ashley B., and Brian B. Peters. "The Desegregation of Land-Grant Institutions in the 1950s: The First African American Students at NC State University and Virginia Tech." *Journal of Negro Education* 88, no. 1 (Winter 2019): 75–92.
Cobb, James C. *Away Down South: A History of Southern Identity*. Oxford: Oxford University Press, 2005.
———. *The Selling of the South: The Southern Crusade for Industrial Development, 1936–1990*. Urbana: University of Illinois Press, 1993.
Colburn, David R. *African-American Mayors: Race, Politics, and the American City*. Urbana: University of Illinois Press, 2005.
Coleman, Willie. "Black Women and Segregated Public Transportation: Ninety Years of Resistance." *Negro History Bulletin* 63, no. 1 (Winter 2000): 17–22.
Connelly, Thomas L. *The Marble Man: Robert E. Lee and His Image in American Society*. New York: Alfred A. Knopf, 1977.

Corcoran, Robert. *Trustbuilding: An Honest Conversation on Race, Reconciliation, and Responsibility*. Charlottesville: University of Virginia Press, 2010.

Crespino, Joseph. *In Search of Another County: Mississippi and the Conservative Counterrevolution*. Princeton, NJ: Princeton University Press, 2007.

Crespino, Joseph, and Matthew D. Lassiter. *The Myth of Southern Exceptionalism*. Oxford: Oxford University Press, 2010.

Custos, Dominique, and John Reitz. "Public-Private Partnerships." *American Journal of Comparative Law* 58 (2010): 555–84.

Dabney, Thomas L. "The Study of the Negro." *Journal of Negro History* 19, no. 3 (July 1934): 266–307.

Dabney, Virginius. *Liberalism in the South*. Chapel Hill: University of North Carolina Press, 1932.

———. *Richmond: The Story of a City*. Charlottesville: University of Virginia Press, 1990.

———. *Richmond: The Story of a City*. Garden City, NY: Doubleday, 1976.

———. *Virginia Commonwealth University: A Sesquicentennial History*. Charlottesville: University of Virginia Press, 1987.

———. *Virginia: The New Dominion: A History from 1607 to the Present*. Charlottesville: University of Virginia Press, 1989.

Dailey, Jane. *Before Jim Crow: The Politics of Race in Post-Emancipation Virginia*. Chapel Hill: University of North Carolina Press, 2000.

Danns, Dionne. *Crossing Segregated Boundaries: Remembering Chicago School Segregation*. Piscataway, NJ: Rutgers University Press, 2020.

Darden, Joe T. "Black Residential Segregation since the 1948 *Shelley v. Kraemer* Decision." *Journal of Black Studies* 25, no. 6 (July 1995): 680–91.

Daugherity, Brian. *Keep On Keeping On: The NAACP and the Implementation of* Brown v. Board of Education *in Virginia*. Charlottesville: University of Virginia Press, 2016.

Dean, Melissa. *Desegregating Private Higher Education in the South: Duke, Emory, Rice, Tulane, and Vanderbilt*. Baton Rouge: Louisiana State University Press, 2013.

Dinnella-Borrego, Luis-Alejandro. *The Risen Phoenix: Black Politics in the Post–Civil War South*. Charlottesville: University of Virginia Press, 2017.

Dittmer, John. *Black Georgia in the Progressive Era*. Urbana: University of Illinois Press, 1977.

Doherty James L. *Race and Education in Richmond*. Richmond, VA: Self-published, 1972.

Dornfeld, Steven. "1969 Bus Strike: Twin Cities Mass Transit Turning Point." *Minnesota History* 66, no. 7 (Fall 2019): 274–89.

Dougherty, Jack. *More Than One Struggle: The Evolution of Black School Reform in Milwaukee*. Chapel Hill: University of North Carolina Press, 2004.

Douglas, David. *Jim Crow Moves North: The Battle over Northern School Segregation, 1865–1954*. Cambridge: Cambridge University Press, 2005.

Drake, W. Avon, and Robert D. Holsworth. *Affirmative Action and the Stalled Quest for Black Progress.* Urbana: University of Illinois Press, 1996.

Driggs, Sarah Shields, Richard Guy Wilson, and Robert P. Winthrop. *Richmond's Monument Avenue.* Chapel Hill: University of North Carolina Press, 2001.

Dunn, Marvin. *Black Miami in the Twentieth Century.* Gainesville: University of Florida Press, 2016.

Dunn, Ronnie A., Donna M. Whyte, James L. Hardiman, Adrennie Y. Hatten, and Mittie D. Jones. *Boycotts, Busing, and Beyond: The History and Implications of School Desegregation in the Urban North.* Dubuque, IA: Kendall Hunt, 2016.

Edds, Margaret. *We Faced the Dawn: Oliver Hill, Spottswood Robinson, and the Legal Team That Dismantled Jim Crow.* Charlottesville: University of Virginia Press, 2018.

Egerton, John. *Speak Now against the Day: The Generation before the Civil Rights Movement in the South.* Chapel Hill: University of North Carolina Press, 1995.

Eskridge, Sara K. "Virginia's Pupil Placement Board and the Practical Applications of Massive Resistance, 1956–1966." *Virginia Magazine of History and Biography* 118, no. 3 (June 2010): 246–76.

Estes, Steven. *Charleston in Black and White: Race and Power in the South after the Civil Rights Movement.* Chapel Hill: University of North Carolina Press, 2015.

Farrisee, Anne. "Heritage Tourism: Telling the Rest of the Story." *Georgia Historical Quarterly* 83, no. 1 (Spring 1999): 101–7.

Feld, Scott L., and William C. Carter. "When Desegregation Reduces Interracial Contact: A Class Size Paradox for Weak Ties." *American Journal of Sociology* 103, no. 5 (March 1998): 1165–86.

Fenn, Richard K. "The Community Action Program: An American Gospel?" *Science & Society* 33, no. 2 (Spring 1969): 209–22.

Fischer, Mary J., and Travis Scott Lowe. "Homebuyer Neighborhood Attainment in Black and White: Housing Outcomes during the Housing Boom and Bust." *Social Forces* 93, no. 4 (June 2015): 1481–512.

Fishman, Robert. "The Garden City Tradition in the Post-Suburban Age." *Built Environment* 17, nos. 3/4 (1991): 232–41.

Fishwick, Marshall W. *Virginia: A New Look at the Old Dominion.* New York: Harper & Brothers, 1959.

Fleischmann, Arnold. "The Territorial Expansion of Milwaukee: Historical Lessons for Contemporary Urban Policy and Research." *Journal of Urban History* 14, no. 2 (February 1988): 147–70.

Flemming-Hunter, Sheila. "Conversations about Reparations for Blacks in America: A 21st-Century Model in Civic Responsibility and Engagement." *Phylon* 53, no. 2 (Winter 2016): 100–25.

Foeman, Anita Kathy, and Teresa Nance. "From Miscegenation to Multiculturalism: Perceptions and Stages of Interracial Relationship Development." *Journal of Black Studies* 29, no. 4 (March 1999): 540–57.

Forsyth, Anny. *Reforming Suburbia: The Planned Communities of Irvine, Columbia, and the Woodlands.* Berkeley: University of California Press, 2005.

Freeman, Lance S. "Commentary: 21st-Century Gentrification." *Cityscape* 18, no. 3 (2016): 163–68.

Frey, William H. "Black In-Migration, White Flight, and the Changing Economic Base of the Central City." *American Journal of Sociology* 85, no. 6 (May 1980): 1396–417.

———. "Central City White Flight: Racial and Nonracial Causes." *American Sociological Review* 44, no. 3 (June 1979): 425–48.

Frost, Jennifer. "Impossible Democracy: The Unlikely Success of the War on Poverty Community Action Programs/Why America Lost the War on Poverty—and How to Win It." *Journal of Social History* 42, no. 3 (Spring 2009): 831–34.

Gadsden, Brett. *Between North and South: Delaware, Desegregation, and the Myth of American Sectionalism.* Philadelphia: University of Pennsylvania Press, 2012.

Gallimore, Mark. "Coordination or Competition: State Regulation of Motor Buses under Private Ownership and the Decline of Mass Transit in Pittsburgh." *Pennsylvania Magazine of History and Biography* 138, no. 1 (January 2014): 39–71.

Gates, Robbins L. *The Making of Massive Resistance: Virginia's Politics of Public-School Desegregation, 1954–1956.* Chapel Hill: University of North Carolina Press, 1964.

Gavins, Raymond. "Gordon Hancock: An Appraisal." *New South* 25, no. 4 (Fall 1970): 36–45.

———. "Urbanization and Segregation: Black Leadership Patterns in Richmond, Virginia, 1900–1920." *South Atlantic Quarterly* 79 (1980): 257–83.

Gavins, Raymond. *The Perils and Prospects of Southern Black Leadership.* Durham, NC: Duke University Press, 1977.

Germany, Kent B. *New Orleans after the Promises: Poverty, Citizenship, and the Search for the Great Society.* Athens: University of Georgia Press, 2007.

Gillette, Howard, Jr. *Camden after the Fall: Decline and Renewal in a Post-Industrial City.* Philadelphia: University of Pennsylvania Press, 2009.

———. *Civitas by Design: Building Better Communities, from the Garden City to the New Urbanism.* Philadelphia: University of Pennsylvania Press, 2010.

Gilmore, Glenda Elizabeth. *Defying Dixie: The Radical Roots of the Civil Rights Movement.* New York: Norton. 2009.

Godschalk, David R. "New Community Development Partnerships in America." *Community Development Journal* 8, no. 2 (April 1973): 60–69.

Graves, William, and Heather A. Smith. *Charlotte, NC: The Global Evolution of a New South City.* Athens: University of Georgia Press, 2012.

Greismer, Lily. "Good Neighbors for Fair Housing: Suburban Liberalism and Racial Inequality in Metropolitan Boston." *Journal of Urban History* 39, no. 3 (Fall 2013): 454–77.

Gritter, Elizabeth. *River of Hope: Black Politics and the Memphis Freedom Movement, 1865–1964*. Lexington: University of Kentucky Press, 2014.
Gutmann, Amy, ed. *Multiculturalism: Examining the Politics of Recognition*. Princeton, NJ: Princeton University Press, 1994.
Guy, Rebecca F., Louis G. Pol, and Randy E. Ryker. "Discrimination in Mortgage Lending: The Home Mortgage Disclosure Act." *Population Research and Policy Review* 1, no. 3 (October 1982): 283–96.
Hall, Eric Allen. *Arthur Ashe: Tennis and Justice in The Civil Rights Era*. Baltimore: Johns Hopkins University Press, 2014.
Hall, Jacquelyn Dowd. "The Long Civil Rights Movement and the Political Uses of the Past." *Journal of American History* 94, no. 4 (March 2005): 1233–63.
Hamilton, Phillip. "Race, Politics, and Education in Tidewater Virginia: Christopher Newport College and the Shoe Lane Controversy of 1960–63." *Virginia Magazine of History of Biography* 119, no. 3 (2011): 245–75.
Hammock, Allan Stanton. "The Leadership Factor in Black Politics: The Case of Richmond, Virginia." PhD diss., University of Virginia, 1972.
Hanchett, Thomas W. *Sorting Out the New South City: Race, Class, and Urban Development in Charlotte, 1875–1975*. Chapel Hill: University of North Carolina Press, 1998.
Harada, Masataka. "The Voting Rights Act of 1965 and Strategic Policy Making in the South." *State Politics and Policy Quarterly* 12, no. 4 (2012): 456–82.
Harold, Claudrena. *New Negro Politics in The Jim Crow South*. Athens: University of Georgia Press, 2016.
Hayter, Julian Maxwell. *The Dream Is Lost: Voting Rights and the Politics of Race in Richmond, Virginia*. Lexington: University Press of Kentucky, 2017.
———. "From Intent to Effect: Richmond, Virginia, and the Protracted Struggle for Voting Rights, 1965–77." *Journal of Policy History* 26, no. 4 (October 2014): 534–67.
Hazirjian, Lisa Gayle, and Annelise Orleck. *The War on Poverty: A New Grassroots History, 1964–1980*. Athens: University of Georgia Press, 2011.
Hedges, Larry V., and Amy Nowell. "Changes in the Black-White Gap in Achievement Test Scores." *Sociology of Education* 72, no. 2 (April 1999): 111–35.
Heinemann, Ronald L. *New Commonwealth: A History of Virginia, 1607–2007*. Charlottesville: University of Virginia Press, 2007.
Helling, Amy A., and David S. Sawicki. "Disparate Trends: Metropolitan Atlanta since 1960." *Built Environment* 20, no. 1 (1994): 9–24.
Hening, William Waller, ed. *The Statutes at Large; Being a Collection of All the Laws of Virginia*. Richmond, 1810.
Higginbotham, A. Leon, Jr. *Shades of Freedom: Racial Politics and Presumptions of the American Legal Process*. Oxford: Oxford University Press, 1996.
Hirsch, Arnold R. "Race and Politics in Modern New Orleans: The Mayoralty of Dutch Morial." *Amerikastudien* 35, no. 4 (December 1990): 461–84.

Hobson, Maurice J. "Ali and Atlanta: A Love Story in the Key of the Black New South." *Phylon* 54, no. 1 (Summer 2017). 79–96.

Hobson, Maurice J. *The Legend of the Black Mecca: Politics and Class in the Making of Modern Atlanta*. Chapel Hill: University of North Carolina Press, 2017.

Hoeth, Thea. "Public-Private Partnerships in State Government." *Public Productivity and Management Review* 15, no. 2 (Winter 1991): 147–50.

Hoffman, Stephen J. *Race, Class, and Power in the Building of Richmond, 1870–1920*. Jefferson, NC: McFarland, 2004.

Holland, Dan. "Forging a Consistent Vision: The People Who Shaped Manchester's Renewal, 1964–2014." *Pennsylvania History: A Journal of Mid-Atlantic Studies* 86, no. 2 (Spring 2019): 254–86.

Hornsby, Alton, Jr. *Black Power in Dixie: A Political History of African Americans in Atlanta*. Gainesville: University of Florida Press, 2009.

Horton, James Oliver, and Lois E. Horton, eds. *Slavery and Public History: The Tough Stuff of American Memory*. Chapel Hill: University of North Carolina Press, 2006.

Howell, Ocean. "The Merchant Crusaders: Eichler Homes and Fair Housing." *Pacific Historical Review* 85, no. 3 (August 2016): 379–407.

Hume, Richard L. "The Membership of the Virginia Constitutional Convention of 1867–1868: A Study of the Beginnings of Congressional Reconstruction in the Upper South." *Virginia Magazine of History and Biography* 86, no. 4 (October 1978): 461–84.

Hustwit, William P. *James J. Kilpatrick: Salesman for Segregation*. Chapel Hill: University of North Carolina Press, 2013.

Iceland, John, Gregory Sharp, and Jeffrey M. Timberlake. "Sun Belt Rising: Regional Population Change and the Decline in Black Residential Segregation, 1970–2009." *Demography* 50, no. 1 (February 2013): 97–123.

Ihlanfeldt, Keith R. "Rail Transit and Neighborhood Crime: The Case of Atlanta, Georgia." *Southern Economic Journal* 70, no. 2 (October 2003): 273–94.

Ippolito, Dennis S., and Martin L. Levin. "Public-Regardingness, Race, and Social Class: The Case of a Rapid Transit Referendum." *Social Science Quarterly* 51, no. 3 (December 1970): 628–33.

Irish Jesuit Province. "Catholics and Moral Rearmament." *Irish Monthly* 67, no. 796 (October 1939): 722–26.

Jackson, Kenneth T. *Crabgrass Frontier: The Suburbanization of the United States*. Oxford: Oxford University Press, 1987.

Jackson, Kenneth T., and Stanley K. Shultz. *Cities in American History*. New York: Knopf. 1972.

Jefferies, Kwame. *Bloody Lowndes: Civil Rights and Black Power in Alabama's Black Belt*. New York: New York University Press, 2009.

Jencks Christopher, and Paul Peterson, eds. *The Urban Underclass*. Washington, DC: Brookings Institution, 1991.

Jiao, Junfeng. "Identifying Transit Deserts in Major Texas Cities Where the Supplies Missed the Demands." *Journal of Transport and Land Use* 10, no. 1 (2017): 529–40.

Johnson-Hart, Lallen T. "Residential Outcomes of HOPE VI Relocates in Richmond, VA." MA thesis, Virginia Commonwealth University, 2007.

Johnston, Richard, and Byron E. Shafer. *The End of Southern Exceptionalism: Class, Race, and Partisan Change in the Postwar South.* Cambridge, MA: Harvard University Press, 2006.

Jordan, William Patty. "Crime on the Bus: Bus Driver Safety in Postwar Washington, D.C." *Washington History* 25 (Summer 2013): 36–51.

K'Meyer, Tracy E. *Civil Rights in the Gateway to the South: Louisville, Kentucky, 1945–1980.* Lexington: University Press of Kentucky, 2009.

Kafoglis, Madelyn L. "Participatory Democracy in the Community Action Program." *Public Choice* 5 (Fall 1968): 73–85.

Kalman, Laura. *Yale Law School and the Sixties: Revolt and Reverberations.* Chapel Hill: University of North Carolina Press, 2005.

Kalmijn, Matthijs. "Trends in Black/White Intermarriage." *Social Forces* 72, no. 1 (September 1993): 119–46.

Keating, Larry. *Atlanta: Race, Class, and Urban Expansion.* Philadelphia: Temple University Press, 2001.

Kelley, L. M. Blair. *Rights to Ride: Streetcar Boycotts and African American Citizenship in the Era of Plessy v. Ferguson.* Chapel Hill: University of North Carolina Press, 2010.

Kennelly, Tamara. "The Quiet Path of an Invisible Man: Irving Peddrew III and Desegregation at Virginia Tech." *Virginia Magazine of History and Biography* 126, no. 4 (2018): 422–66.

Kim, Claire Jean. "Clinton's Race Initiative: Recasting the American Dilemma." *Polity* 33, no. 2 (Winter 2000): 175–97.

———. "Managing the Racial Breach: Clinton, Black-White Polarization, and the Race Initiative." *Political Science Quarterly* 117, no. 1 (Spring 2002): 55–79.

Kinchen, Shirletta J. *Black Power in the Bluff City: African American Youth and Student Activism in Memphis, 1965–1975.* Knoxville: University of Tennessee Press, 2016.

Kinnick, Mary K., and Mary F. Ricks. "The Urban Public University in the United States: An Analysis of Change, 1977–1987." *Research in Higher Education* 31, no. 1 (February 1990): 20–35.

Kneebone, John T., and Eugene P. Trani. *Fulfilling the Promise: Virginia Commonwealth University and the City of Richmond, 1968–2009.* Charlottesville: University of Virginia Press, 2020.

Kruse, Kevin. *White Flight: Atlanta and the Making of Modern Conservatism.* Princeton, NJ: Princeton University Press, 2005.

Kyle, Ethan J., and Blain Roberts. *Denmark Vesey's Garden: Slavery and Memory in the Cradle of the Confederacy.* New York: New Press, 2018.

Lassiter, Matthew D. *The Silent Majority: Suburban Politics in the Sunbelt South.* Princeton, NJ: Princeton University Press, 2006.

Lassiter, Matthew D., and Andrew B. Lewis. *Moderates Dilemma: Massive Resistance to School Desegregation in Virginia.* Charlottesville: University of Virginia Press, 1998.

Lawson, Steven F. *Running for Freedom: Civil Rights and Black Politics since 1941.* New York: Wiley, 2014.

Layton, Robert C. *Discovering Richmond Monuments: A History of River City Landmarks beyond the Avenue.* Charleston, SC: History Press, 2013.

Leedes Gary C., and James M. O'Fallon. "School Desegregation in Richmond: A Case History." *University of Richmond Law Review* 1, no. 10 (Fall 1975): 1–61.

Leib, Johnathan, I. "Robert E. Lee, 'Race,' Representation, and Redevelopment along Richmond, Virginia's Canal Walk." *Southeastern Geographer* 44, no. 2 (November 2004): 236–62.

———. "Separate Times, Shared Spaces: Arthur Ashe, Monument Avenue, and the Politics of Richmond, Virginia's Symbolic Landscape." *Cultural Geographies* 9, no. 3 (July 2002): 286–312.

Leidholdt, Alexander S. "Showdown on Mr. Jefferson's Lawn." *Virginia Magazine of History and Biography* 122, no. 3 (June 2014): 230–71.

———. *Standing before the Shouting Mob: Lenoir Chambers and Virginia's Massive Resistance to Public School Integration.* Tuscaloosa: University of Alabama Press, 1997.

Leon, Warren, and Roy Rosenzweig, eds. *History Museums in the United States: A Critical Assessment.* Urbana: University of Illinois Press, 1989.

Leong, Nancy. "Racial Capitalism." *Harvard Law Review* 126, no. 8 (June 2013): 2151–226.

Levitan, Sar A. "The Community Action Program: A Strategy to Fight Poverty." *Annals of the American Academy of Political and Social Science* 385 (September 1969): 63–75.

Lewis, Amanda E., Mark Chesler, and Tyrone A. Forman. "The Impact of 'Colorblind' Ideologies on Students of Color: Intergroup Relations at a Predominantly White University." *Journal of Negro Education* 69, nos. 1/2 (Winter 2000): 74–91.

Lindgren, James L. *Preserving the Old Dominion: Historic Preservation and Virginia Traditionalism.* Charlottesville: University of Virginia Press, 1993.

Link, William. *Southern Crucible: The Making of an American Region.* Oxford: Oxford University Press, 2015.

Littlejohn, Jeffrey E., and Charles H. Ford. "Booker T. Washington High School: History, Identity, and Educational Equality in Norfolk, Virginia." *Virginia Magazine of History and Biography* 124, no. 2 (Winter 2016): 134–62.

———. *Elusive Equality: Desegregation and Resegregation in Norfolk's Public Schools.* Charlottesville: University of Virginia Press, 2012.

Lowry, Richard. "Yuppie Racism: Race Relations in the 1980s." *Journal of Black Studies* 21, no. 4 (June 1991): 445–64.

Lutz, Francis Earle. *Richmond in World War II*. Richmond, VA: Dietz, 1951.

Lyall, Katharine C. "Public-Private Partnerships in the Carter Years." *Proceedings of the Academy of Political Science* 36, no. 2 (1986): 4–13.

Marlowe, Gertrude Woodruff. *Right Worthy Grand Mission: Maggie Lena Walker and the Quest for Black Economic Empowerment*. Washington, DC: Howard University Press, 2003.

Marsh, Henry L., III, Jonathan K. Stubbs, and Danielle Wingfield-Smith, Esq., eds. *The Memoirs of Honorable Henry L. Marsh, III: Civil Rights Champion, Public Servant, Lawyer*. Hampton Fall, NH: Grant House, 2018.

Massey, Douglass S., and Nancy A. Denton. *American Apartheid: Segregation and the Making of the Underclass*. Cambridge, MA: Harvard University Press, 1993.

Matheson, Victor A., and Robert A. Baade. "Race and Riots: A Note on the Economic Impact of the Rodney King Riots." *Urban Studies* 41, no. 13 (December 2004): 2691–96.

Matusow, Allen J. *The Unraveling of America: A History of Liberalism in the 1960s*. New York: Harper & Row, 1984.

McCoy, Patricia A. "The Home Mortgage Disclosure Act: A Synopsis and Recent Legislative History." *Journal of Real Estate Research* 29, no. 4 (2007): 381–98.

McDougall, Gerald S., and Harold Bunce. "Urban Services and the Suburbanization of Blacks." *Social Science Quarterly* 67, no. 3 (September 1986): 596–603.

McGraw, Marie-Tyler. *At the Falls: Richmond, Virginia, and Its People*. Chapel Hill: University of North Carolina Press, 1994.

McMillen, Neil R. *Dark Journey: Black Mississippians in the Age of Jim Crow*. Urbana: University of Illinois Press, 1990.

McNeil, Genna Rae. *Groundwork: Charles Hamilton Houston and the Struggle for Civil Rights*. Philadelphia: University of Pennsylvania Press, 1983.

McWhorter, John. *Losing the Race: Self-Sabotage in Black America*. New York: Perennial, 2001.

Meier, August, and Elliott Rudwick. "The Boycott Movement against Jim Crow Streetcars in the South, 1900–1906." *Journal of American History* 55, no. 4 (March 1969): 756–75.

Melamed, Jodi. "Racial Capitalism." *Critical Ethnic Studies* 1, no. 1 (Spring 2015): 76–85.

Mele, Christopher. "The Strategic Uses of Race to Legitimize 'Social Mix' Urban Redevelopment." *Social Identities* 25, no. 1 (January 2019): 27–40.

Minchkin, Timothy J. "One America? Church Burnings and Perceptions of Race Relations in the Clinton Years." *Australasian Journal of American Studies* 27, no. 2 (December 2008): 1–28.

Moeser, John, and Rutledge B. Dennis. *Politics of Annexation: Oligarchic Power in a Southern City*. Cambridge, MA: Schenkman, 1982.

Mogulof, Melvin B. "A Developmental Approach to the Community Action Program Idea." *Social Work* 12, no. 2 (April 1967): 12–20.
Moore, James T. "Black Militancy in Readjuster Virginia, 1879–1883." *Journal of Southern History* 41, no. 2 (May 1975): 167–86.
Moore, Leonard N. *Black Rage in New Orleans: Police Brutality and African American Activism from World War II to Hurricane Katrina*. Baton Rouge: Louisiana State University Press, 2011.
Morris, Aldon D. *The Origins of the Civil Rights Movement: Black Communities Organizing for Change*. New York: Free Press, 1984.
"Municipal Segregation Ordinances." *Virginia Law Review* 3, no. 4 (January 1916): 304–9.
Muse, Benjamin. *Virginia's Massive Resistance*. Bloomington: Indiana University Press, 1961.
O'Brien, John Thomas. *From Bondage to Citizenship: The Richmond Black Community, 1865–67*. Milton Park, UK: Taylor & Francis, 1990.
O'Leary, Elizabeth L. *The Carillon Neighborhood: A History*. Richmond, VA: Carillon Civic Association, 2013.
Odum, Howard W. "Some Studies in the Negro Problems of the Southern States." *Journal of Race Development* 6, no. 2 (1915): 185–91.
Olsen, Joshua. *Better Places, Better Lives: A Biography of James Rouse*. New York: Urban Land Institute, 2003.
Overby, Ethel Thompson. *"It's Better to Light a Candle Than to Curse the Darkness": The Autobiographical Notes of Ethel T. Overby*. [Richmond, VA?]: [Overby?], 1975.
Pascoe, Peggy. *What Comes Naturally: Miscegenation Law and the Making of Race in America*. Oxford: Oxford University Press, 2009.
Pattillo, Mary. "Black Middle-Class Neighborhoods." *Annual Review of Sociology* 31 (2005): 305–29.
Payne, Charles M. *I've Got the Light of Freedom: Organizing Tradition and the Mississippi Freedom Struggle*. Berkeley: University of California Press, 1995.
Payne, James Robert. "New South Narratives of Freedom: Rereading George Washington Cable's 'Tite Poulette' and 'Madame Delphine.'" *MELUS* 27, no. 1 (2002): 3–23.
Pearlman, Lauren. *Democracy's Capital: Black Political Power in Washington, D.C.* Chapel Hill: University of North Carolina Press, 2019.
Peeples, Edward H. *Scalawag: A White Southerner's Journey through Segregation to Human Rights Activism*. Charlottesville: University of Virginia Press, 2014.
Perrnod, Virginia Marion. *Special Districts, Special Purposes: Fringe Governments and Urban Problems in the Houston Area*. College Station: Texas A&M University Press, 1984.
Perrotta, John A. "Machine Influence on a Community Action Program: The Case of Providence, Rhode Island." *Polity* 9, no. 4 (Summer 1977): 481–502.

Phillips, Anne E. "A History of the Struggle for School Desegregation in Philadelphia, 1955–1967." *Journal of Mid-Atlantic Studies* 72, no. 1 (Winter 2005): 49–76.
Powell, Lawrence N., ed. *The New Orleans of George Washington Cable: The 1887 Census Office Report.* Baton Rouge: Louisiana State University Press, 2008.
Pratt, Robert A. *The Color of Their Skin: Education and Race in Richmond, Virginia, 1954–1989.* Charlottesville: University of Virginia Press, 1993.
———. "The Conscience of Virginia: Judge Robert R. Merhige, Jr., and the Politics of School Desegregation." *University of Richmond Law Review* 52, no. 1 (2017).
———. "New Directions in Virginia's Civil Rights History." *Virginia Magazine of History and Biography* 104, no. 1 (Winter 1996): 149–56.
———. "A Promise Unfulfilled: School Desegregation in Richmond, Virginia, 1956–1986." *Virginia Magazine of History and Biography* 99, no. 4 (Winter 1991): 415–48.
———. *Selma's Bloody Sunday: Protest, Voting Rights, and the Struggle for Racial Equality.* Baltimore: Johns Hopkins University Press, 2016.
———. *We Shall Not Be Moved: The Desegregation of the University of Georgia.* Athens: University of Georgia Press, 2002.
Pulley, Raymond H. *Old Virginia Restored: An Interpretation of Progressive Impulse, 1870–1930.* Charlottesville: University of Virginia Press, 1968.
Quinn, Rand. *Class Action: Desegregation and Diversity in San Francisco Schools.* Minneapolis: University of Minnesota Press, 2019.
Rachleff, Peter J. *Black Labor in the South: Richmond, Virginia, 1865–1890.* Philadelphia: Temple University Press, 1984.
Randolph Lewis A., and Gayle T. Tate. *Rights for a Season: The Politics of Race, Class, and Gender in Richmond, Virginia.* Knoxville: University of Tennessee Press, 2003.
Randolph, Adah L. Ward. "It Is Better to Light a Candle Than to Curse the Darkness: Ethel Thompson Overby and Democratic Schooling in Richmond, Virginia, 1910–1958." *Educational Studies* 48, no. 3 (May 2012): 220–43.
Renshon, Stanley A., ed. *One America: Political Leadership, National Identity, and the Dilemmas of Diversity.* Washington, DC: Georgetown University Press, 2001.
Ritter, Luke. "The Discriminating Priority of Integration: Open Housing Activism in St. Louis County, 1968–1977." *Journal of the Illinois State Historical Society* 106, no. 2 (Summer 2013): 224–44.
Robinson, Cedric. *Black Marxism: The Making of the Black Radical Tradition.* Chapel Hill: University of North Carolina Press, 1983.
Rodriguez, Joseph A. *Bootstrap New Urbanism: Design, Race, and Redevelopment in Milwaukee.* Washington, DC: Lexington Books, 2014.
Rothstein, Richard. *The Color of Law: A Forgotten History of How Our Government Segregated America.* New York: Norton, 2017.

———. "From Ferguson to Baltimore: The Fruits of Government-Sponsored Segregation." *Journal of Affordable Housing and Community Development Law* 24, no. 2 (2015): 205–10.

Rusk, David. *Cities without Suburbs*. Washington, DC: Woodrow Wilson Center Press, 1995.

Ryan, James E. *Five Miles Away, A World Apart: One City, Two Schools, and the Story of Educational Opportunity in Modern America*. Oxford: Oxford University Press, 2010.

Saito, Leland T. *The Politics of Exclusion: The Failure of Race-Neutral Policies in Urban America*. Palo Alto, CA: Stanford University Press, 2009.

Sanford, James K., ed. *Richmond: Her Triumphs, Tragedies, and Growth*. Richmond, VA: Metropolitan Richmond Chamber of Commerce, 1975.

Satter, Beryl. *Family Properties: How the Struggle over Race and Real Estate Transformed Chicago and Urban America*. New York: Picador, 2010.

Savage, Kirk. *Monument Wars: Washington DC, the National Mall, and the Transformation of the Memorial Landscape*. Berkeley: University of California Press, 2009.

———. *Standing Soldiers, Kneeling Slaves: Race, War, and Monument in Nineteenth Century America*. Princeton, NJ: Princeton University Press, 1997.

Schein, Richard H., ed. *Landscape and Race in the United States*. Milton Park, UK: Routledge, 2006.

Schlatter, N. Elizabeth, and Ashley Kistler, eds. *Growing Up in Civil Rights Richmond: A Community Remembers*. Richmond, VA: University of Richmond Museums, 2019.

Schneider, Mark, and Thomas Phelan. "Black Suburbanization in the 1980s." *Demography* 30, no. 2 (May 1993): 269–79.

Schroeder, Larry D., and David L. Sjoquist. "The Rational Voter: An Analysis of Two Atlanta Referenda on Rapid Transit." *Public Choice* 33, no. 3 (1978): 27–44.

Schuit, Sophie, and Jon C. Rogowski. "Race, Representation, and the Voting Rights Act." *American Journal of Political Science* 61, no. 3 (2017): 513–26.

Schuman, Howard, Charlotte Steeh, Lawrence D. Bobo, and Maria Krysan. *Racial Attitudes in America: Trends and Interpretations*. Cambridge, MA: Harvard University Press, 1997.

Sears, David, Jim Sidanius, and Lawrence Bobo, eds. *Racialized Politics: The Debate about Racism in America*. Chicago: University of Chicago Press, 2000.

Self, Robert O. *American Babylon: Race and the Struggle for Postwar Oakland*. Princeton, NJ: Princeton University Press, 2005.

Shagaloff, June. "A Review of Public School Desegregation in the North and West." *Journal of Educational Sociology* 36, no. 6 (February 1963): 292–96.

Shanker, Amy, and Len Rodman. "Public-Private Partnerships." *Journal (American Water Works Association)* 88, no. 4 (1996): 102–7.

Sigelman Lee, and Susan Welch. *Black Americans' Views of Racial Inequality: The Dream Deferred*. Cambridge: Cambridge University Press, 1991.

Sigelman, Lee, Timothy Bledsoe, Susan Welch, and Michael W. Combs. "Making Contact? Black-White Social Interaction in an Urban Setting." *American Journal of Sociology* 101, no. 5 (March 1996): 1306–22.

Silver, Christopher. *Twentieth Century Richmond: Planning, Politics, and Race.* Knoxville: University of Tennessee Press, 1984.

Silver, Christopher, and John V. Moeser. *The Separate City: Black Communities in the Urban South, 1940–1968.* Lexington: University Press of Kentucky, 1995.

Silverstein, Clara. *White Girl: A Story of School Desegregation.* Athens: University of Georgia Press, 2004.

Simon, Nicole, and Susan Moore Johnson. "Teacher Turnover in High-Poverty Schools: What We Know and Can Do." *Teachers College Record* 117, no. 3 (2015): 1–36.

Sloan, Jerome S. "The Community Action Program and the Social Responsibility of the Local Lawyer." *Virginia Law Review* 51, no. 8 (December 1965): 1545–85.

Smith, Christa A. "Predicting Success or Failure on Main Street: Urban Revitalization and the Kentucky Main Street Program, 1979–1999." *Southeastern Geographer* 42, no. 2 (November 2002): 248–61.

Smith, Douglass J. *Managing White Supremacy: Race, Politics, and Citizenship in Jim Crow Virginia.* Chapel Hill: University of North Carolina Press, 2002.

Smith, Larissa M. "Where the South Begins: Black Politics and Civil Rights Activism in Virginia, 1930–1951." PhD diss., Emory University, 2001.

Smith, Renée M. "The Public Presidency Hits the Wall: Clinton's Presidential Initiative on Race." *Presidential Studies Quarterly* 28, no. 4, Special issue, Clinton Presidency in Crisis (Fall 1998): 780–85.

Sorrell, Andrew V., and Bruce A. Vlk. "Virginia's Never-ending Moratorium on City-County Annexations." *Virginia News Letter* 88, no. 1 (January 2012): 1–33.

Starr, Paul. "Civil Reconstruction: What to Do without Affirmative Action." *American Prospect* 8 (Winter 1992): 8–14.

Steele, Shelby. *The Content of Our Character: A New Vision of Race in America.* New York: St. Martin's Press, 1990.

Stone, Clarence N. *Regime Politics: Governing Atlanta, 1946–1988.* Lawrence: University Press of Kansas, 1989.

Strauss, David A. "The Myth of Colorblindness." *Supreme Court Review* (1986): 99–134.

Sugrue, Thomas. *Origins of the Urban Crisis: Race and Inequality in Postwar Detroit.* Princeton, NJ: Princeton University Press, 1998.

———. *Sweet Land of Liberty: The Forgotten Civil Rights Movement in the North.* New York: Random House, 2008.

Swain, Johnnie Dee, Jr. "Black Mayors: Urban Decline and the Underclass." *Journal of Black Studies* 24, no. 1 (September 1993): 16–30.

Sweeney, James R. "Southern Strategies." *Virginia Magazine of History and Biography* 106, no. 2 (Spring 1998): 165–200.

———, ed. *Race, Reason, and Massive Resistance: The Diary of David J. Mays, 1954–1959*. Athens: University of Georgia Press, 2008.
Taylor, Clarence. *Knocking at Our Door: Milton A. Galminson and the Struggle for School Integration in New York City*. New York: Columbia University Press, 1997.
Teaford, Jon C. *The Road to Renaissance: Urban Revitalization in America, 1940–1985*. Baltimore: Johns Hopkins University Press, 1990.
Temple, David G. *Merger Politics: Local Government Consolidation in Tidewater Virginia*. Charlottesville: University of Virginia Press, 1966.
Thomas, June, and Marsha Ritzdorf. *Urban Planning and the African American Community in the Shadows*. Thousand Oaks, CA: Sage, 1997.
Thomas, June Manning. *Redevelopment and Race: Planning a Finer City in Postwar Detroit*. Detroit: Wayne State University Press, 2013.
Thompson, Douglas F. *Richmond's Priests and Prophets: Race, Religion, and Social Change in the Civil Rights Era*. Tuscaloosa: University of Alabama Press, 2017.
Thompson, Gregory, Jeffrey Brown, and Torsha Bhattacharya. "What Really Matters for Increasing Transit Ridership: Understanding the Determinants of Transit Ridership Demand in Broward County, Florida." *Urban Studies* 49, no. 15 (November 2012): 3327–45.
Tindall, George B. "The Significance of Howard W. Odum to Southern History: A Preliminary Estimate." *Journal of Southern History* 24, no. 3 (1958): 285–307.
Titus, Jill Ogline. *Brown's Battleground: Segregationists and the Struggle for Justice in Prince Edward County, Virginia*. Chapel Hill: University of North Carolina Press, 2011.
Tuch, Steven A., Lee Sigelman, and Jason A. MacDonald. "Trends: Race Relations and American Youth, 1976–1995." *Public Opinion Quarterly* 63, no. 1 (Spring 1999): 109–48.
Tucker, M. Belinda, and Claudia Mitchell-Kernan. "New Trends in Black American Interracial Marriage: The Social Structural Context." *Journal of Marriage and Family* 52, no. 1 (February 1990): 209–18.
Tyler-McGraw, Marie. *At the Falls: Richmond, Virginia, and Its People*. Chapel Hill: University of North Carolina Press, 1994.
Tyson, Timothy. *Radio Free Dixie: Robert F. Williams and the Roots of Black Power*. Chapel Hill: University of North Carolina Press, 1999.
"Unconstitutionality of Segregation Ordinances." *Yale Law Journal* 27, no. 3 (January 1918): 393–97.
Urofsky, Melvin L. "The Virginia Historical Society: The First 175 Years, 1831–2006." *Virginia Magazine of History and Biography* 114, no. 1 (Winter 2006): 185–200.
Wallenstein, Peter. *Blue Laws and Black Codes: Conflicts, Courts, Change in Twentieth-Century Virginia*. Charlottesville: University of Virginia Press, 2004.

———. *Cradle of America: A History of Virginia.* Lawrence: University Press of Kansas, 2007.
———, ed. *Higher Education and the Civil Rights Movement: White Supremacy, Black Southerners, and College Campuses.* Gainesville: University of Florida Press, 2008.
Wang, Jing, and Evgenia Gorina. "Fiscal Effects of Municipal Annexation: Evidence from a Large National Sample of Urban Municipalities." *Growth and Change* 49, no. 4 (December 2018): 612–35.
Watkins Alfred J., and Arnold Fleischmann. "Annexation, Migration, and Central City Population Growth." *Social Science Quarterly* 61, no. 3 (December 1980): 612–22.
Watson, Dwight. *Race and Houston Police Department, 1930–1990: A Change Did Come.* College Station: Texas A&M University Press, 2005.
Weise, Julie M. *Corazon de Dixie: Mexicanos in the US South Since 1910.* Chapel Hill: University of North Carolina Press, 2015.
Wheelock, Darren, and Douglas Hartmann. "Midnight Basketball and the 1994 Crime Bill Debates: The Operation of a Racial Code." *Sociological Quarterly* 48, no. 2 (Spring 2007): 315–42.
Wikstrom, Nelson. *City Manager Government in Henrico, Virginia: Implementation, Evolution, and Evaluation.* Henrico, County VA: Henrico County, 2002.
Wilkerson, J. Harvie, III. *Harry Byrd and the Changing Face of Virginia Politics.* Charlottesville: University of Virginia Press, 1984.
Williamson, Thad, and Amy L. Howard. "Reframing Public Housing in Richmond, Virginia: Resident, Resistance, and the Future of Redevelopment." *Cities: The International Journal of Urban Policy* 55, no. 1 (December 2016): 33–39.
Willie, Charles V., and Susan L. Greenblatt. *Community and Educational Change: Ten School Systems under Court Order.* New York: Longman, 1981.
Wilson, C. R. *Baptized in Blood: The Religion of the Lost Cause.* Athens: University of Georgia Press, 1980.
Wilson, David. "Urban Revitalization on the Upper West Side of Manhattan: An Urban Managerialist Assessment." *Economic Geography* 63, no. 1 (January 1987): 35–47.
Wilson, William Julius. *The Declining Significance of Race.* Chicago: University of Chicago Press, 1980.
———. *The Truly Disadvantaged: The Inner City, the Underclass, and Public Policy.* Chicago: University of Chicago Press, 1987.
Winant, Howard. "Race and Race Theory." *Annual Review of Sociology* 26 (2000): 169–85.
Wise, Tim. *Colorblind: The Rise of Post Racial Politics and the Retreat from Racial Equity.* San Francisco: City Lights, 2010.
Woldoff, Rachel A. *White Flight/Black Flight: The Dynamics of Racial Change in an American Neighborhood.* Ithaca, NY: Cornell University Press, 2011.

Woodward, C. Vann. *Origins of the New South, 1877–1913: A History of the South.* Baton Rouge: Louisiana State University Press, 1971.

Wynes, Charles E. "The Evolution of Jim Crow Laws in Twentieth Century Virginia." *Phylon* 28, no. 4 (Fourth Quarter, 1967): 416–25.

Youngblood, Susan Ashmore. *Carry It On: The War on Poverty and the Civil Rights Movement in Alabama, 1964–1972.* Athens: University of Georgia Press, 2008.

Zeinemann, Robert D. "Overlooked Linkages between Municipal Incorporation and Annexation Laws: An In-Depth Look at Wisconsin's Experience." *Urban Lawyer* 39, no. 2 (2007): 257–318.

Zelden, Charles L. *The Battle for the Black Ballot: Smith v. Allwright and the Defeat of the Texas All-White Primary.* Lawrence: University Press of Kansas, 2004.

INDEX

501(c)(3) tax exemptions, 117

Affirmative Action and Minority Tenant Opportunity Program, 126
Affordable Housing Trust Fund, 206
African Ancestral Chamber, 194
Alexander v. Holmes County Board of Education, 51, 52
Alexandria, VA, 21, 34, 39
Allen, George F., 178
American Civil War Museum, 192–93, 194, 195
Anderson, SC, 38
antiblackness, 1, 2, 4, 48–49, 67, 138, 166, 175
archconservatives, 11, 31
Armstrong High School, 120
Arthur Ashe Monument, 176, 179, 182–85, 186, 192
Ashe, Arthur, 180–81
Atlanta, 36–37, 122, 149, 170
Ayers, Edward L., 165
Azalea Mall, 34

Bagley, Philip J., Jr., 32–35, 38, 41, 44, 95, 131, 158
Baltimore, 38
Bank of America, 143
Bank of Virginia, 123, 143
Banks, W. Lester, 83
Barton Heights, 53, 104
Baskerville, Viola, 52, 82
Battery Park, 53, 104
Beckett, Joyce, 163
Bell, Janine, 166
Bellemeade, 152
Benedictine College Preparatory, 31
Bennett, Lerone, Jr., 47
Berlin, Ira, 165
Berry-Burk Co., 130
Best Products, 130

Biggs, 130
Black-McDaniel, Claudette, 94
Black Panthers, 13
Black power, 25–26, 82, 165
Black Teens for Advancement (BTA), 170–71
Blackwell, 204–5
Board of Realtors, 142
Bobb, Robert C., 130, 181
Bohn, Henry G., 72
Book, Rev. John Butler, 62
Boston, 122
Boushall, Thomas, 128
Bowling, Brag, 177
Brent, Andrew J., Jr., 95–96, 98–100, 102–3
Brent, Andrew J., Sr., 95
Brewer v. School Board of Norfolk, 60
Bridge of Unity, 119, 127, 131
Briley brothers, 129
Bristol, VA, 21
Brown v. Board of Education, 17, 49–51, 60, 66, 110, 168, 208
Bryan, Thomas P., 74–76
Burton, Audrey, 159, 160
Burton, Collie, 159, 160
Butzner, John D., 80
Byrd, Harry Flood, 38
Byrd machine, 4, 38

Campbell, Benjamin P., 135–38, 140, 142–43, 150, 153, 166–68, 171, 173–75, 186, 199, 201, 210–11
Camp Fernlake, 147
Canal Walk Project, 155, 176, 190–91, 192–94
Capital One, 130
Capital Square Associates, 106–7
Capitol Square, 16, 30–31, 104, 147
Carillon (neighborhood), 158–60, 163
Carillon Civic Association (CCA), 158

321

322 INDEX

Carmichael, Stokely, 13, 25–26
Carter, Jimmy, 92–93, 96, 100–101
Carver (neighborhood), 205
Carver Elementary School, 209
Central Fidelity Bank, 144
Cephas, Bernard A., 18–20, 24, 80
Chambliss, Clifford B., 75
Chandler Middle School, 53
Chargois, Paige, 171–72, 175, 186, 188
Charity, Ronald K., 76
Charleston, SC, 38, 179, 196, 211
Charlotte, NC, 91, 98
Charlottesville, 21, 80, 179, 196
Chattanooga, TN, 38
Chesapeake, VA, 39, 40
Chesterfield County, VA, 21, 28–29, 34–35, 38, 41–45, 48, 85
Chesterfield Towne Center, 196
Chewning, Thomas, 184
Chicago–Cook County, IL, 40
Chiles, John R., 75
Chimborazo, 141
Christian, Barton, Epps, & Brent, 95
Church Hill, 24, 79, 80, 82, 123, 141–42, 145, 156–57, 159, 167–69, 205
Church Hill Association, 123
Citizens Against Busing (CAB), 59, 62–3
city council. *See* Richmond City Council
city hall, 17, 20, 24, 26, 30, 49, 71–2, 84–5, 91, 95, 102, 104, 106, 108, 113, 153, 204
civil rights, 2, 3–4, 6, 11–12, 17–18, 20, 23, 30, 37, 46, 48, 53, 67, 71–72, 82, 88, 95, 114, 138, 140, 179–81, 185, 188–89, 191, 193–95
Civil Rights Act (1964), 50–51, 71, 79
civil rights movement, 3, 5, 7, 12, 17, 25, 36, 48, 67–68, 71–73, 82, 85, 90, 111, 136, 140, 146, 154, 157, 165, 180, 208
Clark, Maxine, 163
Clinton, William J., 188, 189–90
Cloverleaf Mall, 129
Cokesbury, 130
Coleman, Christy, 194–95, 196
College of William & Mary, 31
Colonial Heights, VA, 39

Columbia, SC, 38
co-missioner/s, 137–38, 141, 146, 153
Commonwealth Club, 31, 104, 115
Community Reinvestment Act (1977), 140, 143
Confederate History Month, 178, 196
Congressional Black Caucus, 92
Congress on Racial Equality, 12
Cooper, Rev. Roscoe, 119
Corcoran, Robert, 159–62, 169–70, 173, 175, 186–88
Corcoran, Susan, 159–61, 169–70, 173, 186,
Creighton Court, 72, 79, 80, 82, 205
Creighton Court Civic Association (CCCA), 79
Crockford, Virginia Alden, 58–59, 61–65
Crockford, William Hamilton, 58
Crowe, Morrill M., 31, 60, 81
Crusade for Voters, 17–20, 23–24, 26, 42, 73, 86–88
CSX Corporation, 91

Dallas, 37–38
Darden, Joshua P., 117–18
Davis, Jefferson, monuments to, 182, 193
Dayton, OH, 188
Deans v. Richmond, 139
Deese, Emmanuel, 105, 126
Defenders of Freedom, Justice, and Equality, 194
Dell, Willie J., 87, 94, 137, 163
Democratic Party, 188, 190
Dennis, Rutledge M., 158, 163
Department of Housing and Urban Development (HUD), 77, 79, 100
Detroit, 122
Devil's Half Acre, 168
Diamond, The 127
Dogtown, 49–50, 52, 58–61, 63
Dominion National Bank, 144
Down Home Family Reunion, 166
Downtown Club, 115–6
Downtown Development Unlimited (DDU), 95–96, 98–100, 102–3, 108, 137
Downtown Expressway, 21, 22
Drake, W. Avon, 163

INDEX 323

Drumette, Marty, 183
Duhamel, Betty, 75
Duke, David, 178, 196
Dunning School, 165
DuPont, 9, 91

Ealey, Roland "Duke", 119
East Baton Rouge Parish, LA, 37
East Broad Street, 91, 95, 102, 105, 108, 113
East End, 23–24, 32–33, 50, 58–59, 60, 79, 131, 141, 156, 167, 205–6, 210
Ebony (magazine), 91
Economic Opportunity Act (1964), 72, 73
Edley, Chris, 189
Edmonds, Celestine, 156
Edwards, Ana, 194, 195
El-Amin, Sa'ad, 191
Elegba Folklore Society (EFS), 166, 194
Elkhardt Middle School, 62, 210
E. S. H. Greene Elementary School, 210
Esparaza, Monica, 194
Establishment, the, 18, 31–35, 37, 41–43, 45, 48–49, 54, 58, 61, 73, 80, 83, 87, 89, 93–95, 97, 100, 104–6, 108, 114–16, 120–21, 180, 184
Ethyl Corporation, 30
Eviction Diversion Program, 206
Ezibu Muntu African Dance Company, 166

Fairfax County, 39, 80
Fairfax County Federation of Citizen Associations (FCFCA), 39
Fair Housing Act (1968), 140
Falls Church, VA, 39
Fan District, 145
Fay, Frederic, 77
Federal District Court of Columbia, 85
Federal Highway Act (1956), 21
Federal Housing Act (1934), 139
Federal Housing Authority (FHA), 139
Fields, Barbara, 165
Fifth Street Baptist Church, 119
Figgie International, 91
First and Merchants Bank, 143
First Bank of Virginia, 31, 104
First Virginia Bank Colonial, 144

Fleet, Morty, 47
Floyd, George, 204
Foner, Eric, 165
Food Buying Club, 152
Forest Hill, 49
Foster, Gordon, 60
Founding Fathers, 4, 30
Franklin, John Hope, 189
Fred D. Thompson Middle School, 210
Freedom of Choice plan, 50, 52–53, 57–58, 60, 80
Fulton Hill, 82

Gabriel's Rebellion, 194
G. C. Murphy, 129
General Assembly. *See* Virginia General Assembly
George Mason Elementary School, 210
Georgetown University, 32
George Wythe High School, 61
Gerald D. Hines Interests, 96, 99
Gilbert, Frank, 158
Gilmore, Jim, 178
Gilpin Court, 80, 82, 168
Ginter Park, 53
Glass, Ruth, 144
Goldfield, David, 165
Gray, Russell "Block," 129
Greater Richmond Transit Company (GRTC), 148–50
Greek Revival architecture, 133
Green, Joseph, 118
Greene, JeRoyd, 158
Greensboro, NC, 17
Greentree's, 130
Green v. County School Board of New Kent County, 50–51, 60
Greenville, SC, 38
Green v. School Board of Roanoke, 60
Guiner, Lani, 188

Habenicht, Robert J., 31
Hampton, Fred, 13
Hampton, VA, 23, 39, 80
Hancock, Gordon Blaine, 15
Hare, Weston A., 75
Harris, Grace, 75, 163

324   INDEX

Harrisonburg, VA, 21
Hartsfield, William B., 37
Harvard Business School, 22
Hays, Lawrence Brooks, 20
Hayter, Julian Maxwell, 12
Healing the Heart of America Conference, 172, 174–75, 187
Hecht's, 130
Henrico County, VA, 29, 34–35, 39, 42, 43, 47, 130
Henry, Patrick, 168
Highland Park, 53, 145–46
Highland Springs High School, 47
Hill, Oliver White, 16–19, 66, 83, 193
Hill, William M., 31
Hillside Court, 82, 152
Hilton Hotel Corporation, 96, 99, 101, 102, 107–8. *See also* Richmond Hilton Associates
Holsworth, Robert D., 163
Holt, Alto Mae, 79
Holt, Curtis, 72–3, 78–80, 83–8, 105
Holton, Linwood, 59
Home Mortgage Disclosure Act (1975), 140
Hope in the Cities (HIC), 155, 171–73, 175, 185–90, 192–93, 200
Houston, 37–38, 149
Howard University, 14, 16
Howe, Harold, II, 51
Huguenot High School, 210
Hunter, Richard C., 119
Hunton, Williams, Gay, Moore and Powell, 120
Hurd v. Hodge, 139

Initiatives of Change. *See* Moral Re-Armament (MRA)
Interstate 64, 121,
Interstate 95, 125

Jackson, Stonewall, monument to, 182
Jacksonville–Duval County, FL, 37

Jackson Ward, 14, 104, 123–26, 131, 145, 165–66, 205
James River Corporation, 91

J. E. B. Stuart Monument, 182
Jefferson, Thomas, 30
Jefferson Hotel, 104
Jewell, Frank, 164
Jim Crow, 2–4, 6, 8, 11–18, 46, 48, 51, 67, 88, 90, 94, 113, 139, 148, 160, 177, 185, 191–92, 211
John B. Cary Elementary School, 63–4
John Marshall High School, 30, 53, 56–57, 67, 120
Johnson, Ed, 170
Johnson, Harmon, 170
Johnson, Lyndon B., 66, 73, 76, 78
Joint Venture in Youth Education, A, 152
Jones, Ben Lewis, 178
Jones, Dwight C., 202
Jones, Mike, 205
J. Sargent Reynolds Community College, 146
Junior League of Richmond, 89

Kaine, Timothy, 183, 191, 194
Kanawha Canal. *See* Canal Walk Project
Karmas, Jason, 209
Kellam, Sidney, 40
Kendall, Randolph, 75, 119
Kennedy, John F., 66, 73
Kenney, Walter T., 24, 94, 172
Kerner, Otto, Jr., 146
Kiepper, Alan F., 49, 56
Kimball, Gregg D., 164
Kimbrell, Bill, 47
King, Martin Luther, Jr., assassination of, 25, 56
King, Rodney, 186, 188
Kirk, Claude R., Jr., 52
Kneebone, John T., 163
Knoxville, TN, 38
Ku Klux Klan, 178

Laburnum Park, 53
Lambert, Benjamin J., III, 150
Lancaster, PA, 98
Langston, Timothy, 158
Lassiter, Matthew, 29
Laurens, SC, 38
Lee, Lauranett, 165

Lee, Robert E., mural portrait of, 177, 191
Leidinger, William, 104–5
Lincoln, Abraham statue, 193
Look (magazine), 23
Lost Cause, 113, 165, 168, 176–79, 182, 191–93, 196
Louthan, Frank G., 31
Lumpkin Slave Jail, 168, 194
Lynchburg, VA, 21, 34
Lynnhaven Marine Construction Co., 118

Maggie Walker Community Land Trust, 206
Maggie Walker High School, 14
Main Street Train Station, 127
Malcolm X, 165
Manchester Slave Docks, 168
Marriott, John Willard, 102
Marriott Company, 101, 102–3, 106, 107, 108
Marsh, Diane (née Harris), 17
Marsh, Fred, 14
Marsh, Harold, Sr., 14, 158
Marsh, Henry Lavender, II, 14
Marsh, Henry Levander, III, 6, 11–27, 28, 32, 34, 43, 45, 50, 73, 75, 80–1, 84–7, 89, 92–100, 102–8, 112, 114, 116, 118, 201–2, 206
Marsh, Lucy, 14
Marsh, Marian, 14
Marsh, Robert T., Jr., 31
Marshall, Thurgood, 16
Marsh Revolution, 11–12, 45, 202
Martin Luther King Jr. Middle School, 210
Massive Resistance, 4, 28, 50, 52, 160, 183
Matthew Fontaine Maury Monument, 182
McGurn, John M., 121
McQuinn, Delores, 193–94
Memphis, 38
Merhige, Robert, 64
Metropolitan Bus Company, 147
Metropolitan Coach Corporation, 120
Miami–Dade Clounty, FL, 37

Miller, Henry R., III, 31
Miller & Rhoads, 96, 108, 129–30
Minneapolis, 196
Mitchell, John, 177
Mitchell, John, Jr., 139
Moeser, John V., 163, 201–2
Moffatt, Carleton P, Jr., 31
Montaldo's, 130
Monument Avenue, 179–80, 182–85, 196
Moore, T. Justin, Jr., 114, 119–21, 123, 125–28
Moral Re-Armament (MRA), 155, 159–60, 162–63, 168–69, 170–73, 174, 176, 202
Mosby Court, 82
Motorola, 130
Mundle, Winfred, 19–20, 24, 71, 80–81
Museum of the Confederacy, 166, 172, 193, 195

Nashville–Davidson County, TN, 37, 38
National Association for the Advancement of Colored People (NAACP), 12, 17–18, 50, 118, 148
National Civic League, 23
National Conference of Black Mayors, 92
National People Action on Housing, 140
National Trust for Historic Preservation, 194
National Urban League, 12
Navy Hill Project, 203
Newport News, VA, 14, 39, 80
Nieweg, Rob, 194
Nikens, J. Jay, 75
Nixon, Richard, 50–51, 100
Norfolk, 23, 34, 39, 117–18
Norfolk Housing Authority, 118
Northside, 15, 22, 24, 50, 53–57, 60, 67, 120, 124, 139, 141, 205–6

Oak Grove, 145, 152
O'Berry Methodist Church, 14
Office of Community Wealth Building (OCWB), 203
Office of Economic Opportunity (OEO), 73–75, 77–78, 80, 83
Omni Hotels, 107

One America, 189
Oregon Hill, 145, 155–57, 159, 205

Parents of Richmond City Public Schools, 123
Patrick Henry School of Sciences and Art, 210
Peter Paul Development Center, 169
Petersburg, VA, 34
Pettaway, Sarah, 148
Pettus, Robert, 177
Philadelphia, 122
Philip Morris, 30, 91, 123
Planters Bank, 31
Portland, OR, 188
Portsmouth, VA, 21, 34, 39
Potato Patch, 152
Powell, Lewis F., 66
Pratt, Robert A., 138
Prince Edward County, 120, 194
Princeton University, 31
Private Industry Council of Richmond, 152
proannexation, 38, 40
Project One, 89–90, 92, 95–109, 114, 116, 137, 203
Pungo, VA, 121
Pusey, Nell, 74, 83

Race Initiative, 189
Raleigh, NC, 38
Ramada Renaissance Hotel, 107
Randolph, Milton, 53–54, 139
Reagan, Ronald, 122
redlining, 7, 124, 140, 144, 146, 150, 160
Regency Square, 129
Republican Party, 120, 189
Reynolds Metals Company, 9, 30, 91
Richardson, Henry "Chuck," 94, 183
Richmond Afro-American, 24, 26, 86, 87, 119, 156, 184
Richmond City Council, 11, 13, 17–20, 22–24, 26, 31, 33, 45, 52, 58–60, 64, 71–72, 78–87, 89, 92, 96–98, 102, 104–8, 110, 121, 130–31, 145, 149, 157, 175, 181, 184, 186, 192, 194, 200, 203, 205, 210

Richmond Coliseum, 14, 23, 98, 203
Richmond Committee for Youth, 58
Richmond Community Action Program (RCAP), 74–83
Richmond Council of Women's Organizations, 58
Richmond Federation of PTAs, 58
Richmond Forward, 120
Richmond Hill, 167–69, 171–73
Richmond Hilton Associates, 106
Richmond Hustings Courts, 148
Richmond Independent Taxpayer Association (RITA), 97–100, 102
Richmond Police Department, 26
Richmond Public Library, 147
Richmond Public Schools (RPS), 8, 60, 64, 79, 82, 129, 146, 152, 167, 207–11
Richmond Redevelopment and Housing Authority (RRHA), 77, 79–80, 85, 204
Richmond Renaissance Incorporated, 110, 116–17, 119, 123, 125–26, 137, 149–51
Richmond Riot Commission, 26
Richmond Slave Trail, 194
Richmond Times, 13
Richmond Urban Forum, 115–6, 119
Richmond Urban Institute (RUI), 135–54, 161, 163, 200
Richmond Urban League, 81, 119
Ritchie, Virginia, 89
Roanoke, VA, 21, 23, 34, 39
Robb, Charles S., 97
Robert E. Lee Bridge, 34, 41, 49
Robert E. Lee Monument, 182
Roberts, Spencer, 75
Robinson, Spottswood W., III, 193
Rock Hill, SC, 38
Rockville, MD, 38
Rodgers, Edythe M., 137–38, 140–41, 147
Rouse, James, 110, 121–23, 125–28

Sacred Ground Historical Reclamation Project, 194
Sadler, Philip G., 79
Salem, VA, 39
San Antonio, 37–38

Sartain, James A., 53–54, 57
Schwartz, Phillip, 163
Shannon, David T., 119
Shelley v. Kraemer, 139
Sheppard, Eleanor, 24
Shockoe Bottom, 31, 194–95, 203
Shockoe Bottom Memorial Park, 194–95
Shriver, R. Sargent, Jr., 73
Shumate, Stuart, 31
Siemens, 130
Silver, Christopher, 21, 138
Silverstein, Clara, 66–67
Sistah Soulja, 188
Sixth Street Marketplace, 110–11, 117–19, 123–25, 127, 130–32, 137–38, 203
Slavery Reconciliation Statue, 193
Smithsonian (magazine), 178–79
Sons of Confederate Veterans (SCV), 177–78, 191, 193, 195
Soto, Tom, 128
Southern Christian Leadership Conference, 12
southerners, 13–14, 21, 36, 90, 168, 179, 182, 187
Southside, 49–50, 52–53, 57–60, 62–64, 66, 78, 129, 141, 204, 206, 210
Southside Plaza, 34
Staylor, Claude, 118
St. Catherine's School, 31
St. Christopher's School, 31
St. Gertrude High School, 31
St. John's Church, 168
Stone, Clarence, 89
Stone, William F., 31
Stoney, Levar, 151, 180, 196, 200–202, 204, 206–9
St. Paul's Episcopal Church, 104, 112–13, 114, 115, 135
Student Nonviolent Coordinating Committee, 12
Sugrue, Thomas, 33

Taylor, Breonna, 204
Taylor, Nancy Jo, 167, 173
Teaford, Jon C., 93
Templeton, John, 120

Thalhimer, Morton G., Jr., 54
Thalhimers, 96, 104, 129–30
Thomas Jefferson High School, 67
Thornton, Theodore E., 75
Thornton, William, 119
Tidewater region, 39–40, 78, 123
Tinsley, Jesse, 18
Title I, 209
Tobacco Row, 164
Todd, A. Howe, 160
Townes, Clarence L., Jr., 119–21, 123, 125–28
Trani, Eugene P., 163
Tredegar National Civil War Museum. *See* American Civil War Museum
Tucker, Samuel Wilbur, 17, 148
Turner, Sylvester, 168–69, 171–72, 186
Tyler, James W., 63
Tyler-McGraw, Marie, 164

United States v. Franklin, 60
United Virginia Bank, 143
Unity Walk, 173, 176
University of Richmond, 31, 32–33, 53, 165
University of Virginia, 16, 31
Urban America Conference, 35
Urban Renaissance, 122
Urban Reporter, 127
Urban Team, 53–54, 56–57, 63
US Army, 17
US Congress, 20–21, 52, 59, 66, 71, 78, 96, 120, 140–41, 143, 178
US Court of Appeals for the Fourth Circuit, 66, 85
US Department of Health, Education and Welfare, 60
US Department of Justice, 85, 105
US Department of Labor and Statistics, 17
US District Court for the Eastern District of Virginia, 50, 107
US Federal Reserve, 140, 141, 143
US Supreme Court, 16, 86, 148

Valentine, Mann S., II, 164
Valentine Museum, 164–65, 172
Varina High School, 178

INDEX

Violent Crime Control and Law Enforcement Act (1994), 188, 190
Virginia Beach, 39, 40
Virginia Chamber of Commerce, 34
Virginia Civil Rights Memorial, 193
Virginia Commonwealth University (VCU), 137, 145, 152, 155, 163, 165, 166, 172, 175, 195
Virginia Electric and Power Company (VEPCO), 114, 121, 123, 184
Virginia Flaggers, 195
Virginia General Assembly, 15–16, 24, 30, 38–43, 59, 81, 92, 97, 108, 150, 210
Virginia Heroes, 181, 183
Virginia Historical Society. *See* Virginia Museum of History and Culture
Virginia Mercury, 195
Virginia Military Institute, 31
Virginia Museum of Fine Arts (VMFA), 165, 195
Virginia Museum of History and Culture, 165
Virginia National Bank, 106, 143
Virginia Supreme Court, 102
Virginia Transit Company, 61, 148
Virginia Union University, 14–16, 18, 24–25, 75, 119–20, 165
Voting Rights Act (1965), 71, 85, 105

Walker, Maggie Lena, 177, 194
Wanner v. Arlington County, 60
Warner, Mark, 178
war on poverty, 72–74, 76, 78, 80
Warren, Earl, 51
Washington, DC, 38, 39, 149
Washington Commanders, 203
Washington Post, 18, 20, 26, 28, 34, 40, 41, 42–43
Waterside Redevelopment Project, 117–18, 123

Watkinson, James S., Jr., 54
Watson, Rev. L. P., 118
Wednesday's Child, 147, 148
Wegner, Mike, 189
welfare programs, 34
West, Roy Alexander, 108
West End, 26, 31–33, 50, 59–60, 63, 95, 104, 115, 124, 141, 143, 148, 158, 181, 190, 199
West End Concerned Parents and Friends (WECPF), 59–60
Westover Hills, 49
Wheat, James C., 31, 83
White flight, 6, 37, 66, 94, 105, 117, 122, 148, 170, 172, 186
White House Commission on Civil Rights, 189
White House Review of Affirmative Action, 189
White supremacy, 7, 13, 29, 43, 166, 186, 196
Wilder, Lavinia, 148
Wilder, L. Douglas, 120, 150, 155, 181, 191
Wilkinson, J. Harvey, Jr., 31
William Byrd Park, 158
Williams, Michael Paul, 173
Willow Lawn Shopping Center, 34
Wilson, Charles P., 31
Wilson, Gary, 103
Windsor Farms, 204
Wise, H. Alexander, Jr., 192
W. K. Kellogg Foundation, 187
Woodward, Claude, 42
Woolworths, 129
Wright, Frank B., Jr., 62

Yale University, 31
Young, Leonidas, II, 184

Zippy's, 127

RECENT BOOKS IN THE
Carter G. Woodson Institute Series

A Little Child Shall Lead Them: A Documentary Account of the Struggle for School Desegregation in Prince Edward County, Virginia
Brian J. Daugherity and Brian Grogan, editors

We Face the Dawn: Oliver Hill, Spottswood Robinson, and the Legal Team That Dismantled Jim Crow
Margaret Edds

Keep On Keeping On: The NAACP and the Implementation of Brown v. Board of Education *in Virginia*
Brian J. Daugherity

Schooling Jim Crow: The Fight for Atlanta's Booker T. Washington High School and the Roots of Black Protest Politics
Jay Winston Driskell Jr.

The Punitive Turn: New Approaches to Race and Incarceration
Deborah E. McDowell, Claudrena N. Harold, and Juan Battle, editors

Freedom Has a Face: Race, Identity, and Community in Jefferson's Virginia
Kirt von Daacke

Gabriel's Conspiracy: A Documentary History
Philip J. Schwarz, editor

Rambles of a Runaway from Southern Slavery
Henry Goings, edited by Calvin Schermerhorn, Michael Plunkett, and Edward Gaynor

Whispers of Rebellion: Narrating Gabriel's Conspiracy
Michael L. Nicholls

Word, Like Fire: Maria Stewart, the Bible, and the Rights of African Americans
Valerie C. Cooper

Strategies for Survival: Recollections of Bondage in Antebellum Virginia
William Dusinberre

Criminal Injustice: Slaves and Free Blacks in Georgia's Criminal Justice System
Glenn McNair

Segregation's Science: Eugenics and Society in Virginia
Gregory Michael Dorr

The Segregated Scholars: Black Social Scientists and the Creation of Black Labor Studies, 1890–1950
Francille Rusan Wilson

Bitter Fruits of Bondage: The Demise of Slavery and the Collapse of the Confederacy, 1861–1865
Armstead L. Robinson

Migrants against Slavery: Virginians and the Nation
Philip J. Schwarz

Black Prisoners and Their World, Alabama, 1865–1900
Mary Ellen Curtin

Rituals of Race: American Public Culture and the Search for Racial Democracy
Alessandra Lorini

"Rearing Wolves to Our Own Destruction": Slavery in Richmond, Virginia, 1782–1865
Midori Takagi

Enterprising Southerners: Black Economic Success in North Carolina, 1865–1915
Robert C. Kenzer

Free Blacks in Norfolk, Virginia, 1790–1860: The Darker Side of Freedom
Tommy L. Bogger

A House Divided: Slavery and Emancipation in Delaware, 1638–1865
Patience Essah

A New Plantation South: Land, Labor, and Federal Favor in Twentieth-Century Arkansas
Jeannie M. Whayne

Limits of Anarchy: Intervention and State Formation in Chad
Sam C. Nolutshungu

Fire This Time: The Watts Uprising and the 1960s
Gerald Horne

Virginia Landmarks of Black History: Sites on the Virginia Landmarks Register and the National Register of Historic Places
Calder Loth, editor

Cultivation and Culture: Labor and the Shaping of Slave Life in the Americas
Ira Berlin and Philip D. Morgan, editors

Printed in the USA
CPSIA information can be obtained
at www.ICGtesting.com
JSHW080350081223
52985JS00009B/113